FROM PSYCHE TO SYSTEM
The Evolving Therapy of Carl Whitaker

THE GUILFORD FAMILY THERAPY SERIES
Alan S. Gurman, Editor

Ethnicity and Family Therapy
Monica McGoldrick, John K. Pearce, and Joseph Giordano, Editors

Patterns of Brief Family Therapy: An Ecosystemic Approach
Steve de Shazer

The Family Therapy of Drug Abuse and Addiction
M. Duncan Stanton, Thomas C. Todd, and Associates

From Psyche to System:
The Evolving Therapy of Carl Whitaker
John R. Neill and David P. Kniskern, Editors

Normal Family Processes
Froma Walsh, Editor

Helping Couples Change:
A Social Learning Approach to Marital Therapy
Richard B. Stuart

IN PREPARATION

The Process of Change
Peggy Papp

The Practice of Theory in Family Therapy
Larry Constantine

Contemporary Marriage
Henry Friedman, Carol Nadelson, and Derek Polonsky, Editors

Parent–Adolescent Conflict
Arthur Robin and Sharon Foster

Depressed Families
David Rubinstein

FROM PSYCHE TO SYSTEM

The Evolving Therapy
of Carl Whitaker

Edited by
JOHN R. NEILL
University of Kentucky College of Medicine

and
DAVID P. KNISKERN
University of Cincinnati College of Medicine

FOREWORD BY SALVADOR MINUCHIN

THE GUILFORD PRESS
New York   London

© 1982 The Guilford Press, New York
A Division of Guilford Publications, Inc.
200 Park Avenue South, New York, N.Y. 10003

Printed in the United States of America

Third printing, May 1985

LIBRARY OF CONGRESS CATALOGING IN PUBLICATION DATA
Main entry under title:
From psyche to system, the evolving therapy of Carl Whitaker.
   (The Guilford family therapy series)
   "Works by Carl Whitaker": p.
   Includes bibliographical references and index.
   1. Family psychotherapy. 2. Marital psychotherapy.
3. Psychotherapist and patient. 4. Whitaker, Carl A.
I. Neill, John R. II. Kniskern, David P., 1948–
III. Series.
RC488.5.F76   616.89'14   81-22933
ISBN 0-89862-050-3   AACR2

TO OUR PARENTS

FOREWORD

To introduce Carl's selected work is a responsibility, a pleasure, and an opportunity. For the last 20 years I have been trying to tell Carl the meaning of his therapy, that regardless of his iconoclastic statements he has a well-elaborated theory; that his techniques are not only dazzling, creative, and genuinely spontaneous, but also easy to describe, predictable, and therefore possible to map and to teach. I had offered frequently my free services to instruct him on the way he does therapy and produces change, even in the most recalcitrant systems, to no avail. Carl's answer has always been a benevolent acceptance of my need to explain and the offering of an irrelevant, but funny, tale about a distant relative or a close patient or student. The offering, and his comfortable, pseudogenuine farmer naiveté, usually did the the trick. I shackled the message, but didn't lose my hope of being successful the next time. Carl's invitation to write an introduction to this book is an indication of how convincing I have been. But something funny has happened on the road, or in the walking. I have increased my understanding and respect for Carl's work and have lost my wish to explain it.

But this book does it well. You should enter into this book like one visiting an exhibit of the works of a master. If you can, imagine a retrospective of the works of Carl Whitaker at the Guggenheim Museum in New York: the images, metaphors, theories, techniques, explorations, experiments, blunders, hopes are all displayed in the uninterrupted elliptical walls. At the top, where we would start our visit, are the efforts of an early Whitaker. If we watch carefully, we can see through his words the images, colors of the masters—Adolf Meyer, Rank, Adler, Allen, Aichhorn, Jung, Sullivan, and, of course, Freud. Descending the elliptical aisle, as early as the late '40s, we begin to see in all his work a central theme: that the therapist is inexorably linked to the patient in an integrative dance, a dance of mutual growth. His work with Malone, *The Roots of Psychotherapy* (1953), anticipates by almost two decades the innovations on transference and countertransference appearing in the psychoanalytic field in the '70s.

Here and there in our exploration of his work, we stop with amazement to enjoy an early concept that will be repeated again from another perspective, enlarged by Carl's life experience. A 1957 publication, "Communication in Brief Psychotherapy with the Nonpsychotic Patient," deals with techniques of indirect communication, the acceptance of therapists' and patients' irrationality, the therapist's modeling freedom of being, and the experiences of intimacy between therapist and patient. These images will reappear in a major work in 1962, "First-Stage Techniques in the Experiential Psychotherapy of Chronic Schizophrenic Patients," and in the last article in 1981, "Symbolic–Experiential Family Therapy," and, of course, throughout many of the other chapters herein. In effect, what is so interesting in this retrospective is the process of growth of the ideas. Standing at midpoint in the gallery, we could look backward and see the origin and the modifications of certain techniques; projecting forward, we could predict certain variations.

For a man who has objected with such vigor against theory and technique and to whom could be attributed a paraphrase of the W. C. Field quip—"What this country needs is a good dose of nontheory"— Whitaker is remarkably consistent in his philosophy about people, his concepts of therapy, and of individual, couple, or family growth, and in his use of therapeutic techniques. As a matter of fact, this book is extremely rich in techniques and methods of therapy, and it could provide the student with the Ariadne thread to decipher some of Carl's puzzling non sequiturs in therapy.

I will anticipate the reader by suggesting that Whitaker has developed a language of discontinuity as an answer to the absurdity of living. When people insist that the reality they have learned is the only one possible, Carl's response is an impossible question, an absurd answer, a dirty joke, a dream.

It occurs to me, stuck as I am with the idea of retrospective, that it could have been possible for the editors to add an historical perspective to this book. Carl accompanied and, sometimes, led the mental health field through the last 40 years of its meandering. Did the technique of bottle-feeding appear in Atlanta at the time in which the field was concerned with orality, and the arm-wrestling technique when the focus moved to aggression? Was the multiple therapist a prerunner of cotherapy or vice versa, and was this initiated in Atlanta and moved elsewhere? What has been the influence of Whitaker's concept of therapist–patient immediacy in the later exploration of transference–countertransference in the psychodynamic field?

It seems that, in the end, I could help the reader of this book by forgetting my early constraints and share with him or her my observations of Carl's family therapy. Whitaker's therapy is impressive in the range of his interventions. He uses humor, indirection, seduction, indignation, primary process, boredom, and even falling asleep as equally powerful instruments of contact and challenge. He rarely challenges the content of a communication, but he does not accept it either. Any statement presented as complete is turned into a fragment; like James Joyce, Whitaker creates a revolution in the grammar of life. He brings up an association with his own life, an anecdote about his brother, a slightly different comment another family member made, or a joke—"What would I do if God retired?" Though seemingly random, his interventions all are directed to challenge the meaning that people give to events.

Whitaker's assumption seems to be that out of his challenge to form, creative processes in individual members as well as in the family as a whole can arise. Out of this experiential soup, a better arrangement among family members can result.

Whitaker is a destroyer of crystallized forms. If family members enter into a dialogue, it is not long before Whitaker asks a third person a question that is related to the theme tangentially, if at all. The content of family members' communications is stretched to touch areas that are human universals, but which people own uneasily: rage, murder, seduction, paranoid fears, incest. All of this is presented casually, amid commonplace statements. By the end of therapy, every family member has been touched by Whitaker's distorting magic. Each member feels challenged, misunderstood, accepted, rejected, or insulted. But he has been put in contact with a less familiar part of himself.

The materials in this book span 40 years of a master's life. They show the development of his existential theory and the simplicity of his complex techniques; they are a measure of his stature.

SALVADOR MINUCHIN

PREFACE

Carl Whitaker received his Doctor of Medicine degree from Syracuse University in 1936. At that time psychiatry was mainly concerned with the institutional care of the seriously disturbed.

Formal psychotherapy was synonymous with psychoanalysis, and its practitioners were few. Whitaker's career spans and partakes of the growth of the psychotherapeutic enterprise from the orthopsychiatric child guidance movement, to the therapy of schizophrenia, multiple therapy, and finally to family systems therapy. In all of these areas he has made often unacknowledged pioneering contributions. His work has been and remains refreshingly alive, reflecting his own preoccupation with personal growth through professional endeavor.

In addition, he has been disarmingly frank about his aims and methods both in print and in public. His candor makes it possible to trace the evolution of his thought as well as the influences upon it. Fred Allen, Barbara Betz, Harry Stack Sullivan, Freida Fromm-Reichmann—these were some of his teachers. There have been co-workers too whose contribution Whitaker has never minimized— Muriel Whitaker, his wife, and Thomas Malone, MD, John Warkentin, MD, and Richard Felder, MD, three members of the Atlanta Group.

Although Whitaker has written comprehensively, he has, like Alfred Adler and Harry Stack Sullivan, not written systematically. Also, like these men, much of his teaching has been rendered through personal contact and example. Thus, the continuing life of his work is dependent in large measure on the teachings and reminiscences of his pupils and colleagues. Like certain nonlinear anthropological phenomena his work is in need of preservation for use by future students.

However, Whitaker himself would be the last to insist that this work should be embalmed for preservation, or that any of his papers and concepts are in some way "classic," or that his writings represent a finished product. Rather, he would see his work reflecting the course of his personal development, and as a stage in the development of psychotherapy in general.

Within this context, then, the importance of Whitaker's work is threefold. First, his conceptions of normal family development, family therapy, and training of psychotherapists, based on his clinical experience, have immediate practical application. Whitaker's preference has been to remain empirical and avoid metapsychology unless it is of immediate value in the clinical situation. Consistent with this naturalistic orientation is his belief that the abnormal is merely a variety of the normal. "Psychopathology" is not esoteric, or "foreign," but arises by the same mechanisms that produce "normality." Secondly, Whitaker's work reveals the evolution of a perspective on psychiatric disorders from the intrapsychic to the interpersonal to the one family system level. Historically this development mirrors that of psychiatry as a whole, and Whitaker's experience recapitulates that of the field in micro. Finally, his work illustrates the result of faith in his own creative process and in the healing potential that, still remaining "beyond science and beyond technique," needs to be further understood and utilized.

We have grouped Whitaker's writings around four major themes: (1) the nature of psychotherapy; (2) the training and growth of the professional therapist; (3) the structure and therapy of the marital relationship; and (4) the structure and therapy of the family system. We provide a selection of Whitaker's work in each of these areas along with pertinent summaries of important concepts.

We have written an "intellectual biography" to help orient the reader, which should be read before going to the papers; Part Six ("Gatherings") serves up condiments to the papers in Parts Two through Five, to sharpen, for the reader, the flavor of Whitaker's style. These are good chapters for "dipping."

Finally, we suggest that after reading Part One, the reader go on to read the introductions to Parts Two through Five in sequence to get an overview, a picture of Whitaker's work unfolding.

JOHN R. NEILL
DAVID P. KNISKERN

CONTENTS

FROM PSYCHE TO SYSTEM
The Evolving Therapy of Carl Whitaker

PART ONE

BIOGRAPHICAL INTRODUCTION TO THE WORK OF CARL WHITAKER, MD

John R. Neill

Carl Whitaker's contributions to psychotherapeutics span some 40 years. They are of interest to us from two perspectives—the historical and the pedagogic. Whitaker's personal growth and change recapitulate that of psychotherapeutics in general in the period from 1938 to 1978. The interplay between his own development and that of his culture is subtle and reciprocal. The detailing of this interaction is one purpose of this introduction.

Whitaker's work remains instructive. His ideas, his technical observations about the nature of psychotherapy, the training of the therapist, individual, marital, and family therapy remain lively and pertinent. His thinking reflects his own experiences and is derivative of no formal school or system. This is the hallmark of a gifted clinician.

Carl Alanson Whitaker was born in 1912 on a large dairy farm near Raymondsville, New York. Life was dominated by a work routine that was long and grueling, reinforced by a strong Calvinistic religious strain that focused on salvation through good deeds. There was an associated lack of intimate expression and social companionship outside the family. His mother, however, who had wanted to be a nurse, opened the doors of their home to a steady stream of "patients" who spent time in the large family house and eased the social isolation. Whitaker recalls the formative effect of daily exposure to changing seasons and the cycle of life and death, both of which impressed upon him the inevitability of change.

To one who was shy, asthmatic, and sensitive, the family move to a bustling city, undertaken at the beginning of his high school years, was

Quotations attributed to Dr. Whitaker, unless otherwise cited, are taken from conversations with the editors.

quite a shock. Whitaker felt painfully isolated in his own world and verged on a nervous breakdown. In some respects, his experience to this point resembles that of Harry Stack Sullivan, who was from the same "hyperreligious" area in upper New York State. There are, however, two major differences worth noting. The first was the family affective atmosphere. Sullivan's family, as described in Chapman's biography, was cold, distant, and reproachful.[1] There was, in that Catholic ethos, little hope for escape from earthly suffering or eternal perdition. Sullivan became, and remained, isolated, defensive, and pessimistic. For Whitaker, on the other hand, raised in a Calvinist tradition, work could provide a sort of salvation; he could "make something" of himself. He broke out of the cell of his loneliness and forced himself to make friends: "I picked the boy who was top in my high school class intellectually and the boy who was most successful socially and deliberately forced us into a threesome. It lasted through all 3 years of college before I went to medical school. It was as though I structured a cotherapy team to break up my isolation." Here the roots of the man and the therapy begin to intertwine. The themes—forcing growth, the "curative" aspects of relationships, the rejection of isolation—will reappear at every stage. How different from Sullivan's fatalistic view of the human condition!

In medical school at Syracuse University (1933–1936), Whitaker decided to specialize in obstetrics and gynecology, but after a 2-year residency at New York's City Hospital, he keenly felt a need to know more about the psychological aspects of that field, so, in an unorthodox move, decided to spend his final year at the Syracuse Psychopathic Hospital.

At that time, American psychiatry, under the influence of Adolf Meyer, was beginning to emerge from the 19th century. Despite Meyer's focus on processes and reactions, many professionals believed nervous disorders, especially the psychoses, were caused by as yet unlocalized brain lesions or unspecified toxic factors. This was the world of Kraepelin and Krafft-Ebing: descriptive, objective, and intensely hostile to psychodynamic teachings. Save for the recent introduction of tryparsamide and fever therapy in the treatment of general paralysis, the therapeutic outlook was bleak. Whitaker was stunned by what he found and began to wonder, "How had this begun? Was psychosis truly irreversible?" He empathized with the patients' condition and was frustrated by the official attitude, summed up in the phrase "not curable."

In 1940, he applied for and was granted a year's fellowship in child psychiatry sponsored by the Commonwealth Fund. While waiting for the fellowship to begin, he moved, with his wife, Muriel, to Brigham Hall, a private psychiatric hospital in Canandaigua, New York, where he worked as assistant physician. This, too, was a step backward in time, but to the 18th century, for Brigham Hall was a true asylum where "moral treatment" was still practiced. For 7 months he and his wife "lived in" with a number of psychotics in this isolated community. At Syracuse Psychopathic, the patients had been "curiosities." Here, in this true asylum, he learned to know them as people struggling with life. It appears to have been a profound experience for a man of Whitaker's sensibilities, a man who was able, through some curious lack of fear, to spend long hours with these psychotic individuals, as interested in them as he was in himself. In these fellow sufferers, isolated and preoccupied with a vivid inner reality, he found parts of himself and felt a call to help.

At this time he was finishing his master's thesis in psychology, *Without Psychosis—Chronic Alcoholism—A Follow-Up Study*, submitted in the spring of 1941. Although not exemplary research, its conclusions reveal his state of mind at that time.

> Is it possible that abstinence should not be the aim in treatment? Is it possible that the real defect is in emotional maturity and integration? We feel that the study of alcoholism by this panoramic or psychobiological approach may furnish information which we cannot obtain by the use of biochemical, physiological, or statistical studies with their fixation on the objective experimental approach. Clinical progress then should proceed through an attempt to isolate for study not single factors as the sole basis for the pathology but the refinement of the field (i.e., the whole life space) survey, and by increasingly detailed study of the event series leading to the alcoholism.[2]

Here we see the meliorative attitude of Adolf Meyer. Individuals and their own particular reactions to life's stresses must be considered as such. Also, we see the idea that psychopathology is the expression of disintegration or immaturity—less clearly Meyer, more likely Whitaker.

In the spring of 1940, Whitaker and his wife moved to Louisville and began the Child Guidance Clinic Fellowship. He also taught in the medical school, which he found very rewarding. The chairman of the department at that time was S. Spafford Ackerly. He and a number of the faculty had undergone some psychoanalysis, but taught the ideas of Adolf Meyer, emphasizing psychosocial parallelism, reaction types, and getting the "whole picture." The Child Guidance Clinic milieu, however, was heavily influenced by the work of Otto Rank in the person of the chief social worker who had been one of his analysands. Work in the clinic and in Ormsby Village, a live-in treatment center for delinquents, exposed Whitaker to a group of patients as confounding to psychotherapeutic technique as had been the schizophrenics at Brigham Hall.

We can assume Rank's work was of help at this point to Whitaker in explaining the patient's willful resistance to becoming involved in therapy or to change. Rank had found that by sidestepping the battle of wills inherent in the psychotherapeutic setting and by providing acceptance that the therapist could be effective. He had written:

> Here it becomes clear that a constructive psychotherapy for the adult cannot be in any way education, nor reeducation either, by means of love or fear, but must be something else suited to the grown person who cannot be "brought-up" any more, but only can be understood, that is, accepted as he is. The perfect understanding [Rank's appellation for Freudian analysis] on the other hand is a self-accusation. . . . The understanding of the other rests on a love identification; therefore, in the understanding of the analyst we have a phenomenon of identification, a proof of love as the patient seeks, before the other.[3]

And elsewhere: "Experience has taught, however, that as the therapist can only heal in his own way, the patient can only become well in *his* own way."[4] Thus, the therapist was to be a "helper," an "auxiliary ego," and eventually a "friend," according to Rank. The patient was a responsible agent; the therapist *followed* the direction of his growth. Rank also posited a dynamic tension, in each person, between the will to unite and the will to individuate from the other. Separation and union were the focus of the therapeutic effort.

It seems that Whitaker affirmed Rank's notion of the therapist as "creative artist." The creative artist in the Rankian triptych of personality classification creates his own standards from within. He differs from the neurotic whose will is sublimated to that of his group and the delinquent whose will expresses itself in defiance of his group.

Another notion of Rank's that Whitaker imbibed was that of the distinction between truth and reality, that is, between psychological verity and social or consensual opinion. The former must be accepted before the latter is acceptable.

For the only therapy is real life: The patient must learn to live, with his split, with his conflict, his ambivalence, which no therapy can take away, for if it would, it woud take with it the actual spring of life. . . . If he only understands how to live in harmony with the inevitable, that is, with the inevitable in himself, not outside, then he will be able to accept reality as it is. This is no fatalistic and passive acceptance, but rather an active constructive utilization.[5]

• Rank's therapeutic focus was on the "here and now" because "the undischarged, unreleased or traumatic experiences are not repressed into the unconscious and there preserved, but rather are continued permanently in actual living. . . . Here in actual experience, as in the therapeutic process, not only the whole present but also the whole past, and only here in the present are psychological understanding and therapeutic effect to be attained."[6]

The parallelism of present life and the symbolic life was also elaborated by David Levy (who had studied Jungian psychology) in his work with children. That is, rather than positing a "deep" symbolic or primitive level, Levy showed that such material is coextensive with more "conscious" content and is available for therapeutic exploration. Whitaker's ideas about human motivation and action come from Rank and Levy. He turned to another Freudian, to August Aichhorn, for his therapeutic tactics.

From Aichhorn, Whitaker took the notion of the importance of a power base in the person of the therapist. Aichhorn, who himself was "almost" a delinquent (as Whitaker had been "almost" a schizophrenic), is described at work by Federn.

Matching wits from the first moment of their meeting, a time of prime importance in establishing the foundation for their relationship, Aichhorn was on the alert for cues—a defiant shrug, an appraising glance— knowing that he must avoid the extremes of severity and leniency. Undue severity would invite rejection from the timid, whereas excessive leniency would be mistaken for weakness. With infinite balance and delicacy, Aichhorn managed to create the impression that he was an ally, albeit with a faint adumbration of power. He avoided all reference to the dissocial behavior; fully alert to the critical issue of the child's immediate emotional state, he concentrated on topics dear to the hearts of boys and girls, a favorite football player, a movie star, fairy tales, or tales of adventure.[7]

Aichhorn felt that it was necessary for the therapist to mediate between two worlds, that of the delinquent and that of society. At Ormsby Village, Whitaker found this could best be done by splitting the functions of "therapist" and "policeman." The "policeman" was a person (the house mother) who was in charge of administrative details, punishments, and so forth. The therapist, since he didn't "hold the keys," was free to provide a maturing "unreality experience"—an experiential excursion into the timeless present described by Levy and Rank. Later, of course, the "administrator–therapist split" became standard practice in therapeutic settings.

However, Aichhorn was a believer in the epigenetic model of human development, and thus his technique in treatment was a process of uncovering—establishing the narcissistic transference, eliciting and dissolving the infantile neurosis. Whitaker's ideas effect a synthesis of Rank's strategies and Aichhorn's techniques. The stress, therefore, in therapy is on integration (i.e., putting the parts together) rather than on "uncovering and working through."

> The general philosophy of this psychiatrist is that therapy as a relationship is independent of other relationships, requires no historical background, no genetic understanding of the origin of the pathology, nor even an understanding of the dynamics of the fields of force in the personality at the time of therapy, but merely an understanding of the process of helping an individual to mature. . . . It was felt that these hypotheses, now under attack by others, would either stand or fall in this rather rigid test.[8]

The "rather rigid test" was an experiment in treatment of psychopathic (antisocial and asocial) delinquents at Ormsby Village, a "forced psychotherapy" situation, utilizing these treatment principles and attitudes. It appears to have been successful enough to have been continued with the staff in a more optimistic mood. In this experiment, Whitaker began to focus on the importance of certain structured aspects of the therapeutic process. Besides the separation of functions reflecting the "unreality" experience of therapy (and pointing to his later conclusion that therapy takes place in the patient), we have the following:

1. Therapy aims at the integration of one's personality and is distinguished from maturation, which is the learned social expression of one's integration.

2. Integration is the task of the therapist. Maturation (teaching this) is the task of the social worker, counselor, foster parent. Teaching and experiencing are different modes of knowledge about oneself and the world.

3. All therapy is "forced" by either the pressure of symptoms or, as in this case, the wrath of the social group.

4. Resistance to change must be overcome by participation of the therapist as a person: "The perception of the therapist's suffering involved in the patient's effort to inaugurate the relationship on a verbal basis seemed to be the core of the process of helping . . . [as well as seeing] . . . that rejection could cause the therapist real suffering."[9]

Whitaker tried to function as an "assistant" rather than a transference figure, with the boundaries enhanced by separation of function.

At the end of the project at Ormsby Village, he was beginning to turn his attention from the structural necessities for therapy to the proper role of the therapist's own feelings and self in the therapeutic process. These reflections were the first step toward the idea of a "professional therapist," one whose own development was welded to his therapeutic work. Much of this had to do with finding himself as well. He had inquired about psychoanalysis at several major centers but chose to enter psychotherapy locally. A major theme with which he struggled was the need in himself for toughness as well as tenderness, finding too much of the former in the medical students he taught but not enough in himself. Perhaps toughness was selfishness and ran against the religious grain. At this point he was beginning to understand that *both* the therapist and patient need something from the therapy.

When the United States entered World War II, Whitaker, as a civilian, joined Eric Clarke's group at the top-secret Oak Ridge atomic bomb facility. Clarke, in a memoir, described the spirit of the department there.

> As I indicated in my earlier letter, no one ever attempted to define the responsibilities of the psychiatric department, and consequently many things that were quite remote from the strictly psychiatric sphere found their way to this doorstep. They can be classed possibly as mental hygiene problems. The explanation may be that none of us in this section was able to keep quiet when something seemed to be going wrong, and often what were meant to be helpful suggestions bounced back with a terse note to get

busy and see what could be done to straighten it out. It was challenging
even to our inadequate staff. In many ways it was like riding a badly worn
tire. When a blowout occurred, you applied a patch and wondered where
the next blowout would come.[10]

The heavy work load allowed for only brief half-hour sessions, done
"back to back," up to 12 patients a day. Whitaker recalls that the tone
of the therapy was nondirective, allowing for "Quaker-like" silences to
stimulate the production of material. In addition, there was a 10-bed
inpatient unit where group meetings were the major mode of therapy—
the group that met included all the staff as well.

As at Ormsby Village, Whitaker had found himself, as therapist
to delinquent boys, with loyalties divided between his patients and
"society." To some extent the same role conflict was present at Oak
Ridge. Was the therapist to be a military policeman denying his
patients' regressively expressed needs or could he be accepting and
nurturing? Whitaker wished to be the latter. Fortunately, Eric Clarke
was a strong unit chief who could "front" for the therapists' "countercultural" activity. Thus protected, Whitaker devoted full attention in
therapy to developing his tender side, in expressing more caring.

He came to believe that, with psychotic patients, regression must
precede integration, and the therapist must be the "mother," that is, all
powerful, all giving, all accepting of the patients' behavior. This was
dramatically demonstrated on the day when one of Whitaker's manic
patients seized a full baby bottle (left from a child therapy case) and
began nursing vigorously. Over a period of days this man regressed,
while being nursed, to a state not unlike that of a babbling infant.
Then, slowly, he "grew up."

Clearly the therapist's acceptance and participation in the induced
regression was the facilitating factor. The bottle was a concrete symbol
of his acceptance. Regression had to be experienced, not just discussed.
The affect generated by this corrective emotional experience had to be
integrated, not just ventilated or dissipated. For this reason, the induced regressions under hypnosis or during narcosynthesis often
spurred no growth. At the time it seemed that the major effort was to
get the patient to regress. Years later, Whitaker reflected that the major
struggle was with himself—could *he* accept his own childish side, his
own "craziness"? Again, we find personal and professional growth
intertwined.

It was at Oak Ridge that Whitaker first discovered the importance of and his need for close professional relationships. There he met Dr. John Warkentin, who was to be his colleague and cotherapist for the next 20 years. It appears to have been a complementary pairing—Whitaker intuitive and expressive, Warkentin methodical and organized. Warkentin, who came to Oak Ridge after a PhD in psychology at Rochester, an MD at Northwestern, and child therapy work, was, like Whitaker, "inner-directed." Both came from intense but repressive religious backgrounds. Both men were grappling personally and professionally with the experience of intimacy. It appears this pairing in some way gave a needed legitimacy to the investigation of this topic in itself. Whitaker could be sure that his interest was something more than a projection of "personal psychopathology."

Another such intimate relationship grew up between Whitaker and Dr. Thomas Malone. Malone, who received a PhD at Duke, had a strong interest in psychoanalytic theory and had himself been analyzed. Temperamentally, he was aloof, analytic, the opposite of Whitaker. His ability to formulate concepts from experience and apply abstractions to particular situations complemented Whitaker's clinical, concretistic way of seeing. It appears that Whitaker, Warkentin, and Malone were able, over the years, to sustain a very intimate and creative partnership. Out of it came two books, *The Roots of Psychotherapy* (1953)[11] and *Psychotherapy of Chronic Schizophrenic Patients* (1958),[12] and numerous professional papers. It was quite an organic group. Whitaker was the "guts," Malone the "brains," and Warkentin the "will." In the ensuing years together each became more like the other, developing each other's latent capacities.

In 1946, Whitaker, age 34, was offered the chairmanship of the new Department of Psychiatry at Emory University in Atlanta. He decided to take the job, for it offered him a chance to again teach medical students—which he did in a novel program that was evangelical in spirit. Each student was exposed to 200 hours of psychotherapy, including 2 years' compulsory participation in group therapy with his peers. In its later stages the group functioned as therapist to a single patient. Whitaker's idea was to get physicians used to being with patients and talking to patients, before they became enclosed in the professional "character armor" of the bedside manner, forever rendering them at least partially immune to their patients' sufferings. However, the reaction of the students was mixed and often negative.

He had underestimated the magnitude of the job. Inhibiting political pressures grew, support once promised—for a residency program and an inpatient unit—proved illusory, and Whitaker found himself as a student advocate, in a painful triangle between students and administrators. In 1954, he and his faculty quit and formed the Atlanta Psychiatric Clinic, a private practice group.

This experience sharpened Whitaker's recognition of the need for an administrator–therapist split in both his therapeutic and educational work. That is, he found the often "hot" affect given and elicited in productive teaching and therapy was of such a nature and degree as to be incompatible with performing the "cool" administrative task. His resignation as chairman at Emory was more than a career choice, it was the closing of one road to self-actualization—that of administration. Whitaker would no longer attempt to foster change by administrative decree or political maneuvering. The country boy's suspicion of the city slicker was confirmed. In a dilemma no longer, Whitaker chose the individual over the group. His conviction grew that the individual's struggle to grow and change would always be opposed by societal pressures, family restraints, or anxiety engendered in the other. The fact that the therapist intervened on the side of the patient made psychotherapy an "antisocial" activity. Thus, the therapist could not serve both masters simultaneously; he must make his choice.

During the Emory period, psychiatry came alive with the possibility that schizophrenia could be treated, possibly cured, with psychotherapy. There was a great deal of heated controversy about technique, often more to do with scholasticism than substance.[13] Whitaker's group was quite interested in the therapy of schizophrenia and in the early 1950s they worked with John N. Rosen, who was later to develop the method of direct analysis.

Rosen's first paper,[14] in 1946, dealt with his dramatic use of psychoanalytic interpretations to make contact with catatonic schizophrenics. The later-evolved "theory" of direct analysis seemed jerry-built to those who studied Rosen at work, bearing little relation to his actual practice.[15] Whitaker's group believed, like Rosen, that it was of paramount importance to make contact with the regressed schizophrenic patient by active techniques that included physical contact. Both knew that the absence of fear or hostility in the therapist was required, as well as a willingness to identify with the schizophrenic and his plight.

There were deep differences between the two groups centering about the nature of the schizophrenic's symptoms. Rosen believed that pathology was pathology—that the schizophrenic's symptoms were immature, crazy, stupid—and to be attacked then as such to "break the back of the psychosis." Whitaker's group was notoriously "positive" about this point. Symptoms, they believed, were a sign of health, a sign of the schizophrenic's attempts to survive, to care for himself and his family. Symptoms could be creative solutions to a series of vexing interpersonal problems. At any rate, patients were not to be attacked, shamed, or taunted. It seems, in retrospect, that Rosen's influence on Whitaker's work was moral rather than intellectual. That is, Rosen's example gave Whitaker and his group courage to press ahead with their own ideas, however radical, about the psychotherapy of schizophrenia.

This notion that all psychopathology is a manifestation of the organism's attempts to heal itself is also found in the work, widely circulated at the time, of the British psychoanalyst Melanie Klein. Besides positing an inborn tendency for growth, Klein, in her work with children, believed it was crucial to establish contact with the patient's unconscious fantasy, using symbolic (primary process) language and responses.[16] Klein's emphasis on the interpersonal basis of intrapsychic conflict and the patient's use of projective identification as a solution also appears in the work of the Atlanta Group.

If all psychopathology was a manifestation of the organism's attempt to heal itself, then symptoms were signs of "stuck" growth. Further, if this state of affairs was initiated and maintained by untoward affective experience, a restitutive experience might free the patient for further growth: "Therapy at this phase includes the symbolic defeat of the mother's introject at the hands of a mature therapist. Therapy is not simply the replacement of cathexes to the symbolic 'mother' that have never occurred, but the active reconstruction of the pathological cathexes. . . . We must develop in ourselves a biological response to the patient as powerful as that of the original mother during the first few weeks when the baby's cry makes her stomach contract."[17]

The experience of the individual members of the group was "spread around" by means of certain therapeutic practices. Quite routinely one member would consult by sitting in during the second of three evaluative sessions. One of the group was designated "administrator," the other the actual therapist. Often two therapists saw one patient together. There was, as well, a weekly conference at which the data on all new patients were presented for review by the group. The growing sense of intimacy, of shared "combat experience," made it possible to give each therapist an intensive critique of his handling of the case.[18]

Whitaker and Malone gradually developed a strong interest in what they called the "roots" of psychotherapy—what was the nature of this process, the nature of the therapist's contribution, of the patient's contribution? Three half-days a week for 2 years were spent on "the book," both men talking, diagramming, then dictating material that was later reworked and refined. The result, published in 1953, was *The Roots of Psychotherapy.*

The book begins with a rather heady manifesto delineating psychotherapy from psychiatry—the former a culture-bound function, the latter a true science. They felt research on the psychotherapeutic process, in an attempt to reduce the process to a science (i.e., technique), to be pernicious and in a way immoral. That is, research violates the sacredness of the therapeutic relationship and the integrity of the therapist. The latter, as researcher, would have divided loyalties. He would, of necessity, simultaneously think of his patient as subject and object.

Later chapters establish the psychologic principles of energetics, transductions, field principles, adaptation, and entelechic growth. Pathology indicates an interruption of the entelechic growth process, that is, "when the organism extends its own functional capacity, and makes dynamic that which has been potential." In the case of schizophrenia, there is "an exaggeration of a repair dynamic to the detriment of the organism as a whole," much like an immune hypersensitivity reaction. Growth could be catalyzed by therapeutic activity. The measure of growth, which is the goal of any therapy, is not in increase in adequacy or adjustment per se, nor the removal of symptoms. Rather, "The more unconscious the response or the greater the participation of the unconscious in his total functioning, more likely is the individual to function personally and socially on an adequate and gratifying level." The unconscious is seen as the source, the integrator, more like Jung's creative unconscious, rather than the seething, churning cauldron pictured by Freud.

How was growth to be achieved?

Perhaps it would be better to speak of an emphasis on synthesis and integration as against analysis and insight. The therapist's or patient's understanding of the genetic panorama of his current inadequacies assumes less significance than the development of the patient's capacity to function as a person integrated within himself and with the surrounding culture. *This synthesis can be achieved by experience and seldom simply by understanding* [our emphasis]. It may or not be pertinent to understand that his inability to be aggressive toward a parental figure is due to certain infantile fears and guilt. In contrast, the experience of being aggressive toward a parental figure, even if he does not understand what occurs, will be helpful if the patient finds that after such expressed aggression he does not suffer and is not rejected. This is the precise difference between synthesis and analysis, between experience and insight.[19]

Thus, activity on the part of the therapist ("push for growth"), a focus on experience rather than reflection, and a goal of integration (maturity) rather than adjustment (social adequacy), are the characteristics of any true psychotherapy. The remainder of the book details stages and techniques of therapy, the changing role of the therapist in the experience, and the importance of certain affects in the process.

Notice the positing of mutuality and reciprocity in the therapeutic endeavor. Both parties regress; both grow and integrate. The interpersonal field is, in fact, a projection of the intrapsychic state and the other is an "image come to life." The critical difference is the *relatively* greater maturity and integration of the therapist. It is, in fact, the therapist's residual "slivers" of pathology and his ability to identify similar pathology within the patient that makes therapy possible. Whitaker's view is that therapy is of necessity a "selfish" endeavor. Once therapy has begun each party is, to some degree, simultaneously patient and therapist to the other. The proportion of affective investment changes as the pair passes through the natural course of the therapeutic process.

The Roots of Psychotherapy also covers two other important concepts—positive and negative anxiety. Negative anxiety comes from the fear of being overwhelmed by the breakdown of defenses. Positive anxiety is caused by the perception that one is not living up to one's potential for growth. Reparative therapy, aimed at symptom removal, is the antidote for the former. Positive anxiety is what pushes one on beyond the symptoms to growth and integration.

The professional therapist is described as one who has committed himself personally and professionally to his own growth and is thus qualified to catalyze the growth of others. Although there is a basic appreciation of the common human condition (i.e., mutual psycho-pathology), the therapeutic relationship is not an I–thou (humanistic–existential) one. It is that of a professional, albeit one who eschews technique, working with a layman. "Professional" is thus a moral rather than a social distinction. It bespeaks a vocation rather than an occupation. The person of the therapist, then, is again inseparable from the process of the therapy.

As an aside, it is interesting to note the grudging concession made to the necessity for technique in the latter chapters of the book. Technical maneuvers are mentioned in the section titled "Brief Psychotherapy," and are to be used deliberately, but sparingly, when time for one reason or another is limited. In the end, it is the planned use of tactics such as silence and "forced fantasy" that is of concern rather than the activities themselves. The spontaneous unexamined process of therapy can be destroyed by therapeutic strategies. This wariness is redolent of the psychoanalytic therapist's fear of contaminating his patient's free associations.

The Roots of Psychotherapy received mixed critical response. Most reviewers were enthusiastically "for" or categorically "against" the authors. A truly balanced review of the book is difficult to find. (One wonders whether it was ever closely read.) The authors were surprised and disappointed at some of the clearly sectarian, vituperative attacks that alleged their work was inhumane, antisocial, barbaric, and suggested that the authors were in need of a great deal of personal "help." Several points in particular were the target for criticism.

The first was the experiential, even anti-insight bias of the book. This struck at the very roots of psychoanalytic therapeutic practice (certainly "ego psychology"), where insight provided by an affectively neutral, highly controlled and controlling therapist was held to be the curative factor. The converse of this—that the therapist should avoid technique and draw on his own pathology to effect a cure—was extremely unsettling! The world was turned upside down, a transvaluation proposed. A serious attempt to disprove Whitaker's model, however, was never undertaken.

The unabashed activity on the part of the therapist was another starting point for diatribe. The Atlanta Group was known to utilize physical contact with patients during the course of some therapies. This took the form of hand holding, arm wrestling, or occasionally, with schizophrenics, mutual face-slapping interchanges. The psychoanalytic establishment was mortified. Again, there does not appear any clinical evidence cited by the critics to prove their contention that these behaviors were "destructive." This was rancor born or prejudice. Its effect was to strengthen Whitaker's resolve to press ahead with his investigations.

It had become the custom for the staff of the clinic to meet for a 4-day weekend every 6 months in Atlanta with the staff from the Schizophrenia Research Project at Temple University, Philadelphia—Edward Taylor, John Rosen, and Michael Hayward. The Tenth Conference Proceedings, which took place at Sea Island, Georgia, were published in 1958 in a book titled *Psychotherapy of Chronic Schizophrenic Patients.*

At the Atlanta conferences, patients interviewed were discussed. During the course of each conference, all the participants were involved in the intensive therapy of a single chronic schizophrenic patient or the patient and his family. Group, individual, and joint sessions were held, mixing various combinations of therapists. Over the years the group began to focus more and more on the role of the schizophrenic's family in the genesis and treatment of his illness. In case after case, they found the therapist could "extinguish" the psychosis only to have it flare up again upon contact with the family. Whitaker found that in these families, the mother had established an antenatal symbiotic relationship with her offspring that served to fill her own sense of emptiness, the residuum of her own childhood. This turning to the child left her spouse free to seek attachment to nonhuman sources of reward (money, prestige, etc.). This turning away further deepened the isolation of the mother and her intensified fear of craziness. The mother, in these cases, treated the child as the projectively identified "crazy" (i.e., primary process) part of her own self. Thus she becomes what Whitaker calls counterschizophrenic; that is, she counters or blocks the emergence of her own ego-dystonic wishes and socially unacceptable designs by projecting them onto her child. This pairing, with the resultant continuing infantilization of the child, is stabilized by the further withdrawal of the father into extramarital sources of gratification. Only an external event (death, divorce, arrival of a sibling) or biological maturity of the infant can dissolve the symbiosis. At such junctures the mother is threatened with the intensification of isolation, leading to fears of insanity, and the child faces autonomy, which he fears will lead to death (affective starvation). Thus, schizophrenia has its etiology in interpersonal relationships, which are, at the same time, intrapersonal.

Much of the therapeutic work involved manipulating the distance between the schizophrenic and his family to achieve therapeutically useful isolation. Like therapy with delinquents, work with schizophrenics had to be strategically planned—the metaphor of the surgeon preparing the operative field appears often in Whitaker's writings of this period.

The therapeutic strategy consisted in the therapist's replacing the mother as the symbiotic partner in the schizophrenic dyad. The therapist himself had to experientially replace her. He himself had to experience the "agony and ecstasy" of that mutually double-binding relationship. The difference was that the therapist was comfortable with the regression in himself. It was this very regression in herself that the biological mother feared and had defended against projectively, and which stabilized the schizophrenic dyad. Thus the therapist imposed a therapeutic double bind in lieu of the pathologic one. With all avenues of escape literally blocked, the patient was forced to become more sane, more integrated, as he became more counterschizophrenic in response to the therapist's regression. As this happened interpersonally, it was hoped that it happened simultaneously intrapsychically. As he once experienced his mother's projected primary process, the patient experienced and internalized the therapist's projected sanity or secondary process or maturity. Thus therapy was a corrective emotional experience that was in essence intrapsychic. The course of therapy consisted of alternating cycles of patient–therapist regressions and corresponding or countering integrations. Again, isolation from those who would reestablish the old one-way symbiosis was critical.

Achieving this critical isolation was impossible, Whitaker found. Since Atlanta at that time had no suitable hospital facilities, the group first tried nearby private sanatoria but encountered formidable administrative interference. They next tried boarding patients with people in the community, but this, too, resulted in administrative confusion. Finally, they rented a house where their patients could live, but this eventually proved unsatisfactory. The only alternative was to begin treating the schizophrenic with his family.

When treating the individual patient they found cotherapy was often necessary to duplicate the original parental dyad and to facilitate the administrative–therapeutic division of roles. Now, working with the family, Whitaker found the multiple therapist team necessary to prevent the enmeshment of the therapist in the powerful family system.

The single therapist was all too prone to take sides, to become the covert agent of one family member or to avoid involvement altogether. The presence of two or more therapists provided both a safeguard and an opportunity for modeling of more desirable interpersonal behavior for the family. Alternating participation and withdrawal from the family system was taught, rather than permanent enmeshment. In addition, the therapists gained power in their ability to reflect and comment on both their own and the family's feelings and activities. Multiple therapy with the entire family became standard practice at the Atlanta Psychiatric Clinic. How well it worked is not clear, for no outcome research was undertaken, but it is clear that the therapists felt it was an improvement over other forms.

In the early 1960s, as the clinic was growing, the feeling of being a small group striving mightily against strong odds began to fade. Each new staff addition weakened the old "combat experience" bond that had provided so much closeness. Subgroups began to form around certain administrative issues. The clinic was becoming an institution; Gemeinschaft was evolving into Gesellschaft. Whitaker felt the urge to leave, and go on to newer territory, and to resume teaching. In 1964 he joined the faculty as Professor of Psychiatry at the University of Wisconsin at Madison, with the understanding that he would teach family theory and therapy.

The chairman at the time, Milton Miller, recruited a genuinely eclectic faculty. Several had been pupils of Carl Rogers during his tenure at Wisconsin. To these Miller added several Menninger graduates (he himself trained there) and Dr. Carl Fellner, a European-trained existentialist. By keeping the department small, selecting his faculty carefully, and providing a rather charismatic leadership, Miller made possible much experimentation and cross-disciplinary investigation during a time when most departments of psychiatry were preoccupied with squabbles about psychoanalytic orthodoxy.

Whitaker's first formal involvement was as consultant to the inpatient unit under the directorship of Dr. Gene Abroms, newly arrived from Yale. They began first with regular family conferences and moved on to admitting entire families to the ward for treatment in marathon therapy sessions. The details of this experience are given elsewhere.[20] The difficulty of teaching concepts understood through experience—of translating into words for students of what had been private language in the Atlanta Group—had to be faced. It appears that Whitaker felt some resistance to doing this, to squeezing his ideas into print, to conceptualizing what was felt process. Instead, he began therapy with interested residents, using both clinic patients and his own private cases. The addition of videotapes made it possible for him to "sit in" on additional sessions.

This was a period of focusing, again, on himself and his goals, heightened by the end of most of his parenting duties at home and facilitated by the existential ethos of the department at Wisconsin. Again, there was a personal and professional struggle taking place.

> Twenty years of play therapy with children, relationship therapy with delinquents, mothering of neurotic self-doubters, and depth therapy with chronic schizophrenics was coming to a grinding halt. Couples therapy became more and more boring. How could one aging therapist stay alive? Even cotherapy, the 20-year model for patient parenting, felt sterile and stereotyped. It became clear that my personal growing edge must become my central objective in every relationship—if experiential therapy was for my experience, then patient modeling could be for real. If I could change, they might try to. I am time-limited; my marriage is deep, long, and wide-coursing. But only the family lives and has a forever-extended time dimension.[21]

Perhaps the struggle for personal integration came to a close during this time. The "slivers of pathology" had been worked out. The next task seemed to be his exploration of his relationship to the family group. The tension was now between Whitaker as a person and as a functioning member of the group. He would use his "growing edge" rather than slivers of pathology to press for change. During this time, perhaps in the context of his reading of the literature of Zen Buddhism, he felt more free to be openly "selfish" in therapy, to be himself, and to minimize his transference availability.

His formulations of the family system show the influence of the communications theorists of the Palo Alto group, especially Jay Haley. Whitaker saw the healthy family as flexible in assignment of necessary roles to its members—mothering, fathering, and scapegoat positions should be rotated among family members. He described the development of the family unit as it moved along a biologically determined time coordinate. There was always a dynamic tension between the needs of individual members for individuation and the needs of the family system.

His therapeutic technique became more strategic but remained spontaneous in content. It consists of two major elements. Using paradox, mystification, and spontaneous craziness, he sought to raise the anxiety of the family group, to provoke a crisis, by "raising the affective thermostat." Simultaneously, he provoked, badgered, and seduced individual family members into changing their customary ways of responding to crisis toward the direction of a greater maturity. In many ways, Whitaker's approach parallels that of Murray Bowen. Both emphasize the biological rootedness of psychological maturation, and the goal of helping individual family members toward a higher level of differentiation of self within the family. Their technical approaches are, however, vastly different.

It is instructive to recall that this family work took place in the 1960s, a time when many were preoccupied with "doing your own thing," antiestablishment politics, and self-transcendence. However, there are no strains of aestheticism or anarchism in his philosophy. Although he inveighed on the side of the individual, he believed that there was no possibility of individuation outside the cultural dialectic: "The job of psychotherapy may well be changing. . . . Doing your own thing is not enough. It can also grow as you can also belong. Togetherness does not make for growth, neither does 'being your own person.' There has to be a balance, an increase in each, and that's our psychotherapy project."[22]

Self-transcendence takes place through the family group, not in isolation. Whitaker has never questioned human participation in the life cycle. Self-actualization, potentiation, and growth are rooted in human relationships, not esoteric intellectual or physical discipline.

We believe the major theme in Whitaker's work is the search for wholeness or reunion. Man is by nature incomplete. It is the move from the garden of childhood that first rends the fabric. The cultural pattern represented first by the family, then by "public life," divides us from ourselves and others. The two patterns have certain coordinates or cognates that appear in these writings.

Intimate pattern	*Cultural pattern*
Nature	Civilization
Family intimacy	Business roles
Marriage intimacy	Public relations
Schizophrenia	Sociopathy
Unconscious sources for living	Conscious sources for living
Corpus callosum transfer	Right- or left-brain living

We find ourselves, says Whitaker, in a world of flux, of eternal movement. The movement is not random, but cyclic, seasonal, with an ebb and flow. This coming into being and passing away is not tragic, but natural, therefore good. Life, then, is not a journey or a "brief interlude," but a cycle within many other cycles.

A human life cycle, limited in time (time retains for Whitaker a biological directionality) is one of crisis and re-creation. One continually rediscovers that which he is. The kingdom of God is indeed within you, Whitaker would say. Heaven is "being yourself," and "living in your own unconscious." Recall here that the unconscious is a fertile source to be tapped, not a monster to be tamed.

To complete the self one needs communion with others in relationship—parents, spouse, family, generations of family, all of nature. Coming into relationship, the self paradoxically (and for Whitaker the human world is one of paradox) gains in definition and potential as it seems to contradict the laws of nature. What is given away to others remains. This genre of paradox is at the core of the great religious systems (e.g., "He who would gain his life shall lose it"). In fact, Whitaker's self, we suggest, has been lived religiously, unhampered by the pride of pilgrimage.

Within the religious framework is latent a definition of evil. Evil springs from the interference with the natural pattern, with the cycles. Some concrete "sins" that bring groups to therapy are constructing graven images of the self, sacrificing to the false gods of stability. The basic human tendency is not to be evil (i.e., the tendency is to grow). People are evil to the extent that they remain cowardly, mystified, or ignorant. Therapy aims to free both patient (family) and therapist from this bondage.

There is, then, no end, no final state. T. S. Eliot's observation applies, we think, to Whitaker, and perhaps to all therapists.

> We shall not cease from exploration
> And the end of all exploring
> Will be to arrive where we started
> And know the place for the first time.[23]

PART TWO

PSYCHOTHERAPY

A brief recapitulation of Whitaker's ideas about psychotherapy in general are presented here; they are developed in detail in the chapters that follow. Also, the relation of Whitaker's theory and technique to "orthodox" psychoanalysis, and to the language of the object relations school in particular, is considered briefly. Information about Whitaker's debt to Otto Rank's theory of therapy and technique can be found in Part One.

In this section appear those writings of Whitaker that more or less have to do with psychotherapy and individual psychotherapy in particular. It is impossible to specify individual psychotherapy as opposed to or distinguished from family therapy, since all of the therapy is really of a piece. When Whitaker wrote *The Roots of Psychotherapy* (with Tom Malone), he was working with individual patients; his conclusions at that time were couched in a language and perspective congruent with that context. His views on the "roots" or dynamics of $n > 1$ therapy, are to be found largely in Parts Four and Five of this book, and do not supplant this individual work but, rather, are congruent with it. It is most accurate to say that Whitaker's thinking about psychotherapy has not gone through "stages" but through elaborations and variations.

Whitaker believes that it is important to clarify what is and what is not psychotherapy. He believes that valid psychotherapy is a form of encounter. It is a process that accelerates the growth of the person. More technically, it is an identifiable sequence of events that takes place between a professional therapist (or team of therapists) and a patient or system seeking to grow. This growth takes place intrapsychically, bilaterally; it is catalyzed by the therapeutic process. The ensuing psychic maturity is reflected behaviorally as a greater interpersonal competence. As we look at some of these terms of definition more closely, we see that much of what today passes as psychotherapy in fact is not.

Growth

In Whitaker's view the human organism operates teleologically. That is, it struggles unrelentingly to become what it can become—as the acorn becomes the oak. The growth that is provoked in psychotherapy is psychobiological growth, the growth of the entire organism. The human individual struggles toward "maturity," which is an intrapsychic state expressed behaviorally as greater interpersonal and social competence. This drive toward growth and integration is axiomatic, a therapeutic article of faith. There is a basic tension between the individual growth process and the human environment —parents, family, group, culture. These supraindividual forces tend to block the growth of the individual, yet, paradoxically, are required for the growth of the individual to occur. This paradox is the key to understanding Whitaker's attitudes about the individual vis-à-vis the group. The individual does not thrive at the expense of the "other" or the culture, nor vice versa. The presence of this dynamic tension, of inherent but necessary conflict, reveals the relationship between the individual and the other as paradoxical rather than ambivalent.

Encounter

The proper mode of psychotherapeutic interaction is existential encounter. Encounter implies immediacy of relating (i.e., spontaneity), presence, and an exchange with the flinging aside of social role constraints. Encounter retains the notion of conflict, combat, and hostility embodied in its etymology as well as the notion of meeting. In the psychotherapeutic encounter, unpredictability reigns. No escape is permitted; no dissembling, no affective dishonesty is tolerated. The encounter intends to shake all participants out of the restrictions of old satisfactions, ways of acting, ways of feeling. This frankly upsetting experience is necessary, Whitaker feels, to reactivate the stalled inherent growth process.

Intrapsychic Process

Whitaker believes that the "change" in psychotherapy is intrapsychic, perhaps at the neurobiological level. The body changes as well as the "mind." The growth that he speaks of is literal. It is the same as the growth process that pushes the child to become an adult. Perceptual, affective, and cognitive systems all take part and are affected. Some of the growth is restitutive or remedial—bringing the patient to his chronobiological age.

People become "stuck" in their growth to maturity because of the absence of facilitating experiences usually provided by parents or culture. Maturity is a sort of ideal endpoint in Whitaker's view of human development, a state that is rarely achieved, but toward which the organism unremittingly strives. Beyond remedial growth comes the growth toward integration of certain parts of the person. This typically takes place in later stages of psychotherapy. This integration is reflected in better function in all spheres. For example, in an adult one must experience oneself in many roles—and here we distinguish between "playing" and "experiencing." One must live these roles as ego states or states of being. Sometimes they may appear to conflict. For example, how does one, unless one is quite integrated, experience the same person (and himself) as, say, parent of one's child and lover? It requires the greatest flexibility to integrate these ego states (images).

Process

Psychotherapy is a process; that is, psychotherapy is a series of experienced events that catalyze the natural growth of the organism. It involves the therapist moving against his and the patient's resistances, attempting to shape their relationship into an existential rather than a social one. As the patient begins to go deeper into himself, so too does the therapist go into his own self in a series of reciprocal transactions. The notion of depth as Whitaker uses it refers to more and more uncustomary but nevertheless vivid ego states (i.e., states of thinking, feeling, and acting). These states may be described, from a maturational point of view, as more primitive. They are states through which the patient has not grown, due to lack of satisfaction of the needs present in these particular states. The integration (i.e., experience of ownership) of these ego states frees the patient for further growth and at the same time allows him to reexperience these states in himself and with other people with much less conflict. What was once feared and unknown is now known and satisfied.

Bilaterality

Experiencing of the "deeper" ego states is bilateral. Both the patient and therapist experience these altered states of ego consciousness (see Figure 1[1]). There is a significant difference, however. That is, the regression or alteration of the therapist's consciousness is less profound, less total, and reflects a partial participation in the regression. The therapist's more primitive needs to be or to experience himself in this mode, in these ego states, as a "child-self," for example, have been satisfied. The patient's experience, then, is more total, more intense, possibly more primitive, as he reexperiences his unsatisfied needs, satisfies them in the relationship with the therapist, and moves on.

The process of therapy also has to overcome a certain amount of resistance, inertia, or habit. Both therapist and patient have mastered intrapsychic and culturally imposed inhibitions about abandoning role prescriptions and expectations with each other, yet they must enter into the encountering mode. A certain amount of technique (see below) is required to "kick start" the process, to change the mode of interaction from a social to an existential one. Here technique is used in the service of fostering this relationship (facilitation) and not as an end to itself.

Anxiety and Technique

Whitaker lays great stress on the use of anxiety as a means of motivating psychotherapeutic process, of switching the mode from social to existential interaction. Most patients come with some anxiety, but this is often not sufficient to motivate the therapy. Any activity that isolates the relationship, or confounds therapist–patient expectations, heightens anxiety and forces the existential mode. The therapist, for example, may maintain silence in the face of the patient's request for feedback. He refuses to discuss real-life problems, refuses to be the patient's resource person. He will speak only in the existential mode, rather than the social mode, as soon as it is warranted to do so.

A distinction is made between "positive" and "negative" anxiety. Negative anxiety is that which has motivated the patient to seek therapy. Most succinctly, it is caused by what the patient fears about himself, what he does not know, or what he is at that particular moment. Positive anxiety is like the Kierkegaardian trembling before

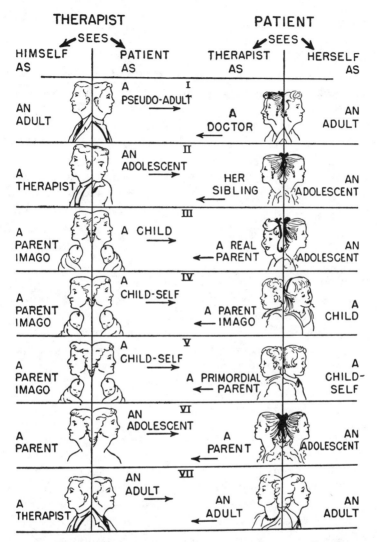

FIGURE 1. SYMBOLIC REPRESENTATION OF BILATERAL STATES OF EGO CONSCIOUSNESS. (From *The Roots of Psychotherapy* by C. A. Whitaker and T. Malone. Copyright © 1953 by The Blakiston Company. Used with the permission of McGraw-Hill Book Company.)

the possibility of freedom to become other than what he is at the present moment. This positive anxiety is compounded of fear and anticipation.

Following the principle of bilaterality, the therapist himself will also experience these anxieties. Clinically, it is the therapist who, by dint of his training, first perceives the presence of differing types of anxiety in the therapy and begins to teach this discernment to the patient. At times the therapist will seem to the patient cruel as he purposefully pushes the patient and himself into greater and greater areas of anxiety. However, the therapist perseveres because of his belief in the basic tendency of the organism toward growth and because he knows that the greater the risk, the greater the gain. By pushing the relationship existentially to new areas of experience, both parties begin to grow and change. One sees the therapy then dominated by "disequilibrium dynamics," that is, a moving toward symmetry and a flip into complementarity (see Figure 1 again). In this light, what was once the symptom, anxiety, now becomes an indicator of the progress of the work. Encouraged by the therapist's courage and his own newfound freedom, the patient learns to tolerate the anxiety, which he now experiences as the anxiety of his freedom to choose.

The Ending of Therapy

Many, perhaps most, therapeutic relationships end before they are, in the therapist's judgment, finished. The question arises as to how this "failure" is explained. Who is to blame—the therapist (poor technique, countertransference) or the patient (unsuitable for therapy, transference)? Whitaker takes a rather sanguine view of this phenomenon. He believes that the patient takes the therapy he needs or can tolerate at a given time. If the therapist has been unremittingly "professional," as described above, we can count these premature exits as punctuation "growth spurts." One doesn't grow up all at once and one doesn't run away from home unless he thinks he can make it on his own. Neither is there an elopement without a fiancée just outside the door.

In a therapy that runs a natural course, there is, near the end, a change in the tone of the relationship.

The latter stage of any psychotherapy ought to include a great deal of give-and-take, a kind of existential peer consultation. It's like two adults, one of whom has had a different kind of, maybe more, or a more sophisticated understanding of a particular area of living, will now share this and meld it with the patient's knowledge and understanding of his own living process. There is no bind involved; no responsibility for carrying it out, since the transference has been minimized. The patient is like a late-adolescent child who has enough of himself to feel free so that he can listen to the parent without being destroyed or losing self-esteem and then go on to make his own final decisions. At this stage, the therapist can even talk about himself to the patient, things he either hasn't solved, or more valuably, things he has experienced in the past that he looks at now with a wry sense of humor.[2]

Valid Psychotherapy

What is *not* psychotherapy is any kind of relationship or intervention that does not aim to produce growth, but which stabilizes the emotional status quo. Therefore, "supportive" therapy, education, counseling, and so forth are not, technically speaking, psychotherapy. Improving communications or insight are not therapeutic in themselves if they do not produce that qualitative change in one's psychic maturity that is the hallmark of valid psychotherapy.

Clearly, then, much of what passes for psychotherapy does not fit this definition. It follows, then, that not all persons who come forward with some problem are suitable candidates for psychotherapy, since they may not be at a time in their lives when they are willing or able to grow and change. Such people must be identified by the psychotherapist and redirected by him to suitable social therapists.

Whitaker's Work and Orthodox Psychoanalysis

If we distinguish between psychoanalysis as a theory of human development and as a technique of therapy we can say that Whitaker has always rejected the latter definition, while embracing the former. In agreement with Freud, he holds that as a therapeutic modality, psychoanalysis, the free-association method, is relatively ineffective. While agreeing that the genetic approach is a useful research technique, he rejects it as useful for therapy because

> the essential dynamics of psychotherapy unfold themselves within a current experience. This current experience modifies the relationship of other current experiences to each other, and integrates the biological effect of past experiences. . . . Such a therapy might be appropriately labeled *experiential*. It is essentially nongenetic, ahistorical, atemporal, and therapist-activated, and deals essentially with id processes. This distinguishes it from ego-level therapy, with the latter's analytical genetic, temporal, historical, and causal emphasis.[3]

As Robert Harper has pointed out, Whitaker's ideas about therapy represent a "regression" to earlier Freudian emphasis on id psychology.[4] Indeed, in Whitaker's view, behavior is largely unconsciously determined. However, this unconscious is not the rapacious infantile unconscious postulated by Freud, but the creative unconscious as conceptualized by Rank and others; it is the unconscious of the creative artist. This unconscious determinism is not tragic (à la Freud) but teleologic. The relation between the individual and his social group is paradoxically interdependent and not ambivalent. That is, the more the individual becomes himself, the more he can be with others, the more effective he is, and so on.

Whitaker's Work and Object Relations Theory

It may be helpful to look at Whitaker's ideas about therapy in the language of object relations theory.[5] In object relations terms, the therapy process as Whitaker has described it consists of the serial replacement or modification of the patient's own introjects with those of the therapist. In some cases, the process is restorative or reparative; in other cases, it pushes beyond past experience.

As mentioned before, the therapeutic mode is one of encounter. The therapist forces in himself an epigenetic series of complementary projective identifications we call "therapist." In this state, he experiences, by projective identification, the patient as his own (the therapist's) adolescent self. The patient internalizes this projection and becomes (i.e., experiences himself as) an adolescent. In this adolescent ego state, the patient then experiences (i.e., projectively identifies) the therapist as a sibling. The therapist, in response, begins to experience himself as a parent and projectively identifies the patient as his own child-self. The projection of the therapist's child-self onto the patient activates the patient's own child-self representation or imago, which is altered by the therapist's projection of his child-self. The most primitive pairing is that of the patient's child-self state and the therapist's "primordial parent state." In this process of exchanging projections, or partial counteridentifications in the language of ego psychology, the patient's self-images are repaired or polished, becoming more acceptable and more accessible to him, less likely to be split. In some cases where intropsychic maturation has been severely stunted, the patient in fact keeps the therapist's good projected image (e.g., an image of an adolescent self). As the patient's "intrapsychic family" of images or introjects becomes more and more accessible and acceptable, they are able to be integrated into a more cohesive self-image. Energy once bound in defensive work—primarily splitting and projective identification of bad objects or parts of bad objects—is freed to be put to interpersonal use.

The primordial parent–child self-pairing lasts as long as it takes to gratify the needs of the patient's child-self—that is, to experience himself as a "good child" or to experience his child-self as good. At some point, the patient begins to grow, that is, to experience progressively more mature ego states, and correspondingly engages in the complementary projective identifications of the therapist. This growth sequence, then, recapitulates in turn the epigenetic states of normal development. The patient leaves therapy not cured or mature but different. Specifically, an intrapsychic change has taken place that now allows the patient to experience and gratify part identifications as being "him" or "self" and to pursue their care and feeding in the world outside the therapy in culturally acceptable ways. He will experience a greater ability to empathize (i.e., experience and accept parts of himself in others) and to be intimate (i.e., sustain mutually rewarding projective identifications) in human relationships.

We can now discuss the notions of positive and negative anxiety as mentioned above in an object relations context. Again, it is negative anxiety that pushes the patient into therapy. This phenomenon accompanies a state of disintegrated living in which he experiences himself as intrapsychically fragmented. In the course of therapy negative anxiety increases each time the therapist responds inadequately to a projective identification. For example, at the point where the patient has introjected the therapist's projection of the therapist's (good) child-self and simultaneously experiences his own (presumably bad) child-self, negative anxiety mounts. The presence of two incompatible self-fragments or self-images may make the patient feel that he is "going crazy." At this point, in order to be adequate, the therapist must respond maximally to the patient as a good primordial parent. (This is the patient's complementary projective identification of the therapist, the therapist's identification of the therapist, and the therapist's identification of himself at this point in therapy.) Since part of the adequate therapist's response to the projective identification is motivated by his positive anxiety in a shorthand way, we can say that the patient's negative anxiety (fear of his introject) covaries with the therapist's positive anxiety (experience of his own good introjects). In other words, when the patient is most deeply experiencing the aspects of his negative self, the therapist must heartily keep up his experiential good projective identification of the patient.

Whitaker retains a great deal of the content of the Freudian developmental model. He holds to the psychopathological division between neuroses and psychoses as based on deficits in Oedipal and pre-Oedipal experience (the traumatic theory of causation). Defenses are acknowledged but are seen as homeostatic rather than simply resistive; that is, defenses prevent growth as well as regression. Defensive structure is also extremely effective and very hard to change, since it is rooted in a biological substrate.

In summary, then, Whitaker's differences with psychoanalysis largely have to do with technique: analysis is rejected in favor of synthesis, objectification for encounter, and neutrality of the therapist for a bilateral experiencing.

As an historical note, we should recall that Whitaker began his work in an atmosphere that was hostile to psychotherapeutic innovation. One could deviate from "orthodox" psychoanalytic practice (the free-association technique) only at the risk of professional censure. Whitaker's early work took place during the McCarthy years, years of political conservatism and public conformism. Surely these factors contribute to a stylistic irritability in some of his early work— that is, the insistence on isolation of the therapy process, the extreme self-consciousness about using such clearly acceptable techniques as mutual sharing of fantasies.

MY PHILOSOPHY OF PSYCHOTHERAPY

Here we have a kind of cinematic show, a "film-clip" view of Whitaker's ineluctable personal and professional development. The importance of people and places far outshines the importance of ideas. A sense of wonder, of wondering about, emerges from this writing. Twists of fate reinforce certainties rather than producing confusion. We see emerging here a man of sensibility more than a man of thought; a man of action, not contemplation. And as he acts, he questions his sensibility, open to new ways of experiencing.

Over the years, his purview enlarges, from the individual to the marital group, to the family, to generations of the family. Intrapsychic constructs are replaced by the interpersonal, the interpersonal by the system. Curiously (and happily) there is no creeping aridity, no abstraction of himself. Whitaker feels as "there" with a multigenerational family as he did with the individual patient, perhaps more so.

Underlying this philosophy of psychotherapy is Whitaker's idea of the therapist as perpetual patient, asking for help from all who come to him. This state, of course, is a place to come to, not to start from. If one would become a therapist, he should first become a patient.

My personal philosophy comes out of character structure. I wonder if I've gone past my childhood dairy farm with the rich sense that Mother Nature was always nearby, nutrient and available? I wonder how far I've gone from the rigid religious protestantism that said I couldn't play on Sunday, I couldn't read except religious pamphlets or the Bible? I wonder how far I've gone from the yen to be a missionary to China that made me go into medicine and avoid being a preacher? I wonder how far I am from the 1940 child psychiatry training, the opportunity

Reprinted by permission from *Journal of Contemporary Psychotherapy*, 1973, *6* (1), 49–52. Copyright © 1973 by the *Journal of Contemporary Psychotherapy*.

to have no residency training programs, no seminars on psychiatric theory, no psychiatric state hospital training, the opportunity of being in my training period when World War II broke out so that I had to learn by filling the service load.

Have I grown since the beginnings of my own personal psychotherapy, which went on and off for 10 years with a total of 5 or 6 years of psychotherapy? In 1941, I began work with adolescent delinquents, and came to sense their pain and the energy they had, and then to Oak Ridge for the total push of back-to-back psychotherapy, 20 patients a day, a half-hour each, and the development of a team approach to psychotherapy.

I wonder how much of my philosophy came from the accidental discovery that you could bottle-feed psychotic patients like infants. Just as Tom Main did in England, we discovered that induced regression by the baby bottle or a physical tussle with the patient was a tremendously helpful experience. Then came 10 years as chairman in Atlanta's Grady Hospital with group therapy for all medical students throughout their first 2 years. We began to use individual houses for the intense co-therapy treatment of an individual schizophrenic à la John Rosen. Those were the years of working with Tom Malone and John Warkentin as we developed an understanding of growth-activating psychotherapy, the double-binding techniques and the use of frequent consultations. Then we began the half-day-a-week writing seminar on our responses to patients and to each other, which went on for 8 years. How much of my present psychotherapy emerges out of the conviction that Baudelaire expressed when he said "Boredom is the ultimate stimulus to crime"? Why did I begin to demand my own growth as a valid base for helping the patient? How much of my own personal psychotherapy philosophy is based on the husband–wife struggle of raising six children and a developing conviction that the intimate character of my growth was not selfish; that the freedom to be loving in psychotherapy was part of being human, that the child–parent model of psychotherapy was so all-pervading that family therapy was the obvious next step?

Out of these and other forces less apparent to me I became more and more convinced that psychotherapy was something I did for myself and the patient merely participated.

Dick Felder and I worked for years to define the line of responsibility between the person who wanted help and became a significant other to me, with whom I could mix my life and gain something for myself. We found more freedom, a push for the growing edge, and a gradually developing determination that unless the person on the other end of the phone stimulated positive or negative affects in me I would stay cool. In the first interview I learned to stay afraid of being a pseudomother, since the freedom to care is not something one can imitate. I became more and more convinced that my own personal involvement was the thing that makes psychotherapy worthwhile for me and for the patients. If so, then they should be stuck with my slivers of pathology just as I was stuck with their problems. I had long before become convinced that I couldn't trust myself and that a cotherapist was the kind of person who could shape my pattern, that he was not a limitation, and that reshaping my pattern was the way toward increasing fun, increasing competence, and increasing usefulness to the patient. Now, almost all my work is family therapy or group therapy.

Behind this philosophical determination was also the conviction that only as I changed was I able to verbalize, since insight, though not a cause for growth, was a by-product, and if there was no growth there probably was no insightful bit of increased individuation and increased togetherness.

During the last 5 years, or maybe a few more, I've been preoccupied with the overall value of a systems approach and have gradually become more insistent that I start with a couple, or better yet with a family, or best with a three-generation extended family or a friendship network. The need to continue with this unit is, of course, another matter. Best to start with as big a base as possible, to keep all of that base in therapy if feasible, but to treat as much of the system as possible.

PSYCHOTHERAPY OF THE ABSURD

During the last 2 years, I've been more and more involved with what I've come to call "psychotherapy of the absurd," an expansion from the paradoxical intention therapy that Milton Erickson and Jay Haley have described. My tactic has become a kind of tongue-in-cheek put-on; an induced chaos now called "a positive feedback"—that is, we augment the pathology until the symptoms self-destruct. It's a kind of accented irrationality with a flip kind of elaboration of the irrational components brought to therapy until the absurdity, like the Leaning Tower of Pisa, is built so high that it comes crashing down.

I believe craziness is where life is. Personal confrontation, like accented fantasy, and sharing my own irrational free associative and symbolic experiences, is a stimulus for the other to expand his own model and mode of operating. I see psychotherapy as beginning in a transference model, with a parent–child quality. When successful it moves from this transference phase into an existential relationship, much like the parent who has grown up enough to stay with the teenager as he finds his adulthood and is then able to be human-to-human rather than parent-to-child.

In the framework of family therapy I find the initial battle is a battle to define my "I" position (Murry Bowen), and that once that has been settled, the second battle is one I call "the battle for initiative," that is, defining their integrity and their status as separate living units. I respect very highly the initial flight into health, and frequently see this as the end of a more or less obvious crisis that has been set up to push growth, whether it's a family fight over divorce or a schizophrenic psychosis. I am convinced that this plunge into growth, whether it's cancerlike or just a slight fever, is the essence of creativity and should be treated with the care and nurturing that it deserves. I am convinced also that lovingness, or as Rogers calls it, "unconditional positive regard," is not enough. Even if such regard is available in me for these particular persons, it demands that I also accord them the status of a worthy foe, that I be willing to mix my life in with theirs. If they are to get help, I'm going to get help, too. I feel it's essential that the patient be given the courage and the opportunity to grow and to bear the pain the growth necessitates. I can't imagine coaching a football team and telling them, "If you get tired don't exercise anymore. It might hurt you." I feel the same way in psychotherapy. Once it's established that we are a team, I feel free to demand of them and expect them to demand of me. Life without pain is an addiction and the fantasy of perpetual happiness is like the "delusion of fusion" that Hellmuth Kaiser formulated.

I am convinced that just as symbolic togetherness "is," reality also "is." The reality of transference has the same validity as the reality of my being hired and of my being available for firing, just like the family carpenter or auto mechanic.

Psychotherapy as a profession in this day and age has moved from the state where it was 20 years ago. Then it was anticultural. Patients came to us afraid because they were going to talk about sin. Nowadays, psychotherapy is not anticultural; as a matter of fact the culture may well have overtaken psychotherapy. Sexual obscenity is only exceeded by the obscenity of brutality, wherefore psychotherapy has become a struggle to help the deviant members of our world find a place in the organized social structure. It's as though now we're expected or pushed into taking the role of helping the culture develop some capacity to deal with the destructive aspects of mass populations. How can we keep people from following the route the rats and mice took in those famous experiments? I have some feeling we're in the position of the Pentagon, which, having developed as a cultural need, is now being attacked. We fulfilled the expectations they had of us. What have we done for people lately? We're all in limbo.

As a person, psychotherapy has been for me a tremendously exciting way to live. I often think of how boring my life might have been as a country practitioner. How dead it would have been as a lifetime, compulsive repetition of delivering babies. I even face the shivers of those moments when I was defeated with a sense of excitement that somehow those who were near helped me through my flashbacks. Through that availability of psychotherapists for me, I had the opportunity to link up with colleagues whose lovingness made the stress growthful. I doubt these would have been available to me in any other professional setting. As John Warkentin used to say, "Imagine spending full time at your own self-development. It's kind of spending your lifetime as a patient or like raising children. We just face the pain and the joy of significant others day after day."

I've always been scared at the hazards of the profession: would I go crazy, would I commit suicide in my despair? Later in life it changed. Would I get calluses? Would it progress until when asked "How are you," I would routinely answer, "Oh, keeping cool"?

The hurt of sharing another's pain that goes beyond the limits of my capacity makes searching for an escape route from that hell a very crucial struggle. But it's great to get to the place where I ask therapy from anyone and everyone who comes to me for help. And what's even more wonderful—I get it.

THREE TYPES OF CRAZINESS

The terms "crazy" and "craziness" appear frequently in Whitaker's writings and require some explanation. In his early work the terms are synonymous with the phenomenon of primary process thinking in the psychoanalytic vocabulary. The unconscious was seen as a source of creativity—the creative unconscious of Otto Rank—and thus to be sane (L *sanus* = health) one had to be able to know and use his unconscious, his craziness.

Later "craziness" grew to encompass all forms of spontaneous thought and action. "Craziness" was defined more by its structural characteristics (i.e., non sequitur, irrelevant, paradoxical) than by content (i.e., primary process language). "Absurdity" becomes a rough synonym for craziness in this context.

Here, in this brief note, we have what could be called a clinical phenomenology of craziness. The three types are defined by three motivations—seeking intimacy, experiencing intimacy, and fleeing. The importance of distinguishing among types of craziness cannot be overestimated. It would be very wrong, for example, to abort an episode of "going crazy" or to take seriously (i.e., give medication to or incarcerate) one who is, facultatively, acting crazy.

It is not difficult to imagine that there are three kinds of psychoses. In our language we say "He was driven crazy," and "He is going crazy," and "He is acting crazy." It seems logical to assume that the person who is driven crazy, typically the psychotic patient admitted to the state hospital, is someone who has been "driven out of the home," out of his world of intimacy, and is trying to find a home in the world. He uses the infantile language of craziness in order to find out if there is someone to respond to him in the primitive, free language of intimacy of his mother. . . . The effort to reestablish his game-playing adaptation is sometimes successful but frequently breaks down with the least amount of added stress. To help him resolve his craziness by going completely crazy, that is, by giving up all the game playing with the therapist, requires a kind of profound intimacy greater than that of his mother with him during those first 2 years of life. It's pretty hard to come by. Most therapists aren't willing to be that intimate and in one way or another give up the effort.

The patient who "goes crazy" falls into a different category. All of us are more or less playing a social game and yet are simultaneously hungry for the opportunity to be "born again" and relive our infantile patterns, thus arriving at truly integrated wholeness. Any patient given the opportunity is capable of going into a "therapeutic psychosis," under the stimulus and support of a competent and professional therapist. Such "going crazy" has remarkable similarities to the 3-day schizophrenia we saw during World War II. It is greatly dependent on context and is an expression of the degree of intimacy between the patient and the therapist. If the therapist stays with it, this therapeutic psychosis is quickly over, and the patient can go on with the rest of therapy, becoming an integrated whole by recurrently dipping in and out of the therapeutic experience of one's own irrational, infantile, primitive self.

A third mode of craziness, that of "acting crazy," is one where the intimacy is very limited. The psychotic who has readapted to the social game-playing world has almost the ultimate weapon by reenacting his craziness on a deliberative facultative level. He may not be aware of this capacity to turn his crazy behavior on and off; he may do it only under stress. However, this "acting crazy" is significantly different from either of the above-mentioned categories because the therapist, who knows him, can turn it off by the simple expedient of seeing through it, laughing at it, disregarding it, or in some other way making it an unsuccessful coping mechanism. However, the fact that the patient needed to act crazy implies a struggle with immature coping mechanisms and the need for some psychotherapy to help him mature his pattern of adaptation to the social structure.

THE PSYCHOTHERAPEUTIC
IMPASSE

with John Warkentin and Nan Johnson

Impasse is always bilateral. The patient or therapist has in some way and for some reason (perhaps anxiety or despair) withdrawn the affect necessary to make the therapeutic process continue. The symptoms are bilateral; the therapist or patient withdraws; the other becomes frustrated. The feeling of "stuckness" is mutual or, more precisely, symmetrical.

The authors describe a number of causes of impasse, most of which consist of the underinvolvement of the therapist (too little affect) in the therapy. There are many ways to curtail or forestall an impasse, but all begin with the therapist's admission of his own "stuckness" or impotence. Where there is no remedy, where the use of an outside consultant has been fruitless, the authors urge a mutual termination rather than referral to another therapist.

The solution of the impasse turns upon a paradox: to confess failure is to begin to move; to experience impotence is to be set free to take action.[6]

In brief psychotherapy it occasionally happens that therapy progresses for a time, and then bogs down. This is more particularly a problem with the type of psychotherapy which depends on the patient–doctor relationship per se, and which utilizes a minimum of reassurance, advice, or interpretation. To limit this paper it seems wise to disregard the problem of inertia in initiating therapy. The purpose of this paper is to describe the impasse, its etiology, and offer methods for resolving it.

The therapeutic impasse is a stalemate or plateau in the process of achieving a therapeutic objective. The impasse might be best illus-

Reprinted by permission from *American Journal of Orthopsychiatry*, 1950, *20*, 641–647. Copyright © 1950 by the American Orthopsychiatric Association, Inc.

trated by the case of a patient who was referred to the clinic for essential hypertension. He had accepted the possible emotional etiology and had made progress in the first five interviews. The relationship with the therapist was good and the patient had worked through two incidents expressing the relationship between aggression and his hypertensive headaches. In the sixth interview the patient stated he could think of nothing to say. He said, "I feel there are still some things I want to discuss but now I can't get at them." This interview seemed unprofitable and before leaving the patient asked, "What do I do now?" The next interview had the same sterile quality and the patient stated, "This isn't helping me the way it used to. I used to feel better after these interviews."

From the above it would seem obvious that both the patient and the therapist face the problem of decelerating progress and increasing emotional hesitancy. It is as though the therapeutic experience has lost its emotional voltage and the patient has developed a new cynicism and fatalism. In this deteriorating relationship the therapist felt increasingly frustrated. He was participating less and the interviews seemed to be a waste of time.

In general, the impasse consists of a deterioration in the relationship. This is characterized by emotional withdrawal in its various forms, such as intellectual discussion, emphasis on symptomatology, interest in real life and its problems, or periods of futile silence. This superficiality results in frustration and irritability. The patient seems unable to carry his own share of responsibility in the interview and demands more direct guidance from the therapist. In his frustration the patient may ask for some substitute for psychotherapy, such as medicine, shock, hypnosis, or amytal interviews. He may even talk about referral to another therapist.

The impasse has been described as a deadlock between patient and therapist. It is not likely to result primarily from poor technique, such as taking a probing history, ill-advised manipulation of environment, giving inappropriate interpretations, or other errors of method. Rather, the relationship is of such a nature that the patient is unable to proceed with the satisfaction of deeper needs. He continues to come back, but something in the relationship prevents the expected progress.

The etiology of the impasse depends upon the dynamics of the patient and the therapist. One patient may be unable to tolerate a therapeutic dependence, because of disillusionment and fear engendered from previous relationships in which he was dependent. Another patient may use the early interviews to allay his anxiety purely by emotional catharsis. Actually, every patient also has deeper needs for which he is unable to find help until the therapeutic relationship is stable enough.

A third patient is afraid that the therapist is not strong enough to help him with what seems to be an impending psychosis. He continues his interviews but is unable to go to a deeper level.

Another patient starts well, establishes a strong relationship, and then is paralyzed by a fear of rejection. Such a patient may overevaluate the slightest indication of rejection on the part of the therapist.

Still another patient is afraid of losing the adjustment he has, no matter how unsatisfactory it is. Such a patient dares not lower his defenses beyond a certain point, because of the confusion that would result. In addition, he doubts his capacity to develop a more satisfactory pattern of living.

Finally, a patient may be panicked by the magnitude of the change needed and may unconsciously maneuver the therapist out of his role and confuse him in his motivation. This may be done with the adroit use of tears, humor, anger, or intellectual seduction.

The question arises as to the possible role of the therapist in the etiology of the impasse. It has been said that an impasse results from the lack of sensitivity and of dynamic force in the therapist. The most experienced therapist may lack force in the interview if he is overworked and too harassed by other responsibility. For example, it is very difficult for a psychiatrist to make rounds on a large number of patients and have much force of feeling left to strive for emotional contact with a single patient in therapy. A similar lack of force may develop in the psychiatrist who has little opportunity for contacts with other psychiatrists and has no colleague with whom to share his changing insights. Likewise, the lack of success encountered by the young doctor in a continued-treatment ward, where therapy is relatively unrewarding, would be a hindrance to sustained effort.

The therapist's role in the etiology of the impasse may be related to his own motivation. The initial clarity of purpose may gradually become contaminated as therapy continues. In the early interviews he was able to function in a giving therapeutic role, but the therapeutic situation gradually assumes an additional meaning for the therapist, namely, to satisfy some of his own unresolved tensions. At first, the therapist may not be aware of the new meaning of the interview for him. He may find himself seeking the gratification of satisfying an affect-hungry patient, and show this by prolonging the interviews. On the other hand, the therapist may be seduced into overidentification by such factors as the cultural background. On the day he has an appointment with a patient of special interest he may find himself wearing his best tie or may even catch himself humming a love tune after the patient leaves. His needs may be reflected in greater interest in the ex-patient of a competitor, or in the wealthy or brilliant patient. There are many factors which make it difficult for the therapist to function adequately and these may contribute to the etiology of the impasse.

The therapist may also be hindered in his freedom by an awareness of one or more of these difficulties. Then he may become increasingly cold and distant until the relationship may reach a stalemate. At the same time, he may set too high a goal for the patient with whom he overidentifies and may thus miss the indications given by the patient who wishes to terminate the relationship. When facing an impasse, the therapist will feel that treatment has been a failure, and he is thus challenged by the failure to go beyond his functional role.

Finally, a major factor in the continued progress of therapy is the conviction of the therapist that the patient is treatable. If the therapist begins to feel that the patient presents too large a constitutional factor to be amenable to psychotherapy, or even that the patient is malingering, this hopelessness will be felt by the patient and interfere with further progress.

Certain methods of approach have seemed useful in meeting the problem of the therapeutic impasse. Even after the impasse is recognized, it is tempting to continue discussing the patient's conflicts and simply try to do this more effectively. However, there is little profit in continuing such a losing battle for change in the patient. It is wiser for the therapist and the patient to recognize their joint problem and come to grips with a different facet of the relationship than heretofore. The therapist must now take the responsibility and initiative for the restructuring of the relationship. He has at least three areas of choice: (1) to consult a colleague; (2) to struggle through it with the patient on his own; or (3) to call a consultant into the interview situation.

The effectiveness of discussing the impasse with a colleague depends on the freedom of the therapist to expose his own feelings to himself or to his colleague. Out of this discussion the therapist may be able to reevaluate the entire relationship. This reevaluation may itself change the interlocking dynamics of the patient–doctor relationship so that the therapist may become more effective. The discussion may be of a supervisory nature on an intellectual basis, or virtually amount to therapy for the therapist. The effect of such a conference may often be apparent in the next interview with the patient.

The therapist is now prepared to challenge his own or the patient's motivation. In this new struggle, the therapist may find a new capacity to meet the patient's efforts to avoid the relationship. He is now more secure in his role and prepared to use more of his own dynamic force. This is extremely delicate, since the therapist must face the possibility that he may be rejecting the patient. For example, the therapist might say, "I'm concerned over the barrier between us. I wonder if I have somehow made you feel I am not as interested in helping you get well as I was. I wish we could do something about the coldness between us." However, such self-criticism may be evidence of a new capacity to participate.

The therapist may not always have the opportunity for collaboration, or he may elect not to discuss the impasse with a colleague. He may be forced to restructure the relationship on his own. The focus for this effort must be on the difficulties within the relationship rather than on the patient. Whereas the therapist had previously concerned himself with the patient's feelings, now he may assume a limited right to express both positive and negative feelings about the impasse.

If the therapist feels sure of his own feelings he may use silence to meet the superficiality which seems to be a retreat from therapy. The tension that develops thereby may help the patient assume more responsibility in the interview. At times it has even seemed that expressions of outright aggression over the patient's inability to participate more deeply served to rupture the patient's cynicism. The therapist may show disapproval of the patient's participation by saying, "This seems like a waste of time to me. You've talked about these symptoms again and again and it has never seemed to help. We're going to have to do something about this bottleneck." The therapist may even recall the patient's right to terminate therapy.

The third alternative is to invite a consulting psychiatrist as catalyst to the relationship. The therapist may introduce this to the patient by saying, "I wonder how you would feel about having another member of the staff in to help us. We can ask him to leave as soon as we agree that he is no longer helpful." It is obviously essential that the therapist be secure with the consultant. The patient is likely to feel ill at ease with the intruder and is sure to resent the introduction of someone who is identified with the therapist. The situation is difficult also in that both patient and therapist become defensive because of the implied inadequacy of both of them. If the patient and therapist are able to express their mutual difficulty, the consultant is more likely to become an effective catalyst to the relationship. In this triangular situation it has seemed logical that the therapist should question his own motives first, so as to provide a better basis for the patient's participation.

The presence of the consultant is also valuable because he is able to carry part of the responsibility for the patient, so that the therapist can express what he had suppressed from fear of his own immaturity. Even if the consultant does not participate very actively, his mere presence may make it easier for the therapist to express some of his own deeper feelings. The entrance of the consultant has the further significance of implying possible therapeutic failure. The patient and therapist may have discussed the possibility of failure, but the entrance of the consultant makes it more imminent. The increased intensity of the therapeutic situation usually results in a greater bond between patient and therapist, who then mutually exclude the consultant. It has been surprising that the patient and therapist rarely ask the consultant for a second interview or second series of interviews.

If our efforts to resolve the impasse fail, it has not seemed wise to refer the patient to another therapist or to introduce therapeutic adjuncts such as hypnosis, amytal, or shock treatments. Instead it has seemed advisable to strive for a joint ending of the relationship. This may be another indication to the patient that the therapist still considers the emotional relationship of primary importance in therapy. It must be understood by the patient that he can always return, and that the therapist will be ready at any time to resume the struggle of solving the impasse. Thus, in the face of apparent failure, the complete frustration for patient and therapist, and their acceptance of it, may precipitate a change in personality dynamics during subsequent weeks and months. Thereby, the therapist tries to help the patient experience the therapeutic value of using his own initiative in achieving a separation even if it means rejecting the therapist.

SUMMARY

The psychotherapeutic impasse has been defined as a stalemate or plateau in therapeutic progress. It has been discussed as the mutual responsibility of the patient and the therapist, because it is not so much a problem in technique as it is a disturbance of a human relationship. The patient may become afraid of being too dependent, or of being rejected by the therapist; or the patient may desire to keep the situation superficial, and may try to maneuver the therapist. On the other hand, the therapist may contribute to the etiology of the impasse by a gradually developing belief that the patient is not treatable, or the therapist may be too busy to devote himself wholeheartedly to the treatment. He may overidentify with the patient in a manner that may satisfy the therapist's needs, or he may have too little contact with colleagues to maintain sufficient interest and motivation in psychotherapy.

The methods described for meeting the impasse include a confidential consultation with a colleague, open discussion with the patient in an effort to evaluate the defects of the therapeutic relationship, or inviting a consultant into the interview situation. This third method has proved valuable where the relationship was particularly difficult to resolve. If it is not possible to recapture the therapeutic process, it seems wise to insist on an ending of some type. If the patient is able to achieve a separation, even if it means rejecting the therapist, this experience may in itself be of some therapeutic value.

GUEST EDITORIAL: THE IMPASSE

An impasse in therapy is like having both ends of the seesaw touch the ground at the same time. Technically, an "impasse" is defined as bilateral symmetry in a relationship controlled by a positive feedback loop. Neither

Reprinted by permission from *Voices*, 1968, *4* (3), 5–8. Copyright © 1968 by the American Academy of Psychotherapists.

party can regain contact with the primary task of the therapy. It is the therapist's responsibility to prevent or terminate an impasse. Usually some person or event from "outside" the closed system is required to provide the needed affect or perspective.

Much of the criticism of psychotherapy is in one way or another related to the problem of impasse. One day we say psychotherapy is no good because the patients don't get anything out of it, that is, nothing moves. Another day we say psychotherapy is bad because it goes on forever. Most patients come to a therapist because of an impasse in their living. Somehow they have been stalemated. If it lasts a long time, we call them rigid or burned out. They also come because they are either beginning to break out, hoping to break out, or determined to break out of their impasse with life. Psychotherapy is a microcosm of life. When psychotherapy does not succeed, it frequently is because that also becomes a stalemate—a kind of cold war that locks therapist and patient in a fixed state.

The impasse problem is not just restricted to psychotherapy. There is a cultural impasse in the United States now [the 1960s] between the black and the white. Neither is able to move in it and the tension of this lockstep condition becomes more and more frightening. The world agonizes daily over an impasse between parents and children. I'll bet even the caveman faced the one between parent and adolescent. Nowadays, most marriages pass through serial impasses. The 10-year syndrome or the 7-year itch are both indications of our social concern with this kind of lock between two individuals or groups of people or states of being.

There is something about the impasse that is like an unhappy bilateral symmetrical dance. Neither of the individuals is able to change the rules of the dance. It's as though they're locked in and neither one can switch to being creative. It includes a kind of mutual disrespect and somehow the process becomes, as they say about a love affair, "bigger than both of us." The 20-year stalemate between Russia and the United States is typical. Essentially, it's a situation such that there is no whole of which each is a part and which transcends them both. It's as though the two units had lost their goal-directed pattern. If the United States and Russia could acknowledge the United Nations they would be out of the impasse and each working for a better world, which indeed may be happening. We know about dead marriages in which the partners rest, each in his individual rocking chair, she reading *True Romances* and he reading *Playboy*, but positioned back to back. Dr. Scheflen describes them as the "gruesome twosome."

Sometimes the impasse is three-cornered.

Father H. was fat, soft, petulant, with temper tantrums like a 7-year-old who was a blustering tyrant but there was no chill in his emotional storm. Mother H. was a tight-lipped fury with every muscle locked ready to spring, yet all was hidden under her idealistic, gentle, agreeable mother image. Impassed with each of these and with their partnership was the 16-year-old son. His lash-back sneer of disdain, his teetering on the edge of delinquency, was combined with a derisive and degrading attitude toward father and a sarcastic pseudosweet snarl for mother. In this case the impasse had a peculiar quality. No combination of two was stable in this unit. As soon as father and mother got together they would break up and father and son would get together in a fight, or mother and son would get together to discipline father. Thus, the triangular impasse revolved around a constant instability, which was in itself very stable.

In the therapeutic setting of a one-to-one relationship the impasse develops after therapy is under way, and after the transference has been established in both directions. The therapist and the patient try to sell *each other* on an image and agree to conceal their personhood behind these images. Once this has taken place there is a kind of mutual enjoyment of the state and the dance goes on and on. The systems theorist would say that the units of which the system is composed are under control of the system, and that the system tends to maintain itself in a steady state.

PREVENTION

Assuming that we are out to do something about the impasse on a deliberate level the therapist is wisest to deal with it as a problem in prevention. Many aspects of psychotherapy can be set up to prevent an impasse. The early establishment of a deliberate, contrived role structure for the therapist undoubtedly prevents subsequent impasses or tends to, if it's well done. If the therapist is in charge of everything that happens in his hospital operating room, the patient is not apt to tie him up in a bilateral unchanging role status. Once this deliberate therapeutic structure is established the therapist is more free to respect the unique custom-made living style of the patient and not invade his life but only his feelings and his personhood. Prevention of impasse probably is also aided by any secondary commentary, for example, an objective discussion of the transference. Thus when the existential and peer relationship typical of healthy late-phase psychotherapy develops, it is not contrived.

It is not new to say that negative affects must certainly be expressed to prevent impasse. Assuming that the impasse is frequently the result of the secretive character of the one-to-one relationship or indeed of much psychotherapy, it follows that the use of a consultant, either early in therapy and later if needed, tends to break up the lockstep. This consultant should be professional but the same result is frequently obtained by bringing in others of the family, even the extended family, and sharing with them the lockup in the therapeutic relationship, or just asking them to participate in the relationship. In the conduct of psychotherapy the freedom for the creative flow of communication tends to prevent a game-playing lock. Freedom on the part of the therapist to leave the scene emotionally, attention-wise or even physically, also helps. If the therapist dares invade his own role stance he creates a happening, and such a happening makes it very difficult to get into a fixed-impasse set.

TECHNIQUES OF BREAKING UP THE IMPASSE

One of the most obvious ways of breaking up an impasse is having a war. When the cold war stalemate is disrupted by a hot war this changes everything. The war may be and frequently is started and won by the patient who ends treatment, walks out, or in some other way breaks up the relationship. Better it should be the therapist who starts so that it can be verbal, affective, and made part of the ongoing process of change. This takes a kind of freedom in the therapist to hang loose, because once the patient has him uptight it's a different kind of world and it's very difficult to reheat the cold relationship. However, a deliberate effort to make the impasse a joint problem is aided (as in prevention) by the humiliation of bringing somebody in from the outside. If it's family psychotherapy, one can sometimes reactivate the family romance. If it's a marital impasse, sometimes one can begin the process of decourting preparatory to the talked-of divorce. The decourting may then change to recourting. The biggest struggle with therapeutic impasse is with the schizophrenic. This necessitates a kind of marriage and divorce between the therapist and the patient, as put forward well in "The Jet-Propelled Couch" (Lindner, 1956). It's a kind of folie à deux.

THE IMPASSE WITH THE SCHIZOPHRENIC

At the risk of being far-out, I should like to postulate how the schizophrenic patient grows in psychotherapy. If the schizophrenic does develop a transference, it's because the therapist is like his mother. His mother was a double-binding person, and so is the therapist. They establish a relationship in which the therapist double-binds the patient, and the patient is able to double-bind the therapist. Gradually this bind becomes tighter and tighter until each of them is locked in step with the other and neither is in charge of any change. Indeed, neither is capable of more than minute quanta of change. This was exactly what he had with mother. We know that when such a patient gets well in a state hospital by some fortuitous and still unknown means and leaves the hospital, it is frequent that mother herself comes into the hospital or goes crazy in some other way. Assuming that this is also true in psychotherapy, our patient dare not get better for fear his therapist would go crazy. On the other hand the therapist went into this relationship deliberately; I assume that for myself at least, my objective for this is to find some more of my own craziness. So at the point where we are impassed in a kind of figure eight reciprocal double bind, I elect to experience some more of my craziness (my growing edge) supported by the homeostasis of that relationship. When I do "go crazy" the patient has no other recourse except to be the counterschiz, if I may use the term, to my schizophrenia. Thus, we are in a pseudo-impasse and each of us is capable of forcing the other, but I as the therapist want to be "crazy" and he is thereby forced to be "sane." Once this reciprocal movement is established the oscillations become wider and wider, assuming all goes well, until we are further separate. One other factor has to be added to this. Once the freedom to oscillate is residual in each of us we are free to love each other, and this is the kind of love that revels in the other's gain, not just in one's own gain. With such love the movement apart, or rather the movement into life on the part of each of us, takes place gradually and with satisfaction in each of us for the life and openness of the other. The love lasts forever, but the freedom is constantly increasing.

Could it be that no impasse in a relationship means no love is developing? So why not go on and break up the impasse with one psychotic after another? I'll tell you why! My society fights my craziness. Each time I have to defy this pressure for social lockstep, and I get scared each time.

THE ADMINISTRATIVE ENDING IN PSYCHOTHERAPY

There is no more profound test of the professional therapist's mettle than his ability to say goodbye when he must. Whitaker reminds us that therapy can be interminable because the therapist cannot bear to terminate. If anything, we underestimate our patients' strengths and overestimate the negative effects of our comings and goings.

Over the years, Whitaker, in his own work, has insinuated more overt and covert interruptions into his therapy. He may tell a patient to stop therapy and go out and try it on his own for a while. Alternatively he may set, in advance, an agreed upon, limited number of sessions. In any case, as administrator of the therapy, the therapist reserves the freedom to make such structured changes as he sees fit.

In his movie about bears Walt Disney shows a scene in which the mother bear drives her two cubs up into a tree, frightens them until they stay there, and then goes off, never to come back. When they get

Reprinted by permission from *Voices*, 1966, 2 (2), 69–70. Copyright © 1966 by the American Academy of Psychotherapists.

hungry they come down and then they're on their own. Mayhap this is more useful as one of the models for psychotherapy than we usually admit. Otto Rank ran a powerful experiment in "preset" ending many years ago.[7] The story was largely disregarded. Each of us from time to time has seen patients who were forced to terminate psychotherapy because of reality details, like changing of jobs, or the death of the therapist. In my recent life story, 65 patients lost their therapist when I moved out of the state. This has highlighted the value of such an ending and recalled for me other experiences which I had shelved. The satisfaction of continuing to see the same patient in an increasingly intimate process over a period of time makes it easy to forget about ending.

Mary was a psychiatric nurse who had been grossly double-crossed by her first psychotherapist many years before. He had used the content of her therapeutic interviews to get her mustered out of the service by a disciplinary board. Since then she had developed severe lung disease and severe alcoholism. I saw her for a period of approximately 1½ years in what was a pretty chaotic and ofttimes explosive therapeutic experience. She pulled out of her cynicism, her alcoholism, and became a warm, responsive person. Then something went wrong. Week after week we tried to break through it but she was getting worse rather than better. This was before I learned to bring a consultant in or learned to add a second therapist if I was failing. In my travail, I decided to terminate therapy. I assumed she had gotten all I had to give. She would have to either find someone else or fight it out on her own. I told her this, and that under no circumstances would I ever see her again. The next week at her regular hour she arrived in the office. I told her I had another patient, and she saw I had no intention of seeing her. She said indignantly, "Well, there's one thing. You can never stop me loving you, and you can never stop loving me no matter what you do," and she turned and left. I have never seen her again, but for over 5 years I received Christmas postcards telling me how well things were going and wishing me a Merry Christmas.

This administrative ending was a variant of what Rank did. It was not preplanned from the beginning of the therapy as Rank did it, but it illustrates the value of administrative decisions about the personal relationship.

In my recent experience I spent 9 months saying goodbye to my 65 patients in Atlanta and moving 1000 miles away. Approximately 18 patients decided to continue their psychotherapy. Part of this was deliberate intent on my part, and seemed to be fairly constructive. A number of patients responded to the termination with conspicuous spurts of growth with freedom to express hostility and intimacy which had been unavailable to them before the pressure of my leaving.

It is obvious but paradoxical that the administrative aspect of psychotherapy is always in conflict with the therapeutic aspect. Professional therapy involves a process of having one foot in the relationshiop and one foot out. The relationship is personal and yet it is professional. The administrative handling of the therapeutic situation could be called a game, yet the therapeutic relationship is a life-and-death struggle. The administration of therapy is mechanical and social and governed by the rules for these, and yet the personal relationship is intimate and profoundly affective. In essence then, the administrative aspect of psychotherapy is a role relationship and the therapeutic relationship, at its best, is nonrole—a purposeless, heart-to-heart relationship. Yet administrative freedom can coexist with therapeutic involvement of a profound character. If the therapist has reality basis for making an administrative decision, he may do this even though it hurts both him and the patient to break their relationship. The child guidance clinic has known for many years that the child needs to preplan his termination visits, and that once they're planned it's important for the therapist to maintain his set and end "on schedule." This kind of joint administrative decision is also possible with adult patients but frequently forgotten in the satisfactions of an ongoing relationship. In trying to understand this I have even wondered whether the therapist was afraid of the deathlike implications of such a termination—does he have a sense that he is killing the patient? Maybe the only thing he is destroying is his own delusions of grandeur. Maybe the patient can live without him.

When the above dynamics are reversed the therapist may become bored with the patient's continued interviews or angry at being stuck with a recurrent symptom pattern, and the kind of dependence that binds him just as it does the patient. Here, too, it is better that the therapist face the patient with his boredom and with his hostility. If they cannot work through this then it is my opinion that he should terminate therapy in his hostility, saying in effect, "I'm so angry at your refusing to get better that I feel I cannot see you any further. You must either go to someone else or fight your life out in some other way than trying to use me as your crutch." The therapist might even say to the patient, "I believe my own hostility is such that I cannot be of any further use to you and I am unwilling to go on with such unresolved aggression, even though the resolution implies the termination of your therapy and my admission of failure as a therapist."

THE USE OF AGGRESSION IN PSYCHOTHERAPY

In this chapter, Whitaker discusses the phenomenon of the therapist's aggression, mainly in a group therapy setting. He believes that we must distinguish between assertiveness and hostility, two different modes of aggression. Assertiveness captures the notion of wanting to define oneself, to find one's "I-ness" vis-à-vis the other. Hostility is a form of aggression bent on hurting or damaging the other. Thus we find that aggression is used to establish, in both cases, a relationship. On the one hand we have a symmetrical relationship, a kind of existential equality. On the other hand, we have a complementary relationship, one of supremacy and submission. It is not the content of the action itself (e.g., shouting) that determines assertiveness or hostility but, rather, the resultant structure of the relationship following the aggressive action.

This chapter might well have been titled "Why Love Isn't Enough in Psychotherapy." If the therapist believes that the patient has (as he himself has) a biological drive for growth and integration and that growth is fostered in an intimate relationship, he must be aggressive. By refusing existential symmetry, the therapist becomes a technician, not a person. He perpetuates the myth of the omnipotent parent and the belief that love and hate do not expand at the same rate in a relationship. The therapist's expression of his own "I-ness" engenders the experience of self-esteem in the other, who is no longer depersonalized, who no longer has the opportunity to project onto the therapist.

We are expert, says Whitaker, at sensing hostility in our patients and expert at concealing our own from ourselves. The guises of hostility are manifold, as we see in Whitaker's discussion. Our hostility, then, in the final analysis, is disenfranchised aggression, the reflexive (unconscious) denial of our right to be ourselves—to define an "I-ness" in the therapeutic context.

I'd like to start to talk about aggression and go about it like a Bach fugue, no reference to George Bach, of course. The scene of aggression I would present the way that Bach does so that one can work counterpoint, against the aggression, to create a theme about the unitary process of psychotherapeutic treatment. It's pertinent that we use aggression because it's the one thing that is least utilized and least acceptable in our social structure. I understand there are a good group of theologians in this association [Group Psychotherapy Association of Southern California] so I quote Christ, "I come not to bring peace but a sword." Aggression is a dialectic which is related to the natural human tendency to become involved with each other. We do have a tendency to get involved and aggression is a part of that.

Aggression in a patient is a truism, and in our culture it is such a truism that homicide sort of wins hands down over sex. If you kill somebody the social structure pays you back an eye for an eye. If you get incestuously involved with your mother we think of it as a "bad thing" but inside we whisper, "The lucky character." So that it's only in the psychotherapist's office that sex wins over aggression in interpersonal relationships and I really think it may be on the way out in the psychotherapeutic process. In talking about aggression in patients, David Levy[8] once said, "The deep affect anger responds only to aggression from the therapist," and yet we try to keep the motivation for help in the patient, we try to maintain that he is the one who is experiencing what is going on, he is the one who must be aggressive.

THE FUNCTION OF THE PSYCHOTHERAPIST

This raises the question, what is our function? Are we sort of missionary do-gooders, trying to help somebody to get where we think they ought to get? Or, are we schizophrenic self-sacrificial people who are tying to help mama be happy? Somebody raised the question whether all therapists had schizophrenic parents. I still can't quite accept it. It's a little disconcerting, but if that's true then are we to reexamine the old question of whether we are really self-sacrificial in the sense that the schizophrenic is? Are we really willing to be "nobodies" in the hope that we'll make mama and papa feel happy, get something out of life, and will sacrifice ourselves in the process? It has been observed that the therapist is a deviant in any group, which is another way of saying the same thing. If we are going to devote ourselves to psychotherapy, whether it's self-sacrificial, some mother-hen quality that we are born with or trained in early so that we learn how to breast-feed people, the question is, can we trust the patient's biological impulse to protect us if we get involved? Is he anxious enough to get well, so that we can devote ourselves as persons or must we say, "I'll stay back and listen, I'll just be a technician, I'll do the smart thing, I'll be careful, I'll keep him in the patient position where I am always safe"?

This is very fundamental because it seems to me that if we get to the belief that every individual has a biological drive for growth and integration, then we can feel comfortable in trying to activate this in the patient and be personally committed to him. I have a suspicion that you can classify therapists by the degree they are willing to commit themselves to the process of psychotherapy. Now, if you did I would be tempted to accept that as a classification of the kind of people they were. This is particularly true in terms of aggression. You can commit yourself to sexual feeling, you can commit yourself to maternal tender feeling; these are socially acceptable. It's hard for the patient to tell whether this is the top layer of "I love you" or whether it's going down to the fundamental aggression. We can always protect ourselves by just saying it was just the social thing to do, we were just being warm and friendly and human. But when you talk about aggression then you have to face the fact that you are sticking your neck out.

UTILIZING AGGRESSION IN GROUP THERAPY

We have been warned many times about aggression. In the Book of Proverbs it says, "Can a man take fire in his bosom and not be burned?" Why must we involve our aggressive feelings? Can't we just let the patient experience his own, isn't our love enough, isn't our closeness, our tenderness and our warmth and our identification with the patient enough? And then again the Bible talks to us, "Open review is better than secret love," or another time, "He that hideth hatred with smiling lips is a fool." Now presumably I am not talking about our professional function and yet maybe we can take some rules from it. I'd like to quote also from Dr. Winnicott, a pediatrician who became a child analyst in London, and in his collected works there is an excellent paper called "Hate in Countertransference" in which he talks about the problems that we are talking about today in a very fundamental way. He says, for example, "The psychotic patient cannot be expected to tolerate his own hatred unless the analyst hates him." These are pretty frightening words, yet the reason we must utilize our aggression in group psychotherapy has to do with this problem.

First, groups are like psychotic patients in several ways, some of them I won't even talk about, but you can imagine those. We can identify all the way with the group, we as individuals become a member of the group, or we can lead a group. But the kind of identification that we can have with patients is not possible with the group. It is a unique structure. You can see it now in family therapy and in couples therapy. In the second aspect of group therapy that makes it like working with a psychotic patient is that the group is repeatedly (I am almost tempted to say always) "one up" on the therapist. He may know it or he may kid himself that it's not true or he may try to brush it off, but I believe it's true. The third thing is that the group is stronger than any therapist and this also has some unique identification with the psychotic patient. I don't say that the psychotic patient is stronger but there are points and ways and times in which he is stronger than the therapist.

To use our aggression in psychotherapy we must do it first of all because the fantasy of the ever-accepting therapist is really a model of the objective research analyst. In contrast, the therapist is a person if he is really going to be a therapist and he is not a technician.

If psychotherapy is an emotional face-to-face relation rather than "studying life," then interpretation is fairly feeble in terms of what is needed. This is particularly true of groups.[9] Interpersonal feelings in any face-to-face meeting are mutual and reciprocal. If you accept this as a statement then the moment of mutuality between you and the group or between you and the patient is often like the discovery that the kid next door is a worthy foe. A special kind of mutuality comes out of the worthy foe interaction. In order to actually go on in psychotherapy and make it effective the patient must come to know the therapist to team with him for autorepair or reconstruction. It is the feelings of the therapist that are the vital factors in the therapeutic intercourse. Whatever these feelings may be, whether they are positive or negative, whether they are socially acceptable or socially not acceptable, aggression is important to utilize. The therapist as a person, even if he were able, must be unwilling to withhold his aggressive feelings. Initially we may withhold it, we withhold it for time, we withhold it in certain areas, but if we withhold it entirely the therapist goes into a very deep kind of apathy and an impasse. Further in the emergence of the group, the opening up has to be concentric; love and hate expand at the same rate. The illusion that you can teach your patient how to love, that you can help him experience the positive aspect of himself without experiencing the negative, is like trying to get electricity out of a battery by just attaching it to one pole.

Now, if we assume these things, what are the prerequisites for a competent therapist to experience his own aggression and how do you utilize it in the relating with the group or patient? The first one and most obvious one is that he has to be a child again and that he has to have been a patient. Maybe this is trite. There are a good many therapists who have the feeling that you can be a good therapist without having had the therapeutic experience of your own. I am not sure this is possible. I wouldn't have anybody working in my clinic with me who hasn't had a pretty extensive therapeutic experience as a patient. Now following this process of being a patient, there is a period, if I can use the theological setting again, of "40 days in the desert." There is a period of aloneness, of Kierkegaardian self-discovery. Beyond this (and we're still talking about prerequisites) one begins to develop the professional capacity of being a therapist. The simplest thing is to develop the capacity to feed, then the mother function if you will, the nurturing, accepting, comforting qualities. Beyond that is the function of aggressive interacting, demanding, the function of castration.

AGGRESSION AND SELF-ESTEEM

In the process of our work, slivers of our own pathology repeatedly break off and stab the patient. In individual therapy these may be small slivers, but in work with the psychotic and in work with groups, these are big slivers. Therefore, a professional therapist who is going to utilize his aggression must have had enough experience so that the major slivers of his own pathology are drawn to himself and are operationally available for working on. And in order not to die, the professional therapist is going to have to push his growing edge endlessly. This means he is going to have to dare to experience, he is going to have to dare to do more than just sit and listen, to do more than nod and say, "Ah, hum." Tom Main, whom you may have heard of in England during the second World War, may well have been a natural father person who worked at his maternal function by feeding all groups of psychotic soldier casualties with baby bottles. Thus he learned to experience the breast envy that we poor men have never gotten around to admitting; we'd rather talk about the woman's penis envy. Winnicott, who I suspect learned to be pretty competent in the practice of pediatrics, then moved into psychotherapy as a way of learning about aggression. He talks about what he calls justifiable hate or "objective hate," he talks about hating a specific thing in a personal way in the same way that one hates in a social setting. As professional people, beneath the capacity to feed we have the capacity to fight. Today we are learning to get ready to fight, how to fight emotionally in our professional efforts. The particular point of our growing edge varies, but our courage to experience it to the fullest requires a maximum of human freedom and the freedom to be aggressive is one of the most difficult to gain in our society.

Let me give you an example. When I was working with delinquent kids we had a cottage-type institute with about 300 inpatients who were picked out of about 2600 court-responsible cases that were handled by social workers in the home and in the foster homes. On the campus there was a group of small children who were standard scapegoats. Most of them were boys. They would ordinarily get from one to six, eight beatings per day from anybody who would happen to come by. Little kids, big kids, faculty, cottage mother, they were really artistic in the way they would attract aggression. I started taking them on in psychotherapy. As they got some self-esteem out of their therapeutic experience, there would come a point when something would break and they would fight. Ordinarily they got beaten up but it didn't seem to make a bit of difference whether they won or lost. But from then on the new feeling in the child was apparent to all the other kids; they were suddenly out of the scapegoat class and into the class of being people. They still had their fights, but no one tackled them just for an opportunity to express projective hostility. And apparently it didn't have to do with the fact they would fight back, it had to do with some self-esteem, it had to do with an inner quality. This is the inner quality we're here to talk about today. The capacity to be a person we may come by in our society only through aggression. In our society we are taught not to be naughty, you must not be angry, to be mad is being a dog, only dogs get mad. Self-esteem may only come to us by our experiencing some efforts to break up this scapegoat tendency. And this may even be characteristic of psychotherapists as a group. If he is free to aggress, the therapist then teaches the group or the patient that aggression is a feeling and can be dealt with as a feeling. It does not need to be projected out, for this is his own capacity now. It is a kind of an insurance policy against acting out in some degree. If the therapist's aggression in psychotherapy is not expressed, as is so characteristically told us in our cultural pattern (keep your anger inside, keep your bitterness to yourself), if you do this in psychotherapy then the patient or the group, poor thing, is loaded with your aggression. Then you're stuck with this accumulated aggression in the patient or in the group which gradually gets to be apathetic and impassed. You are stuck with a very difficult paralyzed setting.

I remember this most specifically in terms of an elderly woman, whom I treated many years ago, whose husband was a vicious character and also an alcoholic, and I guess I was angry at him because he wouldn't come in to the interviews. It dawned on me that I was sticking her with my anger at him. This was very dirty, as I thought of it I was trying to help her stand up to this man and really what I was doing was upsetting the balance between the two of them, which was much more complicated than the question of her just fighting back. I don't believe that psychotherapy is a process of merely teaching the patient to fight back. It isn't that simple. Let me give you an example of this problem.

A schizophrenic woman came because somebody had given her some tranquilizers, some practitioner, and that had made her worse rather than better. I saw her for a couple of years and it dawned on me all of a sudden that she had accumulated a back bill of about $700.00. I had the bookkeeper write "please" on the bill and I brought it up in the next interview, and she said "Yes, I know," and we went on with the interview. The next time I brought it up again. This time I was a little madder. Then she just laughed and said "Well, I'll take care of it." At the next interview I brought it back again and this time she began to get angry and then I went on with the rest of the interview. During the next interview I brought the bill up again and I was getting more angry this time, I was getting personal now, and I was saying, "Not only do I think that you're not going to be able to get anything out of the psychotherapy as long as you are carrying all this guilt about owing me money, but also I am not getting any place as long as I am as mad as I am about this kind of complication and monkey business." Then she got madder and madder but this time there was a flip. She began to be soft. For the subsequent months every time she would make an additional payment on her bill she would rage at me about what an S.O.B. I was. I was a dirty miserable so and so, and she got into some very delicate and tricky aspects. The schizophrenics have a way of doing this. They can pick out all sorts of things. She was identifying me as looking like a dog and she would pick out various kinds of dogs and would explain why and how. Well, this kind of fighting is the kind that we enjoy and the kind that we learn from if we can start it in such a way that the patient then takes the initiative and then we can sort of enjoy their fighting like a 3-year-old buffing at us with his fists. But this is not all that is involved. The problem is, what we do when it isn't a 3-year-old as it was between this patient and myself? For example, when the group starts fighting they are not 3-year-olds and they don't hit you with the soft, warm, facetious aggression that this girl did.

DEFINITION OF AGGRESSION

Now let me back up one step and let me define the different kinds of aggression and I'd like to separate them in a convenient way by the word itself. The word has two different aspects if you look it up. I recommend to you a very interesting book called *Origins* by Eric Partridge, which takes up in detail the background of words. One aspect of aggression is assertiveness, and assertiveness comes out of words that have much meaning as to get fed, to get together with, to walk toward. It's a very interesting word and one we don't usually think of as relating to aggression. The other part of the word is hostility, so assertiveness and hostility are together. Hostility is defined in wedges, one "to assail" and the other one "to destroy." I'd like to talk about the difference between these two also as a way of trying to define where we are with the problem of aggression.

As to assertiveness by the therapist, I am talking mostly about the therapist because I think of the patient as being less important. First we must be able to do something about our own aggression. While you are doing couples therapy it's really fascinating to see how couples sit down together and how each one is very sure what's wrong with the other one. It is very clear that they believe you get going in therapy with the other one, then everything will be fine. This is the way it is with therapists and patients. Whenever we talk, we're sure we can get the patient straightened out, if he has initiative, if he is ready for psychotherapy. So if the therapist has enough assertiveness it will help break up the countertransference factors which keep the patient's biological drive for maturity for integration from emerging. If the therapist can have some kind of assertiveness, some impulse to get to, then you can handle this in the group existentially, direct, open, no holds barred—if you're really asserting yourself. However, if it's hostility, if you are out to destroy, to assail someone else, then it is quite unnatural, actually dangerous unless the group really has asked for it. Then it becomes what Jennifers[10] called "justified hatred" or "objective hatred." When a patient takes my ceramic ashtray and smashes it in the middle of the table, in my office, this is "war." This is valuable in therapy, this is justifiable hate. Why does it get to this point? What is it that made this old maid I have seen for 4 years in group psychotherapy and who has no other life finally feel that she has enough support from this group and that she can do to the ashtray and to my table what she'd like to do to my head? You see the latent background but I am still mad about my ashtray. A therapist has to be mature enough so that he can handle his own hostility in an appropriate way at an appropriate time in the therapeutic relationship. Let's take the patient who comes in with his wife for the first interview or the second interview and carefully spills his mug full of coffee on my nice white rug. It would be inappropriate for me to get angry at that point. It would not be a process of interrelating that's therapeutic, it would merely be social. It would ignore the process of his pain and his hurt at being there. I have the anger all right, it's still my white rug, but I should not burden him with it at this time; he has enough burden already without having to face my anger in the second interview.

If you are able to manage your own assertiveness administratively, if you're in a group setting and deny your own identity, deny your own rights, your own person, then you are heading for an impasse. Let me give you another illustration. One of the most delightful experiences I had with a group of some 5 years ago was the question of who got the chairs around the table. We had a round table with eight chairs. Some chairs were comfortable, some uncomfortable. As is my custom, the group filters in before I get there and I frequently leave and they're still around for a while. The question of what chair I was going to get was something that I fought for. Sometimes it got to be a physical battle, some patient and I would start for the chair at the same time and it was a question of who was going to get there first and who was going to get it away from the other when we had both a hold on. This kind of assertiveness, this kind of definitiveness, being out for yourself to me is an existential candor in relating that is very valuable. It may go on in all sorts of ways; we sometimes have a battle as to whether I have a right to tell my dreams in the group and I'll fight right down to the drop. I've got just as much right as they have; as a matter of fact I have more right because I must be a person.

ASSERTIVE AGGRESSION

This assertive aggression is sharing interacting in which you enjoy the other person's struggle with you. It's part of the lovemaking, if you will, that goes on between a therapist and a patient. If you handle this kind of feeling in yourself by withholding it then you've got trouble in your group. But hostile aggression cannot be expressed unless it's appropriate, unless there is a consultant cotherapist or someone else who can help you handle it. In our clinic whenever we get an impasse because of hostile aggression we invite the original consultant back into the therapeutic relationship and take it up at that point where the patient has someone to help him with the therapist's hostility.

If the patient initiates the hostility, that's something else again. I remember a recent case when one of our staff was treating a girl for a matter of 5 or 6 months once a week. In the process it became more and more apparent that the husband was so paranoid that he had to be included. So he was invited in. The therapist was angry about this paranoid quality in the husband but said nothing about it; he held this for a matter of 2 or 3 months. The husband just sat in and the therapist went on with the interview with the wife. Finally the husband said, "How do you feel about this, my being here? Where do you think we're getting? Is anything happening? Is my wife getting any better?" Then the therapist let him have it; the patient had asked for it. The therapist said, "I don't know whether we're accomplishing anything or not; I don't like the hour, I don't look forward to it, I don't enjoy it, I don't like the way you act about it, I resent the whole thing. But I am committed to your wife. I started out to help her and I intend to work at it, but I assure you it's hard work, this is not therapy as I think it could be, I think you're to blame for it." This was hostility, not assertiveness. Hostility if it is asked for by the patient is much more tolerable and much more able to be worked through than when hostility is initiated by the therapist.

It's much easier if you start out by expressing your aggression during the early phase of treatment. If you put off your aggression until after it's accumulated then you get in trouble and if you lead the patient to believe that you're just a loving mama who's going to sit there and watch her children grow and then all of a sudden you turn your back on it and turn out to be an S.O.B. then you've got real trouble.

There is a wonderful story in this regard about three speakers in Hyde Park on their soap boxes, each talking the religion theme. One of them was saying, "You're all children of God, you're all made in His image and your light shines up to Him and He is happy," and so forth, and the crowd was throwing pennies to him. Down a little farther on there was another man on a box and he was extolling his group, saying that "You're basically fine people, and you're God's children, but you're not living right and you're going to have to get this thing straightened out, you're going to have to get with it." And the crowds were throwing quarters to him. Farther down there was another box and on it there was another man who was saying, "You're all rotten, you're all dirty, you're all children of the devil, you're the scum of the earth," and the crowd was throwing gold pieces to him.

I think this is characteristic. We had a beautiful example of this recently in the clinic; an executive came in, a very competent, capable guy, as you'll see. About the fifth interview he said: "Doc, do you like me?" The doctor said, "Ya, I like you." The patient said, "I mean do you like me personally?" and the doctor said, "Ya," so the executive said, "Now look, I am trying to get something straight, do you really like me as a person? Do you as a person like me as a person?" He said, "Ya, I like you"; the patient then said, "Well would you refer me to someone else?" Being the kind of guy he was, he went one step further and said, "If you really like me as a person then your judgment is not to be trusted." Now, you can go back on it and interpret that he saw in the therapist some similarity to his own parents and figured that the therapist was going to use him just like the parents used him. But I think the patient's point is still well taken.

CONTRAINDICATIONS

Now what are contraindications to the therapist's freedom to be aggressive? Some very specific ones I have alluded to already. Obviously unless you have had therapy for yourself you could not trust your aggression to tempt you to utilize the group or the patient as your therapist or to project upon them your own deep personal needs. If the therapist is unexperienced or without supervision, or without any colleague relating to him, then I guess he will have a hard time finding out how to use his own aggression therapeutically. I might add in here, and I think in spite of anything I can do I am going to be personal too, I wouldn't ever think of practicing psychotherapy alone. If I couldn't have a colleague to work with, I would go back to the farm. I don't think that the kind of involvement I want to be continually giving demands that there be somebody of equal caliber who can cut me when I am beyond where I should be or when I am out of a competent line of functioning. I think one needs supervision in learning how to express aggression or at least some sort of interacting with someone else than the person who comes to you and says, "I am a sick little child, please be good to me and help me." I think some therapists get the feeling because this other person, this patient, is a person also that they have the same status, that this can be an ordinary one-to-one relationship. This is not true. The patient is a person who has committed himself to a certain symbolic role and has committed you to a certain functional role and these are important to become aware of and stay aware of. A therapist who fears experiencing aggression in himself in other areas of life should also be very suspicious about himself if he expresses his aggression in his own professional setting. This I would think of as a valuable time to have a colleague psychotherapist to consult with.

What are the minimum necessary limitations that the therapist must place upon the expression of his own hostile aggression, his own open expression of his personal angry feelings? The most obvious one is the timing of any affect, as in the example of the coffee spilling. It is inappropriate to be aggressive in the first interview. It's been done but I think of it as part of the therapist learning process, and the patient needing a protective atmosphere. Now it may well be different in a setting where you have a captive audience. When we were doing group therapy with medical students (we did this for 10 years) I was sure I could do anything I wanted to in the first session and 2 years later they would still be there. When you're trying to maintain an independence of function in the patient and in yourself then it's inappropriate timing for the overt expression of positive or negative affect. The therapist doesn't throw his entire affect at the patient in the beginning phases of therapy. The expression of aggression, like the expression of affection, can be destroyed if it's offered by a therapist who's insensitive to the interpersonal situation at the time. This reminds me of the story of a therapist who lost a whole group of new patients because of his expression of warmth and appreciation for them. This "I am glad you came to see me" left him without any patients, and a very humiliated guy.

Now let me change the framework for just a moment and try to list for you the characteristics of what I think of as concealed hostility in the therapist, which he cannot contain, and which are really a symptom of his need for help personally, whether it's therapy, or supervision, or maybe confession to the group. You'd be surprised how many things you can accomplish if you all of a sudden make a double take on yourself and become the patient right out in the open, in front of God and everybody. There are many times the group members will use words which will give you some hint of what is happening in you. You don't have the feeling of hostility as such but somebody in the group will accuse you of aloofness or of unexpressed tension: "Your face looks tight, you don't look like you're here." I remember one meeting in my early group therapy days, I came in 1 day late and the group had carefully rehearsed a pattern of my stereotype phrases and they laid them on me one at a time for the next 20 minutes. They were responding to my concealed hostility, which I wasn't even aware of. I don't know why, I don't know whether this had to do with the fact that I was hostile at the work. I felt inadequate for the therapeutic needs of the patient.

CONCEALED HOSTILITY

The sweet denial of hostility is one of the prize ways by which we conceal it. "No, I don't feel angry." Disassociated interpretations of what a group member says: "You know I heard what you said but it didn't really make any dent." "I see this, but I don't feel it, I don't understand why you say it so nicely." These are what I call disassociated interpretations. Now take the me, us, you attitude. Very frequently in group therapy it's tempting for the therapist to become a group by himself and set himself off against the rest. This was valid back in the days when Pratt was lecturing to ulcer patients in Boston in 1922 but it's kind of inappropriate at this time and age. There is another one which is a sneaker with me. That's the identification of the group with my own past. My kids first brought me ahead of this. One of them said one morning, "I know you walked through the snow when you were a little boy and you only got 5 cents a week for an allowance, but please don't tell it to me again." I had the feeling that was the same thing that happened with the groups. Inside of ourselves we say, "Well, now, I can remember when I was like this." This is a hostile pattern. Typical of some highly trained professional people is to hide our hostility with what I call "hot" interpretations where the patient doesn't even understand what we're saying. I am not even sure we do sometimes, we just put one and one together and get four and say to the patient now this is how it is. I recommend to you a most wonderful poem by Baudelaire called "Boredom." Boredom is one of the most subtle ways of hiding hostility, deep, bitter hostility. Also there is the panoramic overseer: "Well, this group is doing fairly well over the last 3 months."

One of the other tricks that we use to hide our hostility is what I call contrived interaction. I want to make clear here in terms of my own experience with psychodrama and the experience of other people that I am talking about contrived interaction that has no person in it. I think if you watch they'll tell you that you're not in it. They'll tell you, "Now doctor, I don't mind your holding my hand, but your hand feels cold." I had a free association when I was making this list. I'll give it to you with no explanation: "A patient is a patient, is a patient, is a patient." Hostility can be concealed under consistency. Some patients will say, "Well now, Doc, this isn't consistent with what you said last week." That's a compliment to me; anybody who is consistent week after week is consistently nobody. A rather standard form of concealing aggression used well in our social groups is "friendliness." When used by the therapist he is a psychopath. Another concealment is kind of subtle. You may have to get your patients' help for you to catch this one: sexual interaction as a substitute for hostile interaction. It's very tempting when one is concealing hostility to develop a kind of banter-ing sexual tête à tête either between you and one, two, or three of the others in the group or to encourage it between them.

About a year ago I set up an anonymous group of couples; nobody knew anybody's name, address, occupation, background, history; the only thing they knew was that all the couples had had couples therapy. This was really an experience. They started throwing names to each other to try to figure out their occupation and then it became a real game to keep hidden. In the course of this we developed a four-way transfer switch. I hadn't seen this happen before. The other's husband–wife attraction within the foursome worked out first and then there was the homosexual attraction also going. I thought we were going to have wife trading. It turned out that most of this happened because of my own hostility. I was inexperienced then, but now I think that this kind of sexual interaction is a way of avoiding the hostile impulses in the therapist. Then there is the nursery school racket: "We in this group do these things, we all play with our own blocks, we don't ever get into the other person's blocks." If you do they'll cut your throat. Another one is the illusion of neutrality. This is a fairly standard one that we all know: the "neutral" therapist. The illusion is that his neutrality is equal to acceptance. We just had an experience with that in the politi-cal sphere with Nehru. His neutrality was for the birds. Another form of concealment is projected aggression outside the group. Aggression about continued alcoholism, continued homosexual acting out, and the like. Here the therapist handles his personal hostility in the group setting by projecting it outside of the group therapy setting into the outside life of people in other groups.

[There is] denial of the deterioration of the group. One of the very strange things is how difficult it is for the group and the therapist to face the fact that their group is in an impasse. It is as if the fact that we have a past history guarantees our present and future. We say, "Let's stay merry and be friends, we'll sleep in separate rooms for the sake of the children." This goes on and I think you find this can be traced to the aggression, the hostility of the therapist. Or take the next one: transferring patients to another therapist. I have given it up, but I understand it still goes on elsewhere. Then there is the all-out attack to end the relationship, the final blast, like this one we had recently: the husband and his wife came in and they had a perfect marriage, until one night the husband came home and said to his wife, "I want a divorce," and he filed the next day. That's the way I think it happens in the impassed group.

THE THERAPIST'S RIGHT TO BE A PERSON

Now let us talk about the other side of this. Let me list for you some of the things I think of as characteristic of a healthy, aggressive, assertive therapist. The therapist should fight for his own individuality right in the group: he has the right to be a person. One of the real compliments I enjoy is when I take an individual patient who enters a group and then comes to me after the first group interview and says, "You know, you were mean as hell up there, you didn't pay any attention to me, in the group you acted like I didn't exist, you didn't introduce me, you didn't tell them anything about me, you're a rat." I think of this as a compliment. If I am going to be in the group I'll tell them ahead of time that I am going to be a person in the group. I am not going to be the pop and they're not going to be my children. This is a round table, I am not going to be the director of that group either. So the therapist is fighting for his own right to be a person in the group. I think of it as a very healthy kind of aggression. One of the other forms of healthy aggression is battling the patient stereotyping the therapist, and they'll do it in the group. They'll stereotype you as being mature in your real life. You know if the therapist says so, it must be true, he must be loving, real loving to all patients and to everybody on the outside and consistent in having an untroubled life of his own; he can't have any personal problems, his dreams must be just healthy dreams. "Wouldn't it be wonderful to be married to a psychiatrist." My wife says, "Just have them talk to me."

The therapist should also have the freedom to be paranoid. One of the real joys of being free to be hostile in the group is the joy of cultivating your own paranoid feeling. It's really delightful to participate in subgroup struggles. You have a personal feeling on the side that started some battle in the group. Get on the side where you belong. You may be surprised what a wonderful time they have beating you. The group is stronger than the therapist except if the therapist is outside of it. If the therapist is in the group, the group is stronger than the therapist. This is an important thing to make it more fun. One of the criticisms they used to make at us was that in our clinic we enjoyed our psychotherapy so it must be that we weren't working. Expressing to the patient your ambivalence, when it's true that you feel both in positive and negative ways, is healthy assertiveness. One of the things that I delight in sharing with a patient when I have gotten well enough acquainted with the patient is trying to make up my mind whether I would like to be married to them or not. It is amazing what this means when it's true and when you do express it. This extends to the type of experience in the group when you make a slip and then you settle down to working at what's going on, what's behind this. Or the patient says, "I don't understand why you were late, and you take it seriously as an expression of your own pathology." This being late is a standard one of mine, nobody's been able to cure it. The offering of spontaneous and insignificant ideas is also helpful. We have a vulgar phrase, if you'll pardon me, in our clinic: "It's characteristic of therapists that they're always waiting for the big shit." You want to get ready so you can make some profound statement that's going to echo down through the years. The patient will never forget, the sharing of free associations by the therapist, mishearing, misspeaking, sharing of fantasies. I remember a fascinating one. My group had gradually broken down so there were only three people left, and this was getting sticky, and I apparently had some feeling about putting anybody else in this group and I didn't realize what it was until, during one group meeting, I had a fantasy. I saw way down at the other end of the long panorama a pig trough and three pigs, and me behind them. I had a club in my hand like you use for feeding pigs. All of a sudden I hit the middle one over the head and swatted the one on the left and I came out of fantasy. Well this kind of fantasy was a little disconcerting to share with the group but if you have that much hostility you'd better not try to keep it to yourself unless you want to go and get some help from a colleague. But it's amazing—the group apparently was not nearly as upset about this as I was. They cut me down to size, but that they had done before.

We're now seeing a family, father, mother, and schizophrenic daughter, four of us serving as a therapeutic team and we see them once a month for 3 hours. It's a single 3-hour session. In the course of a recent session one of the therapists suddenly went to sleep and woke up as he was having this dream about how funny those parents looked with their heads off. We utilize this sleeping during the interview with increasing frequency. At first when we started 10 years ago it was kind of embarrassing, but subsequently it gradually spread. We test whether something is valid by whether it spreads in the group; it spreads through the group until one of our cotherapists for about 6 months would always come up with three dreams just every time he went to sleep in an interview. It got to be sort of a joke.

It's very important at times when the therapist has enough courage to share his outside experiences and his own night dreams, his fantasies during the day about the group or about some outside situation, and again this must be tempered. Constructive aggression by the therapist is his attempt to destroy the myth of the omnipotent parent. Finally, I suggest the idea that castration may be a valuble experience. It is a creative thing when it's done by someone else, someone who loves you. That it is one of the ways that we don't have to castrate ourselves.

Now in summary, the therapist is a person; he experiences aggression in his living. His professional function is a part of his experience and he must share aggression with the patient or the group. When he shares the socially unacceptable phases of his experience with the patient he opens up new vistas in their working team. If he is not heavily burdened with major remnants or negative transference his aggression takes the form of human self-esteem, which we call assertiveness and which obviously includes an equal esteem for the other with whom he is relating. Justified hostility may be shared but with safeguards. Freedom is contagious, freedom to aggress develops the courage for the ultimate freedom, the freedom to be through love and hate all that it is possible for us to become.

TRAINING FOR
THE UNREALITY EXPERIENCE

In this chapter, Whitaker demonstrates the use of an expanded fantasy technique for turning on or "hooking" the nonpsychologically minded or "unsuitable" patient into therapy. Here, in a marital session, as an example, he uses the extended fantasy technique to teach the husband of a psychotic woman how to be receptive to her experience. He opens a window on both his and her world. Whitaker does not say to the husband, "You have to learn to do this . . . ," and so forth, but in fact requires that he do it, and gives him the experience of participating in his own unreality experience.

The professional psychotherapist is a particular type of person subjectively organized and interested in ideas and inner experiences. He naturally tends to enjoy the time he spends with persons of similar life pattern. The therapist finds these psychologically minded patients easy to work with. In doing psychotherapy with couples, the psychiatric attendant–like spouse is a more difficult problem in our efforts to help do something about the symptomatic member of the couple. There are also patients who are very difficult for us. We call them nonpsychologically minded patients, or more honestly, "bad" patients. They live day after day in stark reality and to them the psychotherapist seems like a screwball who lives in an unreal world that they will have no part of. They resemble prepsychotic or latent psychotic patients who are so afraid of unreality that they make us afraid also. This class of "bad" patients includes the grim intellectuals, the cold PhD in physics, the perfectionistic CPA, the man who is immersed in the world of facts, the hard-shelled Christian, and in general the person who doesn't dream.

Reprinted by permission from *Voices*, 1966, 2, 43–46. Copyright © 1966 by the American Academy of Psychotherapists.

Therapists have worked out many technical aids for this problem. I should like to describe one which seems most useful to me. I have previously called it *forced fantasy*. Dr. Hanscarl Luener (1955) has recently written about a similar technique used with great success by his group in Germany. His controlled imagery differs from that described here, in that it is instigated by the therapist on a technical level and is used for diagnosis as well as for its therapeutic by-product.

Our technique is similar to free association in that it utilizes an original stimulus from the patient himself, is utilized for the expansion of an established therapeutic relationship, and is timed usually as the therapist begins to feel bored with this patient.

The episode is initiated by picking up some part of the interview which seems to carry the possibility of opening a window into the patient's world of unreality. This may be a word which seems to carry signal cues of affect load, or a word which seems to imply visual imagery. The word may be a unique one, a word which is used with special significance for the patient, which is unknown to the therapist and possibly to the patient also; or the word may be an ordinary one used in an unusual manner, or repetitiously. The examples quoted below are standard ones of "field" and "wall." It is, of course, possible to force almost any word into this kind of category. A description of a place can be expanded by making it visual; description of a state of being can be expanded by giving it a setting.

Once the therapist has been involved by a next move on the part of the patient, he can push for the visual imagery, the mind's eye picture of the place, and then request the patient or gradually push the patient into seeing himself in this visual picture. It is my custom to then push the patient into seeing me in this setting. Since psychotherapy is the establishment of an interpersonal relationship, it seems important that the dream or the unreality experience be structured in such a way that there is a relationship established in it. The therapist's presence in the dream may also prevent the patient from getting a panic response to the paranoid implications of the therapist as voyeur.

Once the visual construct has been established, the demand on the patient is for progress, change, movement, action. It is probably best if this is instigated by the patient; but if that is not feasible, the therapist may himself propose a kind of action, leaving the patient the freedom to participate, to deny it, or to counterinstigate a movement of his own. Once the movement is begun, the therapist and the patient each are able to push in one direction or another, to add or change the setting or the personnel, and to veto the ongoing process. It seems possible also for each to protest about the other's participation in the fantasy, and even for the two to go separate ways without destroying the fantasy that is joint between them.

The patient was being seen with his manic wife, who was talking in rapid-fire fashion during the entire hour. The therapist asked the husband how he had been moving inside himself over the weekend. He said he had tried to think about himself and found a blank wall. "What does the wall look like?" Patient, "I was just talking hypothetically." Could he visualize the wall? "No, it wasn't visual." I asked him if he would try to picture it in his mind's eye and after several requests of this kind, he said, "Well, it isn't a brick wall." He then repeatedly apologized, tried to back out, said this thing was not real, that he had not thought of such a wall. "Will you think about it now?" He stopped, then said, "Well, I think of a wall of trees." I asked how far apart the trees were, and he said they were touching; it turned out by this he was visualizing a tree windbreak in which the branches went all the way to the ground and were touching each other. I had to drag this picture out of him by repeated questioning. Finally he said, "And Evelyn's name is across the front." He was embarrassed to say how high the letters were or how long the word was, but after much pushing, said the letters were 4 feet high and finally that the sign was 20 feet long. He refused to say it had a structure; suddenly he said, "It's kind of a haze." Could he see over this wall of trees? "No." Could he see himself there? "Yes." How was he dressed? "In a field uniform." Could he see me there? He said no and then under my pressure to be with him, he said yes, he could see me there. I asked how I was dressed. He couldn't picture this and I, for some reason, did not force it. I then asked if Evelyn was on the other side of the trees and he said, "Yes." I asked how close together we were and he was embarrassed and couldn't say, as though he were ashamed and horrified at this visual construct. Then under pressure he said we were close enough to touch with our hands. I then demanded that we go through the trees. He demurred on two occasions and finally said all right. I asked if one of us would have to go first, or whether we could both go together. He said we could both go together. I said, "Are we going?" He said, "Yes, we are going through." I asked if we had made it; he said, "Yes." I asked what was on the other side and he said, "The first thing that came to me was a sunrise." Then I asked if Evelyn was there and he said, "Yes." I asked how she was dressed and he became quite embarrassed and said, "She doesn't have any clothes on." I said, "I guess I'd better duck back through the trees." Then he said, "I suddenly remember a song." The name of the song was "I'll Meet My Darling when the Sun Rises" and we ended the interview at that point.

In the above illustration, the therapist took a momentary fantasy which the patient used, and expanded it with his own fantasy and by insisting on the patient's breaking with reality. Thus, the patient learned something about the psychotic quality of his wife's daily living. If we assume that psychotherapy is aimed toward promoting the dream aspect of life, the "as-if" quality, then the therapist may use his own dream or his fantasy to help the patient to face the fact that his dream is an integral part of his life. The dream life and the waking life are one.

The therapist was seeing a mental health professional who had been in treatment for over 200 hours with another therapist. This particular therapy was like a play within a play, enacted in the original therapist's office and in his presence. It had moved on intensively and seemed liable to rapid termination. In the 10th interview the patient said, "Your last remark opened up an old field. It's an area that seems new, after years of being out of sight." Asked to picture the field she said, "I was talking about a field of interest and a field of attention, not any physical field." I asked if she would picture it as a field. Suddenly the scene became clear. It was a green field. I asked if she was there. She said, "Yes." I asked what she looked like. "I am a blonde [the patient is brunette], 8-year-old girl." Could she see me in the field? She said, "No." Was there anything else there? There was a horse eating grass over in the corner of the field. Asked if she could bring me into the field she hesitated for a few moments, then said she could. When pushed for my physical appearance, she said I was dressed in farmer's clothes. What are we doing? She said I was in another part of the field, walking slowly toward her. Further questioning elicited the fact that she wanted to run to me but was not willing to, and finally in her fantasy I came up to her, picked her up in my arms and she said, "Now I feel safe." Further pushing was not responded to. That episode was ended.

It is as though the patient will accept the visual construct of the fantasy which was instigated by a word or a conceptual term. Usually the patient will accept the therapist into it, if he is concerned and wanting to be there, yet there are specific limits to what can be done. The fantasy usually comes to its own end after a certain amount of time. Yet I have had occasions when the fantasy would go on through a series of interviews. Each episode is alive and they are not expanded between interviews. It is easy to participate in the fantasy once it has been started and has a reality quality established. My fantasy may go along with that of the patient or may be different. If so, I usually share my fantasy. It does *not* contaminate that of the patient. Certain contributions or perceptions of the therapist are acceptable and certain are not. I have on occasion tested the patient's fantasy by insisting that my fantasy went in another direction. We separated. The patient went on with his fantasy and tolerated my fantasy as a separate fact.

The two examples above illustrate recent experiences in this pattern for teaching the patient how to move into unreality with the support of the therapist and with the discovery of a new dimension in his everyday experience. Assuming this is successful, it is possible that the therapist and patient may move on to more experiences in the world of unreality. They may become aware of their own and each other's moments of confusion, or blanks, of interview dozing with dream fragments, of free association, of free fantasy, and of ESP-like experiences and somatic sensations which seem to have no relevance to the interview until they are shared and turn out to be significant.

One of the happy parts about this kind of joint therapy is that it tends to give the therapy a quality of play and relaxed participation. It moves in counterdirection to the ponderous intellectual patterns of the content-oriented interview hour.

THE ROLE OF SILENCE IN BRIEF PSYCHOTHERAPY

with Jerman W. Rose, Frank N. Geiser, and Nan Johnson

In this short chapter we have an interesting catalog of the uses of silence in individual therapy. Silence can signal superficial embarrassment, resistance, or immersion in thought. Of greater importance is how the therapist and the patient can, in the service of therapeutic movement, make use of silent periods. Whitaker has said that the most perfect therapy would take place in silence. This is true because the therapeutic process is an intrapsychic event that requires interpersonal context, one of trust. As the patient withdraws from the world to participate in the "unreality experience of therapy" he goes more "within himself," losing contact with his surroundings. The internal process of change cannot be hastened but can be facilitated. Like the Quaker who waits in silence to be moved by the Spirit, the patient and therapist wait for the inward sign of the patient's growing integration. Sometimes, perforce, they wait in silence.

Most of the knowledge about brief psychotherapy has centered about what is said or done in the interview—much of what goes unsaid must of necessity remain a mystery. Partly for this reason, the therapeutic silence has been neglected as an area for study. Our theoretical discussion is therefore tentative. This paper is an effort to formualte some concept of the silent period: the forces at work during the silence, their utilization in the therapeutic process, and the possible dangers involved in this usage. Silent periods can be separated into two types: those that arise spontaneously between the patient and therapist, and those that are deliberately induced by the therapist. It is planned to discuss first the spontaneous silence and then the induced silence.

All spontaneous silent periods are not of the same quality. For example, in a social setting the silence following the presentation of an intellectual problem is more superficial than the embarrassed silence that follows a slip of the tongue. It is obvious that this embarrassed silence is of deeper emotional significance than that associated with reasoning since each person is precipitated into an emotionally conditioned fantasy.

In therapy there are also varying depths to any silence, which depend in part on the doctor–patient relationship. If the therapist has not become a symbolic parent or successfully attained his professional role, the interview is likely to be on a social plane from time to time and the silent periods may remain superficial. As the transference develops, silences with more emotional meaning may occur. It is as if silent periods have greater import as a result of the new freedom the patient feels in the relationship.

Often during the initial phase of psychiatric treatment the period of silence offers an opportunity for the patient to consider the present status and the future developments of his relationship to the therapist. Silent periods at the beginning of therapy may be frightening or reassuring for the patient. He may be frightened that the explosive force of his own unconscious will destroy him with aggression or sexuality. Another threat may be that the therapist will force him into a fantasy from which he cannot escape. The patient may also fear the therapist's condemnation, his administrative power, or a personal attack. Although these silent periods may follow a cue stimulus that precipitates a fantasy state, they frequently occur with no cause apparent to patient or therapist.

In some patients, particularly adolescents, silence may represent a defiant refusal to say the first word—a battle of wills. This has all the implications of a verbal battle, even though it may not be perceived by the therapist. Evidence of the intensity of the battle may be seen in facial expressions, aggressive sighing, or bodily movements that express tension.

Instead of a sense of fear, the patient may develop a deep sense of acceptance. As he comes to feel the support of the therapist he can dare to explore his own content and struggle with his own unconscious impulses. As he begins to believe the therapist will not reject him, he feels protected from the attack of reality, the censure of social custom, and the limitation of reason. If he is certain of the protection of his therapist the patient can begin to tolerate his sexual and aggressive fantasies. To experience these fantasies in the symbolic setting of the interview is an important part of the therapeutic process.

The silence may be terminated by the patient. This seems most desirable, but there are times when the therapist may end the silence. It should be ended by the therapist if the time agreed upon for the interview is up. The therapist may elect to interrupt if the patient seems to need verbal reassurance. This is more apt to occur in the initial period of therapy when the relationship may be less secure. On the same intuitive basis it is implied that the therapist may return to the verbal level when he senses the danger of overidentification. He need not maintain the silence if it seems apparent that the patient is not preoccupied with his own fantasy. It is always possible that the patient may become too disturbed or go beyond his limits of integration, in which case the silence should be terminated.

The patient's response following the silent period is related to his reaction to the therapist and his reaction to his own fantasy. This may be revealed by content or he may show superficial indifference, disguise his anxiety about the fantasy, isolate the fantasy from the therapist's perception, or he may verbally deny the import and depth of the silence. Occasionally he may leave the interview in a panic or in anger.

As therapy progresses the patient may show more overt responses in the postsilence period. There may be a verbal expression of the value of the silence. Patients have said following a silence, "Time flies when we're quiet," or, "I don't know what came up or where it came from but something sure boiled up." Or, the patient may show the fatigue that follows an emotional explosion, which in itself is evidence of the intensity of the patient's experience. Then the patient may need the therapist's participation either to pull himself back to reality or to gain courage enough to go to a deeper level.

One of the factors that enables the patient to face more of his emotionally charged content is his increased ability to become dependent on the therapist. As he becomes more certain that the initiative is his, he realizes that he will not be pushed to depths greater than he has the capacity to integrate. Consequently, he can dare to ask for help with some of the aspects of his inner self that he has not worked out alone. It appears that the "anesthesia" supplied by the therapeutic relationship enables the patient to fantasize in areas previously blocked. For example, one patient said following a long period of complete silence, "That was the first time I realized I had such violent thoughts. I saw myself doing things I wouldn't even dream of. I recognized that I could, even wanted to, kill someone."

It is necessary for some patients to be silent to experience their own inner drives. They may discover a new capacity to dare to deliberately be irrational and may recognize the fact that joint silence offers an opportunity to live through an irrational experience with the therapist. Patients are often eager for such a period and then the therapist need merely follow the patient's lead and respect silence with silence. Other patients will fight against it as if they feared the irrational state and avoided the silence that would bring it on. The therapist should not assume that it is an irrational experience for the patient, merely because both he and the patient are silent. Certain patients will be able to spontaneously use silence as a means to develop their motivation toward more constructive use of the therapist. Certain other patients need the added force of the therapist's silence.

When the therapist is silent himself the tension increases and it becomes more obvious that superficial material is meaningless. When he maintains a silence, even though the patient has requested interpretation, the demand by the therapist for an emotional relationship becomes more apparent. Then the silence of the therapist or the silence he forces on the patient constitutes an attack on superficiality and becomes a means of demanding greater depth. This is, in effect, an induced silence.

Therapist-induced silence differs from the spontaneous silence we have been discussing. The spontaneous silence arises in any relationship and may be a normal part of it. Induced silence is a threat to the patient, first, because of its artificial quality and second, because the therapist takes the initiative in the conduct of the relationship. It may also be a threat in that the patient feels deserted. Silence then is experienced as rejection and becomes destructive. Silence may be traumatic also if the depth experience of a prolonged silence is forced upon the patient before the relationship is strong enough to support it. Just as an adolescent may be traumatized by too abrupt an introduction to adult sexuality, the abrupt precipitation into a deep emotional relationship induced by a long period of silence may result in panic.

A young male patient whose personality was marked by strong psychopathic trends talked for two interviews about irrelevant historical material. Finally the therapist said, "If you can't think of anything that has real meaning, keep quiet." Fifteen minutes of intense silence followed, in which therapist and patient fought a silent battle. In discussing it 2 months later, the patient stated that he was a lot better.

"When you just sat and looked at me, I started to think. I guess I'm not so different from other people."

From the therapist's viewpoint, there are certain dangers involved in the use of so powerful a therapeutic tool. It is possible for the therapist to use the silence as an escape from his own ambivalence toward the patient or his own rejection of the patient. Silence may serve to suppress his aggression or his sexual feeling, or it may become a means for the immature therapist to misuse his symbolic power in dominating the patient. The silence may in effect taunt the patient with his dependence and convince the patient that the therapist is standing in judgment. The police have discovered this destructive power of the silence. They use it to increase guilt, produce panic, and force a confession.

If the silence precipitates an irrational state the responsibility of the therapist is tremendously increased. Since silence may be a method of attack and of increasing anxiety, ineptness on the part of the thera-pist may result in serious damage to the patient himself. When the patient becomes irrational the therapist's maturity is put to the test lest he be panicked by the primitive force of his own identification or become absorbed by the psychopathology and dissociate himself from the patient.

If the therapist is not sure of his ability to see the patient through a series of interviews on a psychotic level, he should have a locked ward available where the patient may be protected during this phase of the treatment. Desertion of the patient at this level is criminal. Even more dangerous is a silence that serves to disguise from the therapist his own inability to participate at this level.

In taking a more active role, the therapist must recognize that he is the essential factor in the patient's resynthesis and reintegration. It seems apparent that one should not assume this responsibility unless he has had therapy for himself. If he has had a meaningful therapeutic experience himself, he is thereby more able to see beyond the patient's panic to the therapeutic effect of such a struggle.

COMMUNICATION IN BRIEF PSYCHOTHERAPY WITH THE NONPSYCHOTIC PATIENT

This early (1957) work illustrates the use of a number of techniques that can be used to communicate to the patient about the therapy. These "meta" communications contain the following messages: (1) that the patient must take the initiative in the therapy; (2) that therapy will be an experience of intimacy.

These statements about the relationship are communicated indirectly or at the "meta" level, rather than straight out, by the therapist's actions. Telling ("anticipatory socialization") in this context is not as persuasive as showing. For example, the therapist does not demand transparency of the patient, but he himself first models such openness as he speaks of his free associations, dreams, and physiologic experiences. In a sense the therapist broadcasts these messages "over all channels" as well. In the therapy setting, action speaks louder than words because it begets action. Confronted with the transparent therapist, the patient must move toward him or away; he cannot remain stationary.

One of the central problems in the field of psychotherapy is the problem of communication between doctor and patient. For many years psychiatry has put major emphasis on the understanding of the patient, first, in the understanding of his background story, and later on the understanding of his behavior. Still later, with the arrival of Freud and the discovery of free association, we began to interpret the signals sent by the patient in a more comprehensive way. The data accumulated became so fabulous that it has established a whole new scientific language.

Of recent date, efforts have been made to understand more by extensive analysis of recorded interviews, by taking movies of interviews, and Malmo and others have even gone so far as to evaluate evidences of communication in the patient's physiology, including such things as muscle tension, sweating, changes in blood pressure, pulse, and respiration. In this he has endeavored to quantify the patient's signals.

Because of the limitations to these efforts, psychiatry has recently turned to the pure sciences for additional help in the understanding of communication and communication theory. One phase of this has been the study of cybernetics, a whole new field involving the relationship between human function and the function of complex electronic machines. It is trite to say that communication is a two-way process, but important when we realize that psychiatry has spent a major part of its effort in understanding only one side of the two-sided process. Part of our confusion has arisen from the fact that the patient and the therapist are simultaneously sending and receiving. This adds to the misunderstanding just as if two people on a telephone line were talking at the same time. Efforts have also been made to understand the total communication process in therapy. A recent development has been Sullivan's evolution of the use of the participant observer. In spite of emphasis on the patient as sender, however, psychiatry has been concerned in an implicit sense with the therapist as a sender for all of its recent past. Several papers have been presented concerned with the timing of interpretations and, of course, much concern has centered around the problem of countertransference. However, there has been the assumption that the therapist is the "constant" in the therapeutic process, that he is predictable, controllable, and that the patient is essentially the variable. Recent evidence has tended to throw some doubt upon this and to suggest that the therapist's function and the therapist's person is the most significant variable to be encountered. This is another way of expressing Barbara Betz's[11] formulation that the dynamics of therapy is in the person of the therapist. From this it becomes clear that the more wellness the therapist has, the better the patient's therapy will be. The "weller" the therapist, the better will be the communication, and from Dr. Ruesch[12] we get: the more they communicate the better the patient's treatment. Out of these we can derive a final step which is really an hypothesis that the more signals the patient receives from the therapist the more healthy he becomes.

For some time a group at the Psychiatric Institute has pressed the effort to vary the signals sent by the therapist, hoping that an increase in the strength of those signals, or a freer utilization of them by the sender, would move us one step further in the process of becoming more effective as therapists. "Just between us boys," it is reassuring to recall that the communication engineers discovered some time ago that the best reception necessitates a certain amount of background noise. Pure signals are less well received than signals which are superimposed on a background of noise. I say this because I wonder if we psychiatrists have been afraid to send signals with any freedom because we recognize how much noise is present in our usual communication.

Before trying to discuss any of the tactical aspects of communication from the therapist to the patient, it must be noted that psychiatry has recognized for some time that psychotherapy for the therapist or an analytic experience for the therapist has proved a sine qua non for adequate communication. It is our conviction that the adequacy of communication possible from the therapist to the patient is very limited unless the therapist has had a personal experience of such depth and duration as to make him thoroughly conversant with his own function and one that has contributed significantly to his personal growth. The effectiveness of content analysis of the therapeutic relationship also needs no validation here, since it has been proven by the experience of each of us. In addition to this, many people have learned much through the study of electrical recordings of their therapeutic interviews, and many of us who are not clearly research workers realize how much we can get from studying notes taken during an interview, which later contribute to our own professional growth.

It should be obvious that a close relationship and joint functioning with a colleague offers a valuable aid to the professional growth of any psychotherapist, and therefore to his increasing ability to communicate to the patient his own total functioning. Finally, many psychiatrists are quite convinced that the totality of the therapist's responses can never be completely conveyed by verbalized communication. From our use of multiple therapy in the treatment of chronic schizophrenic patients several techniques have been adopted to work with nonpsychotic patients.

This chapter discusses experiences with the utilization of methods long known and employed to better understand the patient, and to adapt these for understanding and improving the sending function of the therapist. Included among these are unrestricted free association by the therapist, the use of manifest fantasy content of the therapist, and the reporting of this to the patient, reporting of manifest content of the therapist's dreams during the interview to the patient, and the communication on a verbal basis of the therapist's behavior responses to the patient, and, finally, the reporting to the patient of the therapist's physiologic responses during the interview. These are all classified as signals arising in the therapist which can in part be reinforced and sent to the patient.

When we try to increase the communication from the therapist to the patient, it is apparent that we alter some of the dynamics of the traditional therapeutic method. When the patient is asked to free-associate, one demands something further from a person who is already emotionally impoverished and repressed. Therapy also increases passive dependence by allowing the patient to do something for the doctor and the relationship may be further disturbed by the patient's effort to express content which will be satisfying to the therapist. When the therapist assumes greater responsibility for communicating to the patient, as well as listening with the third ear, he must push his own "inner truthfulness," as Martin Grotjahn calls it, to the point where he is willing to expose more and more of his total self to the patient.[13]

There is evidence that many therapists free-associate during the interview, although they do not report it to the patient. Anyone who offers his free associations to the patient to activate the relationship by that means assumes several things: one, that the patient will not walk out on him when he "talks in strange tongues." Two, the therapist assumes the unconscious perception by the patient of the latent content of these free associations. Three, the therapist assumes that his wellness is greater than his sickness, and that the patient will not be harmed by being burdened with the therapist's residual pathology as much as he would be helped by the therapist's total participation. He further assumes that the therapist's wellness exceeds the patient's wellness, or at least differs in character, and finally that the therapist's dreams during the interview are specifically related to the therapeutic interview situation and that they are an effective therapeutic vector.

One of the precursors to the development of the techniques here reported has been the utilization of more specific limitations to the therapeutic communication pattern. For example, our group has, for some time, explicitly refused to participate in superficial conversation, and often has refused to answer questions in other than symbolic terms. That is, the therapist comes to respond to much manifest content only for its latent meaning. Further depth in the therapeutic relationship frequently emerges after insistence that the patient does not talk about things which are not understood by the therapist as having symbolic significance. It almost seems that when the therapist forces the patient to stop talking, this brings about a type of nonverbal communication that carries affectively loaded signals more effectively.

What follows serves to illustrate with examples the participation in the therapeutic relationship by the therapist on a level which goes beyond that of deliberate, conscious understanding.[14] The therapist will, of course, try to evaluate what he has said and what has taken place in the therapeutic interview after his spontaneous expression of himself. He must, however, realize that he will be subjected to the kind of embarrassment which was present in his own therapeutic experience and that his own residual pathology will emerge, and may in itself be a significant contribution to the patient's effort to mature. The simplest examples of this are the ordinary slips made by the therapist during the interview. As he participates in the patient's effort, a slip of the tongue will involve him more deeply in the therapeutic relationship and if he denies this slip, or tends to pass over it, the patient will, of course, recognize the therapist as one who participates less than completely in his own effort to grow up. As an instance, the author recently substituted the word "fee" for the word "free" in an early interview with a new patient, and then took up, on a personal level, the basis for this slip of the tongue. When the therapist thus reveals to the patient a part of himself which is obviously interfering with his own functioning, he not only proves his own honesty and his own sincerity, but he also illustrates for the patient what the therapist will expect in the way of participation on the part of the patient. There is no better way to show the patient what we mean by free association than to illustrate it with some free association of our own.

Another example of the therapist's affective participation occurs if he joins the patient in a fantasy relationship. This may or may not be inaugurated by the patient. Frequent openings for joint fantasy are presented by the patient in such a way that if the therapist is ready he can participate comfortably and easily; for example:

Patient said in the third interview, "At times I feel like I'm only half here." The therapist responded, "Where is the other half?" The patient answered, "The other half of me, I guess, is back on the farm with mother and daddy." The therapist asked, "Can you see this half of you?" The patient answered, "Oh yes, I am dressed in a Buster Brown suit and am playing in the back yard."

This switch to the present tense indicated the occurrence of a joint fantasy, and the therapist switched to the present tense with the patient. "Can you see me there with you?" The patient may take this up quite automatically, or the therapist may have to force the issue by asking the patient to look again. At another time a patient noted during an interview, "At times I feel like a little boy." This again left an obvious opportunity for the therapist to paticipate in a bilateral fantasy relationship with the little boy. One patient said, "Yesterday I had a vacant feeling." The therapist suggested that the two of them fill in the vacancy. Another patient said, "I feel as though I am down in the bottom of a well." The therapist participated in the patient's effort to get out of the well, having a good bit of give-and-take before the therapist found the well, went back to his car to get a rope, and helped the patient climb out of the well.

Experience will show how useful it is for the patient to carry the initiative in the fantasies. The therapist waits for the patient to decide crucial questions of movement and finds that frequently if he, himself, tries to decide, the patient will disagree with him. However, the therapist can feel free to push the origin of the joint fantasy.

Patient L.F. had made tentative efforts in the eighth and ninth interviews to recall his childhood relationships and in discussing his inability said, "My past seems like a desert."

DOCTOR: Can you visualize this desert?

PATIENT: Yes, it is one I flew over in north India. (*He describes an actual experience.*)

DOCTOR: Can you see yourself crossing it?

PATIENT: Yes.

DOCTOR: How are you dressed?

PATIENT: Shorts, bush jacket, pith helmet, and two canteens.

DOCTOR: Can you see me?

PATIENT: No. Yes, I can, too. You are a senior partner. (*He begins to take initiative, picturing the jeep, extra gas, and outlines carefully the 60-mile trek, the necessity for precautions, and so forth. Gradually he flips from fiction to reality and into the present tense, describing the two edging along at 15 miles per hour, the terrible strain on arms and legs, of the jolting which necessitates changing drivers every hour. He is sweating and breathing rapidly.*)

DOCTOR: My arms are awfully sore, would you spell me for awhile?

PATIENT: Yes. (*He describes the 130° heat as they stop the car to change places. He notes that they have only made 10½ miles instead of 15 in the first hour. Describes an impassable spot in the road and advises doctor to get out with the carbine and go on ahead. Describes his anxiety when doctor disappears around a bend lest he be deserted, his euphoria at doctor appearing and motioning him on. They suddenly run into a flash flood stream. He gets out to wade it for passability. It is too rapid and he comes back and they hunt for a staff to help steady him. He gets across and motions doctor to bring the jeep, which stalls in midstream. He comes back into the water and dries off the points and they make it to the other side. He expresses his anxiety about the fact they have come only 18 miles in 2 hours; even though they left early in the morning they may well be driving in the heat of the day, which is dangerous. He realizes they cannot turn back and decides that they should go on, but with some sense of desperation.*)

It may not be apparent in the illustration above how adequately the patient is free to disagree with the therapist who offers fragments of his own fantasy, but the patient ordinarily will have no problem with the therapist stealing the initiative once the fantasy is under motion. It seems amply clear that the therapist's participation changes the entire character of the fantasy and makes it much more therapeutically useful to the patient than a fantasy simply told to the therapist and with only the therapist's nonverbal participation.

Patient D.K. returned 1 year after 10 appointments because of feelings of panic about homosexuality. He talked in general about similar feelings, but now said he liked people. Doctor wondered if he had accepted his femininity, but had not yet dared to be a man.

PATIENT: Everything goes blank, now.

DOCTOR: Can you fill in the blankness?

PATIENT: Yes. It looks like a mass of pendulums.

DOCTOR: Can you see us there?

PATIENT: No.

DOCTOR: Can you see yourself?

PATIENT: Yes. I am lying on my face beneath them.

DOCTOR: Are they all the same length?

PATIENT: Yes.

DOCTOR: Can you see me?

PATIENT: No.

DOCTOR: Maybe you can if you look around. (*Thirty-second pause. Patient begins to smile broadly.*)

PATIENT: Now I can see you. You are standing way on the other side laughing hilariously.

DOCTOR: Why am I laughing?

PATIENT: I don't know.

DOCTOR: Can we do something about it?

PATIENT: Yes.

DOCTOR: What?

PATIENT: I can get up and leave.

DOCTOR: Can I go, too?

PATIENT: Yes. I was going to say that.

DOCTOR: Well, are we going?

PATIENT: I want to do something first.

DOCTOR: What?

PATIENT: I don't know, but I am afraid if I don't, I will just fall down on my face again. (*Patient anxious and restless now.*)

DOCTOR: What do you want to do?

PATIENT: Break some pendulums, I guess.

DOCTOR: Do you think you can? Have you got a weapon?

PATIENT: I guess I don't ordinarily think of it so, but I have a weapon. It is my hands. (*Three minutes silence.*)

DOCTOR: Well, do you want some help?

PATIENT: Yes, come on over. (*He opens up his arms to the therapist.*)

DOCTOR: Did I come?

PATIENT: No, but I am coming over there. (*He moves his chair over next to that of the therapist.*)

DOCTOR: Where are we now?

PATIENT: Outside all those pendulums.

DOCTOR: Are you just going to go away and leave them?

PATIENT: No. I want to break them.

DOCTOR: How will you do it?

PATIENT: Just break them across my knee, but we will have to do it one at a time.

DOCTOR: I don't see why you can't do a whole bunch at a time.

PATIENT: I don't know. They may be pretty strong.

DOCTOR: Well, why don't you start out with one?

PATIENT: OK. I'll take the writing one. (*Referring to the problem of extreme compulsive writing habits. Suddenly he grabs imaginary stick and breaks it over his knee. The tension is relaxed and he begins to laugh.)*

PATIENT: Its force is broken and it sure feels nice.

This joint fantasy has illustrated how the therapist was able to communicate by the fantasy his acceptance of the patient's rupture of his childhood enslavement by time and by the compulsive patterns of repressed aggression. It is interesting to note how comfortably this type of fantasy can be interrupted by the statutory limitations of time at the end of the interview. Frequently we continue such fantasies for two or three interviews. Sometimes the fantasy will be interrupted in the middle because the time is up, and the patient will continue the fantasy himself. For example, the patient reported above came back three interviews later saying that while he was waiting for his appointment that day he had completed the pendulum fantasy by himself. This had made him very proud. He said he grabbed another pendulum, and using it as a weapon, had broken them all to bits. He started to examine them on the floor and then decided they could all just go to hell.

Distortion in the sense perceptions of the therapist may also serve as a means of communication. For example, the author, in the middle of a deep relationship with one patient, became convinced that there were tears running down from the patient's left eye. Changing his position in the chair, he realized that this had been an illusion and his free association after he communicated the illusion to the patient was that the tears were the therapist's own tears. He also reported this to the patient.

When we first began to experiment with the therapist going to sleep in the therapeutic interview there was a good deal of embarrassment on the part of each therapist, and considerable hesitation about taking the technique seriously. Later it was possible to develop this capacity so that the therapist could drop into a hypnagogic state or actually into a fairly deep sleep for a matter of only a few seconds or half a minute, and report to the patient the dream which had taken place during this time. The dreams are often easy to interpret, but the therapist makes no effort to interpret them to the patient, since he might then generate excessive anxiety in the patient. When they are reported in their actual character they rarely create anxiety in the patient, and yet seem therapeutic progress. Sometimes these dreams seem to be significant and useful in the patient's therapeutic progress.

Sometimes these dreams serve a fairly simple interpretative pattern. One patient who had been like a servant to her family had brought this as one of her complaints, but had been able to make no progress in it. In the fifth interview her therapist fell asleep, and woke up reporting the following dream: "I was looking at your face and it was replaced by a large silver serving spoon." As the therapist reported the dream he was precipitated into a fantasy of the patient standing on one side of a table, serving her family, who were on the other side, with a large silver spoon and that her right elbow was taped stiff with adhesive tape. The patient supplemented this by saying that she, herself, was probably fed from what dribbled out of the holes in the spoon. This illustration only serves to show how the patient's perceptions and evaluation of her own dynamics can be augmented by additional communication from the therapist.

A final example of the use of dreams within the multiple therapy situation follows. A young psychopath was well along in therapy when the two therapists were precipitated into a series of dreams in one interview. One therapist had the following: "An old lady had fallen on a mass of broken glass. I was amazed that she didn't injure herself." The second dream: "An old lady was standing on a dock in a black lace petticoat." The third dream: "You [the patient] and I were talking about the wind. Somehow a difficult problem was involved. We were concerned. You [the patient] said of the wind, 'Well, it's human, after all.'" During the same interview the other therapist reported to the patient the following dreams. He saw the patient standing on the stage wearing dark glasses. His second dream: a woman was lying on the floor in a very severe attack of hysterical crying. There were two men with her, but there seemed to be no problem involved in the situation. His third dream: something was all packed in ice. He wasn't sure whether it was a coat or a person.

It seems from the above that the dreams in the multiple therapy situation are frequently very fragmentary ones, and probably constricted by the relationship between the therapists. It is also clear, however, that they serve to add another avenue of communication in which the therapist is the sender, and we believe that the patient is able to hear the signals with sufficient clarity that they can be an effective vector in the therapeutic process.

The behavior of the therapist in the interview situation is ordinarily thought of as a problem in the professional growth of the therapist, but as having no true usefulness for the patient. We have come to feel that it is useful for the therapist to take up with the patient, or at least call to the patient's attention, the fact that "I have just crossed my legs," "I am rocking in my chair," "I am feeling sleepy," or "I just loosened my belt." These might be said to indicate respectively, therapist's latent aggression, his oral fantasies, or repression of his own aggression, and the fact of the therapist's introjection of the patient. Ordinarily, it doesn't seem that the therapist needs to interpret these things to the patient, but merely report them. Or it may be that we are not yet adequate to make our interpretations seem effective. Finally, our group has decided to report to the patient in addition the somatic symptoms occurring during the interview. Thereby the therapist indicates his participation in the therapeutic situation. All sorts of symptoms have been reported, paresthesias, reflex coughs, headaches, brief asthmatic-like attacks, hay-fever-like attacks, GI griping, muscular tensions in a leg or an arm, gastric hypersecretion, numbness of a limb, or the therapist's wanting to cry without apparent reason. We know very little about this pattern, but it seems to be helpful to the patient.

FIRST-STAGE TECHNIQUES IN THE EXPERIENTIAL PSYCHOTHERAPY OF CHRONIC SCHIZOPHRENIC PATIENTS

with Richard E. Felder, Thomas P. Malone, and John Warkentin

The remark of Shakespeare's Hamlet that "Diseases desperate grown are by desperate appliance relieved—or not at all" describes the situation of the therapist who approaches the chronic schizophrenic. In order to begin to

Reprinted by permission from J. H. Masserman (Ed.), *Current Psychiatric Therapies* (Vol. 2). New York: Grune & Stratton, 1962. Copyright © 1962 by Grune & Stratton, Inc.

effectively work with these people, the therapist must break through the patient's defensive isolation and provoke interpersonal feeling of some kind. He must move quickly to reduce the mutually felt terror in order to establish an extradelusional relationship with his patient. While moving into the relationship, the therapist must, simultaneously, sever the patient's other pathogenetic relationships.

We see that these tasks must be carried out tacitly, paradoxically, if they are to be carried out successfully. I cannot make you believe I am not afraid or that I care. I can, however, be caring or not afraid. The schizophrenic mistrusts or misunderstands the spoken word and, therefore, the therapist must speak by his actions. For example, the therapist "unconsciously" communicates his lack of fear of the paranoid patient by falling asleep in front of him (see technique discussion in the text). Many of the first-stage techniques are for control and structuring of the interview. The aim is to eventually construct a "therapeutic" double bind from which the patient and therapist eventually escape. The creation of an intimate nondelusional relationship, however, comes first; that is, it is the first stage. We should remember in this light that all techniques are in the service of building such relationships. As an intimate relationship becomes established the need for techniques withers away.

The most frequent failures occur in the early stage of psychotherapy with difficult schizophrenic patients. The authors have found some empirical techniques useful in dealing with these problems. There is little doubt about the diagnosis of schizophrenia on the basis either of the presenting symptoms or the patient's history. Excluded from the group are the pseudoneurotic schizophrenic patients and the schizoid characterological problems. The patients described here do not readily relate to a therapist in any meaningful way. Their transferences are primarily internalized; that is, they are not operative interpersonally. The distortion of their interpersonal relatedness and communication is so gross that the ordinary ways of responding on the part of the therapist are both inappropriate and ineffective.

The difficulties in the early stages of treatment of these patients arise out of their interpersonal poverty and the therapist's consequent dilemma. Effective psychotherapy requires a personally meaningful relationship between the two (Malone, Whitaker, Warkentin, & Felder, 1961a). It is not enough that the therapist becomes meaningful to the patient in terms of the latter's delusional system. The therapist finds himself in a vacuum at the onset. Schizophrenic patients are then meaningful only in terms of stereotyped feelings about "the schizo-phrenic." These are on a similar feeling level with the delusional system of the patient. The therapist somehow has to relate to the patient in a way that the patient becomes personally meaningful. To say it negatively, the patient must reach the point where he is unable to ignore the person of the therapist, either by including him in his delusional system or by withdrawal. In the same vein the therapist must reach a point where he is unable to ignore the patient either by becoming administrative in his relationship to the patient or becoming lost in a labyrinth of concern over psychopathology. Intense reciprocal involvements are usually momentary. A problem in the early stage of treatment is to preserve and extend these periods of involvement in order to assure a solid interpersonal matrix for treatment.

Confronted with such patients, we recently have begun to strive for certain limited objectives. The early phase of treatment takes shape around the achievement of these objectives. They in no way cover the complete treatment program, but are rather limited objectives which we see as necessary in the early phase of treatment in order to provide the kind of therapeutic relationship within which the long-range therapeutic objectives can be attained.

These immediate and limited objectives are, first, *the provocation of affect in the patient* (Malone, Whitaker, Warkentin, & Felder, 1961b). The stimulation of any affect within the relationship is constructive and a necessary forerunner to a transference relationship. Our second objective is *the reduction of terror in the patient and, to some extent, in the therapist*. We think of this as the core affective experience of the schizophrenic. Therapists exposed intimately to this terror frequently experience anxiety allied to unreality feelings. These at times come close to terror. Our third immediate objective is to *establish some sort of relationship with the patient outside of his delusional system*. We consciously and persistently resist any effort by the patient to neutralize his relationship to us by including it in his delusional system. Our fourth immediate objective is *the neutralization of critically patho-genic relationships*. By this we *do not mean* the resolution of patho-genic introject relationships within the patient. This we consider a long-range treatment objective. We do feel that it is essential in the early phase of treatment to neutralize real relationships in which the patient is involved since they currently either bind, immobilize, or terrify the patient (Whitaker, Warkentin, & Malone, 1959).

OBJECTIVE NO. I:
PROVOCATION OF INTERPERSONAL AFFECT

Technique A: Intensification and Reinforcement of Affect

As in other techniques, the patient is kept "off balance" in his perception of the therapist. He is shown that the ordinary social restraints are inoperative, and is likely to get the feeling that "this is the damnedest thing I ever ran into" (Warkentin, Felder, Malone, & Whitaker, 1961).

Example:
PATIENT: (*simple schizophrenic**) I can't trust you—I can't trust anybody.
THERAPIST: You hadn't better—I never fight fair.

Technique B: Direct Confrontation

In our experience, confrontation with factual or logical inconsistencies is ineffective. Forcing the patient to acknowledge his psychosis is useful.

Example:
PATIENT: (*paranoid*) (*looking stealthily at the window*)
THERAPIST: You hear voices outside the window.
PATIENT: (*nods slightly*)
THERAPIST: You're really crazy, aren't you?

Technique C: Deliberate Affect Flip

Schizophrenic patients often elude a relationship with the therapist by a sudden unexpected flip or reversal of affect. In this technique, the therapist pulls the same trick on the patient. The theapist does it by being aware of his own affect and deliberately switching to the opposite, then amplifying it as far as possible.

---

*Abbreviated to "simple" hereafter.

Example:

PATIENT: (*catatonic*) (*time for the interview to be over*) I appreciate your interest in me.

THERAPIST: (*flippantly*) Time's up.

In this technique, as well as in the others, the therapist refuses to make any effort to explain his behavior, or to be consistent.

TECHNIQUE D: CONTRIVED DOUBLE BINDS

The use of a deliberate double bind may be effective in stimulating anxiety and transference (Whitaker, 1958).

Example (This is probably the prototype of all double binds.):

THERAPIST: (*provokes the patient to anger by flipping cigarette ashes in patient's hair*)

PATIENT: (*simple*) (*looking very angry, clenching his fists, saying nothing*)

THERAPIST: If you feel angry, why don't you express it?

PATIENT: (*expresses his anger verbally*)

THERAPIST: (*plaintively*) What are you mad at me for? All I'm trying to do is help you.

TECHNIQUE E: CALLING THE PATIENT'S BLUFF

The purpose is to make fun of delusional systems, inappropriate responses, pseudoaffect, and seductiveness. It presupposes that the therapist can be more cynical than the patient.

Example:

PATIENT: (*paranoid*) (*smiling*) I'm sure you know what you're doing.

THERAPIST: Wipe that shit-eatin' grin off your face.

TECHNIQUE F: NEGATION OF THE SACREDNESS OF THE INTERVIEW (THE HOME)

The ritualistic quality of the relationship is negated in order to make room for the human encounter.

Example (multiple therapy):

PATIENT: (*simple*) Do you think I'll ever get better?

THERAPIST 1: (*speaking to the other therapist and completely ignoring the patient*) Did you get your steps made in the back yard over the weekend?

THERAPIST 2: Yes, let me tell you about it.

PATIENT: Do you think I'll ever get better?

THERAPIST 1: Don't interrupt; we're talking about something important.

TECHNIQUE G: SILENCE

Silence is for us an encounter between patient and therapist with no speaking, no smiling, no movement at all. It may be eye to eye, or staring at a fixed point or into space. This may be empty, useless, and futile and when it is we suspect the ineffectiveness to be due to the self-consciousness of the therapist. Such a silence may include any feelings, for example, love, hate, togetherness, isolation. When it intensifies the isolation of the patient it may provoke overt psychotic responses. Presumably, it produces a vacuum of initiative which the patient may fill. Silence may be continued in spite of the patient's effort to get into conversation. Each time the patient speaks he may be told to shut up, with increasing aggressiveness at each repetition. If the patient speaks with feeling we respect his communication.

TECHNIQUE H: THREATS

The effort to produce affect in the patient by forcing him to take some initiative and some responsibility for himself.

Example:

PATIENT: (*simple*) I'm not getting anywhere.

THERAPIST: You're going to get in the back ward of the state hospital for the rest of your life if you don't get something out of this.

TECHNIQUE I: USE OF PRIMITIVE LANGUAGE

Various types of primitive language may be provocative as well as effective in communicating with schizophrenic patients. Vulgar lan-

guage or dirty jokes, for example, are not perceived by the schizophrenic as offensive or humorous—nonetheless his response indicates
their significance.

Example:
(Any dirty story may be told that comes to mind, assuming the
therapist to be sensitive to the situation and using good judgment.
They are not told as jokes, but presented as parables.)

It conveys to the patient our willingness to go beyond customary
social expression. It is a method of inviting the patient into the psychotherapist's fantasy life. We use this technique intuitively, and on a
trial-and-error basis.

TECHNIQUE J: DESTRUCTURING

We consciously endeavor to devalue the magical quality of the interview situation, so that the patient loses his faith in what the therapist
will do for him and to him. The natural tendency to retreat to stereo-
types is broken. This helps resist the patient's effort to subsume the
therapeutic program under his psychosis. Destructuring disrupts psy-
chopathy as a defensive avoidance system and provokes anxiety or
confusion.

Example:
PATIENT: (*paranoid*) Have you had any insights about me since my
last interview?
THERAPIST: Yes, many; I've been staying here every evening for
3 hours praying for you.

OBJECTIVE NO. II: REDUCTION OF TERROR

TECHNIQUE K: PROFESSIONALLY ACCEPTABLE ACTING OUT IN INTERVIEW

Schizophrenic patients do concrete thinking. They must have some
opportunity to express their thoughts in behavior. If this is forbidden
in the presence of the therapist, then the patient is likely to get in

trouble socially. The involvement of motor and proprioceptive systems in the therapist and the patient tends to modify the awesome fantasies and to provide a kind of interpersonal contact. Provision of symbolic activities which suffice to express intense and terrifying feelings of the patient, for example murderous feelings, reduces the patient's terror.

Example:

PATIENT: (*simple*) What's wrong with me?

THERAPIST: Let's play checkers and I'll show you. (*The patient sacrifices himself endlessly on the checkerboard and this activity becomes symbolically cathected.*)

TECHNIQUE L: COUNTERACTION OF WEDGING EFFORT ON THE PART OF THE PATIENT

Terror is intensified by any feeling in the patient that he can separate the parents. We have referred to this as "wedging" (Whitaker, Malone, & Warkentin, 1956). In individual therapy we have noted that the terror of the patient is increased when he is able to split the maternal and paternal functions of the therapist. He may also try to wedge the therapist and the patient's family. This splitting has been more obvious in multiple therapy. Techniques which reaffirm the primacy of the relationship between the multiple therapists over the relationship of either of the therapists to the patient seem markedly to reduce the anxiety and terror of the patient. In our preliminary contact with the patient, we verbally affirm the primacy of the relationship of therapist to therapist. For example, one patient was told, "We two therapists have been married for years, and we do not believe you can do a thing about it." Other safeguards against wedging include any refusal to accept administrative restructuring, which would separate the therapists. For example, one therapist refuses to see the patient during the absence of the other therapist, where wedging has been a problem. Another example is the refusal on the part of one therapist to accept criticism of the other therapist during his absence from the interview, and his insistence that the patient bring this directly to the other therapist. Another common example is the willingness of the multiple therapist to reinforce the other's decision in the interview situation, even when he has verbally disagreed with him. Sometimes however, despite these measures, the patient is successful in splitting the therapists and his terror is intensified. Techniques for repairing these splits are many. One technique is to place the responsibility on the patient, by saying, "You have succeeded in splitting us, now what are you going to do about it?" Another is to exclude the patient from participating until the therapists can work out the repair themselves. For example, "You have managed to split us, now you shut up while we work this out in your presence."

TECHNIQUE M: PHYSICAL CONTACT

The rationale of the initiation of bodily contact by the therapist, or by the patient, has to do with the infantile functioning of the regressed schizophrenic. In some respects, the therapist accepts the patient as a real child, where words make relatively little difference, and it is important to the patient to have some sense of physical nearness and contact with the therapist (Warkentin & Taylor, 1957). Sometimes a brief touch of the hand can change the course of the interview, or even of the therapy. It is important to remain clear about the fact that the behavior of the patient is motivated by his need, while the behavior of the therapist is motivated by professional awareness of the clinical situation.

Example (touching of hands):
PATIENT: (*catatonic*) I don't know what to do with my hands. (*as he moves restlessly*)
THERAPIST: Your hands seem lost.
PATIENT: (*sits silently, looking confused, questioning, but unable to speak*)
THERAPIST: (*holds out his left hand, palm down, and says*) Could you lay your hand on mine?
PATIENT: (*stares uncertainly for a few moments, then slowly and laboriously lays his hand lightly on the therapist's. Both the therapist's and the patient's hands tremble and seem tense and awkward.*)
THERAPIST: I like the warmth of your hand. (*At this point the patient relaxed, rested his hand comfortably on the therapist's, and seemed ready to continue on a new basis in the interview relationship.*)

Technique N: Sleeping

On occasion we find ourelves going to sleep for varying periods of time during the interview. While going to sleep is involuntary, we tend not to resist it. This may be a powerful technique in reducing the terror of the schizophrenic patient.

Example:
THERAPIST: (*just waking up from a short nap*)
PATIENT: (*paranoid*) Aren't you afraid I'll kill you?

Although in some instances the therapist probably goes to sleep out of anxiety, it is still obvious that he is not afraid of the patient's aggressiveness toward him.

Another reason for going to sleep may be that the therapist is feeling no response to his patient and goes to sleep in an unconscious effort to locate his relationship to the patient. Sometimes as the therapist begins to go to sleep, the patient is stimulated affectively. On other occasions, the therapist may dream of the patient and report his dreams in the interview.

Another effect of the therapist's sleeping is to state in an emphatic way that his responsibility for the patient and for the therapeutic movement has a limit. Finally, sleep seems to be a powerful form of postural kinesis; with the relaxation of the therapist, the patient himself may become more relaxed and this may be a way of helping to reduce his terror. Our sleeping occurs more frequently when the therapeutic situation is in the form of multiple therapy. If the patient begins to go to sleep in the interview, the therapist may or may not interfere with this, according to his feeling about it at that moment.

Technique O: Waiting It Out

The therapit assumes that his just being there is therapeutic. This technique is attitudinal rather than behavioral. The attitude of the therapist includes a casual approach to the interview, no sense of urgency about relating, and no thought of termination.

Example (comfortable participation in small talk with expansion *ad absurdum*):

PATIENT: (*simple*) It looks like rain.

THERAPIST: I expected it would rain yesterday, but maybe it won't rain until tomorrow. (*and so forth*)

TECHNIQUE P: THE PERIODIC ASSUMPTION OF OMNIPOTENCE

This reduces terror in the patient by providing a strong and directive parental image. The therapist communicates his sense of being able to help the patient, his sureness of the relationship, and conviction that the patient is susceptible to interpersonal contact.

Example:

PATIENT: (*a hebephrenic patient who couldn't get to the interview on time because he was having fecal incontinence and vomiting when it was time to come to the interview*)

THERAPIST: You are to come here an hour early and if you have to shit or vomit, do it in the waiting room and bring it into the interview in a bag.

Example:

PATIENT: (*a catatonic patient beginning the interview snaps his fingers three times*)

THERAPIST: Trying to destroy us, eh? (*snaps his fingers three times and the patient jumps*)

THERAPIST: You'd better be careful or I'll do it the fourth time.

TECHNIQUE Q: THE PERIODIC ADMISSION OF IMPOTENCE

The patient needs an opportunity to identify with the therapist. This is not possible if the therapist maintains an omnipotent role. Identification is fundamental in reducing anxiety and terror in patients. Much of the terror in the schizophrenic patient seems to be a by-product of his dependent feelings.

By placing as much responsibility for getting well on the patient as the patient's ego strength will allow, we reduce his terror. This has to be delicately judged. It is better to leave the responsibility with the patient than assume it for yourself. Choice itself reduces terror, particularly in terms of double-bind dynamics. There is no choice if the therapist is God. His admission of his impotence may take many forms.

Examples:

THERAPIST: You have defeated me.

THERAPIST: Perhaps continued psychotherapy would be a mistake.

THERAPIST: If we're lucky we may be able to keep you out of a hospital.

THERAPIST: (*paranoid patient who has seen several therapists over period of years*) I'm no better than the other doctors you've seen.

OBJECTIVE NO. III:
ESTABLISHMENT OF RELATIONSHIP WITH THE PATIENT OUTSIDE HIS DELUSIONAL SYSTEM

TECHNIQUE R: CHANGE OF TECHNIQUE

The therapist must be able to keep the patient off balance. For this purpose, the changing of techniques unexpectedly may in itself be effective. This change may involve a reversal from one technique to another directly opposite. Schizophrenia involves opposites; such reversals recognize this. An example is the use of the technique for the assumption of omnipotence on one occasion, followed by the use of the technique which involves the admission of impotence.

TECHNIQUE S: SHARED FANTASIES OF THE THERAPIST

The therapist relates to the patient's initial limited participation with his own fantasies.[15] These fantasies emerge spontaneously and free-associatively to the patient's limited behavior and speech. They are shared by the therapist without any interpretation. They appear indirectly to present the patient with some underlying dynamic of his delusional system in such a way that the patient has to continue to struggle with the problem within himself. This prevents him from avoiding the problem by the interpersonal extension of it into delusional thoughts about the therapist.

Example:

A paranoid patient, apparently relaxed, closed his eyes. The therapist shared a fantasy which he spontaneously had that the patient had slits in his eyelids, through which he was peeking at the outside. The patient remarked, "I feel ashamed, suddenly. I have never known what a feeling was before. Now after 2 minutes of this feeling, I am completely exhausted." (*The therapist was conveying to the patient, "You are the one who peeks at people—it is not other people who peek at you."*)

TECHNIQUE T: DENIAL OF SECONDARY SYMPTOMS

The patient may present symptoms as an endeavor to avoid relationship with the therapist. The therapist denies these symptoms frontally by calling them fakes, or by pressing for something more real.

Example:

PATIENT: (*mixed*) (*giving a long story of imagined interplanetary travel*)

THERAPIST: (*after repeatedly interrupting*) Are you interested in getting help from me?

PATIENT: I've been needing some help.

TECHNIQUE U: MIRRORING

This is a type of psychiatric judo. The therapist responds to the patient by expanding the patient's delusional presentation.

Example:

PATIENT: (*paranoid*) Is that desk lamp a microphone?

THERAPIST: Of course. The phone is also recording, and the recordings are published in invisible ink in the daily *Atlanta Journal.*

TECHNIQUE V: REIFICATION AND ANTHROPOMORPHIZING

Many times the schizophrenic has distorted people by making them into things. He desperately defends this delusional system until the therapist breaks into it. This may be done by fragmenting his experience in the interview, or by making the therapist's experience identical with the patient's delusional system.

Example:

THERAPIST: (*with no preliminary comments from the patient*) You are a marble statue standing in the middle of a Greek square.

TECHNIQUE W: UPSIDE-DOWN LANGUAGE

The patient's defenses include a kind of denial which takes the form of saying the exact opposite of what he feels. He may verbalize complete hopelessness, particularly on the day that the psychotherapy shows some evidence of getting into motion. Since the therapist cannot directly counteract this dynamic, one technique is to join the patient in talking upside down. Sometimes, this resembles sarcasm on the part of the therapist, although it may not be at all hostile. This is a technique which devalues words, and emphasizes that there needs to be some sort of exchange between patient and therapist.

Example:

PATIENT: (*simple*) I want you to know that my Mama had nothing to do with my being sick.

THERAPIST: I'm sure you're right, your mother is a wonderful person who could help you a great deal now. She has already done everything she possibly could.

TECHNIQUE X: REVERSAL OF THE DOUBLE BIND

The double bind is the outward presentation of acceptance with the meta feeling of cold rejection. In this technique, the reverse is true. An outwardly hostile presentation is made with the meta feeling of warm acceptance. This technique may help break the "spell" of the original double binding.

Example:

THERAPIST: What do you want me to do that for?

PATIENT: (*hebephrenic*) It might help me.

THERAPIST: I'm not interested in helping you.

OBJECTIVE NO. IV:
THE NEUTRALIZATION OF CRITICALLY PATHOGENIC
RELATIONSHIPS

Over the years in our treatment of schizophrenics, the most difficult problem in the early phases of treatment has been the administrative relationship of the therapist to the patient's family. We have utilized a multitude of techniques for neutralizing the family in such a way as to allow psychotherapy of the patient to proceed. By and large, all of these techniques have been inadequate. We have attempted to remove the patient from his family by a variety of isolating techniques. We have attempted to put members of the family into collaborative therapy. We have had the family members as visitors in interviews with the primary schizophrenic patient. In all instances, however, there were serious difficulties. We increasingly were made aware that an essential problem of the schizophrenic person is his assumption of a saviourlike responsibility for members of his family, particularly his parents. All of our techniques have been aimed at negating this self-dedication. It appears now that the most effective way to neutralize critically pathogenic relationships is to treat the whole family of the schizophrenic as a unit (Malone, 1961).

SUMMARY

We have outlined and briefly described some techniques which we have found useful in the psychotherapy of schizophrenic patients in the early phases of treatment. These techniques reflect some general attitudes. First is a willingness to accept the limits of what is possible, with these patients, at this point in psychotherapy. Second is a willingness to take more responsibility for and with these patients than we do with other patients. Part of this responsibility involves relating more directly to the "child" in the patient and the sickness of the patient (Whitaker & Malone, 1953). This contrasts with psychotherapy with neurotics where we relate primarily to the "adult," the wellness of the patient. The primary dynamic of psychotherapy is the human encounter.

PREVERBAL
ASPECTS OF PSYCHOTHERAPY
WITH SCHIZOPHRENICS

Why would a therapist undertake intensive psychotherapy with the schizo-phrenic? It is work that rapidly becomes painfully personal. Whitaker's an-swer is startling: Because he has to. More precisely, in order to do successful work with schizophrenics, one must have some need or wish, albeit uncon-scious, for a better integration of his own irrationality. The therapist ex-presses this wish for himself and his caring for the schizophrenic patient. He communicates this caring in many ways, the most important of which are nonverbal or preverbal. Because the preverbal mode of expression dates from early life, it is less ambiguous and more believable than the words that come later. To the schizophrenic, who has learned to distrust words, this is a language that he can understand and trust. Expression of caring then, is done concretely and unambiguously. In so expressing himself, the therapist also symbolically involves his whole presence in the therapy. Therapy, the schizo-phrenic knows, will not be restricted to a "meeting of the minds," but to the meeting of two whole persons. The therapist also communicates that he will be congruent with himself and expect the patient to be likewise. That is, neither will be allowed in the therapy to say more than he will do and what he does will recapitulate what has been said.

Another message communicated in the preverbal mode is that the therapist, though he cares for the patient, knows and respects his own integrity as well. He will make it difficult for the patient, the schizophrenic, not to do likewise. The reader should recall that "caring" describes a rela-tionship, not a particular set of behaviors. Being caring is also not synony-mous with nice, pleasant, or kindly, as Whitaker's illustrations reveal.

Although my subject has been announced as preverbal aspects of psychotherapy with schizophrenics, I am not altogether sure what the

Reprinted by permission from *Archives of Neurology and Psychiatry*, 1952, *67*, 834–837. Copyright © 1952 by the American Medical Association.

term "preverbal" means. It may be a misnomer, and you may not know any more about what it means when I am through.

I should like to talk to you about the term "schizophrenia." One does not talk about the term "schizophrenia" in a personal sense, and yet it is a very personal subject. One can do psychotherapy with medical students or with neurotics and it can still be a fairly professional situation. In my own experience, when you do psychotherapy with schizophrenics, it becomes a very personal matter. It may become more than just personal—it may become painfully personal. Some of what I am about to say will be very personal to me. As I talk to you, I am feeling my way along, trying to get to know you. I would like to talk to you about some of the experiences we had, what they meant to us,[16] and I hope to find the time to talk to you about what you go through, because it seems to me a little pointless to get up at 2:45 in the morning unless you are going to say something that has some significance for yourself.

Before I go any further, I would like to discuss the framework in which we do our psychotherapy with schizophrenics and the framework of my own thinking, because all of what I say here will actually be the experience of a group of us—some of us here and some in Atlanta—who have been discussing the problem of psychotherapy with schizophrenics for 2 or 3 years now. There will be certain similarities in what I am going to say to what John Rosen has said, what Milton Wechsler has said, and what Mike Hayward has said.[17] If one could understand the similarities and differences, you might say a lot of the differences have to do with the question of verbalization, because to talk about something that is nonverbal is difficult. I am going, to some degree, to stay away from the verbal area, partly because I feel that the verbal area in schizophrenia is relatively unimportant.

The framework has to do with an increasing conviction that the therapeutic relationship must be a personal relationship. It particularly has to do with the feeling that I am going to talk about, my own personal function in the psychotherapeutic relationship. If we wanted a subtitle, you might be able to change the title to say that I want to talk about communications. First we have this verbal communication that is the principal means of social intercourse; under the heading of verbal communication we may subsume the written word, music, and various other forms of communication that are standard. In this connection it is natural also to think of the spoken word, but in that there is what I think I will at least with poetic license subsume under the preverbal—timbre, voice quality, tone, breaks in timing. In the area of psychotherapy one is particularly involved in the inferences involved in verbal communication, and with every patient we ought to utilize in our work the patterns that produce the tension within the patient that necessitate his filling in the interstices in our verbal and in our non-verbal communication as well. It might be better to call it "extra-verbal" rather than "preverbal." In schizophrenia one is not just deal-ing with a child but with a person who has grown and formed different patterns for communicating than a child. Involved in extraverbal com-munication are various patterns of interpersonal communication, in-cluding proprioceptive sensations, posture, muscle tensions—especially the facial muscles, the circumoral muscles, the muscles of the neck, muscles of the eyes, and the muscles of the visible extremities, as well as the muscles of the back of the body. All of these we feel are perceptible to the patient and he is much more sensitive to these than we give him credit for. In addition, we ourselves are influenced by our own tension states. Our mood is set and modified by our own posture, tone, and so forth, and these influence the psychotherapeutic relationship.

One of the other extraverbal communication patterns is visual communication, or as somebody put it, visual intercourse. You already know how powerful it can be to have a patient stare at you, and the patient will tell you how powerful it is when you stare at him. Another aspect that may be as significant is the power of the silence of the therapist or the silence of the patient. There are many different kinds of silence: the waiting silence; the warm, affectionate, loving silence; the silence that goes with a battle of will between the patient and the psychotherapist as to who is going to carry the initiative.

What brings about communication? What is the channel in which communication flows? What is the power behind communication? I would like to narrow this down and temporarily give attention to the patient's communicating to us his affect and anxiety and categorically take up my own conviction that the basis for good results is affective involvement with the patient. You will say, "How can you manage this where you have no communication with some patients, poor com-munication with others, and with still others good communication at times and poor communication at others?" One thing is constant; the patient always wants to get well. He wants to mature. I see no difference between the biological drive of the organism to grow to full physical height and the biological drive of the organism to grow to full maturity. If that is true, then, and the patient is a constant, then the problem is in the therapist, and the inability to communicate with a schizophrenic patient has to do with the inability of the therapist to develop an emotional involvement with that patient and to have enough affect for that patient, enough conviction of the capacity of that patient to get well, so that he can put out enough of himself to communicate with that patient.

Now, why does the therapist get involved? Why does he have affect? Why would he make an effort to get at the patient? You may say, "That is his job." I feel that is inadequate. You don't go through the pain and suffering you must go through to get at a schizophrenic unless you have more than "professional interest." What makes a therapist push through a communicating channel to get at a schizophrenic patient? I feel there are two possible answers. I feel the therapist has the same basic motivation that brings the patient to the therapist, a biological drive to grow and mature and be more of himself. We tend to presume a mature therapist, but if that were really the case there wouldn't be any therapists left. The therapist wouldn't have to mature; he would be mature. I feel many therapists are mature in that they have no presenting gross disturbances in the interpersonal field, but I also believe that there are slivers of pathology in themselves that are still unresolved. It would not be unreasonable to assume that the therapist operates partly at least in this area because of his need to solve more of his own pathology. Maybe it goes beyond the interpersonal entity. It may be that the therapist is in this sort of depth therapy profoundly and personally involved because he has had to solve a deeper type of pathology, perhaps, for example, the pathology of the body image. There must be in the therapist somewhere a deeply significant motivation and needs that make him go into this relationship with the degree of affect that is necessary if you are going to do anything with schizophrenics.

Another concept we ought to get clear before we go into the process of how the therapist pushes himself into this type of relationship is what is he out for technically? In therapy with schizophrenics the therapist is looking for meaning; with neurotics he looks for information content. It may be that in therapy with schizophrenics, we should keep in mind the idea that there may be some reciprocal relationship between information and meaning. If one struggles for information one may fail to get meaning, and if one struggles for meaning one may fail to get information.

Another thing that seems to us very significant is that in order for a therapist to be professionally adequate with a schizophrenic it is necessary that he not only back away from or discard or minimize verbal communication, but that he also to a large degree minimize his own reality function. It is necessary that he deliberately push beyond his own ego boundaries. How can you protect yourself so that you can dare to be this deeply involved with schizophrenics? Most obviously by your own therapy. A second way is by participation in a group. One of the problems of the psychotherapist is that in dealing with a schizophrenic he has to move so far away from his culture patterns of acceptable feeling and thinking and behavior that he must have a great deal of confidence in himself lest he himself be panicked and withdraw from this primitive type of relating. It seems necessary that the therapist maintain a constant duality in his person. One has to be simultaneously a real person and a symbolic person. You have to have one foot in insanity and one foot in the earth. It is sometimes possible, in the depths of psychotherapy, to get both feet off the land, but only if you are fairly sure you know how to get back. Let me illustrate. We started with a new schizophrenic last week and in the middle of the third interview we got involved in a fairly deep symbolic experience having to do with an exchange of pipes. There were two of us and the patient. The other therapist offered her his pipe, but she was unable to smoke it and gave it back to him; he could not smoke it either. I felt he had lost his pipe and gave him mine. He smoked it for a while and gave me his. I took a few puffs on it and then offered it to the patient. This time she was able to smoke it very deeply.

I think our meaning got across: the patient perceived her therapists' expressed love for her and also the expressed love of the two therapists for each other. This gets very deep inside of you. Came the end of the hour, and we said, "Time is up." All of a sudden we were different people. We have broken out of this world we were in together. She said, "OK, I'll go." She didn't go. One of us said, "Well, why don't you leave?" Grossly real. The use of these two parts of yourself is a necessity; the patient needs both. She needs you as something that belongs to her and also needs to know that there is a point at which you belong to yourself and do not belong to her, and that there is a point at which she will not belong to you. A secondary part of this relationship, still nonverbal in context, has to do with general fantasy experience. We have long told patients how to free-associate. I think this is a failure with the schizophrenic patient. It seems to me a valid practice for the therapist to associate first. When the therapist dares to free-associate and leave his ego boundaries behind, he is already showing the patient the way. This merges into the next question of how do you mature yourself to the point of being able to depend more on nonverbal communication? This is one of the ways: you push your own ego function to the point where you are as free of reality as you can possibly be.

This, if I take it historically in our own group, developed as a long series of patterns and mechanisms. First there was multiple therapy. What it can give we would get in every interview, and often fight out with the patient problems of our own interrelationship. As you can imagine, this would make for a trying interview and sometimes for difficult situations even afterward. The results of it and the advantages to the patient of two therapists functioning on such a deep level with each other seem to be well worth the cost. In the process of trying to mature the therapist to the point where he is able to communicate on this preverbal level we have utilized many different anticultural and primitive forms of relating oneself to the patient. One of the earliest was the use of the baby bottle and "breast feeding" the patient, as it were. The first time I did this I was thrown into a panic. I felt the same way the first time I took a patient on my lap; the first time I dared to slap a schizophrenic's face after she had slapped me; and the first time I dared to slap a schizophrenic's face before she slapped me. Daring if you will to move beyond the limits of your own self-control and moving to a point where you are using your own immaturity in the treatment demand certain protections, and the most obvious is the protecting of yourself against your own pain. In this a cotherapist is a tremendous advantage.

Why do you have to go into this area? As far as I am concerned, the use of the baby bottle and nursing the patient with it, which I began in 1945, resulted out of my own inadequacy as a mother. I was ashamed of my maternal feelings. This was the way in which I was daring to push it to the forefront and get it resolved. This effort lasted about 2½ years. Since then I don't think I have used the baby bottle more than a half-dozen times. I suppose I don't need it anymore. The patient gets from my facial muscles, body posture, voice tone, and other nonverbal aspects of my attitude what he wants.

The same thing is true of aggression. In the beginning, my physical aggression against the patient was pathological. It still is. I will offer them my pathology until I mature to the point where it is unnecessary for me to offer that pathology in order to help them get well. You may say, "Maybe they can get well without it." I have my doubts.

Let me take up something else, that is, the problem of how the therapist can develop his own capacity in nonverbal or preverbal communication. Out of the development of silence as a means of communication and the communication in visual intercourse, that is, the capacity to look at each other, there came a conviction that one could demand of the patient that he look at you—that he be with you visually. Out of that came increasing frustration. Out of this frustration grew the reaction of going to sleep. The interpretations, the possibilities of this—the therapist going to sleep—are many; some of them are disturbing. Is it so he can have sexual fantasies? Aggressive fantasies? Or is it just because he is tired? Nonsense! I have dreams, and I come out of my dreams with help for the patient. This is nonverbal communication. I often don't know what the dream means, and neither does the patient. During about the fifth or sixth interview with the patient mentioned above I had about 10 short dreams. The first one I don't recall. The second had to do with an aluminum frying pan; I don't remember that one either; it didn't mean anything to me. The third had to do with a big power house. I was standing up on the catwalk and there was someone with me. The fellow with me was Kettering.[18] He said, "I'll get my men and we'll get to work on it." That was for the patient. The patient knew what was involved, even if I didn't, and he needs it on an emotional affect level. One of the staff brought up the point that it might have been a reaction to utter frustration. I don't know. I don't think so.

Let me tell you one other bit and then I will stop. We had a schizophrenic patient who was being seen in multiple therapy by four therapists and was constantly saying, "Stay away. Don't come near me." We though that over and then went over and sat down beside her. She slapped my face. I slapped her back, and then I dared her to slap me again. She did, twice as hard. Then I could really blow my top. I slapped her as hard as I could. I bring that up because I challenge you to say it is on the level of what interns do in an emergency ward with drunks. In the next interview I had a closer relationship with the patient, and it was not one based on fear. The rest of the way through was a good and loving relationship. You can interpret that in many ways. To me, it had to do with my demand that she recognize me as a person and recognize herself as a person. If I could dare to lose myself, and in a sense, "go crazy" over her, then maybe she could dare to do the same and we might both get better.

THE CONTRIBUTION OF INDIVIDUAL AND FAMILY THERAPY TO THE PSYCHOTHERAPY OF SCHIZOPHRENIA

Here, in a lecture presentation, Whitaker takes us on a sleigh ride across the field of schizophrenia and psychotherapy. As he wonders aloud, bits of autobiography, case examples, metaphor, theory turned inside out rapidly zoom into focus, then fade. Whitaker has always been intensely ambivalent about the use of theory or presupposition as a guide to action. The confounding effect of a theory is that it decreases the clinician's visibility and flexibility (see Part Three). When in the course of this chapter Whitaker asks, "Is it true that . . . ?" he is not looking for the correct answer among possible answers. Rather, he is posing ways of looking at the question at hand, any number of which may be clinically useful. Clearly, the clinician selects the theory that best fits his experience, and that theory which he uses in therapy can come from any source, including his mother! Theories are like training wheels in learning how to do psychotherapy. We see, by Whitaker's examples, that theory can be evocative and facilitative, rather than prescriptive or constricting, and this is how he would have us use it.

I want to lay down certain guidelines. First, I intend to cover my experience, the contributions to my way of treating schizophrenia as distinguished from other people's theory and from my own theory. Secondly, I need to define what I mean by theory! The term is so broad that it can connote almost any "thinking" process. The contribution of "thinking" to this treatment of schizophrenia is a very debatable point in my opinion. Sometimes I see it as a tremendous contribution. Sometimes I suspect it's essentially to contaminate and a problem rather than a contribution. However, if I use theory in the broader sense to include fantasy and creative effort of any kind, then the answer to my question is much less difficult.

When one talks about theory (as I have defined it above) and schizophrenia in the same sentence, one has to ask, "What is a schizophrenic?" Is he a more purified type, representative of all psychotic persons? Is he merely an individual who has been caught in a double bind and broken by it? Is he essentially a scapegoat from a pathological family structure? Or, is schizophrenia an electrochemical change that originated in a psychosocial setting, a change that is now fixed and irreversible? Is the schizophrenic the extruded third of the parental triangle, the "thingified" person, who became a nobody so the spirit of his family could continue? This "thingified" person, by the way, is a social role, like the town drunk, which, as Mark Twain said, was an elected office.

Let's go further; assuming the schizophrenic is a family-chosen counterweight to an overloaded family interlife, is this family unit just a ritualized actor on the sociocultural stage? We don't even know whether the schizophrenic is ahead of us or behind us in his involvement with life. Are we, as we see, I think, in our modern humor, art, music, and literature, trying to catch up with the schizophrenic, or is our therapeutic struggle an effort to help him catch up with us and inherit both his craziness and our cultural sanity? Sometimes we pity him; sometimes we envy him. If, for him, to love is to die on the cross and to be loved is to be killed, has his world been destroyed and are we all then playing the reconstruction game with him? Let me try again. Are the rest of us also playing the same reconstruction game with different rules? Has our world too been destroyed?

If we assume he's needing help rather than that we're needing help, then what is wrong? For years we thought that mothering was bad, then we thought it was his mother who was the person who was out of step. Then some people swung to a conviction that it was father, and that the poison was in the marriage. Then some went back to genetics.

When I think about theory, I wonder about the schizophrenic's opposite—the sociopath. Is his another way of being where, instead of running from the world, he's attacking it? The sociopath is usually less treatable and even less definable than the schizophrenic. Is he part of some continuum? Is he covering up his schizophrenia?

Is he a whole new compound of x parts of schizophrenia and y parts of social maladaptation, thereby making a whole new chemical?

Is a normal family, one that subtly moves on the pendulum of dynamics from a schizophrenialike scapegoat pattern to the social manipulation, we call a successful family? If the family's stabilization process fails in its group operation, is the schizophrenic just ballast that is thrown out to keep from scuttling the ship? What if the family gets too hot and are all crazy like the hippies? Is this too loving for the social structure? What if the family gets too cold and they are all politicians? Is this too mechanical for our social structure? I keep asking myself these questions, struggling for more theories. Why isn't everyone a schizophrenic? Is it possible that the gift of a psychotic diathesis is the greatest gift that the family can offer? A push for profundity?

There are almost as many models of what psychotherapy is all about as there are people practicing it. However, in therapy, as in a marriage, understanding, information, knowledge, and philosophical orientation may have nothing to do with the ongoing process between the individuals involved. If one assumes this latter orientation, then the one-to-one relationship has a certain standard patterning we can study. Variations of a gross nature take place when we introduce a second therapist, making a triangle, or when we introduce a second patient to make a triangle. If it is indeed true that any dyad is a triangle with the extruded third, then all psychotherapy is multiple therapy or couples therapy! Can we then take some theoretical model from this individual therapy and do couples treatment or multiple therapy setting and discover some new aspects of what goes on there? Can we discover the limitations of the one-to-one relationship between two human beings? Can we discover some of the limitations of the triangular relationship, whether it is composed of two patients and a therapist or two therapists and a patient? Is there any difference between these two kinds of triangles?

My own particular prejudice is toward a patterning that involves the freedom-inducing aspects of a third person, whether this makes the patient freer or the therapist more so. It certainly makes possible a kind of mobility in the relationship that is hard to come by with just two people in the room. One of the outstanding dynamics in the triangle is the strength or power move. Two people are obviously stronger than one in most situations. The dangers of reversible team arrangements or fixed team arrangements, of splits between the members of the triangle, makes for a massive kind of interpersonal power struggle. Within this context, each person is more apt to either be more constrained or alternatively more open as a way of increasing his freedom and satisfaction in the setting.

In that guerrilla warfare fighting which is psychotherapy, the useful utility of theory is defined by its application. In my own efforts in this guerrilla fighting it seems to me that my theories come from many places. My really applied theory came from very young children. The play therapy of Melanie Klein and Fred Allen's Rankian process therapy involved a demand learning of nonverbal and preverbal communication. My capacity in the oral dependent area was part of my farm boy loneliness and need for personal contact and physical contact. Some of this came from John Rosen as well as those little children, some of it from my sainted mother. The theory of control and of anal discipline and structure was largely learned from John Warkentin in the capacity to use sarcasm and control that he came by naturally. My use of analytic Freudian theory is from Tom Malone. However, this theoretical understanding was forged in the tag-team wrestling match of multiple therapy. My 3 years of therapy with delinquents forced me into defining theories of my own about the necessity for according the patient the status of worthy foe and of beating him thoroughly if I could. I found increasing freedom in relating to the schizophrenic and his family by way of my own family and my professional family. Our multiple therapy intimacy was not always theoretical.

Broader theories were also contributory to my learning of psychotherapy. Paul Schilder gave me a freedom to fantasize the image distortion in the schizophrenic and his body, the construction of a graven object to worship and a self he might lose. My fantasy and a baby bottle brought the discovery that any body contact was an undeniable intimacy with my body. Does mother's body contact with the baby's body convey a denial of the presence of that body to the infinite self? If so, is psychotherapy the capacity to make contact and stay in contact? From communication analysts I learned a kind of humility about what I knew that only kinesis and linguistics could make legible. They showed me, for instance, how Tom Malone and I cued each other with pipe smoking, yet 7 years later when I did this same thing with a patient, I was still not aware of it until I saw it on the videotape replay. This merely reinforced a belief that my endless suspicion of my function, my own conclusions and observations, is justified. Yet, my theories are only my dreams. Bateson and his group with their double bind, their concept of complementary and symmetrical relating, gave me a push to theorize about families instead of just about individuals. My original orientation toward bottle feeding patients was supplanted by a physical fight pattern that seemed as effective as the bottle when I was ready to dare it. Now both are superseded by a kind of parental power to structure the psychotherapy, to force patients to take the initiative. Then, when my inner feeling and my perception of myself as a person in reference to them is solidified, I have the capacity to deliberately battle for the right to be a self and demand that they be a self in spite of and in defiance of the stress in the relationship. I became "theoretically" convinced that the relationship is not constructed by or dependent upon incidents or aspects of its operations, that neither rejection, hate, disgust, boredom, or love makes a relationship. A relationship arrives *de novo* and lasts forever.

PART THREE

TRAINING AND GROWTH OF
THE THERAPIST

Whitaker has given a great deal of attention in his work to the training and growth of the person who has become a therapist. In Part Two, we detailed the distinction between the social therapist and the professional therapist. The former is someone who serves as a source of guidance and support to the patient but does not have a truly therapeutic experience with him. The social therapist often guides, directly or indirectly, the patient to a professional therapist. The professional therapist, we recall, is one who has committed himself to his own personal growth in his professional work. As a teacher is, in a sense, the "perpetual student," so is the professional therapist a "perpetual patient." This sort of dedication of one's self gives a sense of purpose to the work of therapy. For each patient, then, the professional therapist's own growth is at stake. His hope for the patient reflects his hope for himself and the one cannot be greater than the other. Whitaker's professional therapist is the Western version of the shaman or medicine man. The shaman struggles with his own demons as he struggles with those of his patients.[1] The shaman takes his patient into the world of mysteries, of which both partake before they both return to the real world, cured. The shaman must need to do therapy in order to do therapy successfully, for there is some risk involved. The journey is not to be undertaken lightly. We can see this shamanistic attitude toward the training and growth of the therapist, the relationship among therapists and the relationship between the therapist and the rest of his culture.

First we begin with the choice of professional training. We assume that all psychiatrists pick their specialty because they fear or are intrigued by craziness. They go on to split in two groups—those who give up hope of finding their craziness and those who keep trying to find it. We assume that psychologists pick their profession because they want to study the inside of themselves in a more voyeuristic, peeping Tom manner. The social worker's choice may well be related to the dream that society can be your ultimate earth mother, that you can get the grown-up nutrition and control we all want from the social structure or the group.[2]

Therefore, the person who becomes a therapist has a vocation, a need to do therapy, to push his own growing edge, to find his own creativity. How this need comes about we do not know, but it is probably "learned at mother's knee." Therapists appear often to have been "fixers" or "explainers" or surrogate parents in their own family of origin and this may have something to do with a kind of role preparation.[3]

Because nature is more important than nurture, the therapist's training, with the exception of his personal therapy, is a relatively superficial gloss on character structure. The trainee's personal therapy experience with a more senior professional therapist should be profound. The experience of his own patienthood provides the therapist with a vivid experience of the reality and importance of the symbolic life and the creativity of the unconscious. In his personal therapy, the novice becomes aware of his own needs and psychic immaturities. Some of these are lived through and repaired. Slivers of psychopathology, however, remain. This training for the unreality experience that is psychotherapy and the initiation into the reality and importance of the symbolic life kindles in the trainee the desire to grow further as a person. His accelerated growth in personal therapy gives him the hope that he can grow, a hope that he will see reflected in his work with his patients. Experience in therapy comes best from doing cotherapy teamwork with a more senior therapist. The novice should begin his apprenticeship by seeing families, then couples, and finally individuals. If the trainee begins by "cutting his teeth" on families, he will have the greatest opportunity to experience different transference and role relationships. Families, however, will be the least damaged by his inevitable slipups.

Senior cotherapists provide permission and protection for the trainee to experiment within the therapy setting. This working together eventuates in a shared experience more vivid and more useful in learning than the view from the "super-visor's" chair. Each therapist must find his own style, his own way, and although imitation may be a necessary step in the process, Whitaker doesn't encourage it.

The senior cotherapist teaches the trainee a set of attitudes, not a set of techniques. Some therapists will disagree, of course, with his model. Here Whitaker contrasts his style with that of Salvador Minuchin of the Philadelphia Child Guidance Group and, by extension, others who would insist on imitiation.

> In contrast with the Minuchin pattern, ours is not a vertical model but more a horizontal one. It is assumed that the student's intuitive methodology for making interpersonal relationships is of significant value. It assumes that the experience of working with the supervisor is more valuable than technical indoctrination of a particular methodology. We are quite convinced in contrast with the Minuchin pattern that observation and technical indoctrination by the supervisor tends to make the supervisee less confident of himself and more dependent on a technical method. This, like behavior modification technique, we assume becomes more boring and the therapist less of a person and more of an indoctrinator himself.[4]

The trainee will always be searching for techniques. Whitaker feels that techniques—that is, the deliberate use of certain behavioral stratagems—are necessary for the beginning therapist or the growing therapist moving into a new area. However, all techniques rapidly outlive their usefulness and become restrictive rather than facilitative. Therefore, they should be discarded as soon as possible. For example, the therapist may use silence or confrontation strategically, that is, deliberately, to foster intimacy in the therapy relationship. However, to structure the entire therapy around one such technique restricts the power of the therapist and imperils the success of his work. Too often, the tail wags the dog.

> [The medically oriented therapist assumes] a medically correct stance aloof and superior and possesses expert knowledge to be doled out in the customary manner to the underdeveloped. Therapists training in this mold are known by their still formality and their omnipotent, one-up attitude toward patients. Even when Freudian, neo-Freudian, or existential theories are adduced to underpin the medical therapist's activities, he typically uses them as weaponry to further widen the gulf between the patient and himself, to foster secrecy about his person—in short, to obliterate any sense of his belonging to a common human family with his patient.[5]

Thus we find, for example, Whitaker rejecting psychoanalytic technique, the free-associative method with the analyst, as a "blank screen," as a technique of therapy. Whitaker agrees with Freud's belief that the free-associative method is useful for research but is not potent enough for therapy. In fact, Whitaker's work shows a clear acceptance (see the introduction to Part Two) of much of the psychoanalytic theory of human development.

The use of theory should also be facilitative or evocative rather than restrictive or "constipating." By theory we mean the inductive use of any schema that explains the way things are. As William James and later Adolf Meyer pointed out, theory can result in a blindness to the facts, can restrict our opportunities for action. The reflexive use of theory clearly can block or dilute the impact of the underlying experience of therapy. Each therapist quite unconsciously will choose the ideas that foster his own growth. Theory is only a means to an end. The novice should be exposed to various theories but not indoctrinated. For some therapists, a comprehensive theory of growth and therapeutic practice may not be necessary.

There is no clear rite of passage to mark the end of the protective, nurturant period in the training of the therapist. Perhaps it is when the training program (residency, internship, placement) is administratively over. This may not coincide with one's personal readiness to be done with this period. At any rate, the therapist finds himself in what suddenly appears to be the real world. He quickly discovers two disconcerting things: (1) that he is hard-pressed to maintain his commitment to remaining professional (i.e., the commitment to growth), and (2) that the therapist's role, his role, like his predecessor the shaman, is countercultural.

Personal anxieties and isolation from colleagues encourage stagnation. It is tempting to deprofessionalize, to become a therapeutic technician, not to participate in the work fully. To remain professional in the sense that Whitaker uses the term, the therapist needs, literally, feedback on his own experience so that he may see himself at work. He also needs support for this continued experimentation in a place to detoxify the day's professional experiences, which he might otherwise take home or act out in his private life.

Whitaker sees one answer to the ongoing growth of the therapist in a "professional cuddle group"—a group of colleagues who can provide nurturance, perspective, and discipline. Of course, these colleagues should all be, themselves, professional therapists, who will then be "cuddled" by the rest of the intern group. This same sort of "cuddling" can be had in a more dilute form from one's cotherapist in multiple therapy or from leading a therapy group. If he had this experience available, the professional therapist will be more able to live as he must, in the real world, and the unreality experience of therapy. The two worlds overlap or merge for most of us—we therapeutize our families, we need our patients' love. The risks, however, of working alone are great.

> One wonders what is the result of years of individual one-to-one therapy. The stereotype is that the therapist, psychoanalyst, becomes more and more distant, less involved, less responsive, carrying a fantasy load along with the therapy but with no personal commitment. Is the therapist, the individual therapist, overloaded with affect projected upon him, depressed and enraged by it, pushed to suicide? Or does such a therapist become a technical administrator and help other people do the therapy?[6]

Clearly the psychotherapist, as Whitaker conceives of him, is an artist for whom, like Socrates, the living of life is the *ars artium*. What begins as a technical challenge becomes an aesthetic adventure. His professional work and his own intimate living are congruent. As the years pass, the professional therapist becomes more impressed with, and accepting of, the paradoxes inherent in human existence—that one is most oneself in a group, that closeness requires separateness, and so on. Perhaps he becomes more wise, but *he* cannot say.

THE ONGOING TRAINING OF
THE PSYCHOTHERAPIST

The "professional" nature of professional therapy is the therapist's commitment to his own growth, which makes him the "perpetual patient." By such a commitment, he avoids becoming a mere therapeutic technician. We see in this chapter on exploration the temptations faced by the therapist as he

Reprinted by permission from N. P. Dellis and H. K. Stone (Eds.), *The Training of Psychotherapists*. Baton Rouge: Louisiana State University Press, 1960. Copyright © 1960 by the Louisiana State University Press.

journeys through his professional life; that is, the isolation from community and living the "cross-cultural" role of the therapist.

The isolation imposed by the private practice of therapy promotes over- or underintensity of involvement. The therapist needs some experience, which functions as sort of a governor for this intensity. In order of increasing effectiveness, Whitaker suggests doing play therapy with children, group therapy, cotherapy (multiple therapy), and finally a professional "cuddle group."

This paper describes the dynamics of the "professional cuddle group" at the Atlanta clinic. In their regular meeting, members would present their patients, their impressions, and their treatment plans. There would then follow a kind of free-associative group critique, which seems to have had the quality of a "being in the hot seat" experience. The unanimous devotion to professional growth and strong yet diverse personalities of the members exerted a leveling effect on the group while providing a sense of cohesiveness. This sharing in turn proved antidotal to the isolation inherent in the practice of individual psychotherapy and as Whitaker says, sanctioned a freedom to experiment without license. Is this group therapy? Whitaker says no, since the relationships were "adult-to-adult" and did not involve prolonged regression or dependency. Each member ultimately felt he had veto power, in the administrative sense, over the group's opinion of his case management.

We know of no reports in the literature about similar groups. Perhaps some of our readers will repeat this experiment and write such a report.

This conference has been concerned with the student–teacher setting—the process of training an inexperienced and receptive student. The present chapter is concerned with the fact that training must continue or we die. Many of these problems, data, and findings are similar but take a new twist because we will consider training in a peer setting. Can we teach us old dogs any new tricks?

Howard Potter, Henrietta Klein, and Donald Goodenaugh (1957) note a national "trend away from psychotherapy" which they attribute in part to our monopolylike practices. We are certainly sectarian. Are we also rigid and unregenerate?

HORIZONS—LOST AND FOUND

Those psychiatrists who go into the active practice of psychotherapy after a more or less adequate training period, and with more or less adequate personal psychotherapy, can be divided into four general groups: those who grow professionally, those who hold the line, those who retreat, and those who are routed. It is not too unusual to see psychotherapists who in the course of their practice decompensate into a situation where they are clinically patients, whether this is admitted or hidden. Others gradually begin to retreat—as though they were in a professional impasse with themselves. They become cold, personally isolated from their patients, and usually develop some acting out in their professional setting, even though this may be restricted to a "who listens" kind of indifference. The group who hold the line are like general practitioners in psychiatry. They frequently consider themselves to be eclectic; this may mean they have no real conviction and vacillate from one compromise to another. Much of their professional functioning is of a mechanical quality and may become impotent under any real assault from the patient or the family. Many of these psychotherapists become technical listeners, advisors, environment manipulators, or addicts to a school of practice about which they have no actual convictions. Dr. Charles Watkins might call them "therapeutic technicians" also. Finally, there is the group who become real professionals. I suspect we all belong to this group so our views about the others are prejudiced.

PERSONAL AND PROFESSIONAL GROWTH

The psychotherapist may be mainly motivated to grow personally. (If he has had no experience in the patient's chair this is more serious but may be true of the "blessed" also.) Thereby he becomes the perpetual patient, within the framework of the partially psychotherapeutic situation. His personal growth can only be a by-product of his work with patients and is therefore limited. Such a person uses the slivers of his own pathology in his therapeutic work with the patient. This particular pattern was seen clearly in our training of medical students in psychotherapy (Malone, Whitaker, & Warkentin, undated). It has been described in the literature and is surprisingly effective with the patient.

Professional maturing in the psychotherapist has been assumed to be related to his personal therapy and analysis. This may actually be open to question, or certainly to further evaluation. It may be that the relationship is not as simple as we thought it to be. We have seen several residents whose individual therapy was effective, but whose professional functioning did not reflect this then or later. Their personal growth did not make for greater competence as a psychotherapist. Apparently it wasn't valuable as training.

Professional growth in psychotherapy follows experience and the opportunity for a felt evaluation of this experience.

Psychotherapy is unique in that training experience is only useful if it entails a certain amount of anxiety. The psychotherapist must be able to take a chance with his personal involvement and must somehow push his "growing edge" with each patient. To say it again, the growing professional psychotherapist must maintain open patient vectors in himself although his training is technical.

The Impact of Private Practice

The psychotherapist who practices "in private" must be a symbol to his patient, yet his other functions are varied and overlapping. Each new patient must be diagnosed; administrative structure must be established to handle the realities of possible acting out during therapy and to handle the patient vectors in the spouse or other relatives. Plans and progress reports need to be shared with the referring physician or social agency so that if the community kicks back, the symbolic relationship will be uncontaminated.

For example, the fifth appointment with an "experienced" schizophrenic was pure catatonic excitement. Two hours later her boss called: "Do I have to fire you?" One hour later the sister in authority called in a panic, "Mary must be returned to the hospital, don't you agree?" Three roles and largely incompatible ones.

There is a unique correlation between the findings on sensory deprivation coming out of John Lilly's work at N.I.M.H., Phil Solomon's work at Harvard, Robert Malmo's work at McGill, and what happens to the young psychotherapist. He is not deprived of light, sound, and touch stimuli as the experimental subjects are. He is subject to a type of isolation not usually discussed in conferences like this. To a greater degree than the parent, the boss, or the public official, he is cheated out of the rectifying affects of a healthy one-to-one, now we call it "existential," relationship. The therapist has no one to relate to. He is not the recipient of affect from his patient; that affect is directed past him to the symbol he represents. Most of his working day he is left isolated. Furthermore, his own affect must be as controlled as the blows of a father boxing with a 4-year-old son. His participation must be graded to the physical and emotional tolerance of the patient in transference. In summary then, the psychotherapist is unique in that he is often cheated out of the experience of defeat and reevaluation which teaches many powerful lessons. He is thereby liable to that sick professionalism that we sometimes call the "prostitute syndrome."

HOW CAN THE THERAPIST "BREAK THROUGH" TO PROFESSIONAL GROWTH?

Psychotherapy has a large unconscious component. The dynamics of training a psychotherapist are much more involved than those of ordinary education or training in an intellectual or a physical skill. Are psychotherapists born or made? Does the psychotherapist need to learn a system? Does the psychotherapist need a comprehensive knowledge of psychopathology? And still further, assuming he is well trained, does it also constrict him as it makes him more knowing? If so, then one of the objectives of this chapter is to push for methods of breaking the constricting bands. If social, interpersonal, and emotional security is the reward for conforming to our society, what is the cost of breaking through this for the continuous training necessary to become a good psychotherapist? Obviously, the primary cost is a degree of "break" with the community. As G. K. Chesterton said, "I believe in getting into hot water; it keeps you clean." Further, the psychotherapist must tolerate a high level of personal anxiety and frustration. The roots for this have been set during his residency training, but learning from a supervisor who is the responsible physician and a patient who is asking for help is much simpler than the independent functioning demanded when he moves into the adult professional practice of psychotherapy. Then he must work without supervision and to some degree in opposition to the family. In essence, the therapist needs to incorporate that about his culture which is therapeutic and be sensitive to that about his culture which is nontherapeutic. In the development of these things within himself, he may be able to accept the natural stimuli offered by those around him. If he can correct his functioning in response to these communications from patients, colleagues, and critics, he is fortunate. If he has become addicted to a school or constricted by a technical reaction pattern, such fluidity may be difficult to attain. Responses become stereotyped and decathected and then communicate no affect.

My 3-year-old daughter discovered some time back that the lullaby songs I had used for the previous five children were cold. She refused to listen and insisted I sing only the ones I've scraped up lately and haven't yet "purified."

At the end of his formal training the psychotherapist moves into a situation carrying new responsibilities and demanding greater independence of operation. This inevitably means increased social pressure with a move on his part toward social conformity and a gradual slowdown of his function in the cross-cultural role of psychotherapist. Most therapists break out of this stalemate to a greater or lesser degree and the means by which this comes about are pertinent to our discussion.

The psychotherapist does much to train himself through his work with patients, referring doctors, the patient's family, and community, and by contact with colleagues. However, most of this is tangential and some tends to augment his delusion of omnipotence and tempt him to avoid any reality testing of his professional capacity. As someone has nicely said, practice makes perfect, not only your assets but also your liabilities. The case which teaches a remarkable lesson may lead one further in the wrong direction instead of correcting a misconception.

If insecurity in his new professional situation produces a slowdown in professional growth, then security should be the simple basis for an increasing capacity to relate to his patients. However, the security of belonging to the community, the medical society, the neighborhood, the church, and increasingly to his own family may be an opiate which lulls him into the easy role of the nonlistening therapist. He may be broken out or break himself out of this by his contact with a particularly powerful patient who threatens his omnipotence through negative transference or who confronts him with his nonparticipation. There may also arrive a patient who is personally significant, say, subtly reminiscent of mama or big brother. Maybe the challenge of a local VIP will precipitate new affect and push him to further growth. Sometimes patients who have been treated by another psychiatrist may add the subtle personal overtones that test a man's mettle. At other times a patient who suddenly decides to see someone else may spur him to new effort. Even the necessity for defending the patient against the effort of the family to pull him out of treatment, or the sudden emergence of his own countertransference to the family, will open up new vistas for him.

Dr. A., who had been working for several months with Jim, has been called several times by the wife and by the mother who lived in a distant city. He'd had a bad interview this day and mother and wife were on the phone together. Something snapped; he not only "told them off" in terms of what they had done to his patient in the years past, he added evidence for their own need of therapy, and declared that the patient would probably never get back under their thumb.

This kind of chance taking can produce trouble and I am sure I need not illustrate the various kinds to anybody in this audience. Furthermore, success in this kind of venture may make the therapist more reckless and he may get in deeper trouble with the community. Most often the backwash from such overidentification induces guilt and thereby more compromising of his integrity and of his freedom of function. So failure as an administrator may scare him out of doing psychotherapy although it may move him rapidly toward being a better therapist.

The practicing therapist may also fail in his job with the patient. The patient may stay on and on in therapy—a sort of "haunt"—or leave therapy and perhaps be forgotten. Yet if the therapist is deeply involved, the patient may make the therapist's failure a crude and effective training experience.

Pete was a well-compensated schizophrenic who had had several hospital admissions. After 1 year of intensive treatment he was doing well in his profession and fairly well in his social life. Somehow the therapist took advantage of this steady improvement to try to push him into more rapid adjustment. He shot himself. A year later the therapist was still reverberating and was still fantasying that patient in his daily practice. He had a new sense of the integrity of the patient. He had learned that when the patient is improving it is dangerous to push him to also adjust his new competence to the social structure.

There are two simple technical methods which may help the therapist break through toward greater competence. The simplest of these is play therapy with children. There is something about getting down on the floor with a 5-year-old that does things to the delusion of grandeur with which adult patients ensnare him. Children tend to break up the compulsive devotion to words, to increase his personal participation through the use of toys as objective symbols and by body contact. They force him to use more nonverbal communication, while the unstructured character of play produces a greater release of affect. It's easy to be personal and loving with a 5-year-old and the satisfactions tempt one back into the conviction that people are worth knowing.

An 8-year-old autistic patient dubs me "Fuzzy Face" to his family because of the experience of rubbing his face against my whiskers.

Whenever the therapist steps off his throne he is apt to grow. Group therapy often does this. It's not difficult to maintain a sacred role in "that" chair by "that" desk, but in a group setting one's status may take quite a fall. The strength of the group may not appear at first but if the group grows at all its strength will be greater than his. Once that has happened he will gradually be pushed outside while the group helps each other, or he will become to some degree a patient with the others. Thus another "breakthrough" out of the symbolic isolation.

In 1945, the author, while conducting a group at Oak Ridge, came to group meeting one morning to face a 5-minute mocking imitation of all his standardized responses. He can still feel the humanizing effect of it. The memory is a persistent training force.

The remainder of this discussion will be centered around the training value and professional development stimulated by the give-and-take between colleagues either in the direct sense of multiple therapy or in the somewhat broader interaction between colleagues who practice in a clinic group, which includes staff work on all new cases and routine consultation with each other's patients.

Training Patterns Visible in One Clinic Group of Psychotherapists

We have been saying that there is strong evidence that many solo psychotherapists gradually move into a compromise type of functioning which is inefficient. The pressure of society makes "mendacity" even more useful to the psychotherapist than to the ordinary citizen. To be certain that the psychotherapist continues to develop his own capacity, and that he constantly balances experience with evaluation, is difficult. Psychotherapists are naturally mulish, and they say mules are difficult to teach. The story is told that a city man who decided to try farming bought a mule and then couldn't make the mule move a step out of the backyard. He called for help from an old neighbor who asked for a 3-foot length of two-by-four and calmly proceeded to clout the mule in the ribs on each side and finally on the head. The city man protested that this was cruel (a pertinent word in this discussion), and the old farmer replied, "Mister, if you're gonna teach a mule anything you first have to get his attention." The problem then is how to get the "attention" of the practicing psychotherapist to somehow set up a situation that will prevent his drying up on the vine. One of the best situations I know of is a practicing peer group.

THE GROUP

It is difficult to describe what makes a successful peer group. It's even more difficult to do when so much of one's personal involvement in the work must be under scrutiny. We have tried to summarize this by suggesting that first of all each member must have or develop the willingness to be a patient to or a therapist to any other member in the group. In effect, each person is a trainee and each is also a supervisor. Furthermore, there needs to be structure such that the group itself becomes the director of training. Once this is established, there arises respect—certain common policies develop about such things as shock treatment and tranquilizers. Yet within a broad framework each person must have the right to experiment with his own work. He may need to justify it, he may even feel the pressure of the group enough to seek permission for certain variations. It is as though the individual has a veto right on the group's supervision of him and vice versa. Possibly each colleague merely needs to learn how to tolerate the omnipotent feelings of the others and at the same time feels free to challenge that omnipotence repeatedly.

Doing psychotherapy as a member of a clinic group is an "existential" encounter (May, 1958). Whereas the relationship between patient and therapist is dominantly a problem in transference, the relationship with one's colleague is more personal and builds the capacity to utilize the therapeutic potential in the "encounter" part of one's work with patients. Let's say this in a more prosaic manner. A staff group teaches the therapist how to structure relationships to allow maximum freedom without license. Thus he learns to allow limited access by the patient to his real life or his real "self." This interpenetration of living roles in the clinic group increases the learning even in the patient–therapist experience. Clinic functioning thus prevents the type of walling-off that the therapist is apt to do if no one is peeking over his shoulder. He is less apt to wall himself off from the patient or wall himself off with the patient, either of which is a type of dry rot. Obviously, the give-and-take within a group produces joint experiences from which the disagreements and the consensual validation between the staff members makes for a mutual learning of this "encounter" type.

Dr. A. had seen the patient for the initial hour and Dr. B. was invited in for the routine second-hour consultation. The history was reviewed with him. He questioned the patient and the spouse and they departed. His first comment as the two began to staff this patient was, "That man is murderous." Dr. A. had found no suspicion of this in his own examination. The next five interviews gradually produced proof of the paranoid understructure. Dr. A. had learned a thing or two.

In summary, the general effect of working in a group is to increase the swing toward growth in the dynamic balance between growth and homeostasis. The cost of this professional movement is an inability to develop the compromise-oriented living and working, which is so frequently the defense of doctors and which Sir William Osler extolled in his lecture, "Aequanimitas."

THE PROCESS OF TRAINING IN A GROUP SETTING

In general the learning process seems to take an upswing wherever the therapist involves another person in his professional function, thus breaking up the neurotic quality which so permeates the usual psychotherapeutic tête-à-tête. This is true even if the third person is nonprofessional (e.g., the spouse in the first interview, the whole family group when administrative decisions have to be made, or in the psycho-therapy of couples or family groups). It is more effective if the third person is a colleague, for example, the second interview consultation, the consultant for any impassed relationship, treatment of a patient by two therapists, or two therapists involved in the same group therapy sessions. Further, a psychotherapist's training is augmented whenever he dares an innovation, whether in structure, procedure, or the charac-ter of his own participation, that is, in strategy or in tactics.

THE INTERACTION

In those areas where one is not naturally a good therapist he must learn gradually and painfully how to utilize the patterns that are effective for others. As Dr. Lief said, his behavior may change first and his attitude only gradually. For example, Dr. A., who is naturally soft and mater-nal, had little access to derision as a therapeutic tool, which was natural to Dr. B. It has been a struggle of years to gradually learn how and to make part of his own professional armamentarium this socially unacceptable, but therapeutically useful response. Dr. A. was like the man who was very fond of his pet dog. He just couldn't bear to cut off Fido's tail although he knew it must be done. In this empathy (or was it recipathy) he cut the tail off an inch at a time.

Some have suggested this learning is only artificial, but we believe it to be similar to learning a particular aspect of a golf swing—one may learn it from the pro and not be able to integrate it into his own functioning for some time to come. The type of learning necessary for the professional therapist also demands experience in a situation where the anxiety level is not too excessive. Thus, excessive responsibility for patient care or for running counter to the culture may make learning highly difficult. This limiting of anxiety may well be one reason for the value of group therapy, multiple therapy, couples therapy, close colleague relationships, and the occasional accepting community (e.g., New York City).

About 2 years ago it was decided that every new patient be seen jointly with a consultant before psychotherapy was advised. Several of the members of the group thought this was pointless, at least in many cases. The results have been almost frightening. Many of those patients who were thought to be routine turned out to be problem cases where the therapist was grossly in error on his initial evaluation. It almost convinced them that countertransference is like love at first sight.

Dr. A. was referred to a Negro belly dancer who, although pretty, didn't seem particularly a problem. When the consultant came in everything seemed to go routinely to Dr. A.; however, when the case was brought to staff the consultant was in stitches about the doctor's complete inability to present the history. His slips of tongue were revealing, as was his restricted history. We all sympathized.

DIAGNOSTIC STAFF MEETING

A typical diagnostic staff meeting starts a half-hour late and by the time everybody is there those who were ready first are piqued. Dr. A. says, "I have a new case, a 17-year-old who was messed up by a psychiatrist in Wisconsin in 1955 and messed up by Dr. D. here last year. The family is mad at Dr. D. and came to see me. Only lately has the patient begun to like Dr. D.; only now is he even calling for his own appointments." Three staff members jumped Dr. A. for his obvious presentation, not of a clinical problem but of a problem between him and Dr. D. Then Dr. A. recalled that the patient was a schizophrenic, that really he was surprised that Dr. D. had been able to get this much relationship, and that he guessed that was why the family was now raising a ruckus. Dr. A. gradually formulated his own function in the situation. He would line the family up and fix it so that Dr. D. could go on with his therapy of the boy.

The next new patient was a girl Dr. C. had treated for 1 year. She had been having an affair with a local VIP, had "blown up," gone to a private sanatorium, and later tried short-term therapy with two other psychiatrists. Some of the staff wanted to decline any further treatment of this problem because of the acting-out episodes. Others insisted that the clinic was in a responsible role and shouldn't back out on a technicality. In the give-and-take that followed the staff decided to itself supervise her further treatment and warn her that any break in appointments could necessitate termination of her treatment here. Dr. C., the therapist, felt comforted that he had gotten a vote of confidence and reassured that the staff would say "or else" in a situation where he had found it difficult to do so.

The third patient was a fairly simple problem and the therapist got only mild censure for his overeagerness to push the patient into therapy.

INTERPRETATION

The first therapist expressed his covert hostility to the other staff member, which all realized later involved a current problem and the social tension of the day. He immediately got the counterattack he asked for from half the staff group. His hostility and guilt were relieved. He then accepted his role in the treatment problem and when the staff member in case three was reprimanded he quipped, "They're easy on you. It's lucky you weren't first up." In the second case the therapist feared censure for failing with a treatment case and for precipitating some acting out. He wanted the relationship but feared the public relations aspect of her reverberations to further treatment.

The Monday morning diagnostic clinic sets up a series of dynamic balances between the staff members. This has an ebb and flow quality. Almost routinely there is sarcasm, aggressive punning, dependent cries for help, and defensive talk. There is a constant process of grouping and regrouping. The general pattern of individual veto stays in balance with group control of individual functioning. Also there are a good many as-if interchanges, and from time to time an actual push by one or more on the growing edge of one staff member, or even a move to push the entire group into a new pattern.

Two years ago Dr. B. began to find claustrophobia in almost every new patient. In working this through he went through the following stages: (1) derision by the staff whenever he presented a new patient with claustrophobia as the central complaint; (2) Dr. B.'s increasing conviction that these people were untreatable; (3) the staff's gradual decision that his treatment of these patients must include the spouse and a second therapist in four-way interviews; and (4) the gradual assault on Dr. B.'s personal "sliver" of claustrophobia, during staff meeting and casually over coffee. Within the next 2 months Dr. B.'s concentration on claustrophobia in his presentation of new patients gradually disappeared and has rarely recurred in the last year and a half since then.

Summary

A staff member had expressed a need for help in evaluating new patients. The process of training was covert, yet often forceful. The doctor developed a new insightfulness about patients and a freedom to participate more personally in the trainee–teacher activity of the staff.

Experiment

To evaluate one avenue of learning the author taped an interview in which he had a consultant in with him and a long-term schizophrenic whose treatment was going sour. The tape was played back to a group of four for their conclusions about what and how the therapist had learned from the consultant. I am summarizing eight pages of notes. The therapist learned by regressing as he described the impasse. He began to blame himself and suddenly saw his identification of this skinny physician patient with his own medical-student body image. He only saw his overprotectiveness when confronted with it by the consultant. This was reinforced by the therapist's sudden anger at the consultant when the latter faced the patient with his psychopathlike irresponsibility. In the protection of the consultant's office the patient then accused the therapist of prolonging the breast feeding.

Summary

The therapist, by going with the patient for help to a consultant, was able to find new free associations, new perception of the patient's maneuvers, and a new freedom of function.

The Resistances to Ongoing Training in Psychotherapy

It's probable that each person is a "natural" or a nonprofessional psychotherapist to one or more types of patients. The move from this happy state to the discipline necessary for professional functioning involves the breakthrough of many defenses. This is best done by stimuli of colleagues who want him to be more adequate. Patients try to keep the therapist as he is. Each of us has his own protective mechanisms against peer supervision. In this group, Dr. A. blocks out any contrary ideas with straight silence. Dr. B. ordinarily maintains a quiet, "you can't be mean to me after I've worked my fingers to the bone for you" attitude. Dr. C. oozes the conviction that all is well, thus making anyone else feel like a villain for disrupting his euphoria. Dr. D. classically accepts help with the most delicate appreciation and it's only later that one runs head-on into a stubborn refusal to be influenced. Dr. E. maintains his professional function with such a well-structured exactness that one has the feeling nothing can penetrate it. Dr. F. seems to resist by a "poor little me" look, and Dr. G. by requesting help in such a way that one feels put upon and tempted to refuse it even when requested. Some other maneuvers are extremely complex and could be diagrammed over a period of months or years. Nevertheless, they each contain the seeds of a request for help at the same time that they try to maintain the delusion of perfection.

The identification of an individual with his peers is always ambivalent. Each person alternates between the desire to emulate and the desire to destroy the other and maintain his own omnipotence (Meerloo, 1954). The resolution of this requires multiple checks on both phases of the ambivalence, whether the group is breaking up a pet theory of one of its members or the erroneous evaluation of an affect-loaded case. (So often it seems that the professional therapist is like the woman who was about to get married for the fourth time and suddenly realized that he too was an alcoholic, as all the others had been.)

THE CONDITIONS FOR PROFESSIONAL LEARNING

Central among these is the fact that massive reorganizing or organizing insights are probably illusions. The fact that these "ah ha" reactions "feel" so good probably is associated with this particular case situation. In fact, the crucial case that one thinks is going to change his whole professional career probably has a very limited effect and even that may be in the wrong direction. One of the most significant generalizations coming out of this group's work is that whenever a member has been "caught" with a particular faux pas they assume that this will happen repeatedly and that his changing will be gradual and painful to himself and to the rest of the group.

How does one identify valuable learning that has been accomplished? An obvious example is the therapist who gets an erotic response to an hysterical patient during the first interview although he well knows that what she is searching for is a dependent relationship. The consultant's participation clarifies this for him both intellectually and emotionally, and yet when the patient returns for the next interview the therapist feels a twitching in his scrotum. It appears that learning only takes place under the pummelling of someone of equal power.

Dr. A. and Dr. B. were seeing a schizophrenic girl in multiple therapy. She came in one day and precipitated sexual affect in one of the therapists, which he handled with directness and forcefulness. As he walked out congratulating himself the other therapist noted, as though he had not been aware of the above, that the patient was certainly expressing affect hunger and dependency in a primitive way. Therapist A. was shocked and thought that B. had certainly been blind. It occurred to him later that this was probably a selective bilateral blindness. Mayhap each participated in a facet of the patient's need and each learned as he felt the relationship between the patient and the other therapist. Thus each learned on a deeper level the possibility that he himself could respond as had the other therapist.

Each person makes his covert or overt request for teaching from someone around him in a manner unique to his own character and past training. In the mature therapist, this is usually direct. He may discover an uncomfortable sense about a particular relationship or interview, or even a specific area of his professional function. Some seek help by asking a consultant in to an old, continuing treatment situation. In fact, Dr. B. makes it a regular practice to have a consultant visit with each long-term therapeutic patient every 6 months no matter how well treatment seems to be progressing. To say this more specifically, the request for learning is as serious as the depth of the trainee's involvement and as valuable as the power of the teacher.

A standard problem in the training of the psychotherapist has to do with the difference between learning and therapy. In the young resident the separation may be difficult and each may involve some of the other. With a professional therapist the separation is more clear-cut. The request for psychotherapy is the request for a specific isolated dependent relationship in which the therapist carries a personal responsibility for the patient. The teacher is not responsible in this sense for the mature colleague and the trainee is not asking for a dependent relationship, merely for a shared experience.

There is always the temptation in the teacher to make the teaching experience into an experience which is therapeutic. This problem has been handled administratively by deciding that training is only valid if it's kept in its professional setting.

Who can teach us pros psychotherapy? It is probable that the experienced psychotherapist cannot learn much from patients. Here the power of the trainee requires a type of relationship which is bilaterally balanced. Probably the best teaching is done by each person in his own particular manner, a manner probably consonant with his character structure. (This is the positive side of the coin Dr. Riess spoke of when he said the character problem of the supervisor interferes with supervision.) That is, the best teaching involves the natural response of the teacher. One member of this group does it by tender, loving, infiltrating insights, one by an often derisive irritant comment which feels like a knife between the ribs, another by the extension of one's own perception to include a wider field (e.g., pointing out how the defensive response of a patient is also a ploy for participation), another by presenting a rigid right–wrong structure, and still another by a facetious ribbing which seems almost offhand. This is not the whole of training—merely the dominant pattern in the one-to-one learning situation repeated daily.

Professional development is probably influenced by any expansion of the therapist's creativity (e.g., music or painting, the study of philosophy, comparative religion, or great literature). Any participation by the psychotherapist in the nonrational aspects of the culture lessens the stress of his cross-cultural therapeutic work. This is true whether it is personal (e.g., the weekend painter) or a joint fantasy—reading Dylan Thomas.

Finally, there is no doubt that one of the most powerful stimuli for professional learning emanates from a satisfying personal life outside the professional situation. We are all aware of the dangers inherent when professional setting serves to satisfy personal needs, but we often neglect to credit professional growth to the learning readiness brought about by a rich nonprofessional life. Thank God for the wife and kiddies.

ACKNOWLEDGMENT

The author is indebted to John Warkentin, Thomas P. Malone, and Richard E. Felder for their suggestions and criticisms of the present chapter.

MULTIPLE THERAPY AND ITS VARIATIONS

In the 1940s, Rudolph Dreikurs, an Adlerian therapist, reported his experience with what he called multiple therapy, using more than one therapist working with a single patient or marital couple, in the training of psychotherapists. Whitaker and his colleagues expanded on this pattern when they found, at Oak Ridge during the war, where time for case conferences was nonexistent, that if they had another therapist "ghost in" for a few minutes of each session both would be able to discuss the case later. He and his colleagues went on to use cotherapists (i.e., multiple therapy) in just about every possible position. Most commonly, in Atlanta, a cotherapist would serve as a consultant on the second session of the intake interview. Later Whitaker and his colleagues found cotherapy was necessary for working with schizophrenic individuals and later with their families.

Elsewhere, Whitaker has detailed the advantages of using multiple therapy as both a training and treatment modality.[7]

1. For the trainee, cotherapy provides a foxhole or roost from which to watch the melee. He can feel the bullets whiz by, sense the old soldier's gait, his stance, feel the pressure on him. He can watch, take notes, masturbate,

Reprinted by permission from G. D. Goldman and D. S. Milman (Eds.), *Innovations in Psychotherapy.* Springfield, Ill.: Charles C Thomas, 1971. Copyright © 1971 by Charles C Thomas Publisher.

and occasionally take a step outside. It is a graduated stress, one which the trainee can escalate and deescalate at will, in and out of the family, in and out of responsibility.

2. The post is an ideal clinical research method. When scared, or bored, the trainee can take more notes. Not only does he learn dynamics, but he learns dynamics that have probably eluded the old master. Combat is a good analogy because of the stress, but the apprentice to the artist or craftsman is probably better.

3. The trainee gets a lot from the supervisor. One of the best things is that the supervisor is dethroned. He stammers at times. His patients quit therapy at times. He doesn't always understand. He isn't always loving. What a relief to both that he is a human being.

4. Not only that, but if they are to make the cotherapy work, both parties have to respect and like each other as persons. The trainee can't always be pretending that he is fighting with his father, though he will do some of that, and the supervisor has to get over his dependence on his status. The latter has to rescind the pseudosuperiority of expertise.

5. The supervisor can provide the trainee with a rare and powerful opportunity to be creative, to try out maneuvers and explosions and forays with the assurance of skillful support when he inevitably gets into trouble.

6. The trainee has access to the supervisor's feeling life, instead of just his thoughts about something. He sees his involvement with the treatment process, and therapy is less likely to seem like a chess game.

7. Feedback is in the air. The supervisor criticizes the trainee on the spot, when it is alive for both. The trainee critiques the supervisor, an unusual opportunity. What a relief for both that can be—and helpful to the supervisor. This real feedback is not painful or destructive, because it has a function. Both are jointly treating the family and feedback is an essential component of their work together.

8. The family will likely critique the cotherapists by risking an attack on one, carefully reserving the other to maintain stability of the therapy. Without the pairing, this feedback would be less likely.

9. Cotherapy enthrones the family as it dethrones the supervisor. The family owns itself and the therapists are less likely to get caught up in its struggles outside the therapy hours.

10. Administration of a case is taught in the process of treatment as it is negotiated between the therapists.

11. Process is kept in focus, rather than the painful rumination on abstract theoretical issues common to much supervision.

12. In general, therapy is taught as a personal experience, not a function or technique.

For a practitioner, the use of a cotherapist not only dramatically extends the range of therapeutic technique, but it fosters growth in both cotherapists as well. This kind of growth is very important in initial training and most important in the "maintenance" of the professional therapist.

It doesn't take much thought to realize that the individual therapist who works with seriously ill patients is grossly in need of some support. To say it as I sometimes say it to schizophrenics, "It's just as lonesome on this end of our relationship as it is on your end." For the therapist to go beyond the treatment of a neurotic and treat the schizophrenic, ambulatory psychotic, or geriatric patient with psychosis, or to treat couples, groups, or families, necessitates more than the usual technical competence and more than the usual amount of human interest. How to resolve this problem? Add a second therapist. Of course, it's preferable that the cotherapist be of equal professional stature and respectful of his colleague; however, if there is a human respect between the two, it's my conviction that this is better than working alone.[8]

Dr. S. Spafford Ackerly once said many years ago that Freud held psychotherapy back 50 years.[9] He was pointing out by this rather radical statement that Freud's devotion to research in and understanding of the intrapsychic aspects of the individual made progress in the understanding of the process of treatment, of patient recovery, and of therapist function a much delayed and little studied procedure for many years. It was only in very recent years that the American Psychiatric Association had a section on psychotherapy. Part of this delay arose after the discovery that research with individual patients many times was very therapeutic. Thus the pragmatic study of psychotherapy as such was delayed until more recent years.

Probably the biggest breakthrough was in the mid-'40s when Rudolph Dreikurs began to bring his young trainees into his own interviews with individual patients.[10] The author's work in multiple psychotherapy began in 1945 at Oak Ridge with Dr. John Warkentin.[11] Whereas Dr. Dreikurs began his innovation as a training technique, we began ours in an effort to increase our communication. When one of us burst out of a one-to-one interview with great excitement, the other one was not interested in hearing the story. He had not been part of the live experience. Thus we decided that the two of us would treat the patient together.

The new freedom to communicate created a better understanding of our bilateral experiences and facilitated many gains in our relationship to each other and our treatment of patients. A second important gain from multiple therapy was the development of more power in the therapist and confidence in his functioning. With a second therapist present, each therapist was more free to be a person and not just a symbol. Much of the research approach to patient treatment suffered from the fact that the therapist became a symbol and, to some extent, the patient also became a symbol. Thereby these two communicated by a kind of secondary process which kept them at some distance from each other. This not only limited the interaction between the two people but also prevented each of them from being themselves.

One other gain from multiple therapy was the therapeutic and professional protection and the increased flexibility thereby available for response to the patient. Each person could get a feedback not only from one other person but from two people and had the opportunity to compare the two feedbacks. In multiple therapy the legal protection also avoided those disturbing episodes which happen from time to time in any psychotherapist's practice.

COTHERAPY AS A TRAINING AID

Jim began his psychiatric residency with a great deal of insecurity. He had gone into the field partly because his mother had been mentally ill in years past and he was anxious not only to find ways of being helpful to her but to try to make sure that he himself did not suffer a psychiatric breakdown. The first week on service he was put into a state hospital ward, and although he had supervision he was immediately plunged into a personal relationship with two new, acutely psychotic female patients. He spent his regular hours interviewing them and feeling increasingly frightened. His discussions with the supervisor and with the ward chief psychiatrist only served to prove to him how little he knew about what was going on and how responsible he should be for their care and their recovery.

He began to develop nightmares and shortly started taking tranquilizers so that he could sit through the interviews each day without having to be in a tremor and acute panic. One of these women looked remarkably like his mother; the other one had an incisive way of digging at his own personal anxieties until he was literally beside himself. He gradually increased the number of tranquilizers until he was comfortable and casual about the interviews and thus began his development toward becoming the kind of psychotherapist who can say, "Who listens?"

In order to avoid the kind of tragedy outlined above, there is a need to protect the new trainee from his own tender feelings, to teach him in a personal and comfortable way how to respond to very sick patients, and to give him some sense that he can make a contribution to their recovery. One way is to teach him psychotherapy by having him sit in with someone who is comfortable, someone who is competent; he can then participate to the degree possible for him in the ongoing therapy conducted by the more experienced man. The two of them, having lived through a common experience, can also talk in a much more significant and personal way about the ongoing process in the patient and in the interpersonal relationship that is psychotherapy. Once the trainee has had the experience of working in a safe setting with even disturbed patients, he can begin to develop his own pattern of interaction.

Although psychotherapy is usually taught in very small groups,[12] it is possible to have four or five residents plus two or three medical students plus two staff persons making up the therapeutic team for the treatment of even one patient. Such a process is vastly more efficient than the use of movies or the 1 hour of supervision for each hour of interview system. There, words become the means by which individuals play games with each other about an experience that one of them replays in his mind while the other one is trying to get the picture from words alone.

Multiple therapy or cotherapy as a training method has an extra advantage. It produces a different quality in the "as-if" relationship so characteristic of one-to-one therapy. The characteristics of a triangular or multiperson group are much different than the secretive and highly symbolic quality of the one-to-one relationship.

Ideally the new trainee might be introduced to psychotherapy by sitting in with an experienced colleague in the treatment of a married couple. The married couple is probably the least demanding therapeutic unit. The husband and wife, newly married or within the first few years, are largely transferred to each other. The therapist is free to move into and out of the relationship without particular strain and without the grave responsibility involved in other types of therapeutic intervention.

Once having gone through the treatment of a couple with an experienced colleague, the young trainee will be in a position either to do the same thing with a peer or to move on to treating an individual with a more experienced colleague as cotherapist or to the treatment of a group with a more experienced colleague. With this background the trainee can comfortably and efficiently go on to the treatment of an individual with a peer and at that point is ready to treat his first couple without a cotherapist.

Once he has had the experience of treating a couple alone and possibly running a group alone, he is ready to treat an individual patient in a one-to-one relationship without either undue panic or the distortions in perception which are so typical of the beginning psychotherapist. With a peer as cotherapist he should then be ready to take on a couples group. Maybe then he can inaugurate the more difficult procedure of treating a family with one of the senior therapists of the training staff. It is the author's contention that training should always begin with patients who are less seriously disturbed, although there are some who feel this is not true.

Parenthetically, the author must confess that one of the great gains in the use of multiple therapy for training is the feedback he gets from young trainees whose knowledge of such modern additions as systems theory, information sets, and existentialism is a tremendous asset in his effort to grow and to expand his understanding of the therapeutic process. That we learn from these young trainees must of course be kept secret from them lest they lose their reverence for the establishment. The author has been consistently amazed at how comfortably VIP private patients take the introduction of a young resident into their personal psychotherapy. It is as though the only real problem is whether the supervisor is willing to take the chance of being one-upped by the wisdom of the novitiate.

THE USE OF MULTIPLE THERAPY FOR THE GROWTH OF THE THERAPIST

Although every therapist is a mature person, some of us recognize that there are bits of growth we can still gain. In the one-to-one relationship such feedback to the therapist is fairly limited. In the first years we suffer the strange experience of the patient growing past us, and we learn from some of the things they experience how to be different in our own living. However, as we become more experienced, patients do not have that much significance for us and do not ordinarily rock us to such a degree that we are forced to change.

Multiple therapy changes all that. The presence of a triangle— even in the treatment of one patient, or several triangles in the treatment of a couple—makes possible certain unique things characteristic of triangles which are not true of dyadic relationships. In a triangle, one can have the formation of an alliance when two members team up to help the third or all three members team up together. A triangle also can and frequently does make possible the development of collusion, when two people team up against the third. This can have some very painful and sometimes very growthful reverberations in the therapist. When both the cotherapist and the patient agree that the other therapist is off base or is distorted in his perception, it is very difficult for him to use ordinary rationalizations and excuse-making about how immature the patient is, and certainly he would not be able to challenge both.

A third factor characteristic of triangles is the possibility of mediation. The mediator in this case may be one of the therapists or it may be the patient. The experience of having a patient resolve discrepancies between the two therapists or having one therapist mediate the painful struggle between you and a patient is a very growthful one.

Further facilitation of the growth of the young therapist (of course, the older therapist has no need for such experience) is brought about by the unique advantages of seeing yourself in the other therapist. It is very disconcerting to be in the middle of a profound interpretation or a very cogent observation and have both the patient and the cotherapist agree that you are out of order or that you are playing some fancy game that they can both see and you had not been aware of.

Although these dynamic factors and the experience of collusion, mediation, and alliance are all of great help, one of the most obvious gains in the multiple therapy setting is the mere fact that the experience is closer to everyday reality living. This not only necessitates that the therapist be more himself, but it also makes the patient more responsible for his living process rather than just responsible for telling it all to good old mother.

THE USE OF MULTIPLE THERAPY
AS A RESEARCH TOOL

Dr. Al Scheflen[13] first pointed out to the author that in the extensive use of multiple therapy he reported the process of the interview with a greater proximity to the actual experience as seen in the camera than most other therapists they had seen in the Temple Research Project. In the one-to-one relationship the therapist must be a supportive, nutrient mother figure offering intimacy and understanding while he simultaneously carries an administrative, reality-oriented, and structured father function. This double role can be split between the two therapists.

The use of multiple therapy enables each therapist to function on the intermittent time base. Dr. Scheflen discovered that the therapist ordinarily works on a 6- to 8-minute schedule, and after this period he withdraws his affect from the patient for a short period before starting another 6- to 8-minute episode. In the multiple therapy setting the two therapists alternate so that it is possible to continuously interrelate with the patient. Simultaneously, during the period when the one therapist is carrying the initiative, it is possible to study the ongoing process between the patient and the other therapist or to reflect upon the experience you and the patient have just completed.

It is also of great use to the patient for the two colleagues to discuss their joint experience openly during the interview by checking out their observations with each other and with the patient. This freedom to do research—or, if you will, clinical observation—with a live interaction and a present-tense communication gives the multiple therapy setting many advantages for upgrading the therapeutic process.

The patient may make great contributions to this study because, in his involvement with the two therapists who serve as prototype,[14] he will report back his adaptation of the therapeutic experience in his own living. For example, if the two therapists are free to fight with each other, the patient may well return and describe the relationship between the fight he had with his wife last night and the fight the two therapists had during the last interview. This gives the therapist a very exact extrapolation of the interface between them and an opportunity to evaluate their own relationship to each other, the changes in it, and the use of it in the therapeutic process with the patient.

THE USE OF MULTIPLE THERAPY IN TREATMENT

We have been discussing the use of multiple therapy for training, for the growth of the therapist, and for research. It also has unique advantages in the specific problems that come up in the treatment of patients.

One of the most obvious ones, as implied above, is the entrance of the therapist into any new territory. Whereas work with psychotic patients on an outpatient basis is very rewarding, it is also very arduous and particularly difficult during those first few years as a psychotherapist. The use of two therapists in this setting makes for a greater freedom and a greater learning experience; once one has become comfortable in treating such patients, then the multiple therapy need not be continued.

Cotherapy or multiple therapy is also useful in other expansions of the therapeutic territory; for example, the development of a couples group, working with families, working with adolescents, working with severe alcoholics, as well as the intensive personal involvement necessary for work with serious psychosomatic illnesses. The newer work with several families in a group or with a friendship network, à la Ross Speck,[15] also suggests two therapists. The advantages of taking on a cotherapist for working with seriously ill patients for its obvious gains in the freedom for creative innovations in your own therapeutic development is only one of the gains that the author believes to be unique to multiple therapy.

CHOICE OF CASES

One of the serious challenges for a psychotherapist is how to treat a patient who has been to two or three other therapists, each of whom failed. The treatment of such a failure is always tricky. Each time the patient fails he gets twice as cynical about psychotherapy. It is exciting to think that you could take on this woman who has had 10 years of treatment with an expert in a distant city, but it is more painful to discover that 10 years later you are right where he left off. It is simpler to start out with the humble admission that you are probably not any better and that maybe you would be smarter to start out with all you can get on your side rather than trying to test your mettle.

Parenthetically, multiple therapy is also a way to inaugurate the treatment of those VIPs who are frightening when they first arrive; be it another psychotherapist, the mayor of your town, a beautiful woman, a millionaire playboy, or your old college chum—each can be a hidden threat to your own daily equanimity. An ounce of real-life significance can outweigh 5 pounds of your therapeutic competence.

We have all had experiences also with those loaded combinations sometimes called "the gruesome twosome." The hysterical woman and her latent homosexual husband make a good combination for the first few interviews, but it is very difficult not get caught in the throes of their triangulation so that you are on the bottom and in trouble. The alcoholic wife and the hypertensive husband can be just as dangerous. Beware also of the schizophrenic and his widowed mother.

When one is deciding what cases to treat with multiple therapy, there are many factors to take into account. Most of the above are obvious. It is not so obvious that if you are planning to see the patient in multiple therapy, it is better to make the decision before the first interview.

CHOICE OF COTHERAPIST

The choice of cotherapist is even more crucial than the cases.[16] The most obvious thing is to choose a psychotherapist who is personally compatible and whose training and personality are complementary to your own.[17] However, this is not always available, and in some settings discovering any cotherapist who is willing to work with you is a difficult process.

My residents have taught me that my presumption of years past was equaled only by my assumption that I knew the answer. They have shown that it is not necessary for the therapists to be deeply personal in their relationship to each other. In the beginning the cotherapy relationship may be like a pseudomutual family. After the first fight, which certainly should take place in front of the patient or the couple, the cotherapists then may deal with each other in a respectful but personal interaction which does not necessitate intimacy or even profound compatibility outside the interview. Cotherapy can be a time-limited "affair." However, if a cotherapist is available with whom one becomes gradually more established, this is most helpful.[18] Surprisingly, almost any two therapists can work together, although it is equally true that any two therapists can be phony with each other and therefore of little help to the patient.

In using the cotherapy pattern as a way of supervision, compatibility certainly is not a requirement. However, there are some people with whom a cotherapy relationship is very difficult. This seems to be related to a difference in basic philosophical convictions about life rather than technical differences in treatment. For example, since the author tends to work on a base of paradoxical intention, any effort to do cotherapy with a therapist who tries to do psychotherapy on a base of education is apt to be self-canceling.

VARIATIONS OF COTHERAPY

We have been discussing some of the characteristics and uses of co-therapy as a process. There are many variations which should be mentioned in passing. One of the most obvious is the use of the second therapist as a consultant in the ongoing therapeutic process. The pattern utilized by the Atlanta Psychiatric Clinic during their years of developing multiple therapy is fairly routine. The therapist who is going to see the patient takes the initial history. The second interview is joint. A second therapist comes in as a consultant. The first interview is reviewed with him. He expands the history, and the two therapists then, either in front of the patient or after the patient has left, staff the situation and make variations on a plan for treatment.

The original therapist then presents this plan in the third inter-view, and the patient or patients are informed of the alternative plans. It is suggested that they consider the situation, and if they decide to go on in treatment they may reapply. This use of the second therapist as a consultant also has the advantage of completing the initial diagnostic contract, and renegotiating a new contract will set a new framework for ongoing treatment. If the decision is to have the treatment done by one therapist, the consultant is still symbolically in on the continuing treatment and can be brought back as consultant either at the request of the therapist or at the request of the patient. This use of the consultant in the ongoing process of psychotherapy is also of great value whatever the need.

Dr. A., in the seventh interview with his beautiful adolescent patient, began to be suspicious that he was not free to be fully honest and that he indeed was probably overinvolved. He asked the supervisor in, presented his problem in front of the patient, and in the presentation of it the three were able to work through to another level of relating, such that she was clear she needed a therapist, not a boyfriend, and he was clear that he could treat her as a patient and not get her confused with his own girlfriend.

Dr. B. did not discover until near the end of the second interview that the young man he was seeing was actively suicidal. At this point he interrupted the interview, went out and found a peer who was not actively involved in an interview, brought him into the interview, and presented him with the problem they were facing; the three of them were able to arrive at a decision that this suicidal impulse was indeed of such character that outpatient treatment would be feasible. Dr. B. was, of course, also able to sleep that night.

Dr. C. had been seeing Mary Zilch for 6 months and although in the beginning he had dreams of converting this somewhat dried-up old maid into a live, vivid human being, he sensed during the last six interviews that he was becoming more and more bored. Because of this he asked his supervisor to come into the interview with him. The supervisor helped the two of them face the situation for what it was. They developed more realistic plans for the ongoing treatment and the expansion of the one-to-one interviews to include group therapy. This helped Dr. C. get out of the rather awesome corner of being the only man in this 40-year-old woman's life.

One of the implications in the consultation episodes just presented is the usefulness of multiple therapy or the consultant interview as a method of supervision. *In vivo* supervision, either by the regular supervisor or by a peer, allows for an expanded experience as well as learning about psychotherapy. We have talked casually about the relationship of the consultant therapist to the therapist in one-to-one therapy as though it were a one-interview solution. Sometimes this is not possible; the second therapist may continue to stay in the therapy, or he may come back for every other interview, every fourth interview, or when invited. In some patient settings it becomes quite clear that the initial contract between the patient or patients and the individual therapist is quite untenable.

For example, Dr. Joe had agreed to see Mr. and Mrs. Q. because of Mrs. Q.'s severe body symptoms, which included intestinal cramps, rapid heart action, insomnia, and episodes of heart pain. He assumed that

her rather passive husband would be a kind of helper in the psychotherapy. Within a matter of three or four interviews it became clear that
the husband was actively suicidal and a fairly severe alcoholic, both of
which had been concealed. At this point it was clear that they should be
seen in multiple therapy because of the severity of the situation.

One of the most efficient uses of the second therapist is in the
facilitation of the ending process. The author some years ago was
seeing a psychotherapist and wife, each of whom had had considerable
previous treatment, yet the relationship between them was still quite
stormy. Over the course of a year the therapeutic process was intense
and fairly effective, but the patients showed no inclination to break
loose and continue without further treatment. At this point the author
invited one of his colleagues into the interview without any prewarn-
ing. Halfway through the interview this colleague suggested that they
sounded as though they were both bored with psychotherapy and he
thought they should give it up as hopeless. They accepted this a bit
wryly but in the 2 years since have been very happy about the resolution.

As one becomes more comfortable with custom-tailoring the psychotherapeutic process rather than having to follow a preestablished
plan, it seems very useful to also utilize a second therapist whenever
one is expanding the treatment base. If treatment is begun with a
couple, it is advantageous as treatment goes along to add a second
therapist for the initial interview with the children present. If one is
doing family therapy, it is useful to have a second therapist in for such
different episodes as a home visit, an open interview with the extended
family, or an interview to which the family invites the husband's
colleague or the wife's best girl friend.

CONCLUSION

We have discussed the use of multiple therapy as a methodology for
expanding the power, the safety, and the creative freedom available to
the therapist during his workaday world. We have tried to point out
some of its advantages in the realm of training and in the growth of the
more experienced therapist, its technical efficiency in the treatment
process, and variations in the use of a second therapist in the ordinary

ongoing practice of psychotherapy. The days when psychotherapy had to be secretive because it was concerned with the sinful aspects of the patient's life are past. Our basic concern now is with therapeutic efficiency and the discovery of more effective methods for helping individuals find their own life as well as learn how to function in this game-playing world we live in.

THE COMMITMENT TO INTIMACY

What is the commitment to intimacy? It is a conscious act, a "leap of faith," which the therapist decides to undertake. A movement toward intimacy destroys any preconceived contexts and creates its own. The purpose is "encouragement"—giving courage to the patient by the therapist's example. The patient may flee, but with the therapist in dogged pursuit. Intimacy is not a set of behaviors—it may involve kindness or cruelty. It is a mode of being that emerges as a property of a relationship. In therapy, as in "real life," it will be experienced only transiently and with great effort. Paradoxically, the ability to achieve intimacy fosters the ability (and perhaps the desire) for solitude, which is really intimacy with oneself.

Once a therapist has accepted a patient for treatment, there are certain ethical responsibilities which are implicit, as well as certain legal responsibilities which are many times explicit. Recent literature has emphasized the manipulative aspects of psychotherapy and although the tactical and strategic phases are certainly significant and must be developed to the point where they are an aid in the patient's recovery, I believe that there must be more than a game pattern for the psychotherapy to be anything except a method for relieving symptoms. If the therapist believes in helping the patient expand his living and deepen it, the relationship itself must be deeper than a game.

Reprinted from *Existential Psychiatry*, 1967, 6 (23), 355–356.

I can decide to see a patient. I can decide to not commit myself to that patient for more than a game about his symptoms and a game about my function as a therapist.[19] When therapy goes beyond the game stage, the clarity of control is not automatic. I cannot decide to commit myself to the patient on a preplanned basis, although once having committed myself, I can, within limits, decide the pattern of that commitment. However, this deciding is usually based on denial of response, rather than the choice of response. Beyond the decision to play the game, the therapist commits himself with the danger of uncontrolled involvement. Commitment implies a future time and is not merely a present state. The therapist plunging into the relationship presumes a decision that the endpoint of this relationship will be tolerable for him. Such a commitment has certain similarities to becoming pregnant. It may be possible to interrupt it, but this is a difficult and sometimes dangerous thing to do.[20] However, to allow it to continue may, and frequently does, involve a lifetime of responsibility, with the constant challenge of being vulnerable to that person.

The object of committing oneself to intimacy with a patient is to obtain a heightened consciousness of oneself as a way of responding to crisis. Psychotherapy is an endless crisis, a rhythmic crisis of surge and ebb—a surge of intimacy, and the ebb of loneliness. Anxiety is part of the surge to intimacy just as despair is part of the ebb to loneliness. Yet, it is only by committing oneself to this rhythmic surge and ebb that one attains a state of aloneness, which is not loneliness (interpersonal isolation).

As each new patient-hour arrives, it's my own inner life that is at issue. Will I look at him and see an insignificant other, or, like the optical illusion, will I look at him and see my very self? Will I manage to be more and more naked with this other of myselves? Can I use him to be more with myself? Will he hurt me? Of course. Will I hurt him? I hope so. Can he take it when I hurt him? Yes, if I enjoy it. Can I make this a time when my significance to myself is increased one more quantum? Can I keep from hiding the impulse to lead his move to openness by one of my own? Can I expose my aloneness? Can I be available to an "other"?

Such commitment necessitates certain prerequisites. The therapist must first win the battle for structure.[21] He must have been clear that this was his therapeutic process and that he is in charge of it. This is not just a meeting of two strangers. This is a meeting in which one person carries responsibility for the "unknowing" process, its timing, and the reality factors in it. The therapist must win the battle for initiative or for joint beingness; that is, the therapist must force the patient to be and not act the patient role. This can only be done if the therapist insists on not being subject or object. He must insist on being himself and in his most intimate way, endlessly asking himself in front of all who care to listen, where am I? How am I? Is my inner self being or waiting? Being or doing? Being or refusing to be? Can I dare to share my inner self with me? Can I dare to be more full of myself? Each crisis is the effort to force myself to a greater commitment to intimacy with myself. From that, and only from that, can the patient get encouraged to be; that is, to commit himself further to intimacy with his person.

If I can commit myself to greater intimacy with myself, the patient will in his reciprocal aloneness be pressured to commit himself to a self-intimacy which is, in itself, authentic.

WHEN NOT TO SHARE YOURSELF WITH A PATIENT

Sharing oneself with a patient may be done in the course of therapy if it is done with specific goals in mind. Usually the kind of affective participation required in sharing occurs after the game-playing or "battle for structure" stage in the therapy and is part of what Whitaker calls "the battle for initiative." The therapist must know clearly when to share himself, what to share, and if he is affectively able to share at the time. The patient needs to know where the therapist "is" if the therapist cannot fully be with the patient because of some other focus of attention.

Thus, the use of affect in therapy—here in the form of sharing—is done strategically. To say it another way, the therapist decides to be intimate. The affective participation called sharing is not played out theatrically or contrived, however, even though it is done to further the process of therapy. So we see that experiential sharing is not "wild," nor the same thing as saying (or doing) what comes into your head.

In developing an existential position, it's important to share yourself. There are limitations to this, however, including:

1. Not directly with new patients when you are really not a psychotherapist but a psychiatrist or psychologist or social worker.[22]

2. Not big major personal problems but preferably sliver problems, bits of pathology, bits of your own eccentricity, and bits of your own craziness, your free associations, your fantasies, your psychosomatic symptoms (particularly the ones that happen in the middle of the interview).

3. New personal problems probably should not be shared since they have an affect load which would burden the patient already struggling with his own affect.

4. Parts of yourself which are shared because the need for help with them is prominent. That immediately flips the situation so that the patient is warned to "be good to mama because she's very tired."[23]

5. When there is no other help for the therapist that's usable or available. This is probably more apt to be a problem when the therapist has not had therapy or when there is no other person that he can consult with or feel dependent on.

6. It's probably not bad to expose the therapist's family struggles. If the patient angers him because she looks like his wife, it's not appropriate for him to say that. He may say the patient angers him because she looks like somebody that is important to him and with whom he has an ongoing painful struggle. It's also important that he not burden his wife with the retaliatory transference or his children with the retaliatory transference that comes from exposing them in this way. For example, if the therapist has a symbolic sexual involvement with a patient, he has the right to express his feelings. But if the *patient* gets wind of the fact that this means his marital relations are inadequate, she may well take painful advantage of this when she meets his wife at the next cocktail party.

In any of the above situations where *full* exposure of the self is not appropriate, feasible, or desirable, one can allude to why he is not "all there."[24] For example, "I'm sorry I'm not as alive this morning as I would like to be. I had to stay up all night with my baby who was sick," or "I'm sorry I'm not so adequate this morning. I have a hangover from a big party last night," or "I'm sorry I may seem strange to you. I'm having a personal struggle which is not related to this which captures part of my interest," or "I'm sorry, you will have to give me 5 minutes of recovery time. I just got out of a big loaded situation in the previous interview and I haven't gotten it out of my hair yet." Any one of these indirect references gives the patient the message that he is not fully responsible for your current existential state and allows him to recalibrate his own response to you by the fact that you are not a steady state instrument for this particular experience. This use of indirect reference is very similar to saying where you are now or where you want to be with the patient. You may say, for example, "I'm sorry I don't respond openly to you. I haven't gotten to like you yet," or "You still feel like a stranger to me," or "I'm still a psychiatrist and don't feel like I'm a psychotherapist," or "You make me feel so much of my masculinity that it's hard for me to feel like your physician," or "I enjoy your teasing and I know you're inviting me to go to bed with you and I am not making any promises, but I don't think you have what it takes to break me out of my therapeutic set. I hope you'll keep trying though."

GROUP ENCOUNTER: THE NOW SELF OF ME

The therapist's vocation is himself. In different contexts, he finds, expands, and integrates his various selves, or is it (as Whitaker asks) different aspects of one self? In the course of this effort, the professional therapist becomes kaleidoscopic even to "himself." And who is it that experiences these different selves as different selves?

Whitaker believes there is something particularly catalytic about the therapeutic group that can shed light on the question. Experience in therapeutic groups can hasten the departure of the illusion of the "graven image" mode of experiencing oneself. Whitaker finds the marathon group the most powerful. It seems to be a synergistic combination of the forces that power encounter groups and traditional therapy groups. He identifies these as permission for experimentation and pressure for personal congruence (e.g., among "me, myself, and I"), respectively.

The reference to Zen Buddhism in the first paragraph suggests the image of oneself as a koan. The koan is a riddle or puzzle posed to the novice Zen

Buddhist for contemplation by the master. The solution of the koan, which involves a nonlogical, nonlinear jump in thinking, bespeaks enlightenment. Whitaker suggests that the professional therapist is out to solve the koan of the self. How can one self appear to itself and others as different selves in different contexts?

The basic sin in Zen Buddhism is any attempt to teach Zen. In like manner, one of the major social sins in our psychotherapy world is to write in the first person. This is generally based on the concept that when we talk about the self we are generally talking about an image we have of ourselves. The biblical taboo, "Thou shalt not worship a graven image," is a good way of expressing the danger and the impossible aspects of talking about the self. There is no name for God; He is sometimes called the Great, or God says, "I am." In the careful parody developed for Popeye the Sailor, he repeats endlessly, "I yam what I yam."

Herewith, then, I insist on talking about myself, and you can take it as narcissism if you will or you can take it as a somewhat painful but very personal effort to increase my experiencing of myself. Lord knows I'm not writing for the reader. I should like to make it clear also that I am neither a trained psychoanalyst nor a trained philosopher and by living I'm trying to expand my own personal experience of myself. That's why I revel in being a therapist.

When I first dipped into Kierkegaard many years ago, I found myself utterly baffled by his discussion of the self and its many different facets. I have since become more confused. My experiencing of myself isn't captured in the old familiar frameworks of id, ego, superego, nor by the ancient Father, Son, and Holy Ghost, nor by my childhood trinity—me, myself, and I.

The general question, "Can I be *a* self?" involves knowing one's "self" in the carnal sense, that is, experiencing one's self and a whole series of variants—being on top of myself, being bugged by myself, in tune with myself, and in opposition to myself. In addition to these linguistic evidences of the struggle for *unity*, there are a whole series of terms denoting division. As well as "beside myself," I can be "lonesome for myself," trying to "find myself," trying to "learn about myself," trying to "know about myself," talking about myself, looking for myself, and many others that denote a kind of pseudoobjectivity.

In different groups, I encounter different selves. The group encounter that we're centrally concerned with here can be divided into three general types: the traditional group therapy encounter, the interpersonal awareness or sensitivity training encounter, and the more coercive marathon group encounter. There are overlappings in each of these but for sake of conversational clarity I should like to separate them.

GROUP THERAPY

The original group therapy movement developed as a framework of one-to-one therapy done in the presence of a group. As the concept of group therapy expanded, it became more possible to separate group therapy from "therapy in a group." At this stage it seems quite clear that the group, once it has been unified, can increase the intrapsychic unity of my relation to myself. It's an exercise in the fitting together of me, myself, and I. There develops a time when I don't have to wait for Godot and a prototype of my "family to be" or for a corrective experience to be superimposed on the family I now belong to. Traditional group therapy also offers two-person feedback from the whole group and its subgroups.

BASIC ENCOUNTER

The basic encounter or sensitivity training group activates another dimension of my self. Basic encounter employs a framework different from that of traditional group therapy. All humans need training in relating the self to the other, whether it's a significant other, a frightened other, or a strange other. A sensitivity group is a microlaboratory for experiencing the outside world that we live in with the security of a leader and the experience of moving beyond the standard patterns we learned in our early life experience. The encounter group allows each individual the right and freedom to experience some of his own craziness. If craziness is the right to be free of reality and ego constraints, then the awareness group enables us to move past their logic-tight compartments; *it allows me to be a people with other people.* In the past each of us could be crazy in his professional self to a degree that was useful, but nobody was permitted to be crazy in the people-to-people world.

To say it in another way, the current effort to increase one's responsiveness or sensitivity is a countermovement to the 12 or 20 years each of us has struggled against being desensitized by our culture and by our school system. In school the man-child is not allowed to relate to any "other," but must center his life on things, whether toy trucks, an "A" in history, success in football, or making enough money so that "they" would not let him starve to death in his old age. This is what the encounter culture counters.

MARATHON GROUP

Group therapy and awareness groups overlap in function and the marathon group is the logical extension of these two into a whole new entity. The marathon group essentially is an effort to use time and space to increase the pressure for growth. A large group of people are put in a restricted setting where they cannot escape each other for a specific period of time. Under such stress they often develop an interpersonal turn-on toward one another or they serially build up such an interpersonal voltage that the whole group becomes turned on and each individual develops a sense of belongingness so that he can transcend that outside culture which has constricted him in the past. Although there is no hard research evidence that this episode has an enduring effect, many of us are convinced that it carries a special kind of voltage.

Over the course of the marathon I think we each develop a kind of incorporation identification with the other, a kind of intrapsychic unity matched with a sense of interpersonal separation which is equally unique. With that incorporation and the recognition of an equally potent interpersonal separation, I sense that I will not lose myelf in the "other." Only then does the experiential risk of involving my "self" more deeply with the other become possible. I chance a more significant experience than would take place in any short-term contact. One of the unique things about my marathon experience is that it seems transferable to the outside world. Let me say this in yet another way. It seems as though my marathon experience breaks a crack in the cultural code that I live with. The space pressure, the tick-tock time pressure, and the

eyeball-to-eyeball pressure coincide to weaken the intermittent interpersonal ebb and flow character of person-to-person time. The effect is
intensified by the knowledge that it will soon be over. It's now or never!
I seem able to change my style of living for that space and time and itch
as I watch for the spillover.

My experience of this phenomenon begins with a gradually increasing withness of myself, then passes on to an increasing withness in
my relation to a significant other in the group, and from there to a
greater withness related to the stranger, the strange other, and the
nonnatural other. Once I establish my safe, close, fear-free intimacy
with my "enemy" I develop a sense of unity and freedom to separate
from the subgroups and maybe even the whole group. It is as though
the marathon is a microcosm of the lifetime of me. "Oh to be a child
again, just for tonight." I fight for that microreliving of my own saga
each time.

Why do I experience group this way? It seems that a central factor
is the sense of my own need, my need to grow, my need to expand, my
need to belong. When I examine my group turn-on, it seems to be
related to a sense of fullness in myself which is without content and
with a sense of oneness, a sense of weness related to my contact with
another, whether that other is a single person, a couple, a subgroup, or
the full group. As the group gets under way I begin an inner search for
myself almost in defiance of the stress of this group of strangers. I want
to unite with myself before I reach out for or try to unite with any
other. The experience of finding my aloneness, defining and admitting
my need, seems essential as a preliminary step to any further challenge.
Basically that period is more useful to me if it is without talk, without
any oughtness, without any past, without any future, and really without any thought. The attainment of a state which I call vegetative
makes me most unified with myself. Once this state has been attained,
I find myself more available to input from the surrounding people.
Then I feel a desire to move out, a desire to invite others in. Many times
my own freedom to be with myself produces free associations, dreams,
somatic symptoms, and those transference slivers that produce the
secondary gain of an interpersonal turn-on. It's kind of an instant
redoubling of self, a kind of simultaneous transference, countertransference synchrony, between me and the other. One could call it the
arrival of the Holy Spirit. In the experience of confronting myself I
arrive at a state of exposing that noncontent me and expanding it to a

we, or at least offering such expansion to another or such others as I find myself open with. As is true in social relationships, I find myself taking a half-step, then I wish and wait for the other to take the next move. It's kind of a psychosocial courtship. I make paradoxical jabs and then let be in hopes the counterjab will free me to go further. I may suddenly find myself participating in an outgoing joint fantasy with the other, either in an overt, verbal, or behavioral give-and-take. At another time the move may be a covert one. I may offer my own fantasy or somatic sensations along with the pervading fear and the now state of my own beingness. As my involvement becomes more pervasive, I tend to do and less and be more free to share the significance of my beingness with the whole group. As I shared my aloneness they pushed me to change to a state of withness.

To define the process in words is very difficult. There is a level of objectivity and below that a level of subjectivity and below that the capacity to be objective about our subjective experience. This is hard to talk about. It's as though I use the other or the group to let me happen more fully to myself. I bounce back with my relation to another me, inside, to precipitate an increased selfness in me. When I bounce this off other persons they force increased selfness in me. They then use a subgroup or even a full group to increase my trust and my recklessness to that turned-on stage which I prefer to call my craziness, a type of integration such that my usual caution and fear about being falls away and I'm full of my aloneness in the intimacy of knowing they are full of their being. As I let the others happen to me so then I can let me happen to them. It's very strange to me that the process as it proceeds seems to move from an increasing sense of unity with another or with the others to an increasing sense of aloneness. It's as though the more I feel one with them the more I can feel separate from them and one with myself. As I let myself be then I can let them be and we can be more than either of us without the other.

LETTER: SAUNA BATH AND SNOW PLUNGE

You asked for a letter about my home and its significance in "keeping me alive." You also asked for pictures and I found I was avoiding that. It suddenly occurred to me that the home as a picture isn't what matters. It's my inside response to "home" that keeps me alive. I used to think of home as an escape, a refuge, a place to run to after the exhaustion of the day. Gradually it dawned on me that home was the place I went to after my day of role playing. Even though my effort in therapy is to get past roles, I have not yet fully arrived.

For many years it frightened me to sense that I was more mature in my office than at home. Then it became apparent that at home all of me was engaged; therefore, the risks were greater but the satisfactions were greater also. The difference was between participating with a segment of myself and participating with my whole person. There is still enough of the New England farmer in me so that I relish my aloneness, and I find it important at times to "not be anybody," or anything, and this is best done at home. The freedom that I strive for is more difficult to attain at home, but more valuable by far to my aliveness than that which I find in the office.

My home is also the arena for the struggle involved in my most special partnership, the ebb and flow, the fluctuation, the freedom for greater closeness and thereby, for greater separation. The anxiety in the change of direction, either toward or away from my wife, is what makes the sparks and what keeps home like a sauna bath or the snow plunge. It's *that* exciting segment of the day that keeps me alive.

When I think seriously about how to stay alive, I see it as directly connected with a slowly developing sense of commitment. (Please excuse the trite word.) A sense of security in my insides which seems to give, rather than a tendency to sit down, an increased excitement about

Reprinted by permission from *Voices*, 1966, 2 (1), 33. Copyright © 1966 by the American Academy of Psychotherapists.

forging into the outside. Looking back now, I smile wryly about the struggle for complete intimacy that went on through the years. Now I see a certain kind of separateness alternating with intimacy which should dynamically expand as I am more able to be alive.

How can I keep myself alive? Can I gain the kind of strength and recklessness that makes me push to enjoy myself, to "kill off" old concerns, to renew the home romance, to feel free to hate, to force myself out of the affect mire that I get myself into, to edge myself repeatedly into corners where decisions are necessary? Can I mount the courage to struggle with my body image, which is like a free association? It alters without warning, and only if I'm listening closely do I hear the change.

PART FOUR

MARITAL THERAPY

In this section we have grouped together Whitaker's writings that discuss both marriage and marital psychotherapy. As should now be clear, however, any groupings of Whitaker's papers is somewhat arbitrary and tends to obscure the communalities that unite all his work. Marriage is a perfect example of this, since for Whitaker it stands as a midpoint between the individual and the family, and between the family of origin and the family of procreation. To discuss the functions of marriage is of necessity to discuss the individual and the family. Whitaker confronts this fact directly in the first chapter of this section when he states, "The more you are free to be with others, your wife specifically, significant others, the more you are free to be with yourself."

ASSUMPTIONS ABOUT MARRIAGE

Much of Whitaker's method and orientation toward psychotherapy flows directly from the assumptions he makes about marriage. These assumptions remain implicit in much of his writing but are explicitly stated in the chapters in this section of the book. Whitaker sees these assumptions as stemming from "the patterns of our personal living." Once again, we see Whitaker's psychotherapy stance and psychotherapy techniques understood by him as an expression of his orientation toward life in general. This orientation does not change as the unit he treats changes. Therefore, the similarities among Whitaker's individual, couples, and family therapy are to be expected.

The assumptions that we see as most crucial to Whitaker's psychotherapy concern the choice of a marital partner, the functions of a marriage for the individual, and the rules of a marriage. These assumptions and the others discussed in the chapters of this section convey an almost mystical reverence for marriage.

CHOICE OF A MARITAL PARTNER

Whitaker believes that the choice of a partner for marriage is invariably done with wisdom and purpose. This choice is made both consciously and unconsciously, although it is implied that the unconscious processes predominate. One's understanding of the reasons for marital choice, whether one's own or that of another, is always partial at best. For the therapist to question this choice, to wonder if the marriage was a mistake, or to consider seeing one marital partner in therapy because he or she is sick or healthy may communicate to the couple a belief that the marriage is not a viable one. For Whitaker such feelings or behavior are indicative of some inappropriate fantasy of the therapist about the couple. The preferred stance is one of neutrality about a decision to divorce and a sense of appreciation about the "rightness" of the marriage for the couple.

A corollary of this assumption relates to the joint responsibility couples have for all facets of the marital relationship. Whitaker explicitly does not believe in the reality of unilateral behavior and feelings in a marriage. Just as the decision to marry is viewed as mutual, wise, and purposeful, so too are decisions for extramarital affairs, fights, agreements, and so forth. It may be within the role of the therapist to understand the meanings and purpose of behavior for couples, but it is not his role to pass judgment on the behavior, or to encourage a couple's fantasy that one of them is sick or irresponsible.

THE FUNCTIONS OF A MARRIAGE

Few therapists we know of view marriage as so important for human development as does Whitaker. The unmarried person for Whitaker is a biological cripple, unable to reproduce himself or herself, and incomplete in other ways as well. A marriage is an attempt by the individual to complete himself or herself. This biological grounding of marriage is as important to Whitaker's marital psychotherapy as was biology to his individual psychotherapy (see the introduction to Part Two, Psychotherapy).

Man's incompleteness causes a yearning for closeness and communion with others. Marriage functions as the most acceptable arena for experiencing that closeness available in our culture. This experience of intimacy is crucial for human well-being. As Whitaker puts it, "People are good for each other according to the degree to which they are intimate together."

RULES OF A MARRIAGE

Whitaker believes marriage is a unique relationship, one in which the concepts of fairness, decency, politeness, and factual honesty are inappropriate or of no real importance. This assumption is difficult for many people to accept or tolerate, but is crucial in understanding Whitaker's work. Whitaker believes marriages operate at a more important and primitive level where social conventions, consistency, and communication are of little need and are often counterproductive. Whitaker is fond of making the point in lectures by saying, "Telephones are great. Every home should have one, but they shouldn't be expected to heat the house."

MARITAL PSYCHOTHERAPY

It should be noted by the reader that most of Whitaker's writings related to marital psychotherapy were written relatively early in his career as a marital–family therapist. This, we feel, is due to the fact that, although his assumptions about marriage continued to be of use to him, the treatment of couples as a unit separate from the family was short-lived. Whitaker, in these chapters, describes his treatment of couples more as a variant of individual therapy than as a form of systems therapy. Few techniques or descriptions of process are included. Whitaker continued to work with couples, but by the mid-1960s his couples work had become family-system-oriented. A discussion of this period is to be found in the introduction to Part Five, Family Therapy.

FUNCTIONS OF MARRIAGE

As Whitaker discusses the functions and types of marriage in this chapter, he reveals a great deal about the assumptions he has about marital health and sickness. In particular, health relates to the ability of a couple to change—to be, in Whitaker's terms, in a state of flux. More than that, however, Whitaker believes that marriage should be an intense relationship where normal rules of social interaction are suspended. Couples are not fair or polite to one another, nor should they try to be.

The most important function of marriage is to increase the stress and anxiety in a person's life. Unless one keeps in mind Whitaker's individual psychology and the important and potentially positive contribution made by stress, this increase in anxiety may not seem like an important or positive function. Whitaker states explicitly that "nobody lives as hot a life if they aren't married." This belief helps shape his therapeutic work with couples. The therapist's job is to augment this anxiety, not to alleviate it.

There are so many ways you can go after the discussion of marriage. You can take up the functional concept of marriage and what mariage does to the individual and what he gets through it and what happens to him in the process. I'm going to deliberately stay in a state of flux about it. I think if it's going to be of any use to you, it's going to be an experience in thinking about it with me, instead of an experience in taking notes, so that you can take something that I told you should be so and prove it wrong.

Now, in order to talk about marriage, you have to have some concept of what man is, some idea of what the individual is before he combines, and what the functional aspects of the combination results in. I think one of the obvious things is that man is a biological cripple. I am a biological cripple; by myself I have no continuing time extent, I am cut off. I am crippled because I do not have any kind of a bust or a vagina. I cannot reproduce myself. This crippling is part of the functional background of the yen of one for the other. If you just bypass the instinct of reproduction, you realize that the problem that I have as a person is that of being incomplete. I am missing parts that are part of the biological necessity of myself. So the part of what has to do with the background of marriage is the concept of my own crippling.

There are other things that have to do with the individual: the whole concept of transference; that you transfer feelings from one state to another. The homeostasis; the effort of the individual to maintain security, a stable state. The phasic character of oneness; that you can get to other people and then lose them. That you are with yourself at one point and beside yourself at another. This ebb and flow in the living process makes it hard for us to be satisfied with where we are.

You can also assume that there are some aspects of our growing that are culture-bound—and I'm not going to list all of these because I couldn't. One of these is the yen to be a child—a continuing effort to make life simple—to be dependent and to hang on to the Garden of Eden and make believe that God didn't really drive us out, He was just kidding. And then the yen to do something about someone else, to be a therapist, to make mama happy, to solve the problems of the world, to be the Christ, and so forth.

Now, in the framework of that, when you talk about marriage, you have to talk about the definition of a marriage. I guess the simplest one is that marriage is an adult model of intimacy. It's a kind of oneness and separation which is part of the adult pattern of our structure. It has the qualities of all the other marriages, if I can use the term to denote oneness in a broader sense: mother–child, partners' or pals' relationships, the marriage or combination of enemies. (You can notice over the last 10 years the peculiar quality of our relationship with Russia, where at first there was a bitter negative tension and now you can feel the other side of this ambivalence. The same is true of the marriage or the combination of enemies.) I've often had the feeling that most marriages are often like 69—and if any of you have grandparents that makes 73, with four looking on.

There are essential differences between the family as a pattern and culture as a pattern. One of the differences is that the regulations, the rules that cover the two, the covering generalizations are essentially different. I look at those people who conduct their marriage as a public relations project, and they stand out with such a crass difference—like a salesman who doesn't understand why she doesn't stay sold—why he sold her and it worked all right and gradually the whole thing went to hell. His basic problem is that he just doesn't understand why she didn't stay sold. I'm seeing a dentist now who came in and said he had a difficult problem. He had to threaten his wife with divorce because she kept sleeping with this man and wanted to give up their marriage and the children to go live with him. He said, "Of course, I wouldn't do it, but I thought if I made it sound serious enough, she would break it off with him and come home." This kind of public relations rule applied to a private situation. It's in contrast to the other kind which is classically the schizophrenic, who has a private relations system with everybody. He wants to have the kind of intimacy—the unconscious to unconscious relationship with the guy he meets on the street and has just said hello to. So these two contrasting sets give you an idea of the differences between what I think marriage conceptually lives in—which is a framework of intimacy and has a set of rules and regulations versus the public relations world which you and I live in and which at this point we're still communicating in.[1]

I quote from Dr. Warkentin: "All is fair in love and war, and marriage is both." In this sense the rules of public operation and public relations don't apply in marriage. In marriage, there had better be war and there had better not be fairness; there had better not be politeness. One of the characteristic things a schizophrenic's mother wants when she comes in to see you is, "If you just get Johnny so he talks nice to me—he's so horrible—if he'd just be courteous—and he's so nice to other people—he treats me so uncivilly—he talks to me as though I weren't another citizen."

There are various kinds of marriages. If you take the marriages you see coming through your offices, you can type them fairly simply. The problem is that they are not exclusive types—they keep overlapping. One of the simplest types if the playmate type—the people who are just good friends and they decided they will live 10 paces distant but be married. They want to keep 10 paces away and they found someone else who wants to keep 10 paces away so they set up an arrangement.[2] They are two silent partners and neither one runs the store. Each owns a half-interest and neither is selling any. Incidentally, Margaret Mead has come out with a beautiful proposition about two kinds of marriages. Have you all heard about this? One is a marriage which is legally permissible and for which there is a certificate and which is set up on the understanding that the wife will take the pill and there will be no children. After a certain time, they can renegotiate this and decide if they want to be married for reproductive purposes. Then, they get another license, have a formal ceremony, and they are free to have children. This is like the companion marriage which swept the country 25 years ago, except it has a legal gimmick.

Then there is the bilateral adoption marriage—sometimes it is a unilateral adoption marriage. Here a good psychiatric attendant finds a patient and they legalize the relationship. You then have all sorts of fascinating experiences. I had one a couple of years ago, except it hadn't quite been legalized yet. He had had 4 or 5 years of work with a Rogerian and was having a good, stable, operating, living process and ran into this schizophrenic gal who was so exciting, verbally and otherwise, and they decided to live together. So they lived together for a couple of years and things were getting pretty explosive and so he brought her in to me to "straighten her out." This worked pretty well until I noticed how they were both equally crazy. This was going to be a problem when his craziness came out in the open instead of him having fun watching it at a distance in her. Then she began to get better, and as she did, he developed anxiety and they decided it was too much—they weren't bargaining for this. This was an adoption process —he was obviously her psychiatric attendant and she was just his *life*; this is the reciprocal relationship. He had become deadpan, cold, frozen, and she was going to electrify him. She was just as much his therapist as he was hers. To me, this adoption process is a pseudo-therapeutic one. It is what we call a bilateral pseudotherapeutic marriage, and is probably the standard American marriage, or the one that mine or most people I see would fall under. Each person tries to help the other. One of the prototypes of this is beautifully written up and is called *The $100 Misunderstanding*—it's a lovely little book. A 14-year-old unlettered Negro whore and a 22-year-old, maybe an 18-year-old, Yale sophomore, whose father is head of his community's anticursing league—try to work out a way of helping each other. It's very short and well worth getting hold of. This pseudotherapeutic marriage is almost inevitably reciprocal or bilateral and this is characteristic of all marriages—they are reciprocal—they are essentially mirror images—not one-sided.

Then, of course, there is the homosexual marriage—the marriage of two men or two women who happen to have physically different bodies so that they can get legally married, but they are working on an essentially competitive level. Then there's the perverted marriage—the most common is the asexual or nonaggressive marriage, like Henry Ford's—they lived together for 50 years and never had a fight. This to me is a perverted marriage.

Now, in a sense, one of the interesting ways of thinking about marriage besides Eric Berne's, which, by the way, I adopt in all policies, is the one which is what we call the pseudotherapeutic one—the mother and father feelings or roles and child's role that each of the partners has, and the male and female back of them; these are forced characteristics of all human relationships. When I'm here with you I take on the role of mother and father and you be very obedient and quiet and swallow regularly and take on the role of the child and make believe that's all that's going on, when actually we are adults reacting to each other as adults. But if you take the marriage of these two people, with all that complexity, and assume it is composed of his maleness and his femaleness and her maleness and her femaleness, then I think you can assume that in any marital relationship there are complexities of that combination—that her maleness and his maleness can be interrelated, and that her maleness and his femaleness can get together, and his maleness and her femaleness can form a combine, or the femaleness of the two can form a combine. So, when you talk of homosexual marriage between a masculine type woman and a feminine type man, you'll not be just talking about a homosexual combination but all the possible combinations of these four that are represented here. By the way, Ambrose Bierce has a nice definition of marriage in his *Devil's Dictionary*,[3] saying it is a community consisting of a master, a mistress, and two slaves, making, in all, two. He's talking about the same thing as Eric Berne except that he preceeded both of us by about 50 years.

Besides characteristics of the marriage, it is worthwhile to talk about the changes in it. (Incidentally, there are some other kinds of marriages that I'm not going to talk about. The affair, for instance, the marriage in which there's a legal affair and it continues for a long, long time—the only communication that they have is that they sleep together. It is an arrangement where the vagina and the penis have an attachment and the people aren't there. They are at various other places at various other times and they put their bodies together from time to time.) When you talk about marriages, you also talk about something that has a time dimension and in the time dimension, certain things take place. Let me talk about it in what is to me like a physiology first, then in terms of some of the nodal points you can find as you watch it over years. For instance, one of the functions is to increase the rate of metabolism. It does this momentarily but it also does it in a general sense. I suppose that nobody lives as hot a life if they aren't married. The bind between the stable legal contract and the flexible pressure and movement of the emotional involvement makes for an increase in the internal heat, which I doubt that you can get anyplace else. I'd be willing to fight with someone about that, because I suspect it's not an obvious thing to some folks, and maybe not even true. But marriage functions as a precipitator of stress and an increase in anxiety, an increase in affect, both negative and positive, and I think of this as one of its great contributions.

Marriage also precipitates an alienation from the past. It's a kind of forced existential experience which tends to drag you away from the past; and I think that probably you could make some proposition for the fact that people who get married, in general, are less apt to be tied to their mamas and papas and their childhood than those who don't. Sometimes the facts are hard to put together, because you see such distortions; but I think, in general, it tends to alienate the individual from the past. It also precipitates creativity, and not just biologically, but in a general sense, and it does this by disturbing the homeostasis, by disrupting the individual's organization, his solidity, his quieting down. It's more difficult to burn out at 25 if you suddenly find yourself a mate, and you settle into a permanent battle as to who's going to do what to whom with whose gun.

I think it also precipitates physical changes, changes in the body image, changes in the self-concept. One of the interesting things you may not have noticed, but that you may pick up if you watch for it, is that there are a number of women who are flat-chested but will develop greater breasts after marriage, uncaused by pregnancy. You can say it's hand-pressed or not, that's up to you.

Now, I guess you have to postulate the opposite. I don't know about this. Having been brought up on a farm, I tend to see everything from a positive aspect. I wouldn't be surprised if you could postulate that some people after marriage develop negative physiology and body symptom problems like arthritis, for example. I'd be very interested to know if statistically, the number of people who develop arthritis after marriage would be significant.

I think that marriage also precipitates integration. It seems the pressure, like going out for the football team, precipitates into a development. You may not get what you want, you may not even make the team, but if you go out for it you precipitate a physical change in development, and I think the same is true for marriage. It precipitates integration because of the very fact of its disruption and its stress. I think also that it results in an increasing homeostasis and increasing stability, and it may be that's the thing that develops last.

If you move from there into the business of how this happens, what are the dimensions, what are the axes around which this takes place, then you run into this thing which I think is true about a lot of this stuff in marriage, the fantastically paradoxical and strangely dialectical quality when you start talking—that's why I keep getting confused. You know, I start out in one direction and go a ways, and all of a sudden, I'm going in the opposite direction. You can resolve some of that, for example, if you say that two people live together, and there is nothing going on—and I think it is very difficult to prevent something—then they grow closer together and farther apart at the same rate. This is a weird kind of business, but the closer they get, the more separate they are. If they don't grow more separate, they can't grow closer. If they can't increase their individuality, they can't increase their oneness. This is hard to talk about because you have to set yourself up with a double bind. I have to either have a background in logic or philosophy and I don't have either. Sometimes, I feel like a general practitioner who got raked into psychiatry and don't know how to talk about it. The more you are free to be with others, your wife specifically, significant others, the more you are free to be with yourself. The more you are with you the more you can be with her. And if I can be crude for the moment, it's like physical intercourse. You can't plunge in and stay there. It's a process of movement back and forth—it's a state of flux—no pun intended, except it really takes off on a wonderful research project, I think it was Jerry Frank's, during World War II. He was running a huge compound of psychopaths at Fort Knox for the army and he was using filmstrips and trying to do something about 2000 men, and figured out something about flux. He said it was sort of ebb and flow, in and out, up and down quality of life and it was very important that there be some flux in everyone's life all the time, and without it life was dead and uninspiring and uninteresting. You can imagine what 2000 psychopaths did with that. They really got together on the concept of, "Have you had your flux today?"

Among these dialectical and paradoxical things, the business of love and hate is one of the most obvious ones. I don't know whether it is true that as love increases, hate increases, but I would assume that marriage moves from a distance to a closeness and that the closeness is compounded of the two sides of this loving and hating, that the vulnerability and the intimacy make for an increasing temperature of love and hate.

Let me take it now in terms of time, a period of time. If you assume that the beginning of marriage is a transference phenomenon, that the choice of marital partners is infinitely accurate—it's unconscious to unconscious. It's done in the same kind of exactness that you would expect a computer to answer a question. Computers make mistakes (so do we, God knows), but the combination of husband and wife is an extremely accurate one. I think, as far as I can tell through clinical experience, this is true even though the two partners are damn sick. It's as though the interlocking is at a level below that of psychological disturbance. I don't know, but I think it is a transference phenomenon. Once they get past this initial honeymoon of "This is the dream I've been carrying all the time, and now it's here in person," the honeymoon breaks up and then there is another period, which is kind of a second kind of transference—there ought to be a term for it. It's a period between the breakup of this dream transference and the breakup of the whole therapeutic relationship some 7, 8, 9 years later. It's been called the 7-year itch; we call it the 10-year syndrome: the time when it gradually dawns on these people that they can't reconstruct each other. The man—it gradually dawns on him that she will never be what he thought he could fix her up to be, and she's never going to be able to straighten him out into what she wanted. This is another kind of honeymoon flop—the end of a second type of honeymoon.

[Question from the audience: What do you mean by transference?]

I marry my mother—you know—I transfer to this woman who suddenly takes on these feelings that I had for my mama—or my parents—the combination of papa and mama or the combination of my parents and their parents.

The combination which is set up is composed of fantastic numbers of components, and I think probably the transference is part of it. Transference to me is something that isn't as simple a factor as we talk about. We talk about it as just like somebody marrying his mother. I don't think that's it—it disrupts the analogy because it isn't that simple. I think there are factors in his mother that he looks for and that he leans to. There may be factors in the girl which turn him on, which were factors which he was excited about in his father or grandfather. The whole gamut of information is put into a computer and you have to be, or I try to be, awfully careful not to oversimplify it. It would be nice—it would relieve a lot of my irritation and panic and distress from not knowing, but I don't think you can say it that simply. I think people have been trying to, and the reason it doesn't stick is because of this factor—it is so multiple. Because if it were true that if you married someone like your mama, everyone would be convinced of it, and it would be settled, but it isn't settled, culturally, so there are all the various doubts you see about it, up and down the line.

The end of this 10-year period or 7-year period, there gets to be what you would see or I would call a therapeutic impasse. It's a kind of transference–countertransference jam, and the whole thing just gets deader and deader. They'll say to you, "You know, we have the same fights that we had 6 years ago. We start out with the same things, we say the same things to each other, and it's no different." And this is because it's therapeutic. They're having the 7000th interview, and it's just like the first one, or the fifth one. And so if it's an impasse, then it's the same question that you are stuck with when you get in an impasse— what do you do now? Do you just discharge the patient and take a new one, like a divorce and a remarriage? Do you get a cotherapist in and try to do something about it, or do you find some way of disrupting this lock by introduction of another person? One of the obvious things to do, which has been done, is to have an affair—and this raises another aspect of marriage and then I'm going to stop because we've been at it long enough—and that is that the marriage itself is a superorganization, above the individuals who are in it, that the things that happen in the marriage are by order of the combine. He says, "You're frigid"; she says, "You're premature." This goes on for a while until they decide that something is going to have to be done to increase the temperature of the marriage, and they decide that Johnny would be a good guy to increase her temperature, and then they decide that she must do this behind his back, so that he won't have to feel cuckolded, and then when he discovers it, he's horrified, you know; and this is by arrangement, so that they agree that then they will go back together, which was originally planned before this amateur psychotherapy attempt. The temperature will be increased and they will have broken through the impasse and be on to more intimacy and a more signficant relationship with each other. And fairly frequently it results, works out just that way, that the temperature is increased, he's mad as hell and they gradually get through that, and every time the thing begins to cool off again, she makes eyes at somebody and the temperature shoots up another couple of degrees, or in some way they arrange that this old therapeutic experience will be brought out. She will find herself another therapist, or he will say, "Well, you had a therapist, now I'm going to find a therapist." And she will say, "Not that blonde," meaning, "Don't tell me about it, but go right ahead." But if you break through this impasse, which we call the 10-year impasse, either with the amateur triangle therapist or a professional, then you set in for another period of instability and growth; and I think you probably get around to the 20-year impasse, which usually is caused when the kids leave home. All of a sudden, one sits on one end and the other sits on the other end and there are all these people in between, so they don't have to worry about themselves, and all of a sudden, those people disappear and the table shrinks and there's nothing left to do but live together or throw the whole thing over. This 20-year impasse is another kind of lock between them; if it's broken, they then move on still further, to the facing of death and the profundities of older life, which necessitates the kind of background they've had to make it a constructive part of their living, too.

PSYCHOTHERAPY WITH COUPLES

As one reads this chapter, it is important to keep in mind that it was written in 1958, when almost no research had been published with regard to the outcome of marital therapy. Its purpose is to investigate the feasibility of effective psychotherapy with a couple or with an individual in the presence of the marital partner. Although it is not sophisticated research, it did pro-

Reprinted by permission from *American Journal of Psychotherapy*, 1958, *12*, 18–23. Copyright © 1958 by the *American Journal of Psychotherapy*.

vide an early demonstration of the effectiveness of marital psychotherapy and includes some speculation about the process of therapy and the mechanism of marital change.

This is to report psychotherapeutic treatment of married couples carried on during the past 2 years with a limited number of cases by a single therapist. For the most part the psychotherapy has been fairly brief in character and variable in results.

Early studies of psychotherapy were done from the point of view of one patient. The great need for research into the psychopathology of the individual was such that little work was done on the interpersonal relationships of the patient except as seen through the subjective experiences of the patient himself. Over the years this has produced a sacredness about the one-to-one therapeutic relationship which has further restricted our investigation of the patient in relation to his closest associate. In addition, society frowns upon so-called marriage counseling and most psychiatrists thereby hesitate to treat couples as such.

Sullivan and the Washington School of Psychiatry have done much to expand the idea of the psychiatrist's role so that it includes a study of the interaction between people. This is not generally assumed to include psychotherapy of the interpersonal reaction itself, except for those specific interpersonal reactions between the patient and the therapist. A recent book by Eisenstein, *Neurotic Interaction in Marriage*,[4] highlights our increasing concern with the marriage relationship. Previous to that, the GAP Committee on Family Study put out a brochure called "Integration and Conflict in Family Behavior" which attempted to describe the breadth and depth of the family disturbance. This was extremely valuable but leaves the psychiatrist with a sense that the complexity is such that he had better not become involved. In the book, most of the reports are from one side of the marriage or the other and are largely descriptive. However, Edith Jackson speaks of the bilateral fixation between the marriage partners and the feedback systems involved. In this book also is postulated a specific thesis that the partner who comes for psychotherapy is the one who is least disturbed. All of these data makes it more obvious that psychotherapy with the marriage couple would be a commonsense procedure if it were possible.

We are faced then with the question, "Is it possible to do effective psychotherapy on a couple as such, or on the so-called patient in the presence of the marital partner, either with increasing participation of the nonpatient or with the nonpatient remaining as participant observer?" Furthermore, we must determine, if treatment of the couple does not develop, will individual treatment for the patient in the presence of the marital partner be effective, or will individual treatment be possible after the contaminating effect of psychotherapeutic efforts directed toward the couple.[5]

METHOD

This report covers the development of a pattern of psychotherapy with couples as a method of treatment. The author has been engaged with a group of colleagues in exploring variations in psychotherapy. Dual therapy, since called multiple therapy, was one of the early techniques. Subsequent work was done with affective assault as a method in therapy with certain types of patients. The success of these methods led us rather naturally to study the forms of nonverbal communication between patient and therapist and then between husband and wife, as well as the interlocking transferences between the marital partners. The present report concerns a series of 30 couples treated by the author between January 1955 and January 1957. The diagnostic procedure included a history by the author taken with the couple jointly, followed by a joint interview with the couple, the author, and a colleague. The case protocol was then presented at staff meeting. Criteria for selections of patients for this procedure included the following: (1) interlocking psychopathology, so that individual therapy seemed relatively unpromising (e.g., alcoholic husband and mothering wife); (2) specific pathology in the asymptomatic partner which might jeopardize individual therapy (e.g., paranoid attitude in the husband); (3) fragility of the marriage so pronounced that individual therapy with the patient would probably lead to divorce (e.g., unfaithful husband and naive wife); (4) bilateral emotional immaturity so severe that a limited objective for psychotherapy is the only wise procedure; (5) the patient is mildly psychotic and the marriage partner must participate to serve as a nonprofessional attendant. As well as deciding whether individual therapy would be a difficult problem, the staff considered the question of whether multiple therapy for the patient, or the couple, or therapy of the couple by individual therapist was indicated. In arriving at a choice of therapies, consideration of other factors was included, such as the severity of the sickness in the presenting patient, the severity and character of the sickness in the spouse, and the compensatory character of the interdependence between them. The staff also considered the possible danger of acting out, either in a delinquent pattern or in explosions of psychotic behavior.

Once the decision was made, the couple was seen only as a unit by the author. The therapeutic management varied with the situation at hand. If the problem was primarily a marital struggle for closeness, major emphasis was aimed at breaking up the interdigitating transferences between the spouses. Where the problem was more serious (e.g., a long-standing neurosis or incipient psychosis in one partner) the therapist was careful to maintain the twoness and to establish preliminary stability in the marriage before turning his own affect toward either the sick patient or the overcompensated spouse. In trying to maintain the twoness, effort was made to point out those aspects of pathology in one partner that were also present in the other, or to indicate how the pathology or the dynamics in one partner were necessary to the adjustment of the other. The couples were seen only as a unit to avoid precipitating paranoid feelings about the triangular character of the situation. In the later phase of therapy it is possible to change this rule and see one member alone when the therapist is certain that the triangular tensions have been worked through to some extent and the absent member would be fairly sure that the therapist was working for the couple and not for the spouse. The therapist reserved the right to interrupt this one-to-one relationship at any time or to maintain insistently that the other member come in for the individual therapy to balance out any reverberations which might have taken place. The delicacy of this situation was illustrated at one point when a wife came in for a second interview without the husband and when she was challenged about this she brought out the fact that the husband had brought her up to the office and said he would wait for her down in front of the building. She was then told to go and get him and it is probable that if she had not, this particular couple would have broken their therapeutic effort.

The nature and purpose of the treatment effort was similar to that in individual therapy and group therapy as practiced by the author. The therapist tried to avoid participating in the patient's real-life decisions, but instead to stimulate his own affective investment in the couple. He also endeavored to allow them and even to push them toward utilizing the interview time for more intimate discussion between themselves than they were able to do at home.

RESULTS

The patients seen in this series included a group of 30 couples seen by one author in a therapeutic relationship which seemed to be valuable from the therapist's perception and which seemed to be worth further investigation. Only six couples withdrew from the therapeutic experience and none of these because of the author's refusal to see them in individual therapy. Ten of the couples ended without apparent therapeutic process taking place in one of the members; that is, one member seemed to have been only a participant observer. In two cases the couple therapy was preliminary to individual therapy with one of the partners and in both of these the therapy of the couple did not seem to interfere with subsequent therapeutic process of the "patient."

Retrospective evaluation of this series shows some interpersonal dynamics and certain differences from individual psychotherapy: (1) the verbal content of the interview was somewhat restricted but much less so than had been expected; (2) the temptation to interpret on the part of the therapist was greatly increased and it became more and more apparent that these interpretations furnished the other member of the couple with ammunition for the next family squabble and that this was a valuable contribution. Much interpretation involved the obvious interlocking of the neurotic needs of the two, for example, passivity-aggression, impotence–frigidity; (3) it seemed apparent that the degree of illness of the two partners was approximately equal although the symptom presentation was different. The marriage in the couples treated was clearly serving profound needs in the neurotic compensation of each partner; (4) however, the personality strength or the wellness of each partner was also utilized to a great degree by the spouse; (5) the ebb and flow of neurotic symptoms in the members was very closely related in a reciprocal fashion. The therapist could easily watch the seesaw, for example, increasing anxiety in one partner causing increased repression in the other.

ABSTRACT—MR. AND MRS. H.J.   No. 55-2203

Each 25 years old, seen first in November 1955. He is a prepsychotic hebephrenic schizophrenic; she a rather typical hysteric with the severe affect hunger of the orphan. She had been brought up in an orphan asylum. She had considerable nymphomania quality, had been sleeping with many of his friends while he was traveling on his job. It was felt that therapy with her as an individual would not only be long and arduous but that it would impair their marriage relationship further and might well precipitate a psychotic break in her husband. It was assumed that the therapy focus would be around her problem of depression and her feeling that he did not give her enough sense of closeness. Over the succeeding year and a half she had gotten past her depression and her anxiety, has finally told him about her sexual behavior, which threw him into a psychotic rage and an equal state of horror at the fact that he could not leave her. His original symptoms of confusion, disorganized thinking, and feelings of unreality have been relieved and therapy is progressing nicely.

ABSTRACT—MR. AND MRS. L.T.   No. 2715

Mrs. L.T. was referred because of depression, anxiety, and phobia of disease following the birth of her second child. Her husband is a professional man, extremely able intellectually and quite successful in his business, but a very severe compulsive–obsessive who has compensated by an extreme amount of social and community activity. Her hysterical decompensation did not respond to reassurance by her physician. It was decided by the staff that her sickness was intimately related to her worship of him, and to his narcissism; was tied in closely to her complete dominance by his mother and that less than a therapeutic experience for both of them would merely serve to disrupt the shaky adjustment they had made. Over a period of 9 months the two of them were seen once a week. She developed considerable transference and he stayed in each interview, participating in a fairly casual way, wanting to be involved but not knowing how. However, his implicit gains were considerable and he allowed her to take some responsibility in the marriage. The adjustment of the couple to each other and their two children has improved considerably. Her symptoms have disappeared and it is assumed that she will not return for more therapy unless she becomes decompensated again.

ABSTRACT—MR. AND MRS. J.G.   No. 2524

A 40-year-old woman was referred by a gynecologist who called her a "typical crock." She had a history of being a chronic complainer for many years, had been treated in 1954 with electric shock treatments, and had several isolated appointments with various psychiatrists. She had a total of 10 different medical diagnoses over the past 5 years with four surgical operations. The symptom picture seemed to have been precipitated by the husband's circumcision 10 years ago, since when, she says, he has been premature. He insisted she had always been frigid. Her endless whining and complaining are in marked contrast with the husband's complete silence. Over a period of 1 year with weekly interviews, he probably never said more than 20 words in all. After about 8 months of therapy she discontinued treatment, having stopped her three phone calls a day to the gynecologist and all visits to the general practitioner for a period of 3 months. Four months later Mr. G. called to say that they were coming back again. She did not want to come back, feeling that there was no hope for her, but he insisted upon it in spite of the fact that his attitude toward the interviews had always been one of cynical aloofness. He said he wanted to come back because he thought it would be helping "them." His paranoid character has been held in solution and her hysteria has been improved, and the therapist has not had to lie awake over the problem of the husband's paranoid delusions. Five months of further appointments worked well.

CONCLUSION

This is a preliminary report on the treatment of couples in psychotherapy as a method which is psychotherapeutically useful. This method of treatment limits the transference involvement with the therapist and minimizes countertransference problems. It is a method of choice with certain diagnostic categories and also seems to picture some new patterns in psychopathology. It allows a unique opportunity for the utilization of the therapist's spontaneity and his creative interpersonal affects. He is more free to be a person and less pressured to be a "professional." It also serves to further develop the professional capacity of the therapist since it presents him with a new perspective on interpersonal relationships and a new view on some of the dynamics of individual therapy.

PSYCHOTHERAPY
OF MARRIED COUPLES

In this chapter Whitaker lists many of the assumptions and attitudes he has about marriage at approximately the midpoint in his transition between individual and family psychotherapy. As he mentions, when he wrote this he was seeing half his patients with their families. Of more interest, however, is the evidence in the paper of a growing conviction that everyone should be treated within a family context.

It is characteristic of all of Whitaker's writing that he offers the readers lists of his attitudes, rather than truths or arguments for a particular position. He is not asking us to accept his assumptions, but to examine our own and to realize the importance they have to our treatment. This process parallels his therapeutic stance; he does not lead patients to the truth, but rather challenges them to examine their view of life by offering his own perspective.

I want to discuss our thinking as well as our experience with multiple therapy. Let me explain the setting in which we work so you get a feeling of where the pattern came from. Actually, Dr. Warkentin and I began multiple therapy back in 1945 at Oak Ridge, Tennessee. Each would come out of an interview and say, "You should have been in on what happened to me!" Neither was interested in the other's news. We decided we were not communicating. What if we saw a patient together? Then we could communicate about what we were having as a joint experience. In the beginning it was just an effort to work with each other, yet the use evolved, till, for the last 9 years, I have rarely seen a patient without inviting a colleague in for the second interview. In that sense I am always using a multiple therapy pattern even if no one ever comes in again. The second interview is one in which I am evaluated, and the doctor–patient relationship is invaded by another therapist. This does make a difference. We leave it up to the secretary to see who she can get in the two schedules to be the consultant for each new patient. If, in the staffing afterward, we decide the situation is serious enough so I'm scared to treat them by myself, I say to the patient, "I need to have my consultant in with me every fourth time," or every 10th time, or if it's bad enough, every time.

We work in this kind of intimate interlocking relationship all the time, and from this has emerged an interest in relating to more than the single patient. At this point, approximately 50% of my treatment cases are with couples or families. In trying to conceptualize this, four of us spend a half-day a week struggling with the problem of conceptualizing, and have for some 10 years now. We have gradually become convinced that it's impossible to see an individual without including the "significant other." I myself have not accepted any patients for the last 5 years who would not come for the first interview with the spouse if there is one. If they insist there is no one, I sometimes accept that, but it never turns out to be true. You know, mama lives 400 miles away and he hasn't seen her in 3 years but her "spirit" is in the interview within 15 minutes of the second visit. I sometimes have the feeling that there will come a day when I'd say, "You save up money first and bring mother up, and when you get mother here for the first interview, we will see whether it is possible to start psychotherapy. No mama, no psychotherapy. Even llamas have mamas." This is our framework.

Now for the actual use of multiple therapy and the therapy of couples: I think this probably emerged first in the medical school teaching. We had so many medical students treating patients that we were short of patients. So we started pulling them out of the waiting room. The husband would bring the wife in. The wife would see Dr. Joe, but Dr. Bill didn't have any patient. So I would go out and get the husband and say, "How about coming in and talking to Dr. Bill about what's going on in your house?" This turned out to be a natural. It never seemed to backfire and gradually we insisted on it. When we moved into private practice in 1955, we naturally started the same procedure.

Conceptually, there has been a growing evidence that "craziness," if I can use the term advisedly, is the nodal point around which growth and change take place. It has been true in poetry, and art, literature, and other fields. There was a desertion of the logical, the reasonable, the systematic, and the compulsive. Society sensed that the spontaneous and the exotic and left-wing, if you will, was the basis for change and for growth. This is the same thing we have been saying in the staff room or the lunchroom of the state hospital. The patient comes in; the doctor sees him, goes in to have lunch, and says to the other doctors, "I saw papa and mama also and they're crazier than the patient." This is the same idea; the patient is the nodal point, the focus for the movement in the family. I guess if you want to go back to the Bible, this is what the prophets were to Israel.

The child guidance clincis also discovered the same thing. They began saying that the child who comes into the child guidance clinic is merely mother's symptom.[6] Mother is the one who wants to come into the clinic and the fact that the kid wets the bed is merely incidental. As a matter of fact, when I was at the child guidance clinic in Louisville in 1940, we had what I always thought of as a storybook experience. Mother called for an appointment for her son who was 8 years old, and had been wetting the bed ever since he was 2. At 2 he had been well trained for 4 or 5 months, and then started wetting the bed. He hadn't missed a night for 6 years. So in the typical child guidance pattern, the social worker said, "Well, you come in and talk with us for the initial interview and then we will make an appointment for Sonny to come in and talk to the psychiatrist and then you'll come back and talk with me." So the mother made the appointment, but 4 or 5 days later she called up and said, "By the way, I called up to cancel my appointment." When the social worker said, "Why?" she said, "Well, you know, it's a funny thing, Jimmy hasn't wet the bed since I phoned you and I thought I would just wait until he started again and then we would make another appointment." The social worker tried to get past this "resistance," but it didn't work, so he just cancelled the appointment. Six months later mother called back. "I just thought you folks would like to know that Jimmy has never wet the bed since I called up about the appointment." The child guidance workers discovered that the child was a symptom the family used to get help.

More recently we have become convinced that the disturbance in a marriage is of the same character. One partner carries the symptoms and the other partner carries the repression and the stability.

Once you arrive at a concept like this, you start playing with it and discover all sorts of fascinating things. For example, I was treating a woman, who was a bad alcoholic, and her husband was very indignant about coming in. He had 5 years of analysis and he certainly didn't need any more help! After 6 months or so came Christmastime and she arrived at a decision not to drink. For the first weekend in several years since they had been married she didn't touch a drop. The next week hubby tossed away a fifth and a half in 2 days and a half, which was better than mama had ever done. We came to a second conclusion that we call a "marital seesaw." When the symptoms disappear on one side they appear on the other. This is really no different again from the old cliche that whenever the schizophrenic child begins to get better, the mother goes crazy.

It seems clear to us that the psychological disturbance in the marital partner is the symptom of the disturbed marriage, of a disturbed interpersonal relationship, and the obvious thing to do is to treat the interpersonal relationship. If you start doing this it turns out that you have three patients. You have not only the husband and the wife but also the marriage. Many times this third "patient," as we have called it, is at least the most immediate and sometimes the most difficult patient to treat.

Out of this kind of thinking has emerged diagnostic ideas about different kinds of marriages and the nodal point at which stress develops and the method by which the marital partners work out the expression of the pathology that goes on between them. I would like to now read you a more formal discussion of this. Then we can go back to a more informal interaction about it.

This really starts out to be our assumptions about marriage, but also about the psychotherapy of the marital setting, of the couple and of the pathology within them and between them. In the wisdom of everyday life it has been said that marriage is an impossible situation; the only thing that is worse is to be single. Marriage has also been described in *The Devil's Dictionary* as "a community consisting of a master, a mistress, and two slaves, making, in all, two."[7]

Focusing on our own experience, Dr. Warkentin and I, who wrote this formulation, are convinced that our professional attitudes toward the treatment of families in distress are profoundly influenced by the patterns of our personal living. We see as healthy such aspects of marriage as we find pleasing in the experience of our family. We call it "psychopathology" when it is an experience which we do not enjoy in our own family living. Hence, the personal experience of the therapist extensively determines his work in family therapy. The conclusions which we have come to we derive from both our personal family experience and our work with patients. These assumptions and attitudes came to our atteniton primarily as patients noticed and challenged them. They are not absolute to us, but define the direction of our thinking. In addition to asserting our value system in regard to family process, these assumptions also indicate limitations which are inherent to human nature.

First, we assume that people are good for each other according to the degree to which they are intimate together. Marriage is the vehicle and epitome of adult intimacy established by long-standing custom and it is the one acceptable, great arena for experiencing human closeness.

Second, we assume that in marriage the whole is greater than the sum of its two parts. You can see how this is a direct take from multiple therapy. It is very clear if you do any multiple therapy that two of you are much more powerful than either individual.[8] Marriage is a whole field of dynamic forces. When we treat a couple in therapy we treat the three patients, the husband, the wife, and the marriage. The force or power of the marriage is greater than the algebraic sum, greater than the positive and the negative summation of the two people in it.

Third, we assume that marriage must become characteristically a sexual relationship or else it becomes a perverse relationship, and we use that word in its broadest implication as well as in its specific sense. Dynamic forces in the field of marriage other than sexual are secondary. For example, a major age difference between marital partners, if it becomes the primary action of the dynamics of the marriage, makes the marriage perverse and sick. However, the marriage can be profoundly satisfactory despite the major age difference if the relationship is characteristically sexually loving. The legal ceremony of getting married is necessary and useful. Not only does it place legal sanction and definition on the "closest relative," but it provides the framework to enable people to live together enough years to become thoroughly married.

Fourth, we asusme that marital partners have chosen each other with great wisdom, with the wisdom of social propriety, with the wisdom of their bodies, as well as the unconscious awareness of how they complement each other's person. The exquisite accuracy of marital choice repeatedly amazes us even where psychological sickness was present in the choosing. This sickness does not appear to alter the validity of the love or of the marriage itself. If you accept this kind of assumption, new things appear in the framework of your conviction that these two people are good for each other. That this is why the couple set it up this way. Of course this not all new information.

Voltaire discovered it sometime back, but we discovered it again. Voltaire said that each person gets the thing he wants. The only problem is that you don't know what you wanted until after you get it. Then, we insist it really wasn't what we wanted at all.

Fifth, we assume that the feeling relationship between the marital partners is kept continually balanced, mutual, equal, reciprocal both as to type and intensity. As a couple get married they seem to agree on a feeling temperature which they will regulate between them. The emotional thermostat can then be reset only by agreement of both parties, otherwise if the one tries to be too hot the other will compensate by being too cold, thus to maintain a stable overall temperature in the marriage. The feeling flow in a marriage as a whole can be changed only by the participation and support of both parties. We are aware that the behavioral presentations of the two partners may be very different from the underlying feeling tones we are here discussing. The best example of this is one I ran onto not too long ago. The husband and wife had been married 6 years. The first 3 years the wife was very sexy, warm, and pushing. Then their situation changed fairly dramatically in various and sundry real ways and for the next 3 years it was exactly reversed. The wife was cold but the husband was sexy, and pushy. The temperature remained the same for the entire 6 years. A change in feeling by one marital partner is smoothly accompanied by a reciprocal change in the other. This does not mean that their behavior will be similar: their feelings will be the same, but no matter how aware they are of these differences, and they may differ in how they behave.

Sixth, we assume that the usual rules of human social behavior do not apply to marriage nor to other intimate relationships. For example, fairness is not appropriate. Dr. Warkentin has a wonderful quote: "All is fair in love and war and marriage is both." I don't know whether he made this up or picked it up someplace but it's good enough to use anyway. Another example: consistency is impossible in feeling relationships. Woe be to the therapist who tries to be consistent; the only thing worse is a parent who tries to be consistent. Furthermore, such considerations as decency, face saving, factual honesty are all of minor significance in marriage.

Seventh, marriage ordinarily begins when people are "in love." We assume that a normal marriage progresses through a series of impasses as the years go by. For example, when people "fall in love," they experience a bilateral transference relationship with hysterical dynamics in the forefront. The transferences are gradually exhausted within what we have come to guess at about 10 years, producing the inevitable impasse due to the detumescence of the being "in love." At this 10-year point, which we call the "10-year syndrome," there is likely to be a civil war which results in the freeing of both slaves. If at this 10-year period, the partners find a deeper person-to-person love for each other, they may well live for 10 more years before the next impasse arises. This next impasse may develop at about the time they lose their children. However, if they do not resolve their civil war of the 10-year level and just continue living under the same roof, then such a continued impasse is likely to result in a perversion of their relationship. We can state this assumption in another way. It's only after a couple has fallen out of love that an adult, warm, loving, person-to-person marital relationship is possible. In our culture the 10-year syndrome is probably the first opportunity for a couple to have a really full-hearted marriage.

Eighth, we assume that both marital partners bring secret goals to their association and that these secret goals supersede all the obvious reality. The secret purposes, largely unknown to the partners themselves, determine the dynamic lines of force in the whole field of their marriage. It is as if the two partners constitute the two poles of a magnet with invisible lines of force between them which only on occasion come to their conscious attention. As we have worked with couples and families we have detected such secret goals as the following: that the marriage should provide the partner with the means of increasing freedom from childhood attachment and atittudes; that the marriage should help the partner become less ambivalent to making personal decisions. Or the young bride or groom may secretly expect that the marriage should activate their personal emotional growth by increasing sensitivity to all stimuli as well as concomitantly increasing personal toughness when this may be called for in the interest of personal economy. This is one partner using the other as the interlocking compensation for his own inadequacies in personal structure.

Finally, an occasional secret purpose in marriage has been to destroy the built-in graven image of the self. The husband says, "When I was a little boy, Mama told me that I could grow up and be president. It was years and years before I discovered that I wouldn't be president. The process of destroying this image, of being the Christ who would solve the world's problems, was a long, slow, painful one. My wife wasn't much help in it, you know. She didn't believe from the beginning."

In conclusion, our understanding of marriage, whether it be our personal marriage or the marriages which we study professionally, is grossly inadequate. Perhaps we are now at the threshold in our understanding of marriage. As yet we see no marked master key to marital relating.

PSYCHOTHERAPY OF MARITAL CONFLICT

It is clear from this chapter that the assumptions and attitudes described in Whitaker's earlier marital works are crystalizing into an integrated approach to marital psychotherapy. The tone is less experimental and tentative and more certain. For the first time Whitaker is willing to include sections on diagnosis of marriages, and marital psychotherapy techniques and process.

In contrast to most marital therapists working at this time, Whitaker suggests a therapeutic style that keeps the therapist in the center of the interview. The therapist's presence and insistence that each individual communicate with him rather than with each other helps break the pseudotherapeutic pattern found in most dysfunctional relationships. This style of therapy, with its injunction against extrasession discussion by the couple, is clearly not designed to improve communication or to reduce marital conflict. Rather, it is intense psychotherapy designed to treat individual psychopathology and thus alter the pattern of relationships.

Two people who are tied to each other are obviously against each other. This short statement makes a beginning for any discussion of marriage. We may then ask the question, "Why do couples ask for psychotherapy?" It has been traditional in our society for the psychotherapist to treat the individual. To a large degree patients still come as individuals, asking for symptom relief or in a search for identity. Then comes an opportunity to structure this referral so that it becomes the psychotherapy of a couple. In this event it frequently becomes the psychotherapy of marital conflict. As the news spreads couples *request* psychotherapy for the marriage conflict itself. Yet, why do couples come for psychotherapy? Frequently couples come out of desperation. The stress of their conflict is so great that each of them is willing to ask for a moderator. Sometimes they come out of hope; they have seen other couples who have broken through into a new level of relating. Again, they come because of reality pressure. They have gotten in trouble with the law or they have been forced to seek help by family pressure or job pressure. As in individual referrals they also come to break away from family dependence, in a rebellion against being children to their original families. Many couples come because of growth instability in one of the partners, based on a social therapist who has pushed him far enough so he drags the spouse to the *professional* therapist. In summary then the couple usually gets into psychotherapy because *their relationship* which had been stable or homeostatic or interlocking and well impassed *becomes unstable.* In this sense *the unstable marriage is the healthy marriage. The marriage in conflict is the marriage in movement.*[9]

We can now ask several significant questions. How does the therapist participate in the treatment of the marriage? Is he a participant observer, an advisor, a member of a new triangle, or an experiential psychotherapist to the relationship? Is he the therapist of one person while the spouse is an observer, or does this vary from case to case and even from moment to moment? How does the countertransference develop and how does it operate? Is the couple symbolic to the therapist of his own parents? Is this an Oedipal triangle that he is walking into? Is it possible to do individual treatment in the setting of couples treatment? For example, can we treat the symptomatic member with the spouse as observer or treat each spouse alternately? Can couples treatment replace individual treatment for the two partners, or is it a supplement? Would it be ideal to use couples treatment whenever possible, or is family treatment really the ultimate approach (we define family treatment as any treatment involving two or more generations)? What is the ideal outcome of couples treatment? Should it change gradually into individual treatment? Should it move from couples treatment to couples group therapy, or should the couple end as a twosome? What are the possible dangers in couples treatment? What are the chances of an impassed triangle with the therapist? Does it precipitate psychological explosions or psychosomatic explosions? Does the suicide rate increase? Is acting out more of a problem? Finally, is it possible that the whole process is too superficial to be valid as psychotherapy?

DIAGNOSIS OF MARRIAGE

LONGITUDINAL DIAGNOSIS

The diagnosis of the marital illness can be pictured both in a longitudinal and in a cross-section pattern. It is easier to see the marriage in a longitudinal framework if we assume that most marriages begin as a transference process. The honeymoon becomes a joint fantasy with a carefully maintained distance, a structure which suppresses real intimacy and provides an interlocking fantasy repetition of the parental marriage. The couple are each reenacting and reliving and recapitulating their parents' pattern, following a known model. *It is not an experimental relationship* but is at least new for these partners. This fantasy will fade, due to the effects of time and reality. Gradually there develops a new joint fantasy negatively based upon the hard realities of these two real persons. For example, the arrival of the second child or the loss of economic security may tip off a whole new set of conflict patterns in the marriage. This too may fade or be resolved and a new joint fantasy develop around the 10th year of marriage in a pattern John Warkentin has called the 10-year-syndrome (i.e., the bilateral pseudotherapeutic process comes to a grinding halt as each one gets convinced that his therapeutic adventure is failing). This also may be resolved or compromised and another joint fantasy with reality overtones may emerge when the children leave home or later when the couple move into retirement and there is a relaxation of reality stress and the increased insight of "second childhood." Longitudinally we may also see the joint fantasy of old age with the arrival of grandchildren and its accompanying sense of fatalism *or of transcendence.* Each of these foci may produce marital conflict of a severe degree.

A CASE FRAGMENT

Background: Ezra and Eva have been married 3 years. Ezra had a dominating mother whom he loved but wanted to be free from. Eva had a dominating mother whom she loved but does not emulate.

The Action: Ezra fell in love with a shy little girl who was the product of a dominating mother who had squelched her.

Projection: Ezra senses that the little girl can become a powerful woman and he won't always have to fight for freedom. Some day he can give in and be dependent on this wife. Eva fell in love with a boy intent on freedom from a dominating mother by succeeding as a man in the world. Eva senses that she can get strong and that he will help her be on top in the years to come. In fact, Eva and Ezra have established a dominant–dependent axis with reversible roles at any moment of mutual desire for change. They will struggle in their conflict, sensing and gradually confirming that they are equal in strength. Neither is beatable by the other and if things go well they will become satisfied with that as an interdependent relationship with enough *instability* to continue growing.

Here, we see one pattern for the bilateral character of a marriage. This marriage is alive; that is, it is unstable and will *remain alive as long as the roles are reversible,* in this case along a dominant–dependent axis. Diagnostically, a marriage can be called sick when it becomes symptomatic and the dynamics become impassed and irreversible or, as we say "stable."

CROSS-SECTION DIAGNOSIS

To diagnose in cross-section we merely search out the main axis of conflict. Assuming that one anthropomorphizes marriage as we do, it is fairly simple to characterize the marriage by such truisms as growthful (i.e., anxiety-laden or pseudotherapeutic or infantile or bilaterally homosexual or barren or a marriage characterized by somatizations). Further, one may also diagnose the interlocking neurotic patterns along the axis of conflicts, for example, dominant–submissive, socializing–isolated, psychotic–psychopathic. In this way we try to describe the *division of labor,* or if you will, the *division of concern* between the two partners. One may be outer-directed and one inner-directed, one may be socially oriented and one isolated, and so forth. In such event each individual maintains the role assigned to him and *helps the partner* in *his maintaining the role they* have worked out for him, as well.

DEPTH DIAGNOSIS

There is one further aspect of diagnosis which seems important to us. It is helpful to diagnose the emotional significance of the marital relationship. We all know that there are some marriages which seem to have very little voltage and we have tried to identify some of the things that make us sense when a marriage is significant to the partners. We will list these: (1) the presence of a seesaw of symptoms and moods; (2) the presence of any extreme interpersonal feelings (e.g., jealousy, competitiveness, pouting, temper, etc.); (3) the presence of children; (4) the sexual experience of the partners; (5) craziness or silliness experienced together; (6) an earlier period when the marriage was acknowledged to be a significant part of the life of each of them.

In order to clarify further discussion I must explain that our work is done in a nine-member private practice clinic where the use of a consultant in the interview and the use of dual or, as we call it, multiple therapists has been going on daily for over 15 years. Further, all interviews are conducted in the round.[10]

Our usual approaches have been inadequate in the therapy of married couples. (1) Individual treatment for the symptomatic spouse assumed that the relief of these symptoms would fix the partner and the marriage. It was often ineffective. (2) Placing each spouse in individual treatment by different therapists sometimes worked, but many times did not. (3) The treatment of both spouses in individual treatment with the same therapist seemed to be less effective than the systems above. (4) Forcing the unwilling partner to participate in couples therapy may also fail. Psychotherapy of a couple may also fail when both partners are transferred so deeply to each other that they unite in opposing professional help. Couples therapy may fail also when both partners act out their feelings in the community or when both partners are psychotic, although these problems do not always forbode failure.

TECHNIQUES

Our present techniques began with the utilization of two therapists working with the couple and in four-way interviews only. Now we also use one therapist in the treatment of a couple where the situation is relatively workable, the affect in the marriage is apparent, the motivation for growth is visible, and there is no acting out and no psychological decompensation. We are committed to having a consultant in during the early phase of all psychotherapy and couples therapy is no exception. Currently, we also employ family psychotherapy if indicated by the dynamics of a responsible family group which involves two or more generations.

PROCESS OF THERAPY

The actual process of psychotherapy with a couple is not really very different from individual treatment. It is obvious, however, that it must involve different dynamics and that structuring takes more effort and greater exactness. We emphasize our need for both members of the couple in the preconsultation phone contact and usually postpone making an appointment until the couple have agreed to come together, at least for the first session. We bring a consultant into the second or third visit to expand the history and to expand our own perception. Following this consultation and staffing we bring back a report of our opinion and our recommendations to the couple. Thus we set a pattern of the couple relating to the therapist and to the therapist with his consultant. We do not always refuse individual interviews, but we do not use them except under special circumstances.

We believe the therapist is related to three entities: the husband, the wife, and the marriage, which is also a patient. He usually assumes that the initial patient is the marriage since the reinforcement of that homeostasis makes the framework in which the two individual patients can later satisfy their own therapeutic needs. This treatment of the marriage often consists of helping the individuals to see the identification between them and to see the interlocking dynamics in their relationship. They gradually learn that what goes on between them is a *joint project* and that the spiral origin of any particular bit of behavior can be traced to first one and then the other if one goes back in time. As the therapy moves along it becomes possible to interpret dynamic patterns to one partner so that the other partner will understand them. The subtle pseudotherapeutic efforts of the partners toward each other must be broken and cathected to the therapist. We sometimes do this by highlighting the aggression in each patient as it emerges and sometimes by directly countering the therapeutic moves of one partner and insisting that these belong to the professional. Our own particular pattern of couples therapy does not tolerate the therapist being a monitor to couple fights but tries to keep the therapist "in the experience" so that the couple are relating to each other through the therapist or each is related to the therapist. We advise each individual to keep his individual dreams, and his observations or interpretations about the other person, for the interview hour. In contrast with popular dogma we *warn them* that *home* fights or long talks are one of the ways to keep from getting their money's worth in the interview.[11] We try in deliberate ways to *break the pride* and *the delusion of grandeur in each against the rock of their significant other.* We directly attribute both credit and blame for symptom formation to each equally, and *insist that the sickness and the strength on two sides of a marital pair is equal.*

In the therapy of marital conflict the therapist is operating in a role. He functions in a largely nontransference setting and interpretations are easier and more acceptable than in individual treatment. Much of his communication is in the present tense although he does interpret patterns in the history if they arise and helps with dream work much as in individual interviews. Many times these dreams differ from the dreams in individual interviews in that they represent an interpersonal event. Couples psychotherapy is thus more existential than individual psychotherapy.

SUMMARY

Therapy of the marital couple or marital conflict demands extra diagnostic skills and formulations. Its use is contraindicated if the therapist has not had adequate treatment and does not have adequate consultation for protection against overinvolvement in this highly loaded situation. Our present procedure is to treat the couple in deep, intense psychotherapy. We believe the method is effective in the treatment of the individual pathology of each partner as well as the marital conflict between them.[12]

A REEVALUATION
OF "PSYCHIATRIC HELP" WHEN
DIVORCE IMPENDS

with Milton H. Miller

The primary message of this chapter is a warning to psychotherapists that they be aware of the effects individual psychotherapy can have on a marriage. All psychiatric intervention, whether individual, marital, or family, can be expected to have a profound impact on all members of a family system. An intervention at a time of potential divorce is used as an example because it is a time when many individuals seek help, and because an intervention at that time can produce a permanently disrupted relationship.

This chapter suggests that the time of impending divorce, although fraught with danger, may constitute an opportunity for a breakthrough in individual growth and a reengagement of the couple in a more intimate way than prior to the crisis. A psychotherapist may work against this possibility by intervening in the situation at all.

The authors raise a number of important issues about divorce and the potential impact of psychiatric interventions, but do not try to propose a set of rules for handling these situations. Their goal is to increase the sensitivity of the clinician to the effects intervention may have on a patient's family system. They do offer their experience, however, which suggests that the involvement of all potentially affected individuals in treatment (e.g., children and parents of the couple) is the most effective treatment technique.

It was Hippocrates who said, "Physician, at least do no harm!" In attempting to provide aid to those couples who are experiencing marital discord, the members of the family, the would-be friend, and the psychiatric clinician alike may well take heed. Marriage is a complex

Reprinted by permission from *American Journal of Psychiatry*, 1969, *126* (5), 611–618. Copyright © 1969 by the American Psychiatric Association.

matter and divorce no less so. Each marital unit represents a system all its own—no two are alike. When trouble occurs, no simple formula gained from past success will necessarily apply.

Before consulting a psychiatrist, most couples in difficulty have struggled together for long periods and have talked individually with their friends, possibly with their minister, occasionally with the lawyer. Then, one or both turn for assistance to the psychiatrist. We suggest that in a circumstance where divorce impends the ordinary and customary styles of reacting to an appeal for help characteristic of general psychiatric practice may be inappropriate, ineffectual, or, at worst, substantially detrimental.

Although the courts have held that "a high degree of intelligence is not essential to understand the nature of the marriage contract," the significance of that contract and the factors that go into its maintenance or its dissolution are by no means well understood. Many "well-adjusted marriages" dissolve, whereas other marriages, characterized by storm, travail, highs and lows, episodic fisticuffs, jealousy, recriminations, and occasional trips to the lawyer appear to sustain and satisfy.

Key words in understanding a marriage appear to be "engagement," "involvement," "locked in together." It is ordinarily a lessening of "engagement" in a marriage that leads to a provocative act by one partner or the other. Thus, in a cool marriage with a marital temperature dropping slowly toward the freezing level, there may occur an incident that on the one hand seems to provoke divorce but that may, conversely, represent an impetus for "reengagement," "reinvolvement," "getting locked in together." The provocation for divorce may constitute simultaneously a possibility for a heightening of engagement in a marriage that had grown stagnant. Clearly a turning point. Enter the psychiatrist.

PROVOCATION LEADING TO ENGAGEMENT NOT WITH THE MATE BUT THE THERAPIST

CASE 1

Mrs. B., desperately agitated, thinking of suicide, tearful, was referred to a psychiatrist by her girl friend. Mrs. B. had been separated from her husband for 3 weeks as a result of his great anger when she confessed an act of infidelity 1 week before. Her husband of 7 years—rather critical and cold, a frequently unfaithful man—was powerfully hurt by what his wife told him and after a week of passionate rejection and reconciliation, he struck her and she left.

She was in great turmoil, as was her husband, who was quite certain that she had left him to return to her lover. Her lover was, however, in Mrs. B.'s eyes, something of "an innocent bystander." During the first few interviews with the therapist she was terribly depressed and anxious, alternately defensive, ashamed, and filled with proclamations of love for her husband, followed by statements of indignation at his treatment of her and determined announcements of her intention to seek redress.

Mrs. B. was a sensible, proud woman, 30 years old, the product of a somewhat distant home with considerably older parents. In her marriage she and her husband appeared to take turns in periods of anger, hurt, and withdrawal. They had difficulty coming together in a loving way. They alternated in turning down the heat on their marriage burner. She was more outwardly loving, though masochistic; he was more domineering, perhaps less secure. Together they developed something of an indifferent marriage. Indeed, they were unaware of how involved they could be with each other until the interval after Mrs. B.'s infidelity.

Because of the level of the patient's despair, the therapist saw her two or three times each week in a supportive manner during a period of 4 or 5 weeks after she first consulted him. He attempted to play a nondecision-making role, reflected her feelings, expressed confidence in her ability to make an ultimately sound decision, questioned her about the coldness in the marital relationship, but at the same time reassured his patient that the problem in the marriage was not hers alone.

Four weeks after Mrs. B. was first seen, there was a joint interview with the husband. However, the husband was greatly threatened by what he experienced as a coalition against him. He responded with a belligerent assault on his wife, calling her "a cold whore" and warning the therapist not to be deceived by the wife as he had been, and so forth. The husband was incapacitated when he faced his wife's newest allegiance and he put on a very bad performance. He felt outnumbered, outgunned, in danger of assault or humiliation.

The impact of this interview was perhaps decisive in leading to the divorce that followed. The therapist concluded privately, "He's worse than she told me." In the succeeding weeks both the husband and wife were involved in casual sexual contacts outside the marriage. Approximately 3 months after the initial separation, both the husband and wife had discovered that there was little steam left within the marriage. The glue had dried with the partners separate. The engagement, weakened before, had become a disengagement.

For Mrs. B., however, her hours with the therapist assumed the central position in her life. She was grateful to her therapist for his support to her during the most trying period in her life. Her husband, from whom she became divorced 3 months later, continued to resent the therapist very much and referred to him as "her $30 lover." She appreciated the fact that her doctor had not tried to influence her decision. From our vantage point, he was more influential than she knew.

THE IMPACT OF A DIAGNOSIS—
A SICK MATE OR A MARITAL PROBLEM

CASE 2

Professor R., a 36-year-old language instructor, called to request an appointment with a psychotherapist. When questioned over the telephone, he explained that he was very concerned about his inability to consummate his marriage of 3½ months. When he was asked to come with his new wife for the first appointment, he protested that the problem was strictly his, that he had had psychotherapy off and on for a number of years, and that there were matters he did not want to discuss in the presence of his bride. The therapist was insistent, however, and after some protest the two appeared together for the first appointment.

The husband proved to be a most eccentric man. He was deeply entangled with his widowed mother, a woman given to spiritualism and a belief in the living occult and who, over the years, had demonstrated a determination to protect her son against sinfulness. The mother had opposed the marriage. She appeared to take poorly to strangers.

The husband had experienced transient homosexual contacts throughout most of his life but he had never experienced sexual intercourse. Although he had informed his wife about past periods of homosexuality, she had not been discouraged about marrying him. She had been a graduate student in her husband's department and had "loved him from afar" for many years. She was, however, very upset about his inability to consummate the marriage. She proclaimed her love for her husband, as he did for her. She was alternately self-castigating and very angry with him. She was 33 years old, had never been married, but had had a few prior sexual experiences.

Psychiatric examination revealed a very eccentric and narcissistic man, creative but extremely conflicted in the sexual area. He carried to that first interview a Rorschach protocol, one product of a psychiatric examination he had undergone a few years earlier. The protocol hinted broadly, and perhaps not incorrectly, at a psychotic diagnosis. His manifest problems were considerable; the latent problems overwhelming.

The patient's wife appeared to be a much more stable person. She was very attractive, shy, extremely proper, and very female. It is easy to become overidentified with the sexually deprived mate in a psychotherapeutic circumstance and she was that kind of person. Despite the obvious problems of the husband and the apparent stability of the wife, this couple was viewed as sharing in a 50–50 way a need for help to resolve the heterosexual difficulties of the marriage. Despite efforts, first by one, then by the other, to gain an individual appointment, they were always seen together.

After a period of approximately 6 weeks of reassurance, support, and relatively gentle interpretation, the husband and wife together had successfully consummated their union. They were lovingly proud of having worked through a very difficult problem together, an achievement undiluted by major involvement of a third person. The couple was seen at intervals over the next 6 months, always together. They were first seen some 7 years ago and since that time Christmas cards with the growing family pictured and an occasional letter from both speak of the successful union.

The therapist saw himself as a catalyst to the love and desire for success that was present in this union. Had one person been labeled in the marriage as "the sick one" (albeit with some basis), a less desirable outcome might well have resulted. And importantly, there was time later to go toward a more elaborate therapeutic endeavor if necessary. The demonstration of psychopathology, the search for a basis for the husband's anxiety, analysis of his homosexual conflicts, or the explication of the wife's reason for picking a sexually reticent mate were not precluded later if this simple, more direct intervention in the marriage was not successful.

In this instance the husband was not without reason for seeking psychotherapy. He qualified by most standards as warranting psychiatric therapy. The therapist's choice, however, was to take no step to take the action out from the marriage and to take as few steps as possible that put him, the therapist, into the marriage. The therapist viewed his task as one of getting the mother-in-law out of the bedroom, replacing a former student with a wife, assuring the husband that it was okay to enter the bedroom, and keeping himself, the therapist, out of that bedroom. Perhaps most important, the therapist elected to assign heavy weight to the fact of the marriage, recognizing its fragility but affording it particular reverence nonetheless.

RETURNING THE UNWANTED MATE TO A PARENT OR A PSYCHIATRIST

It is always good to know that one's mate of 25 years will not be badly hurt by being divorced and/or that one could divorce one's mate and at the same time, in absentia, take care of her (or him). One way is to provide a rich divorce settlement. Another is to find a lover for the abandoned mate. A third system is to return the mate to his or her parents; a fourth is to find a psychiatrist who will take over.

CASE 3

Mr. D., a 44-year-old lawyer, confronted his wife with the news that although he loved her he loved his partner's wife even more, and he wanted a divorce. Their marriage of 22 years had been quite civilized and in some ways rather productive and fruitful.

He had become a very successful man in his profession. Apparently he had been somewhat threatened by the departure of the older of their two girls for college and on that occasion, 2 years earlier, he had his first extramarital encounter. Puzzlingly, this first affair, although supposedly unknown to the wife, seemed to warm up the marriage slightly and moved it from its rather habitual and civilized form into a period of brief excitement. This did not last too long, however.

Mrs. D., a socially active club woman, was devoted to her family but somewhat on the distant side. She was extremely upset following her husband's announcement, and her husband immediately referred her to a psychiatrist in order to help her through the difficult period. The psychiatrist saw Mrs. D. several times, then insisted that the husband should come for an appointment. At that time, Mr. D. explained his deep affection for his wife and his expectation that they would always be, in one way or another, friends, voiced great concern about her suicidal threat, and with great feeling repeated his hope that the doctor would take good care of this woman. That evening, as if to underscore her husband's words, Mrs. D. made a suicidal attempt, ingesting 10 sleeping capsules.

The psychiatrist found himself catapulted into caring for this woman in the hospital and, despite his ambivalence, accepted her as a psychotherapy outpatient. He worked with Mrs. D. through the enormous ordeal of her impending divorce, saw her through the anger, despair, animosity, and humiliation of the divorce itself, and worked with her for another year afterwards. The loss of her husband was, she felt, endurable only because of the assistance that he had provided.

Two years later the husband, who had ultimately failed in his attempt to marry his partner's wife because of the latter's reconciliation with her husband, committed suicide.

USE OF THE TELEPHONE DURING ENFORCED SEPARATION

CASE 4

Mr. R., a handsome, likeable, 28-year-old, married, unemployed, thrice hospitalized, only son in a prominent Milwaukee family, returned to his parents' home unexpectedly in the middle of the night from the Texas university community in which he and his wife had been living. His wife remained in Texas. He seemed mildly dazed, had been drinking heavily, and spoke in vague terms about his inability to find meaning, and the like. Diagnostically, he seemed to be on a seriously troubled continuum with severe character problems and poor controls, strong sexual conflict, alcoholism, and, more ominously, a strong paranoid predilection. Attempts to arrange therapy at the time of earlier hospitalization had, as with so many of this man's plans, washed away.

He had been married for 3 years to a college classmate. His wife was teaching in a Texas high school. He had drifted out of college 5 years earlier, and his work record in the succeeding years had been very spotty. He was somewhat vague about the status of the marriage but had been living with his wife prior to coming to his parents' home. He had left the evening before without much discussion with her.

In considering this young man's situation, the psychiatrist felt that one of his solid therapeutic assets, and he had few, was a 3-year-old marriage to an apparently more stable and loyal wife. The therapist asked the patient to be in touch with the wife the first day by telephone. The second day, therapist, patient, and wife, by three-way phone, held a 10-minute discussion of treatment plans, reviewed the possibility of continuing therapy "there or here," reviewed the wife's ideas as to reasons for current trouble and her explanation as to why previous recommendations for therapy had been overlooked, and so forth.

Mr. R. had a long history of ineffectual moves in the face of stress. Drifting from the marriage toward his home appeared to be the newest in that series. He needed help. It developed that there were psychiatrists in Texas as well as Wisconsin.

DISCUSSION

The psychiatrist confronts a number of complex professional questions when he is called upon for assistance by a person who is one of a marital pair. He walks a fine line between wishing not to intrude into the intimacy of a marriage and, at the same time, honoring his own credo, which holds that any person who needs professional help should find an answer to his appeal. As a result of these often conflicting pressures clinicians have explored various therapeutic deployments and assignments to make it possible to work with a married person without disturbing the marital relationship. A number of patterns have been tried, but as yet no predictably satisfactory system of intervention has been developed.

Intervening therapeutically on one side or another in a marriage remains a risky business. A number of unsatisfactory results develop. It may be well to list a few examples of what we mean. There are a great many instances of prolonged individual therapy for one or both mates followed by divorce; therapists have worked in prolonged psychotherapy with one partner who does very well in psychotherapy, matures, and grows, while the mate is unable to keep pace; there are those particularly uncomfortable occasions in which a patient sustains a dreadfully barren marriage by embarking on a prolonged "therapeutic marriage" with a doctor that becomes intractable because the termination of therapy threatens the termination of "both marriages."

Of course, the technique of deployment of one or more therapists is perhaps less important than the attitudes of the therapist, his sense of his own therapeutic role, and his unconscious fantasies about the patient (or patients), and the possibility of the patient's divorce. When the therapist is asked to mediate in an impending divorce situation and he agrees to work with one or both of the pair, his own feelings about himself, his own marriage, and his patient's marriage will inevitably play an important role in determining what happens next. The most natural course is to go where his own life is going: that is, if he himself has never been divorced, he can watch the marital pair progress toward divorce or reunion and extrapolate from his observations answers to questions of what could happen in his own marriage.

The third option, perhaps the ordinary stance, is for the therapist to move toward a state of apparent neutrality, asserting, "I am neutral. I will not take sides. The matter of a divorce is for them to decide. I want for them what they want." The patient or patients, however, particularly in the kind of stressful situation represented by marital discord, may utilize the therapist's "neutrality" to project onto him a sense of support for their private decision making, thereby moving on toward their own fantasied objective.

The patient or the couple may pick a side for the therapist, put him on that side, and act as if he said "OK" even though he does not know what side they have put him on. They may make it clear to each other that the therapist wants them to get divorced and thinks that they should become divorced because he frowns at the end of the second hour, or they may decide that the therapist obviously wishes them to stay together since he smiled when they talked about the good old days.

The stance of neutrality is comfortable for the therapist. In theory, when he assumes no responsibility, he may be in a position of such strategic weakness as to contribute negatively to the outcome of the therapy. That weakness may be understood in this way: the gradual, manageable psychotherapeutic transference that often occurs in one-to-one relationships is not easily available in therapy with a couple. The couple are ordinarily substantially "transferred" to each other. Unless the therapist moves in such a way as to displace the mate, he becomes a kind of bystander and he is either a catalyst in their relationship or he is nothing. When the therapist elects to talk seriously with the couple about their impending decisions, which after all may be the result of 10 or 20 years of struggle and ambivalence, he faces an almost insurmountable problem. He ordinarily lacks the power needed to move such an entrenched team.

Even when the marital tie is a very powerful one and where divorce is not an imminent question, treating a married person and hoping that the result will generalize into the marriage usually does not work. Where the marital tie is weak and divorce threatens, intervention with one of the pair seems routinely to be disruptive. We are impressed that moving unilaterally into a marriage relationship, taking one of the two as the patient and referring or ignoring the mate, is very often a tactical blunder.[13]

What is the alternative? A psychiatrist ordinarily moves toward a person who calls for help and offers to listen to him and to see him again. What should he do when there is a marriage in question? The therapist ordinarily feels that in almost any situation something useful can come from honest and open discussion. What should he do if one member of a marital pair wishes to talk unbeknown to the mate? What should the therapist do when there is a suggestion that one member of a marital pair is emotionally disturbed and needs some kind of assistance?

CONCLUSIONS

We believe that psychiatric intervention when divorce impends cannot be regarded as a routine matter. The therapist should view his entrance into the situation as calling for his broadest perspective. He must see what is going on between him and his patient, already a difficult task. Even more than that, he must see what is implied by the fact that he and his patient are sitting down together without the mate. Any move by the therapist that discounts the significance of the marriage may be unexpectedly influential. Thus, the ordinary medical system of replying affirmatively to a request for help by one person in a marriage, excluding the other, may in effect be an intervention favoring divorce.

In working with a married individual, or with a couple who contemplate divorce, the therapist confronts a system under stress. He would do well, ordinarily, to respect the marriage as a continuing fact until the legal divorce is complete. No matter what the degree of complexity, no matter how seemingly collapsed the patient's marriage is, the therapist should not presume to discount its ongoing power, its possibility of resurrection, its beating heart. If there is to be a death certificate, the trial judge of a divorce court of record is the one to sign the document.

Accepting in therapy one member of a troubled couple should be viewed by the therapist as very possibly a step toward preventing a reconciliation. For many couples on the verge of divorce, the therapist becomes an alternate mate no matter how scrupulous his efforts to avoid it. In the history of many, many ongoing marriages, one finds episodes of apparent cruelty, of separation periods, of affairs, of litigation, along with an episodic move toward divorce followed by reconciliation. Therefore, the therapist should be aware that he may be intervening and changing a process that, when nature takes its course, will heal. In a general way, we feel that the burden of proof is on the therapist who elects to work with a couple in such a way as to take the action out of a marriage, either in the first or during subsequent interviews.

Divorce inevitably has many ramifications for children and families of origin. These others, significant others, should be considered for inclusion in the psychotherapy. Our own experience suggests that involving the children and parents of a couple in the midst of marital discord is often a powerfully helpful device. The majority of our patients who were asked to bring family members in for interviews have agreed and in no case did we regret their presence. That the technique is often a useful one we feel quite sure. We are less certain why. Whether the inclusion of other family members offers an opportunity for correcting basic discord or whether its usefulness rests upon a symbolic proof of the seriousness with which the therapist views the possibility of dissolution of the marriage, we are unable to decide. Bringing the other family members in, however, coincides with our general philosophy that it may be better to err on the side of too much respect for the fact of the marriage, particularly in the early interviews.

We often find it necessary to remind ourselves that as therapists we are in no position to offer a real substitute relationship for the mate who will be disappearing; not at the time, not in 1 month, 6 months, nor in a year, and certainly not 4 years hence. This may be especially relevant if the therapist himself is comfortably married and enjoys a marriage where there is parity, affection, and reliability. A comfortably married person is rarely able to anticipate or appreciate the loneliness, despair, and tedium in the life of a divorced person. Even statistical studies that appear to demonstrate rather conclusively that divorce is hardly a road to happiness (Srole, Langner, Michael, Opler, & Rennie, 1962) tend to be forgotten when one is working with an aggrieved, or apparently aggrieved, member of a marital pair.

An observation passed down through the generations advises that almost any couple during a lifetime of marriage could find ample opportunity to break up, depending upon who is around when divorce impends. We hope that it will not be one of us.

PART FIVE

FAMILY THERAPY

It is in these recent materials about family psychotherapy that Whitaker draws together and integrates his concepts and ideas about individuals, marriage, and the family. Whitaker came to family therapy, as is true for most family therapists, because of both the unique importance of the family in human development and because of a mounting frustration with the results of individually oriented psychotherapy. As Whitaker states in "Acting Out in Family Psychotherapy," "Family psychotherapy seems to be almost the ultimate challenge for the therapist as well as his great opportunity to learn about people and to grow as a person" (p. 259, this volume).

The reader should note that within this section Whitaker evolves from a position that implicitly views family therapy as a therapeutic technique to a position that explicitly recognizes family therapy as a philosophic viewpoint. As he states in the final chapter of the section, he is not a psychiatrist who sees families in therapy but a family therapist, regardless of whom he sees in therapy. The chapters in this section, although an outgrowth of those earlier, supplant and encompass his previous work. Whitaker did not turn his attention from individual to marital to family therapy; rather, each led to the other in a gradual transition. This transition and growth continues in the same direction as Whitaker increasingly includes nonnuclear family members in his family psychotherapy.

Whitaker's style of family therapy has been called by many names over the years—therapy of the absurd, existential family therapy, experimental family therapy, and so forth. Most recently, Whitaker refers to it as symbolic–experiential family therapy, a name that, although cumbersome, aptly reflects the combination of "real" relationships between the therapist and family and the unreal, transferential aspects of the meetings. Each aspect is important and potentially leads to growth and change. The real and the unreal are woven tightly together in Whitaker's approach and cannot be dealt with separately. Both are reflected in each of the major areas of the therapy that we have chosen to discuss: the objectives of treatment; the therapist's stance and role; the process of therapy; and the techniques of therapy.

THE OBJECTIVES OF FAMILY TREATMENT

Most families enter therapy at a time when their processes of growth and change have ground to a halt. They endlessly repeat the same pattern of behavior and feelings. Most simply stated, one goal of family therapy is to disrupt this pattern and to thus force the family to develop new ways of relating. Such a view of the goal for family therapy, while accurate, ignores the majority of the therapist's values and assumptions about health, pathology, and family life.

According to a survey of family therapists conducted by the Group for the Advancement of Psychiatry, eight goals were cited by respondents as being of primary importance for all families: improved communication, improved autonomy and individuation, improved empathy, more flexible leadership, improved role agreement, reduced conflict, individual symptomatic improvement, and improved individual task performance.[1] Of these eight, only two, "improved autonomy and individuation" and "more flexible leadership," are viewed by Whitaker as important goals for family treatment. Two of the other eight goals are specifically cited by Whitaker as probably undesirable, "reduced conflict" and "improved individual task performance."

For Whitaker the ultimate goal of family treatment is to increase the members' sense of belonging to the family and simultaneously to increase the members' freedom to individuate. He believes that an individual can only be separate in the degree to which he belongs and vice versa. The two change together or they do not change. In Whitaker and Keith's chapter in The Handbook of Family Therapy are cited 10 mediating goals for family therapy.[2]

1. Increase the interpersonal stress
2. Development of a family nationalism

3. Expand the family's relationship with the extended family
4. Expand the family's relationship to the culture and community members
5. Development of the family boundaries
6. Separation of the generations
7. The family learning how to play
8. Development of a cycle of separation and rejoining
9. Explosion of the myth of individuality
10. Each family member becoming more of whom he or she is

Another important, although largely ignored or denied, goal is the therapist's intent to aid his own growth. Whitaker maintains this view despite opposition from most therapists and states it to his patients frequently. Whitaker "uses" honesty and overt statements about his personal agenda not as a technique to trick the family into changing but because he feels any dishonesty weakens the bond between patient–family and therapist.

THE STANCE AND ROLE OF THE THERAPIST

It is important to bear in mind while considering the role of the therapist in family therapy that for Whitaker the preferred model is that of cotherapy. The therapy team often functions as a unit, a model marriage, but also separates and differentiates functions during the family session. It is also important to note that the role of the therapist team evolves during the process of therapy, not unlike the role of parent as it evolves in response to the growth of children.

At no stage in the process, however, is the therapist in charge of family life outside the session. The team refuses all efforts to assume the role of expert or magician. This stance is not based on a decision that it is better to let families decide even though the therapist could decide "better," but rather is based on the belief that the therapist does not have better solutions for the family. It is additionally felt that suggestions by the therapist would not influence the family even if offered.

Primarily the therapist team and individual therapists are models for the family. They model separation and joining, having fun, fighting, and being crazy. The team provides a model for the marriage and the individual therapists are models for the individual members. The therapists do not teach and rarely interpret or explain, yet they are active members of the therapeutic suprasystem. The family therapist is like the coach of the family team; he is not a player.

The role a family therapist plays with a family in treatment is in part determined by the way in which the family views the therapist and the potential power that results. For example, the therapist is not able to rely on the transference of feelings from prior important relationships as providing the power and content material for the psychotherapy. In contrast to individual therapy, the family members' interrelationships remain stronger and more salient than the relationship of family members to the therapist. This fact allows the therapist a freedom to be more "real" with families than the individual therapist whose words and actions are overvalued and distorted by the therapist. This freedom is the freedom that comes from being impotent, not from being powerful.

THE PROCESS OF THERAPY

The process of family treatment is different for every family treated. It is similar enough from family to family, however, to allow for the discussion of the typical phases of treatment. Similar issues and problems arise in the treatment of almost every family at similar times during therapy. The process of family therapy is considered by Whitaker to involve three basic phases: the early or beginning phase, during which the family and therapist establish their positions and responsibilities in the therapeutic system; the core phase, during which the family works on restructuring their system; and the termination phase, during which the therapist and family separate and end the therapeutic contact.

The beginning phase of treatment involves in part what Whitaker frequently refers to as the "battle for structure." This battle determines who is to be the rule-maker about the interview process. This battle often begins on the phone prior to the first interview and goes on for varying lengths of time. Frequently the issue is fought in large part around the issue of attendance at therapy sessions. Whitaker typically wants the entire nuclear family present for every interview. Implicit in Whitaker's discussion of who attends is his feeling that who attends is often less important than the fact that the therapist clearly establishes his right to make that determination.

In addition to the administrative decisions about therapy (i.e., who, when, where, how long, etc.), the therapist must assert his control and dominance within the interview. For Whitaker, the early phase of therapy is a political and manipulative process and the therapist needs to maintain a position of strength or his usefulness is seriously impaired. The therapist needs to have the freedom to join and separate from the family and to engage with the family at whatever point he chooses.

The second part of the beginning phase of treatment is termed by Whitaker as the "battle for initiative." The battle for structure defines the integrity of the therapist and the battle for initiative defines the integrity of the family. Most simply put, the family maintains total control of their life and life decisions. The family also determines what is discussed in the therapy hour and is responsible for initiating any changes in the family system.

The model for the process of therapy is the evolving parent–child relationship in a family. It begins as parent–infant, where the parent has new total responsibility for decisions, moves toward the parent–adolescent relationship characteristic of the core phase of the therapy process, and finally emerges at the adult–adult peership characteristic of the successful termination phase of therapy.

It is in the core phase of therapy that lasting changes are made in the family structure. Underlying all of the therapist's tasks in this phase is the attempt at catalyzing change. In the process of family therapy, the question of the direction in which a family will evolve is of less importance to the therapist than is the problem of sufficiently unstructuring the family to allow change. Whitaker states, "If you can screw it up so they can't enjoy the way it is going anymore, they'll work out ways of making a more adequate and effective methodology for living which will give them more enjoyment" (p. 221, this volume).

As the core phase continues, the treatment process requires less and less input from the therapists. It gradually becomes a time and place for the family to work on itself. When the therapist is no longer needed to catalyze change, the therapy process can be ended.

The termination phase of family treatment is most often instigated by family members rather than by the therapist. For Whitaker it is not uncommon to have members drop out gradually as the usefulness of therapy for them diminishes. Any move on the whole family's part to terminate contact at any point in treatment is supported and encouraged.

THE TECHNIQUES OF FAMILY THERAPY

Whitaker has always been wary of techniques in psychotherapy. In part, this stems from a view that techniques are not enough and that the purpose of technique is to transcend technique. He also fears that the use of techniques potentially blunts creativity and growth in the therapist. The repeated use of techniques in therapy with the family may also communicate to them a belief in rules, magical formulas, and consistency, which are anathema to Whitaker's view of healthy family process.

Whitaker's repeated warnings about the danger of technique and theory (e.g., "The Hindrance of Theory in Clinical Work," pp. 317–329, this volume) might lead to the idea that Whitaker is proposing intuition as the model for psychotherapy. A careful reading of these papers, however, should lead one to an appreciation of Whitaker's suspicious attitude toward intuition. Whitaker does not suggest that intuition is the secret for psychotherapy. Being "not technical" is not the answer—there is no answer.

In his discussion of techniques, Whitaker comes most close to the teaching of Zen. As do Zen masters, Whitaker offers the therapist not an answer but an impossible problem. Reliance on theory, technique, or intuition all hinder clinical work. None of the three can be avoided in clinical work, but they are not offered to the family as anything other than what they are, and always with a sense of benign absurdity.

In Whitaker's most recent writing, he offers the reader extensive lists of techniques that he continues to find useful in his clinical practice. What Whitaker refers to as techniques are perhaps better described as common strategies that therapists may find useful with families. For example, he considers augmenting the despair of a family member and treating the children like children and not like peers as techniques. The art of family psychotherapy is to convert these attitudes and strategies into the relationships that constitute family therapy. As Whitaker puts it, "More important than explicit techniques are the metatechniques, such as timing, application of emphasis, how and when to apply pressure, when to back off, or when to be cautious" (p. 359, this volume).

In summary, Whitaker's approach to family therapy subsumes and extends his previous work as an individual and marital therapist. The importance of the person and growth of the therapist is maintained; his trust and belief in the biological and the unconscious still underlies his work. His role as a therapist, however, has shifted from being the primary process mother of the schizophrenics of the 1950s to a grandparental role with the families he sees today. As grandparents do, he accepts parenting functions only temporarily and remains free to return them to the real parents at any moment. A grandparent is involved and loving with the children and grandchildren but is not essential to the function of the family.

OBJECTIVES OF FAMILY TREATMENT

This short chapter is included herein because it articulates the relationship between Whitaker's conception of individual therapy and family therapy. It is a difficult and often paradoxical statement. As we have frequently mentioned, for Whitaker the essence of life is contradiction and ambiguity. He states a part of this contradiction here, but leaves the reader to unravel it.

One of the objectives of family treatment that's frequently hidden or emerges later in the process is the growth of the individual members. The question then is raised, "How do individuals grow or get individual therapy in the middle of a group?" Probably what they come out with is the discovery that there is no way to not be alone. There is no place more apt to perpetuate the delusion of togetherness or symbiotic living than the original family and the discovery that you are the only person inside your skin, that you are really alone, and that there is no way to not be alone is probably best learned in the bosom of the family. It is possible also there and the good family therapy experience should bring about the discovery that you can be alone with yourself or you can be alone with someone else (who is also alone with you).

This concept that you can be alone with yourself or be alone with someone else, which is an old definition of friendship (someone you can be alone with), is an extrapolation from Edwin Land's paper in which he discusses the problem of living as being directly related to the two kinds of persons we can be—the two states of personhood. When two or more of us are engaged in some common process, some common parameter, some common project like a quartet or four psychiatrists or nine baseball players, we are in a state that he calls "multiperson." That is, the components are related to each other. The baseball players bring their function as baseball players, the part of them that's included in baseball player in relationship to that similar part in the other person, as two therapists working with a patient become another unit. And the patient knows that this twosome is a unit—it's not just two people. Or a group becomes a group—it's not just eight persons and a therapist. There is another state which he calls the singular person in which all the components of the individual are united with themselves. That is, I, me, myself are all together and we are alone. He then defines the fact that in living the problem is how to move comfortably from one state of the multiperson to the other state of a singular person and that many people have trouble shifting gears. Each of us probably has a predominant tendency toward one or the other. For example, the psychopath is most adroitly a multiperson and the schizo is most obviously a singular person, and in between all the rest of us fit on a continuum.

Family therapy should be the place where one can discover the most of how to be a multiperson and the most of how to be a singular person. Inasmuch as the family is the place where the biological component is the most powerful unifier we are most powerfully related to those others in the group. On the other hand, in the time when we learn to be alone the safety of the family and its loving state should be the place where we can be most alone and most safely unrelated to those around us, except for the security of their presence and the fact that they also are free to be alone, separate from each other.

After you've learned that you can't stop being alone and discover that you can be alone with somebody then you can gradually learn how to be more alone with somebody and the bilateral aloneness can mean more and more intimacy. You can be increasingly yourself.

THE TECHNIQUE OF FAMILY THERAPY

Much of this chapter is ostensibly a discussion of the family therapy style of Nathan Ackerman. In discussing Ackerman, however, Whitaker reveals many of the techniques and assets that he feels are essential to the competent family therapist. The traits he chooses to highlight are the therapist's ability to use power, seduce the father, accept uncertainty, avoid overt power struggles, individuate from the family, and value craziness. It is apparent that these traits are possessed by both Whitaker and Ackerman.

It is a rare opportunity to read a master therapist's commentary about the work of another master therapist. In a real sense one can be more disclosing about oneself by commenting about a respected other than when describing oneself. Whitaker in part uses Ackerman as a blank screen upon which he projects and describes the traits he finds most useful in his own work.

I am glad to have a chance to talk about family therapy. I have a sense that each time I talk about it, it changes me a little. First, by way of introduction, I would like to take the position that knowing is important but sometimes unknowing is more important. I had a very exciting experience in Texas 2 or 3 years ago. I was ushered into a family interview, and the family turned out to be the identified patient, her

Reprinted by permission from P. Sholevar (Ed.), *Changing Sexual Values and the Family*. Springfield, Ill.: Charles C Thomas, 1977. Copyright © 1977 by Charles C Thomas Publisher.

boyfriend, and the boyfriend's sister. I had the feeling that I had been "took"—in this strange territory with no real friends and no real sense of warmth, and I get this kind of distorted family. I started fooling around with it and after about 10 minutes I decided "Oh hell! It's a dud, I have had it, and maybe this time it's a flop, and maybe next time it will work." It was as though the admission of defeat to myself threw me into a state of being alive, and all of a sudden the interview became real, human, and moving. I discovered ever since that whenever I can get to that step of facing my own defeat, it seems to make a new point of departure, a new sense of belonging with and going along with what is happening and so is the value of unknowing.

It is a rather unique and touching thing for me to be giving the Ackerman lecture. I was not quite sure about the wisdom of the community, whether I was given the opportunity because I am a nonpsychoanalytic layman-type therapist or because I am turned on by kids, whether because in my old age I am another dirty old man like Nate or whether because I am closer to death, I should know more about it. Actually, I was only professionally acquainted with Nate. There are so many people who have been intimates of his, family therapy children and grandchildren as it were, who know him so much better and I feel so much more humble in trying to say something about Nate and his fantastic contribution to this field. He was certainly one of the seminal minds if not the actual grandfather. When I was taking my second year of Latin, one of the examiners asked about Virgil, and I said he was the father of all Roman poets, which turned the teacher on. So I think that Nate was that. I also wondered if it was a way of honoring my Jewish inner-self. I discovered some 6 or 8 years ago that I am a disenfranchised Jew. Being brought up in the Adirondack Mountains as a good Methodist, it was 13 years that I lived in the Old Testament. My fairy stories and murder mysteries and sex education all came out of the Old Testament. I was a good Jew and all of the sudden when I became 13, someone said that "I'm sorry about this but you don't belong to them. You're out of that, you belong in the New Testament." All of a sudden it turned out that I was not a Jew after all, and I was disenfranchised (I still grieve with all that). Maybe this is a chance where I can wiggle my way back in by being one of Nate's children.

I would like to say something special about Nate because he was a very special person. The things that have occurred to me I will list for you. I think he was a specialist in a multidisciplinary approach. In a strange kind of way, Nate by himself was a group. He was a grandfather one minute, a grandmother the next, a boyfriend, a husband, a flirtatious lover; he could flip from one role to the next so fast that it would make me dizzy watching him from the distance. I never was quite sure about his homosexual boyfriend competence, I think of that as one of my assets, but I never did date Nate so I'm not sure how much his competence extended in that area. I think of it, by the way, as a very important area. In fact, it's one of the rules I have from one of my residents. "If you don't seduce the father in the first interview, you've had it." The other is that family therapy is like chess; you had better not move the queen until you have your game well into midphase. The residents come back time after time saying, "Hey, look, I've just lost a family," and I ask what they did to the mother and they say, "Well, mother and I did have a fight," and I say, "Too bad about that. Talk to your analyst about it."

Nate had a way of what I have thought of as guerrilla invasion of the family. He sneaked into the family by all kinds of manipulative modes and gyrations that were so subtle, that before you knew it, he belonged more to the family than the members themselves, which, by the way, is not infrequent. I saw a family recently in which the older son had come back from the West Coast to straighten out mom. Papa had died and mom had taken to drinking. In the course of the first few interviews, I asked him how much he belonged in the family since he had been living away for so many years, was married, and had several kids. He said that he did not feel that he belonged to the family at all anymore—of course he stopped his job and came all the way back to stay for several months. I said, "How long have you been out of the family?" and he said that he never had belonged in the family. So then taking his cue, I went around the group, and there were several of them there, and there was not a single one who felt he belonged in the family. So one of the secrets that I think Nate was an expert at was a conviction that the family was a whole, that it had a sense of unity, and that is one of the biggest things to get under way when you first begin seeing the family.[3] If you don't discover it is a unit, they may not discover it and they may have been living in it for many years and having no sense of belonging to it. They just happened to be around.

Nate was also an expert in the use of power. With him it was so natural, he had so much of it that it wasn't much of a problem. But I suggest to the rest of you that you think of it as a very important part of family therapy, because uniquely different from individual therapy, family therapy is a political process. It's really a naughty word nowadays and I am really sorry to have to use it but I couldn't think of another word (so you try to Watergate the family). You do have to develop a sense of power that the family has and if you can't find your own way for taking over, you probably are not going to be of much use. Let me see if I can suggest a way of talking about it for a moment. Think of five or six people who have been living together through thick and thin, and there is a lot of thick in any family—you know, divorces and death, fights with neighbors and attacks by the rabbi, financial trouble and financial luck, which is almost as bad—you name it, and they have gone through it. Along comes this character who thinks that by a few extra words he is going to change their way of living, and that is pretty weird. The whole process of assuming that any individual is going to walk into a group of five or six and take over is weird. If you don't think so, ask any athletic coach what it takes to handle a team to make it operate effectively or to take over from a previous man who had it operating effectively. It's a major move; it's a massive political group process and you need to get started with some sense of how important it is for you to carry some kind of power, some kind of political know-how. There are many ways of doing this. One of the most important and simplest ways is to do something in the beginning that makes it clear that you are going to set the rules.[4] Everyone shows up except papa—thereupon you agree to charge them and not see them and send them back. They are indignant and refuse to come, and so forth. So you lose a case. You get a conviction in yourself that there is such a thing as an important father. It's really very difficult. Margaret Mead was really right when she said the father is a social accident. He just happens to be around. But in the family structure, he is a very important individual and if you lose him, you are probably going to lose the family. That is the advantage of being homosexual or better, homosocial. If you can work out that process of becoming a significant person in the beginning, you have a way to start. Bobby Fischer did well when he was getting ready for that match in Iceland. It is like that but it does not have to be quite that devious or stress-inducing but I think a lot of that quality is important and Nate was a master at it.

One of the other things I think is an important component and is partly an extrapolation of Haley's notion is that the expert therapist uses indirection. That really is a further extrapolation from Esselin's notion, that one of the important things about the theatre of the absurd is that it deals by indirection, that the covert message is the one that produces change and the overt message quaintly enough produces recognition and nothing else. I had a very interesting experience when I took chemistry. I had a great faculty man; the old prof himself was doing the initial lectures in organic chemistry. He moved from inorganic chemistry through the beginning of organic chemistry. I sat with my mouth open, just fascinated, and for 6 weeks I sat there drooling and then we had an examination and I got a 36. I caught on to the fact that recognition was not enough, somehow I had to learn that stuff. I think many times we have a sense that direct information is all that is needed to produce change. I would like to warn you ahead of time that it's usually something they have heard 30 times before and there are very few new things except things that will confuse them. If you can get something that confuses them, that may help. Nate was an expert in the put-on. Help the family get confused, and I frequently help them sense the fact that this is what they are there for, and I'm not trying to get them anyplace, I am trying to confuse them so they won't go on the way they have been going. We had a bunch of nonprofessionals who were running an alcoholic rehabilitation center in Atlanta, and they finally got around to inviting the professionals in, and they were trying to tell us what they were doing for a few years and doing very well. What they ended up saying was, "We are just trying to screw it up so they can't enjoy their drinking anymore." I sometimes have the opinion that that's one of the important things to learn about family therapy. If you can screw it up so they can't enjoy the way it is going anymore, they'll work out ways of making a more adequate and effective methodology for living which will give them more enjoyment.[5] There is another way of looking at this put-on, this induced confusion. I have come to call it "forced transference." It's really surprising what happens when the family comes in for the first interview and you say "Hello, sorry there is someone missing, can you get them on the phone?" and they can't and then you say, "Well, we'll have to charge you for the interview, if you can get the family together call me and we'll make another appointment." "Well, aren't you going to see us?"

"No." "Why not?" "The family is not here." "Well, we are all here but Joe." "Sorry about that. No family without Joe." "Well, can't you see the rest of us? Why not?" "I won't feel right about it." "Well, how about next week Tuesday?" "Sorry about that, I don't think we should make another appointment." "Why not?" "Well, I'm not sure that you can get the family together, you didn't do it today." "Well, we'll get him here next time." "Why don't you see if you can get him and then give me a ring." In a strange kind of way, it does both things of making sure you have a "legal" contract that is going to be binding on both sides but it also means there is going to be a whole new sense on their part of how important the missing member is. One of the things that this "forced transference" is—can I be Christian for a minute—I think that is what we are talking about in the Christian end of this world when we talk about the Holy Spirit. It is the sense of wholeness. A sense that we are an entity.

Barbara Betz said a long time ago, and I think it is still very pertinent, that the dynamics of therapy are in the person of the therapist, not in the techniques, not in the process, and not in the understanding. I think Nate was uniquely adequate in this sense. As a person he conveyed a tremendous amount of power, wholeness, and the willingness to accept and face confusion, to live in a state of uncertainty. One of the things I value in myself is my endless suspicion of myself. There is almost nothing I believe in. I keep reorganizing my theories and each time have the feeling that this time I made it. When I was doing child psychiatry in 1941, my first private patient was a 3-year-old and I got through my fellowship and was allowed to take private patients. It was great. I said hello to mama at the door and sort of sneered at her under my breath. I took the 3-year-old in and we had fun and I handed the 3-year-old back to her at the end. I did this for 10 sessions and got a call from the father, whom I had not seen or heard of and who was a physician. I did not know whether to charge him the $3 every interview or not, and he said, "Hey, you know, that's great stuff. My daughter is much better and it has changed my wife and I think I'm different too!" I thought that I had found the secret of life! It has never happened to me since. So, my dynamic theories are up for suspicion.

Nate had this loving-heartedness that I think was conveyed to the families and gave them the freedom to be loving which is a hell of a hard thing to get. I find pearls as I go along, and one of the pearls for me is a small child. You can cuddle a 3-year-old, you can pummel a 5-year-old, you can play sex-talk games with little kids, which you can't possibly do with parents, and it's as though you were cuddling mother or daddy, as though you were talking directly to the parents when you are just talking to the kid. You say to a 9-year-old, "Listen, did you ever think that the reason your mom is mad when dad comes home 2 hours late is because she thinks he is playing with his secretary after hours?" She says, "What do you mean?" "I don't know, I just had this crazy thought." "How's school going?" "Oh, pretty good." And you have, by indirection, left a pill in mother's and father's teeth that they can't deny and they can't not have heard and all sorts of funny things happen in the next two interviews, including the possibility they won't show up. Don't hope that they will show up. Leave that for them. It may be that the most important treatment you have is the treatment you don't give. For example, we have a family that came in from out in the country. Father was all upset because the teenage daughter was "about to become delinquent." He probably was afraid that he wasn't going to be in on the fun. About the second interview, mother's passivity in front of father's panic and daughter's hostility about father's jealousy erupted into a small-time explosion. Next interview, dad said, "Hey, can we start any earlier, I'm losing work." I asked him why he came and he said, "I thought of not coming, the damn stuff is not helping anyway." I said, "You want to leave now, you will only lose a few hours." He said, "No, I think I'll stay to the end of the hour." "You know you don't have to. I'll charge you anyway." He said that since he came, he might as well stay. I said, "Mom, is it all right with you if we stop?" She said, "We just got started." I said it was a shame for dad to lose all that work. She said, "I'm not going to put up with all the stuff I have been putting up with." I said, "I don't know, he may be different if you're that way." To the daughter I said, "What is it to you?" "Hell, I didn't want to come from the beginning." "Well, are you willing to stay for the rest of the hour?" "Sure, if this is the last one." So they stopped, and they stopped because it was not helping. In terms of my way of looking, it may have been the most important thing I did in those three interviews; to let them accept the failure and take the responsibility for really running their lives. It was as if the group agreed that they did not need a psychiatrist, that they were a family that would make their family work themselves, and that may have been more important than a whole mass of understanding, and communication training, and so forth. So, I am even suspicious of my therapeutic competence.

One of the other things I think Nate was a master at was the power of paradox. The power of the dialectic, the power of never being caught in the corner so they have to either accept what you say or fight you. If you can always leave the inferences up in the air, when they decide to pull them down and insert them in their own heads, they do it on their own initiative or they can just let them float there. You're really not set with some conviction that they have to buy. In this way the family begins to gradually take the initiative for their own living process. I think that's a very crucial kind of process. I think part of this came out of the fact that Nate had graduated from the voyeurism games of psychiatry and he did not have to play peeping Tom on the family and figure out all the things that were cooking with them. He was willing to have the dynamics emerge, change, or stay the way they were. I think that's all right for me too. I think it's all right if the family takes the initiative for their life, and to live the way they want to live. Now, if mom wants to be a lesbian, and pop wants to be a homosexual, the kids want to relax and let the world go on, I think that's their right. I have some objections to suicide because I have a feeling that it lets the implicit murderer in the family get away with murder and I don't like that very much. Every once in a while, a gal says after the first interview, "Do you think I should divorce him?" I have developed a stock answer—one of the problems of old age is that you get stock answers. I say, "I'll tell you what, I've been married 36 years and 10 months. I think I'll probably stick with her. What do you want to do with yours?"

Part of Nate's power tactics was a process of how to enter the family, which I spoke of before. There is a second component of what I think of as good family therapy that Peggy Papp and I were talking about last night and that is how to get out of the family. John Rosen was probably a master at this. I remember watching John talking to a schiz one day and he was talking about how her mother's milk had been poisoned and how his milk was pure gold and she could have him forever and he would always be there and it was really quite tender and all of a sudden he turned to the guy standing next to him and said, "Hey, Joe, let's go play golf," turned, and walked out. The first time I saw that I could have slugged him, because I had a sense that it was not fair to treat a sick human being like this. Over the years, I have discovered it is a very important trick because if you walk in and become a Jewish mother who is symbiotically locked into the family or patient, it is no big deal. It is important to get there, but if you can't get out, you're just like the previous one and you don't help at all. How to get out is a very important process and one of the ways I get out is to become more convinced of how absurd I am. I decided recently in the middle of an interview while I was bored and trying to think of something interesting, that God must be getting very old and probably is going to retire and when He does if He asks me to take over, I am going to work out some plans. I have been working on that ever since. I have decided that we are going to switch sex every 10 years. Man is going to have the first baby and you can borrow time from those people who don't want it. We are going to have detachable penises where we switch sex. I have been wanting to be a female for many years and have never made it. Maybe I can make that part of my initiation rites. Each family member is looking to individuate in a way, to join without being locked in, and to individuate without being outside, and the therapists better know how to belong, be loving, be hurt with pain, cry with, and at the same time be able to back out and be separate. He should know that his life and the patient's family life are different and separate. He should be in charge when he makes those moves in and out and that becomes more and more difficult when you get past the first and second interview, when you become as vulnerable as the family. That's when the real ____ hits the fan. As long as you are in the first or second interview, you can be a technician. By the time you get to the third, fourth, or fifth, you are probably a human being and you had better watch out because you are vulnerable and they can get you and they outnumber you and outgun you and for me; that means I should have a cotherapist.

Now, the things I don't know about Nate are about Nate as a person. I did not get the opportunity to be close to him. But I can guess about his joyfulness—and God protect me from a family therapist who is not having any fun—if I have to take him as seriously as he takes himself, I will never make it. Harold Searles is famous for a lot of things about schizophrenia but one of the things was that if the schizophrenic can get to laugh at himself, he is on his way out. And I have the feeling that the same thing is true of the family. If the family can get to the point of laughing at itself, then you have made it over the top and from then on it's coasting down. I think Nate had a joyfulness

that made for real wholeness. Again, let me flip into my Christian
upbringing. Someday, I am going to teach a course in schizophrenia
with Christ as the continuous case study. Isaac Singer said there are 300
Christs in Jewish history. He said that the kingdom of heaven is only
available if you become a little child and heaven of course is living in
your own person, in your own unconscious. How do you become a
child and how do you get the family to have the courage to become
childlike? Part of it is playfulness, the freedom to be ridiculous, to be
irresponsible. We had a couple we had been working with, both crazy
as hoot owls, a schizophrenogenic kind of family—the daughter went
off for a year's trek into Africa, came back, and really did not need the
family, and went off to college, so we went on seeing the parents. They
came in a few weeks ago and the mother said that she did not have
anything to talk about. I said that we could go for a beer and the
resident said, "Great, let's go." So we got up and went out. We got
downstairs about two or three floors and daddy, who was a responsible
physician type, said, "Shouldn't we have the interview?" and I said,
"Mom, quick, goose him before he gets another thought like that." So
we went over and had a beer and a hamburger and probably had the
best interview we had in a long time. On the way back, dad says, "Well,
we'll see you next Tuesday." And I said, "Not me you won't," and he
asked if I would see him again, and I said, "Well, I guess I can if you
are convinced that it is necessary, but this seemed to be such a good way
of saying goodbye that I would hate to mess it up." That was 3 weeks
ago and we have not heard from him. The thought that they can get
along without me is shattering, but several other people have. So this is
the kind of playfulness, joy, silliness. One family came in for a first
interview and the problem was that their teenage daughter had "poor
ego boundaries." I put a big "X" in the middle of a paper and was
going to put notes on and give it to her in case she needed ego
boundaries. It is a way of getting out, of separating yourself, a way of
showing the family how to individuate. It's really an extrapolation of
that famous book, *"Where did you go?" "Out." "What did you do?"*
"Nothing," which is a kid's way of telling his parents to get off his
back, but doing it in such a nice Jewish double-bind way that you don't
know what to do with it, you don't know how to handle it. I think the
therapist should learn from that. One more step in this process, one of
the other ways in finding the kingdom of heaven, is to be crazy. About
30–40 years ago, and I am just guessing, art became crazy. Then about

5–10 years later, maybe, drama and literature became crazy, then gradually music became crazy. Science got some crazy impulses there but it's kind of hard put, really. I think we are now in a stage where it is all right in the world culture for people to be crazy. It is all right to break out of the linear, crazy, organizational, structured life that we have made the law of reason or rationale and really be crazy. So, I advocate that you learn how to be crazy, to take those crazy parts of yourself and amplify them, that you follow your impulses, follow your irrationalities, that you share with the family and God knows the family is safe, if there is one thing true of the family it has homeostasis like you don't have any knowledge of. There is no danger of you, the therapist, harming the family, say I from on high. The only question is if you make any dent at all. The question is whether you will be just one more flea that will happen to pass by. I don't think there is any danger of your doing any harm. So with that in mind, you should be able to share almost anything; I say "almost" because we used to teach our medical students back in Atlanta many years ago, and one day this lady showed up with her policeman brother. The student that had been seeing her was honest and said to the girl that he would love to go to bed with her. It was said very honestly and I hoped it was a symbolic statement but the policeman brother did not appreciate this at all. He did not think it was symbolic. He didn't think it was even therapeutic. A little bit of judgment you should use already.

There is another tremendous value in being crazy and that is that if you develop a symbiosis with a schiz-identified patient (I like schiz because I think it is a disease of abnormal integrity; they are really doing their thing and I say it with a reverence and do not say this with any facetious overtones), I think that that is what craziness is, abnormal integrity, a creativity that brooks no interference. Now the problem is that most of the people who end up in the state hospitals are also stupid. I make money out of being crazy; Picasso not only made money, he also had fun. Now that kind of craziness they should all have. All crazy people have the kind of opportunity Picasso has. If you become symbiotically involved with a patient then you have done that because you are like the mother. You lock-in and double-bind the patient and the patient double-binds you and there you are, tied in a figure 8. The difference is that when you have been locked like this, in contrast with mother, who is terrified about going crazy, hopefully you want to learn about how to be crazy. When you make the move into craziness, the patient symbiotically has to move into the sane position and then you have the way for curing the schizophrenia. This is an extra pearl because as soon as this is reversible, then the patient has a new sense of his capacity to be sane and of course you learn about the freedom and opportunity of being crazy. So these two become flexible. When the patient becomes sane, he becomes scared, so you have to stick around and teach him how to learn and then you move back and forth. Let me tell you a story. This 18- or 20-year-old schiz (we had been working with the family for a year or a year and a half), the daughter, had really gotten the family on the ropes. She had been screwing around all over the place and had VD several times and this very nice family was upset. She arranged to have herself kicked out of college several times and dad finally decided that he can't support her if she is not going to succeed in college. She got herself kicked out of her apartment and came home to live with family and then started bringing men in, which was all right with the family for dating purposes, but dad very carefully went to bed saying to the boy that it was time for him to go and woke up the next morning to find him still there. The mother then blew her stack at the daughter, said, "Out of my house, my doors are locked, you can't live here anymore." Twenty-four hours later the mother called me to tell me that she has to let the daughter back in, so I said, "Tell her, don't tell me." So she called up the daughter and said, "Look, I was wrong, I can't say goodbye to you; you are my daughter whatever and I'm stuck with it." Twenty-four hours later I got a call from the police. The policewoman said, "We have a girl down here who came in to report a murder. She said she's been murdered." It really did not do much for the policewoman. She really did not understand. "I called the mother and she said for me to call you." I said, "Well, you don't have to worry about her, we have been seeing her for a long time, and she is well able to take care of herself. Thank her and send her along." She said, "Well, she wants to talk to you. Will you talk to her?" I said, "Sure," and so she put her on the phone and she said, "Hey, Mr. Whitaker," which is what she always called me, part of the integrity, as I was no damn doctor to her and it was a very complimentary thing. I said, "I think it was awful nice of you to report the murder to the police and by the way, if you see any more murders, would you please report them too because the police should know about all of them." She burst into this gale of delighted laughter and said, "Thanks, very much," and hung up with a bang. What had happened was that the mother said, "I love you." To the schiz this means, "You are dead," so she had been murdered. What I had said was, "Congratulations for admitting the murder and if you find anymore, bring them in because you may run into two more before the morning," which was saying that "I am crazier than you are," at which point she became sane and delightfully real and human. So learn how to be crazy, but learn also to be smart.

COUNTERTRANSFERENCE IN THE FAMILY TREATMENT OF SCHIZOPHRENIA

with Richard E. Felder and John Warkentin

Whitaker believes that although countertransference is not therapeutic, to be therapeutic it is essential for the therapist to be involved with the family to the degree that countertransference emerges. Without this level of involvement, the contact between therapist and family will not produce growth or change. In a sense it is the same situation as is found in a marital relationship; a polite, friendly marriage does not facilitate growth in the same way an irrational, loving–hating, intense one does.

For Whitaker, the process of family therapy involves the therapist repeatedly joining the family, helping to disrupt their process, and then separating from the family. The therapist comes to this process with his own needs, wishes, and fears, as well as responding to the needs, wishes, and fears of the family. Here Whitaker and his colleagues examine both of these types of countertransference and suggest specific techniques for their handling and use in the service of therapy.

It is the presence of the therapist's countertransference, the reliving of his own family of origin experience, that makes family therapy so frightening to many therapists and also so potentially growthful. Whitaker and his associates offer useful guidelines to the family therapist to resolve the use and

Reprinted by permission from I. Boszormenyi-Nagy and J. Framo (Eds.), *Intensive Family Therapy*. New York: Harper & Row, 1965. Copyright © 1965 by Harper & Row, Publishers, Inc.

resolution of his countertransference feelings without becoming overidentified and/or overinvolved or without remaining isolated from the family.

Countertransference remains, in our opinion, the major problem facing
family therapists. The recent reliance on techniques and tricks within many
schools of family therapy can be seen as an attempt to avoid these feelings of
countertransference. Whitaker and his colleagues offer an alternative to this
stance of the therapist as a technician.

There has been a conspicuous increase of late in the discussion of
countertransference problems encountered in the general field of psychotherapy. Recent studies have included specific research based on
tape recordings, detailed observation of interaction, films, and linguistic analyses of communication. These studies consistently indicate that
the therapist is much more involved in the therapeutic process than we
have previously dared to realize. The increasing tendency to treat
patients in the setting of their family has also activated new insights
into the therapist's involvement. The use of two therapists with one
patient expanded into the use of two therapists with a married couple
and has gradually given us such courage that we are now treating the
family group. As a result, this experience has led to the treatment of the
schizophrenic in his family setting. This chapter proposes to discuss
the therapeutic problems involved in this effort, specifically those that
emerge in the therapist himself. No effort will be made to evaluate the
patients' problems or the process of psychotherapy as such.

In letting himself get involved in the family of the schizophrenic
patient the therapist inescapably must be able to resonate to the group
and also to identify with first one and then another of the members. He
then challenges them to disconnect some of the octopod vectors that
they have been living with and reconnect in such a manner that each
can find a new separateness and be free to interact with the therapist. In
breaking into the family, the therapist is clearly activating his own
open valences. The therapist must bring to bear in this new setting
those securely interdigitated defensive patterns which were associated
with his own original family setting, not just those related to his
parents as individuals. Presumably these latter transferences were
worked through in his own analysis. There is a hidden danger, for he is
relating to a family and yet he has never experienced therapy in the
setting of his original family.

As the therapist faces a schizophrenic and family in treatment, countertransference problems of even the experienced therapist become more obvious than in other forms of psychotherapy (Whitaker, Felder, Malone, & Warkentin, 1962). When he accepts the family as his patient the therapist begins to expose the immature residuals of his own person. No matter how the therapist tries to participate with mature warmth, he will reveal some infantile or pathologic responses in spite of himself. During the interview itself he may not sense what has happened, but he can discover the slips from a study of taped records or with the help of a colleague.

SETTING AND TREATMENT APPROACH

The work reported here was done in a private clinic where the nine therapists maintain a close working relationship. They are in daily multiple therapy and consultative work with each other and in the process have developed a shared ideology of psythotherapy.

The theoretical framework of the authors is designated *experiential* psychotherapy (Malone, Whitaker, Warkentin, & Felder, 1961a). By this term we denote a pattern of sequential overlapping between the transference relationship and the existential relationship, the existential relating dominating the later stages of psychotherapy. Every effort is made to increase the expressive and emotive aspects of the therapist-patient relationship within the limits of clinical judgment (Auerbach, 1963). This approach to the schizophrenic and his family necessitates increased specific involvement in the countertransference aspects of treatment. By countertransference we denote the distorted feelings of the therapist. We include in these not only the counterfeelings which develop in the therapist to the transference feelings from the family which is his patient, but also those from the subgroups within the family. We also include in the term countertransference those affects which develop in the therapist and have to do with his direct transference. The group or subgroups or individuals may symbolically represent to him someone in his own past, that is, his brother, his father and mother, or his family group. We also include under the term countertransference the identification process which takes place in the therapist so that, for example, he becomes so involved that the schizophrenic patient is something of an alter ego to him and he sees the schizophrenic patient as though that person were the therapist himself. Finally, we do not differentiate between overt and covert feelings in the therapist, since in either case the therapist is anxious. Yet, if his feelings are expressed to the family they may be more useful to the family than if they stay hidden (Whitaker, 1958).

Parenthetically we must warn that countertransference is non-therapeutic but that the depth of involvement which it evidences is necessary in the successful treatment of any psychotic patient. A mature therapist can attain such depth if he is willing and able to resolve the countertransference pathology so that his relating will be free and in the patient's interest. The overt expression of the therapist's "pathology" to the family must be controlled by his clinical judgment of its danger. However, unwillingness to share it is frequently based on his pride and embarrassment, and in this event only produces a secondary type of confusion in the relating.

In this chapter we are discussing the treatment of a family group seen as a unit even though the overt symptoms are expressed through a clinically sick child. In our development as a clinic group we have spent many years working with groups, working with couples, and using multiple therapy in all the areas of psychotherapy. We utilize multiple therapy as a method of resolving the countertransference tendencies of the therapist and making him increasingly competent to deal with those defense patterns which weaken his therapy. Our study of countertransference has been made largely on the basis of taped interviews and observations which emerge from the multiple therapy setting where each therapist is able to be an observer of the dynamic patterns emerging in the other member of the therapeutic team. In contrast, his own countertransference is usually not apparent to the therapist during the interview.

In our clinic the father or mother ordinarily calls for the initial appointment, at which time we ask that the entire family come in together. We do not see the schizophrenic patient by himself at any time, nor do we see the parents without the patient. We decide in the first interview whether to include siblings. We treat the family as a unit and insist that unless the entire unit is present we have no "patient." We sometimes dramatize this structure by calling our patient the inter-locked group or, graphically, a "people salad." Each member is con-fined in a network of interlocking relationships which is like a Jello salad with each person embedded in it. For instance, on one occasion the father in a family interview, when asked if he planned to buy a new car, said *"We* didn't have that on *my* mind."

The description of family treatment is a difficult job, since one is really facing a whole new definition of the primal scene which now becomes not a sexual scene but a total two-generation interactional unit. We assume that the schizophrenic child is the sacrificial lamb who, in order to meet the family need, is being repeatedly put through the crucifixion gesture. In family psychotherapy it becomes our job to help the child complete the therapy of the family so that each member can be free. If the therapy is successful, then the result must bring about freedom in the parents from their involvement in the "people salad" that includes the child and the two parents.

In contrast with individual psychotherapy, we are here presented with the actual home relationships which in ordinary psychotherapy are transferred to the therapist. The child is relating to his actual mother and his actual father, and the three of them are involved in a group to which the therapist is related in a separate manner. In other words, individual therapy is based on a symbolic relationship; group therapy is based on a social matrix; and family psychotherapy is based on that biosocial unit which is the basis for our entire society. No wonder the therapist has for years past not dared to walk into the middle of this situation and try to alter it. The dynamics of the family unit arise from the neurotic interlocking between the parents, a love which is both real and symbolic and reinforced by the affect developed in this union by the birth and growth of children and the experiences of many years of living together. In contrast to family psychotherapy, group psychotherapy involves a transference relationship between the members and toward the therapist; these relationships develop in a gradual, symbolic cathecting. In family therapy, the relationship within the group has been operating for many years; it is deeply invested with affect and is not only systematized but well defended in many different directions. The family comes to the therapeutic situation with greater power than the therapist has; and the therapist himself is an outsider. The process of family psychotherapy is one by which this powerful group is for the first time beginning to make deliberate efforts to break up interlocking defenses and patterns that hinder growth.

DYNAMICS OF PROCESS

The process of change in psychotherapy is a major subject and is not to be covered in this chapter. However, we must note that the process of change as described for the individual patient and the process taking place in the psychotherapy of a family are quite different. Family psychotherapy is also different from psychotherapy of a married couple. *A family as defined here consists of at least two and usually three or more persons who compose a two-generation unit.*[6] The very fact of this two-generation spread changes the dynamics of the therapeutic process. In addition, the presence of a cultural breakdown of the family as an institution, as evidenced by the psychotic patient, adds a new vector to the complexities of family dynamics. The natural homeostasis of the family unit is, however, reinforced during psychotherapy by the group allegiance which Bion describes as developing in "the face of a battle" (Bion & Richman, 1943).

We all know that stability prevents change, but the fluidity of groupings and regroupings within a family also prevents change.[7] This fluidity is as protective as the compliance of the man who never disagrees with anybody. Any anxiety in a member is compensated for by reassurance of the member or attack on the therapist by another member of the family or by a subgroup of the family. The therapist as an added force may even freeze the interaction at any one point and cause group panic and the sudden fixing of allegiances, just as he may expose new counterbalancing antagonisms and symbolic identifications. With the therapist as obstetrician a few of these hidden alignments exposed during the panic are delivered into consciousness. When the homeostasis is thus disturbed, a secondary flurry of recompensation may develop and still other interpersonal alliances are exposed and hopefully integrated into the dynamics of the whole.

Family therapy, then, includes a break-up in family loyalty, with the development not only of new subgroups but also of emerging tension systems which have been covered for many years. In family psychotherapy, the therapist must unite with and help with this disruptive effort and the subsequent new alignments. *If the therapist is to be at all useful to the family, the stress of such deep involvement must eventuate in a primitive countertransferencelike attachment* (Rosen, 1953).

COUNTERTRANSFERENCE PATTERNS

We have said that countertransference is unconscious during the time that it is operative; however, it may be forced to the therapist's attention during the experience, or he may become aware of it soon afterwards. When the therapist approaches the psychotherapy of the family, he brings certain specific attitudes which are already part of his personal response to any therapeutic situation. Because he is accustomed to treating one patient, he approaches a family situation as though in search of a person to treat. This is a natural result of his past experience, but it sets the stage for countertransference problems. Actually, then, the therapist may approach the therapeutic situation with more anxiety and more affect than does the family. They are a self-contained group set to relate defensively; they have experienced many years of conflict with others who challenge their integrity as a group. They have resisted such attempts and have a deep unconscious conviction of their own power. So the therapist is off balance, and the patient, in this case an entire family, is very much in balance; it has stability and certain group and subgroup methods of handling stress.

Some data seem to indicate that the therapist uses his work with the family as a way of experiencing some of his own tensions about the social structure in which he grew up. He could not change the community in which he grew up; therefore, he will change this part of the social structure. In this fashion is his missionary zeal stirred.[8] He may at least change this family.

Although we have elected to use the conventional term "countertransference," it may be that most of the distorted affect in the therapist should be labeled transference. He is reliving his early life experience in a sense not possible in his analysis or even in his present home. He can exercise infantile omnipotent control of this family, can become lost in this family group, or can run away from home like Huck Finn. He has the ideal "as-if" family, and the temptation to "act out" is all but irresistible.

One therapist, after working with a family for 13 months in a multiple therapy setting, suddenly in the middle of the hour had a fantasy of cutting off the head of each of the parents. This countertransference problem had undoubtedly been present for many interviews, and it is our conviction that if it had *not* been shared, it would in effect have weakened the therapeutic relationship. Since it was shared, it was one step in teaching the family to alter their own patterns by sharing feelings which seem too horrible to reveal.

To us the only effective counter for this kind of countertransference seems to be a cotherapist who can help make the personal needs of the therapist a current problem of the treatment situation. One therapist would be eaten alive and lost in the "people salad."[9]

ENGAGEMENT PHASE

In the initial phase of his relationship to the family the therapist is facing an excessive anxiety. He develops a plan for this new family, *his* new family. Maybe he is going to be the parent to this group and make them over in the image of his fantasy, his first family. Whatever his plan is, it is likely to be different from what he later discovers himself doing in his relating to the family. In his effort to commit himself to the family, he is very likely to become lost in it and absorbed as a member of the family. If so, he has already developed a transference. He may experience this transference as an impulse to assault the family homeostasis. He tries in effect to break the family in much the same way that John Rosen (1953) talks about "breaking the back of the psychosis" with the individual schizophrenic patient. He may fail miserably because of his involvement, as did the therapist in the following case fragment.

MOTHER: Well, Doctor Jones, what is your idea on sending Pat to a private school, and what type, and where?

THERAPIST: I don't think the problem is with the school. I think you are right when you say his problem has existed for years and that the school only catches the problem already present.

MOTHER: Well, Doctor Jones, all right, the thing is, if there was any end in sight in taking him out of school, all right, but he can't stay out indefinitely, and he has been out 2 months this year.

THERAPIST: Do you see what you're doing as you talk?

MOTHER: No, I have no idea.

THERAPIST: Do you, Dad?

FATHER: No.

THERAPIST: Do you, Pat? (*patient, 16-year-old*) (*no answer*)

Therapist: John? (*younger brother*)

John: No.

Therapist: I was pointing out that the problem is right here in the office.

John: (*interrupts*) Right here?

Therapist: Yes. And then Mother immediately switched our talk back to "what shall we do about school?" as though the problem were at school.

Mother: The problem is getting an education for him.

Therapist: I don't think so. That's what I'm saying. I don't think that's the problem. The problem is that he has to put his dirty shoe on my $80 chair, and his father doesn't do a damn thing about it. That's the problem. (*Therapist is angry about dirt and with father.*)

Father: What can you do? (*meaning what can you [the therapist] do*)

Mother: How can you take anything that big and put clean clothes on it? You lay them out and tell him to put them on and he doesn't put 'em on and he pays no attention to you whatsoever.

Therapist: I think that's beginning to narrow down the problem all right.

The therapist's effort to get away from the subject of school to the present situation failed. In trying to point out an immediate problem between patient and father, the therapist not only failed but became a part of the family's depersonalization of the patient ("anything that big" and "put clean clothes on it"). Mother would not have talked this way if the therapist had not, in the face of his own anxiety, participated in the family's hostility to the "patient." Listening to the rest of the interview, one is aware that the therapist remains impotent, inundated by the fixed family dynamics, and unable to extricate himself. Had two therapists been present, the other therapist would probably have been able to insure that the first therapist could have been stable in his own setting and in being himself. Thereby he would not have needed to "belong to" the family just because he was deeply concerned for its movement. *The therapist decompensated into "wishing" and "trying" prematurely.* A half-step would have been: "How much of your family problem seems to be here in this room, right now?" or "Did any of you pray for me in this interview?" or "Does my office seem like a place for you, Dad, to fight your family to a finish?"

INVOLVEMENT PHASE

As the therapist becomes increasingly involved, he may find himself identifying with the child of the family and attacking the mother as though he were going to protect the child from her malicious impulses. In a secondary way, he may also be endeavoring to replace her in the child's inner life and to become himself the mother in the family structure. On the other hand he may identify with the mother and endeavor to double-bind the schizophrenic child in the same way she has done, either because of his effort to capture a patient or because of his competitive feelings with the mother; for example:

MOTHER: Well, I guess there are things that come up that you don't want to do. But there has been a time when you wouldn't do anything you were asked to do.

SON: I don't feel that's . . .

MOTHER: If I feel the need of asking you to do anything now, I would ask you just like I would any of the rest of them that was around. I tried to give advice and tried to teach you all while you were young—in other words, and after you get grown I feel if you don't know it from me—so I might as well not give too much advice. I have to give you a little about some things because of—well, I reckon you don't think it through.

SON: I think it is very important that you give an opinion about this business. We don't have any idea of knowing what you think. In other words, if you don't say anything, we are at the place we've always been because we don't have anyone to say to us authoritatively if we are right or wrong, exactly where we were.

THERAPIST: (clearing his throat) Well . . .

SON: I know it is an improbable thing, but I am sure we would both like to know what you think about it. If I am wrong in my feelings—I mean, I know I am not wrong in my feelings. I know how I feel—but if I am wrong in my thinking, I have to find that out too.

THERAPIST: That's right. That is the reason why I don't comment. Because I am here to try to help you understand each other and have an experience with each other in which I can participate and possibly make this experience different from others you have had with each other. I don't have an opinion as such that occurs to me. If I have anything that is useful in participating with you, I won't hesitate to say it.

SON: I can't feel like she thinks the way she does about things, and I still don't feel the way I do.

THERAPIST: I'm sure that's true. I expect *that* to continue for a long time. I don't expect either of you to change overnight.

SON: I admit to you that we were both upset going back home last time and probably will be this time.

THERAPIST: I would like to say that much about it and I can give you that kind of opinion. This is the kind of opinion I think I am useful for. (*clears throat*) I think whenever you get upset by being in here that it is going to help you. Anytime you are upset by what happens in here, you can congratulate yourselves on the way home by having accomplished something, because just as long as this is just a peaceful talk, it isn't going to make you more able to go to work.

MOTHER: Well, maybe I'm wrong about this. He says I'm never positive so I can't be positive about this but I can say what I think and what the actions has made me think. If I were to tell Howard he was wrong about something he wouldn't pay any attention to me, he wouldn't think it was, he would think he knew. If you were to tell him something was wrong, give an opinion about something, he has a right to respect what you say more because you taught in this and you know about it, I don't. On the other hand, I feel like that as long as I have been here, if I hadn't learned a little of the true experience I must have been awfully dumb to start with. And with all the things I've seen and experienced myself, and I don't want to give any of them the wrong advice at any time because they might take it. I don't think they will. I don't think Howard is going to take much of my advice if I give any but I just wondered if it's not that way.

SON: I keep wondering, although there is a wide gap in our ages, how two people can have the same situation and get such different results from it. I feel that one of us is not looking at it right.

MOTHER: Well, I do too and I don't feel like it is all me. Maybe I'm too complacent and maybe not complacent enough. I will go a long way to keep from having an argument with a neighbor.

SON: I say you would.

MOTHER: I don't know of anything my neighbors have done to me. That is what I have been trying to tell you. You say I will take anything and I don't think I have.

SON: Would you say that you have never had an argument with anybody about anything?

MOTHER: Oh, I have had plenty of arguments.

SON: I've never heard you make a statement that can be construed . . . (*both talking*)

MOTHER: I have never had occasion to have an argument where you were present that I know of. The fact of the business, I stay home all the time and don't see very many people . . .

SON: Which is something else.

MOTHER: Which is just a little while at a time. It is just another habit, because I've stayed home so long now I don't want to go and I think I am entitled to that. The fact is I have never cared to get out in public much and I had to go to work and that was enough.

SON: Would you make a comment, would you generalize it and say what a relationship between a mother her age and son my age, what should they do? I don't mean specifically, but generally. I want to know.

MOTHER: Tend to their own business, I guess. I don't believe you asked me though. In other words, that is putting it pretty flat.

SON: What are my private affairs and what are her private affairs— what things should we, two people, mother and son, not as a personal element . . .

THERAPIST: I think the personal element is very important.

SON: Well, you refuse to say.

THERAPIST: Howard, I am not interested in setting up a theoretical mother and son, but a real one. I will be glad to say what I think you are talking about this morning; the fact that you feel dependent on her and resent that, which is the normal relationship between mother and a little child of 4. Where the child is dependent on the mother, she supplies his food, she is the most of his world. But he resents this because he wants to be a big man and be out in the world, and that part I can see in this relationship so far.

Mother and son have taken over and are going around in a closed circuit. Son tries to involve the therapist, mother starts to interfere, then changes her mind. Son doesn't like therapist's comment ("I think the personal element is very important") and provokes him ("Well, you refuse to say") as he provokes mother. Therapist becomes mother and answers sweetly, but double-binds (and thus confuses) the patient ("I am not interested in setting up a theoretical mother and son," etc.), but before the end of the paragraph he is speaking to the patient, of the patient, in the third person. The transition from "you" to "he" is very subtle.

As a third bind, the therapist may, of course, become impotent and soft and endeavor thus to carry the balance of power as the father does; the therapist then stimulates the child to become sacrificial at one moment or stimulates the mother to be overtly dominant and sym-biotically double-bound at the next moment (Winnicott, 1949).

As this involvement phase continues, the therapist is often bound in such a way that he begins to isolate himself from the group artifi-cially to prevent further absorption into this "people salad." He may think of this isolation as becoming objective or interpretative. We con-ceive of it as a split in the family so that the therapist is simultaneously related to the child and related to the parental couple. Family therapy is a unique kind of experience for the psychotherapist and something which he may be unable to perceive because he is dealing not in a symbolic, historical situation but in a current dynamic system. We have been so impressed by this experience in the therapist's counter-transference that we have been tempted to generalize and say that every therapist is dynamically the product of the distortions of another family, his own family of origin. If this supposition is true, the thera-pist faces the possibility of reinfection. His own sense of reality may be weakened, his ego defenses reinforced for protection, and his loss of integration may become a fact instead of a danger.

A significant part of the distortion in his relationship to the family is involved with his positive identification with the patient. We psy-chiatrists have for many years idealized the schizophrenic patient, idealized his insightfulness as being magical and omniscient, as though we believed his delusion of grandeur. We have idealized his mysteries, whether neologisms or symbolic formulations which we could not interpret. We even equate the schizophrenic's insightfulness with ther-apeutic capacity as though his insightfulness meant that he would be the ideal therapist in our fantasy of what would make *us* mature. We absurdly assume that the schizophrenic patient understands life better than his parents do, and because of this assumption we wallow in an induced hostility to the parents.

In addition, because of our training, we have a deep appreciation for, and preoccupation with, the symbolic experience; but we distort the communication within the family and accuse the family of creating a "sick" person. Because we idealize this sick person as noted above, we may thus formulate a rather nice double bind for the family, and, of course, this is returned in kind: the family then can double-bind the therapist, usually on a nonverbal level.

It is not unusual for us to picture the schizophrenic patient living in the framework of his sacrificial effort toward a family and to bypass entirely his narcissism. We say in effect, "You are wonderful." The patient says, "You are wonderful, too." And with this kind of feedback system we overidentify with the patient and become lost in a standard transference–countertransference jam. Another time we say to the patient, "Get better but keep the craziness you have. It is your creativity, and we admire you for it." In fact, it may well be that sometimes we become so preoccupied with the artistic enjoyment of symbolism that we use it for its own sake and form a little artistic entente with the patient. At another time we may idealize the schizophrenic child by saying, "He is the only honest person in the family." This compliment is obviously false since the family pattern is certainly unified.

Another countertransference pattern is an extension of the above in which we asexualize the schizophrenic child. Our picturing him as transcending sex is in itself a way of rejection and avoids any sexual countertransference affect. One of the other countertransference problems is associated with the therapist's tendency to become destructive of his own person. It is as though he accepts the patient's code of being sacrificial and becomes himself sacrificial as the patient is to the family. He says, "Here am I, Lord, take me." Our idealization of the schizophrenic may at times spill over to an idealization of the family itself. We tend to close off our third ear so that it is unable to hear the psychopathic maneuvering which takes place in this kind of therapeutic situation. It is obvious that schizophrenics are very adroit at maneuvering people; they maneuver deliberately and they maneuver with real affect. If the therapist loses sight of these two patterns, he becomes enmeshed in the situation.

The therapist sometimes develops a pattern of countertransference which has to do with his own identification with the mother. She says to the child, "How can you do this when I work my fingers to the bone?" and he says almost in direct echo, "How can you all be unappreciative of me when I have sacrificed myself for you?" He is saying to them, "You must appreciate me, else you are not worthy of my love."

This situation reconstructs the child's original dynamic setting and entangles him in a very primitive manner. Thus involved, the therapist faces a very serious countertransference problem. He may resonate to and enjoy the relationship to the family as a unit as he did with his own family group. He is not a working therapist but the child of the family.

In contrast, at times the countertransference problem builds up negative tension patterns within the therapist. These may simply disrupt his function, or they may develop to such a point that he resolves them by means of an affect explosion into the family setting. ("This family just will not go along with my plan for them.") At another level, he may become lost in the subgroup power struggle within the family either by attaching himself to the parental group or to some other subgroup (mother–son or father–son) or by attaching himself to one of the individual members of the family group. In any of these eventualities he is involved in such a way that he becomes therapeutically impotent. If he avoids the Scylla of overinvolvement, he is immediately faced with the Charybdis of isolation. Finally, the therapist may become countertransferred in such a manner that he deftly switches from one side to another in a type of alternating transference which not only keeps him from becoming aware of his involvement but also keeps him from being an adequate therapist.

Thus we see the therapist in a loaded situation. The family is intact and he is enacting only a functional role. His normal warmth in relating to an individual suddenly becomes a countertransference vector. His affect must be attached to the family unit, yet he may not belong to it. He must help the family to break up their group loyalty, to develop new subgroups, and gradually to sense their right to "belong" yet not lose their identity in the group. (Is it possible that *any* subgroup is healthier than the whole family?) Through all this process he must be "in," yet not "of," the family and its subgroups. He must be available to each person of the family, yet belong to none; he must belong to himself (Whitaker, Warkentin, & Malone, 1959).

DISENTANGLEMENT PHASE

It seems very difficult to understand the final phase of treatment of the family. Experience is limited, the situation is complex, and even the multiple therapist tends to become unavailable as an observer because of the significance of the experience to him as a person (Whitaker, Warkentin, & Johnson, 1950). If family psychotherapy has progressed to the stage of disentanglement, failure is a relative term. Many families do not stay in treatment until they have gotten all that is possible out of psychotherapy, in our view, but does that mean the case is a failure? The "break" out of treatment which stops the interviews may originate in the marriage of the patient, father getting a new job and moving to another city, or the gradual withdrawal of the family unit from treatment. We try to participate in any such movement. We express our reservations and our satisfaction, our sense of loss and our relief; yet through it we maintain their right to decision. This is the right we have trained them to take. Only time will tell whether the pattern will recur.

If the therapy of the schizophrenic and his family has been successful and the "people salad" has been altered, there develops in the middle phase of treatment a situation in which there are three separate people who have a rather tenuous relationship to each other. Each of them is becoming an entity, and they may be "out of phase" with each other, that is, no longer reinforcing each other's pathology. If the disentanglement phase is effective, there must develop a stable parental subgroup which forms a base to which the child can relate in a voluntary manner. He is free to attach himself to his primary parental group and detach himself at will. The twosome is available to him but is not enmeshing him. The parents in turn can enjoy his attachment, and when he is separate they can enjoy each other to a greater degree. They feel free to fight for the marriage as the central concern to them. The patient is secondary. Finally, the parents can each be separate, yet a part of the marriage.

We see then that to maintain his separateness throughout the therapeutic process, the therapist must avoid not only the countertransference problem of overinvolvement but also the countertransference problem of isolation. As a prototype he must be a part of the group. He must be involved and not merely carrying a role with the family, yet he must avoid being absorbed into their quicksand kind of meshing.

RESOLVING COUNTERTRANSFERENCE PROBLEMS

The resolution of countertransference problems has at least two foci. There are certain specific countertransference problems that are resolvable in specific ways; yet in the overall sense, countertransference problems, inasmuch as they are implicit, are best resolved by a general reorganization of the relating of the therapist and the "patient." Thereby, the dynamics which keep the countertransference operative are gradually dissipated. The most obvious way of resolving countertransference is prevention. The prevention of countertransference is aided in an overall way by several specific moves. The most obvious is an adequate therapeutic experience for the therapist so that he comes to the treatment process with a maturity and freedom to become involved in the relationship without losing his own integrity or without becoming pathologically transferred to the treatment situation. He needs an adequate background also in the sense of a training experience in which he has grown as a person. He should have an opportunity to experience his patient needs in more than one setting, for example, as a patient in group therapy, in an opportunity to do therapy with small children, or in an opportunity to face his own tendencies toward countertransference in a multiple therapy setting. Adequate supervision of this varied therapeutic work also helps prevent countertransference problems. The simple therapeutic settings also help him learn how to work through countertransference affects and help him grow by this struggle. This background of growthful experience as a person should, of course, be complemented by a fairly lengthy experience as a psychotherapist. He thereby may have become a "professional" therapist rather than someone who still does psychotherapy for the love of it—what we call an amateur. It is important that the psychotherapist let himself become involved in his work to the extent that it becomes stressful. Through stressful experiences he adapts himself and increases his strength to function in his professional role.

Since the therapist must live and work with one foot outside the social structure, it is very important that he be secure in his membership in a professional group. A research institute or a hospital staff may supply this security. If not, his isolation from the community may be a serious burden. If he has a group of colleagues, his freedom to walk in the valley of the shadow of psychosis will be increased. It may be that family treatment of schizophrenia is impossible without this kind of support.

One of the most significant assets in the prevention and the resolution of countertransference affects is the strength the therapist has in his own family life outside the office. A psychotherapist who is deeply related on a constructive and satisfying level to his own wife and children is much more likely to function as a competent person in the treatment of a sick family than one who is living in deep stress at home.

If the therapist is adequate in the above areas, countertransference factors are likely to be resolved if the therapist can muster the courage to bring to the therapeutic interview a type of extreme honesty and affect sharing. His honesty and sharing is the model around which the family can pivot; they can compare their own method of relating and be tempted to be more nearly honest themselves and more sharing of their feelings than before. In effect, the therapist's self-image serves as a prototype for the family and its individual members. The therapist should obtain supervision of his relationship to the family, either by way of tape recording or through actual participant observation by a colleague. In fact, even a technical ploy on the part of the therapist to bring his own affect concerns to the family may alter his affective involvement.

As prevention, we have found it ideal to utilize multiple therapy in the treatment of these families. It may be that as we become more and more adequate, multiple therapy will not be necessary. "When I get over my head I want a cotherapist to push me on through or debunk my distorted effort" (Whitaker, 1958).

Techniques for Resolving Countertransference

On a technical level, there are several things which we think of as helpful in the resolution of countertransference patterns. It is valuable if the therapist can maintain an overview of the family as a whole. His affective relationship to the family group is one effective way of keeping himself from becoming countertransferred to subgroups or individuals in the family. At the same time he must ride the other horn of this dilemma and be involved with the individuals and the subgroups. Thus the resolution necessitates a type of fluidity and strength in his moving in and out of the family situation. To be strong and fluid the therapist must "be," and in his "being" stand and move in his own personal uniqueness and his own spontaneity. Continuity in relating is less valuable than authenticity. In essence, the therapist finds himself involved in a series of Oedipal triangles, and he must be competent and free to disrupt these triangles from time to time in a very deliberate fashion and to re-create them or allow himself to be pulled into them in the same free rhythm with which he may elect to back out and destroy them. When he does this, of course, he becomes a professional therapist carrying on a professional role, which by itself is not enough to constitute a therapeutic relationship but is a necessity in the resolution of the various countertransference slivers which inevitably develop.

Technically, the therapist can also help in the resolution of countertransference by deliberately leaving the initiative for the conduct of the interview to the family members themselves. This kind of withdrawal sometimes is very clearly a process of rejection of the entire situation and as such may precipate tension patterns which will then have to be worked through, but it is a process that can be invaluable at times. A fairly standard example is that of an interview when the entire family is depressed. The therapist is tempted to step in and reassure them, to participate in the depression and its resolution, and to be himself their saviour. However, frequently when he steps in he is expressing his own countertransference. Technically, it seems more valuable to activate the depression, to push the family depression to a new depth, and to come through it rather than to back out of it. It is as though the therapist denies his loyalties to each member of the family and asserts his relationship to the group as a whole.

An awareness that the parents' marriage is a figment may prevent one unreality tendency. To see them as premarital adds a freedom to help them become a healthy subgroup.

If the treatment involves multiple therapy, it is possible at times for the therapist to resolve his countertransference problems by retreating to his relationship to the other therapist, and the therapeutic process then becomes a process of two groups relating to each other. The therapist is thus free to have his major loyalty to his own group and break up his overidentification with the sick family. It may even be that this relationship between the two therapists with its "incestuous" understructure resolves some countertransference problems by making the incestuous relationship between the members of the family less guilt-producing and more satisfying.

In the usual family pattern the mother, with father as her collaborator, accomplishes her purpose by using one sacrificial goat—the patient; with the single therapist she may be able again to structure a sick "family"; with two therapists she is helpless. They form their own group. Since the therapists have their greatest affect with each other, the family is left with their own misery and may thereby rededicate themselves to the therapeutic effort.

If the treatment of the family is not by multiple therapy, then the technical maneuver of bringing a consultant into the interview may serve the same result. If the therapist has no consultant he may well become lost in the group dependency of the family. In breaking the congealed "people salad" by the addition of another person, the therapist may become free to move in and out of his involvement with the family rather than be frozen into it. In contrast, we suspect that attempts at resolving this kind of countertransference by supervisory discussion are ineffective since the experience is unavailable to the therapist for overt discussion. However, the use of taped interviews may produce enough reactivation of the original setting so that the therapist is able to resolve some of his countertransference problems by listening to the tape with a colleague. This suggestion may seem overcautious unless we all agree that the therapist's involvement is not neurotic or technical. He is investing his own deep psychoticlike feelings, those of the primary process itself. This investment is one of the differentials between family psychotherapy and group psychotherapy. Family psychotherapy involves primary process dynamics, whereas group psychotherapy uses to a large degree secondary process dynamics. The therapist's feeling participation must follow the appropriate pattern.

CONCLUDING REMARKS

While the therapist of this generation has had no personal experience of being the patient in his family setting, the next generation of psychotherapists may well include some individuals who got part of their psychotherapy in their family group and who, in so doing, resolved not only their transference problems but also the transference problems of their relationship to their entire family group as a unit. In the meantime, the preparation of a therapist for working with the extremely powerful families who have as their presenting symptom a schizophrenic child necessitates an extensive personal therapeutic analysis and much experience in being a professional psychotherapist. Furthermore, the therapist must be significantly related to his own family and with enough security there so that he is not emotionally liable to major countertransference jams. We assume he also needs the security of a group of colleagues to whom he is deeply related and with whom he can work in multiple therapy.

An extensive experience in supervised family psychotherapy, whether the supervision is individual or group, might make it possible for the therapist to avoid many countertransference problems in family psychotherapy. His training should also develop the capacity to diagnose family dynamics. This latter experience is probably not attainable in the individual consultation room or the ordinary hospital training, but must be obtained either in a mental hygiene clinic or in work with families in a social agency. Only in this kind of training will he develop a security in the strength of the family group so that he will approach this family with respect rather than with disgust, curiosity, or fear.

We trust it is clear from the above discussion that the psychotherapist who gets involved in this kind of work is in essence developing a kind of split within himself. He must be simultaneously involved with the family and separate from it; he must be an entity in himself and at the same time a member of the group, and a primary group at that. He must be able to identify with the child in the family without himself becoming a child. He must be with the parents, yet not a parent. This capacity emerges from experiences which make this kind of openness and this kind of involvement something he can move into and out of rather than avoid. His training should help him know that the family is more powerful than he is and at the same time make him able to participate in the family situation and its alteration without being overwhelmed by its strength or without trying to utilize the group for himself. In this latter sense, the work with families is the ultimate challenge, the ultimate excitement, the most dangerous, and at the same time the most deeply satisfying work that a psychotherapist can attain. It is a real life and death struggle, and "the life you save may be your own."

ACTING OUT
IN FAMILY PSYCHOTHERAPY

Although written prior to the previous material on countertransference, we have placed this chapter following because acting out is the behavioral expression of a countertransference problem. Acting out by any member of the therapeutic group reduces the anxiety for the whole group and thus prevents forward movement of the psychotherapy.

Acting out is considered to occur both by members of the patient group and by the therapist. Whoever acts out, however, it is considered to be a joint decision by the whole therapeutic group. The purpose of acting out will vary, depending upon the phase of the therapy process. Several types of acting out are described and possible remedies are suggested. The methods for dealing with acting out are similar to those suggested for countertransference in the previous chapter.

The beginning of multiple therapy in 1945 as a technique of investigation and exploration of more difficult treatment problems gave us a new sense of strength so we began family psychotherapy a few years later. Since 1950, this has opened up a set of treatment problems previously kept in the shadows. Our group was so constantly involved in teaching psychotherapy and so routinely challenging each other's patterns in the multiple therapy setting, that by 1955 we had moved away from collaborative therapy and were pushing every referral toward couples or family therapy framework.

The multiple therapy supervision system makes the problem of acting out a team problem. In the one-to-one therapy effort such release for anxiety is a personal attack on the other. We have previously defined the difference between acting out and a therapeutically valuable behavioral interaction (Whitaker & Malone, 1963). Acting out by

Reprinted by permission from L.E. Abt and S.L. Weissman (Eds.), *Acting Out: Theoretical and Clinical Aspects*. New York: Grune & Stratton, 1965. Copyright © 1965 by Grune & Stratton, Inc.

any member of the therapeutic group tends to minimize the affect developing between them. In contrast, where the behavioral interaction does not tend to minimize the affect, it is a contributing force in the therapeutic process. Where it does minimize the feeling or prevent the forward movement of the psychotherapy, it should be called acting out, and is in effect the behavioral expression of a transference–countertransference disequilibrium. This does not mean that an impasse or a transference–countertransference jam exists. We clarified in the reference above the fact that any acting out to relieve the affect level is by joint agreement of the persons involved. It is probable that not only is there an implicit and covert arrangement as to who shall burst the affect bind, but possibly even how it shall be done. For example, in looking back on my early work in Ormsby Village,[10] a school for delinquents, I think it quite clear that some of the car stealing my patients did was in direct response to my vicarious enjoyment of their antagonism to the social structure. Simultaneously the acting out served as a mechanism for covering up the panic precipitated in us. They were powerful persons. I was a young therapist. Actually, I didn't feel much more adequate than they did.

THE DEFINITION OF FAMILY PSYCHOTHERAPY

"Family psychotherapy" is defined as variously as the centers that utilize it.[11] The term may or may not include the psychotherapy of husband-and-wife couples. It may include the collaborative treatment of husband and wife by different therapists or the simultaneous psychotherapy of the entire family by several therapists, each in a separate office. Some centers include several varieties in what is called a "multiple impact approach." We operationally experience the family as a biological unit and consider that, with few exceptions, this unit is the patient. The family is an institutionalized microsociety with its own unique cultural patterns, most of which are not revealed to the outside world. It is, of course, a psychological unit and a social unit in the sense that any primary group constitutes an entity. However, for our purposes and for the purposes of this chapter, the family is a two-generation group. We will discuss this group as the patient and restrict it to an artificial model consisting of father, mother, and one or more children.

In family psychotherapy, the chief complaint may vary. The son may have been stealing cars, the daughter may be shy and withdrawn, or indeed one of the adults may have become psychologically crippled. A second series of families present themselves with the chief complaint of a generalized family symptom. The adults have decided that their family is not maturing adequately, that there is not enough warmth at home, or there is too much tension, or in some situations the families want to increase their own creativity. There is a third group of families who come to psychotherapy as an extension of their previous, more specific, work with a psychotherapist. Father says in effect, "I am better, my wife is better, our marriage is healthier, but we want the children to participate in this growth, and we want the family to have the kind of satisfactions we have gotten from our individual therapeutic efforts."

THE THERAPEUTIC TASK

The therapeutic task with the family should be defined accurately. Although we follow the general principle that a new experience is the significant objective, family psychotherapy highlights the complexities of the therapeutic endeavor. We have been forced to admit that family psychotherapy can be effectively undertaken only by a team of two therapists. A good surgeon can do a routine appendectomy, but even a good surgeon wouldn't attempt a major abdominal operation without a colleague of equal adequacy across the table. We believe family psychotherapy is a major operation. Moreover, we are convinced that no team is powerful enough to *"handle"* the family. Manipulative psychotherapy may be sufficient in minor operations, but it does not seem effective in major operations. Although we do manipulate transference feelings, it is impossible to gain "control" of what goes on in a family. Furthermore, it is not possible at this stage of our knowledge to *understand* the family. We do not know enough, we are not clever enough, and God knows we are not mature enough, to be subjectively involved in a family and still be objectively perceptive of our own subjective involvement and its relationships to the family process. By implication, then, our task in family psychotherapy is to be available as a team to move as participants in the psychological and social patterns of this family, and thereby to aid the family unit in its autopsychological reparative process. If we are also able to jar the psychobiological patterns, we can have some assurance that nature will help to make this a constructive intervention.

ACTING OUT

Acting out in the one-to-one interview is carried out by the patient under an implicit doctor–patient agreement. In family psychotherapy that behavior which drains off affect can be by the therapeutic team, by the family group, or by one of the therapists, or by a subgroup within the family, or even by an individual in the family.

Acting out in the family setting has similarities to acting out in group psychotherapy. Since the dynamics in the family are to a large degree expressed interpersonally, all dynamics are in a sense behavioral. The dynamics in one-to-one psychotherapy may be within the person of the patient, and may be with or without behavioral expression in the group therapy setting. The forces at work in the family are experienced within the therapeutic group and are subtly and delicately communicated among the members of this close-knit unit. The family has been developing its covert behavior language for many years. Its exactness is phenomenal.

Acting Out by the Therapist

As mentioned above, we assume that any acting out is by joint agreement with the rest of the therapeutic group. Therefore, acting out by the therapist, whether by the team or one of the individuals, is by joint, usually covert, arrangement with the family. To minimize complications in our chapter, we will assume that the two therapists who make up the team are trained, experienced, mature persons and that their professional relating is stable, solid, and personal. The multiple therapy involvement with individual patients and couples serves as good training before they undertake the therapy of a family unit.

In spite of this, and with no apology, the first and most prominent pattern of acting out will often be a split in the therapeutic team. Therapist Joe will suddenly find himself saying to his cotherapist after the interview, "Bill, you were too rough on that mother today." It is as though their unity had been disrupted so that Joe was intent on making Bill protect this mother the way he wanted to himself. Of course, if the team is more open, such division can be expressed within the interview and thereby become a part of the therapeutic process. The fact that it occurred after the interview is prima facie evidence that Joe was trying to minimize the affective involvement.

Second, the acting out on the part of the therapist may become conspicuous through administrative slips. These may include poor interview timing so that one therapist is tardy, allowing the bill to accumulate so that the family is more dependent, or slips of the tongue by one or the other therapist, indicating an effort to break out of the involvement.

Third, the therapist may try to escape from the therapeutic process by an affective spill consisting of nighttime dreams about the family, fantasies between interview hours, or inappropriate bits of behavior during the interview.

Fourth, the therapists may discover they are involving one or more of the usual distancing procedures. These may include intellectual interpretative "chaff," generalized indifference, aloofness, wandering of attention, preoccupation with "scientific objectivity," or just plain withdrawal.

Fifth, one or another of the therapist team may within the interview regress technically to a more primitive form of "helping." For example, he may use reassurance, inspiration talk, haranguing, or threatening.

Sixth, a prominent pattern is the temptation to attract one of the family members into a one-to-one interaction as a way of avoiding the affective power of the family as a whole.

Seventh, the therapist within the interview may project hostility in a direct manner. For example, Joe says, "Father, you remind me of a sergeant I had overseas." Or he may project sexual feelings. For example, Bill says, "I suddenly became aware today that Susie walks just like my wife does." Finally, the therapist may, of course, retreat into guilt about his inadequacy. The fact of his impotence is a beautiful excuse for using that same impotence as a ploy.

We assume that any acting out by the therapist should best take place within the interview. It is then not only a problem to be worked through by the entire group, but is valuable since the other therapist can use it to diagnose the ongoing therapeutic process. Furthermore, since not all behavior is sick, this kind of acting-out honesty, if it is brought into the therapeutic relationship, may become not just a way of avoiding affect, but secondarily, a way of expressing rather than decreasing affect.

FAMILY ACTING-OUT PATTERNS

With the ongoing process of psychotherapy, there develops a gradual unification of the family group, an increased intimacy between its members, and concurrently a new intimacy with the therapeutic team. Their acting out serves to relieve this anxiety, and varies in character with the stage of the psychotherapy itself. In the early phase of therapy it may serve to evade the development of the relationship. In the middle phase it modifies the pressure necessary for change, and in the latter phase it is mainly a functional effort to delay the ending of the relationship itself. We will not try to separate the patterns of acting out as they apply to these various phases, since the scheme is highly synthetic, and certainly the patterns overlap to a great extent. One comment, however, seems indicated. We assume that the rubber fence patterns which Lyman Wynne talks about are probably most characteristic of the middle segment.

Within the Interview

The pattern of acting out by the family in psychotherapy is almost as variable as the culture of the family, and reflects not only the solidity and style of the family but also its group structuring. The "pseudo-mutuality" of the early interviews may be mistaken for proof of the family's unification. Nothing can be further from the truth. It is an implicit effort on the part of the family to "cooperate the therapist to death." The theme is apt to be, "Doctor, we need help, please do something." This kind of plea is exactly the same kind of ploy that the immature hysterical patient uses in saying, "I don't know what to do, please tell me." The pattern may be accentuated by masses of factual data. This is their contribution, and the resolution is left to the doctor. Next the family may develop a kind of closure against the therapists. They engage in twin talk which has a subtly paranoid character. If the therapists are not secure with each other, they may feel put upon and ostracized, as indeed they are. If they survive this test, or to put it another way, if they are ready to tolerate a greater load of anxiety, the next move may be a denial by the family of its unitary quality. The interview becomes a cocktail party, and the whole group unites in an effort to snow the therapist with a mass of one-to-one relationships.[12] A variant of this acting-out pattern is what we have come to call "group prostitution" for the therapist. Each person evacuates the problems of the week, with the anticipation that the therapist will answer all the situational questions and formulate rules for a better week than "the week that was." As the therapy frees more anxiety, the family begins a series of *role battles*, the variety of which is almost infinite. A struggle may evolve over who will be the spokesman or who will confess the family stress area.

Scapegoating is one very frequent role. For years the entire family has developed life patterns in which one special person carries the symptom of the family illness. This is usually a child, and in the acting-out defense, the family returns to this pattern. It may be varied. Annie, the oldest one, may be castigated for being withdrawn; Susie, the middle one, may be accused of being irresponsible; and Bennie, the little boy, may be attacked as "too childish." Once the general scapegoating patterns are explored and the anxiety relating to them integrated, the family may attack or even exclude the father. Margaret Mead has said that fatherhood is a social invention. It does not take much imagination to realize that in this biological unit, the mother and children have a bond which is experienced in a most profound manner, while father is merely a psychological and sociological appendage.

In family therapy this may begin a dance in which the therapists and the father are excluded together. As the working-through process continues, the family may act out the increasing anxiety by a split into subgroups. They may also unify around the protection of the "hurt one." This kind of old maid clucking about one member's limitation serves as a means for the entire family to withdraw from the therapeutic scene.

It is also easy to move from general withdrawal to the establishment of subgroup battles within the family. The children may unite to fight against the older generation, or father and mother may join to criticize the kids. It is equally frequent for the male segment of the family to get together to defend against the female subgroup. Underlying these mechanisms, there is an undercover agreement with the therapist.

The group should be developing enough integration of its anxiety and enough common cause so that acting-out patterns are less a deterrent, and the therapy is moving to a more significant depth. Yet part of this effort to form a growthful therapeutic community may be interrupted by a simple jam in communication. The old network of communication within the family is breaking up, and the signals of the nonverbal network may directly counter the verbal formulations. Confusion becomes profound before freedom to be open and honest is attained.

It should be clear that any review of possible dynamic patterns of the interview setting must be incomplete. We cannot close without noting the peculiar seesaw of projections or hide-and-seek that goes on with the therapist. It is an expression of the dependent hostility patterns which emerge as therapy becomes more significant to all the persons involved.

Outside the Interviews

We have artificially separated the acting out within the interview, which is most apparent, from the acting out which takes place surreptitiously between interviews. This second form may be very disruptive. One of the reasons for trying to thus separate these groups is the possibility that the therapists can interdict the outside behavior by direct instructions to the family. The usual problem between interviews is to continue interview talk outside the office. Families come to therapy from a lifetime of talking with each other more or less openly. As the therapy increases their capacity to communicate raises the level of their anxiety, and it is natural for them to recapitulate, to argue, to debate, or to begin trying to help each other outside the interview. This process directly decreases the amount of affect brought to the interview, and is, of course, an excellent system for dissipating anxiety in the patient and in the therapist. Since some insights may accrue from this pseudotherapy, the family may never discover that this is diminishing the amount of affect available in the professional setting.

Another frequent pattern is the escape to a surrogate therapist. The entire family may suddenly decide to go for Sunday dinner with grandma and discuss the entire process with her; one or two members may go to talk with the pastor, or the family doctor; the kids may gossip to the school counselor. Father may mull the whole thing over with his golf partner or his secretary and mother with a neighbor or even the maid. This dissemination of affect makes the next interview very relaxed, and, of course, almost useless. They may even bring some cute little insights picked up during the week to bribe the therapist. Then he can't be too personal.

The family may also disseminate anxiety by administrative battles with the therapeutic team. As the level of affect increases, the level of acting out takes on greater seriousness. There may be a gross explosion of affect. For example, Sonny may get into an auto accident which makes therapy impossible on the family budget. Father may lose his job. There may be serious delinquency or a new outbreak of previously latent asthma or stomach ulcer. These explosions may also be closer home and consist of a direct break with the extended family. Then it is the professionals versus the home folks.

How to Meet the Threat of Acting Out

Repairing the damage of acting out is like bringing about the correction of a transference–countertransference jam. The best method is prevention. Such prevention necessitates a clear and feeling presentation of the therapist's conviction that family psychotherapy is a struggle for both sides of the group, and that anxiety is present in both the therapists and in the family as a whole. The family must become aware that any acting out within or outside the interview is partly their responsibility. Furthermore, they must accept the fact that the correction of these recurrent pathological detours belongs to both the therapists and the family. Parenthetically, the therapists cannot communicate such a conviction if they do not believe it.

Prevention of intolerable anxiety rests upon the freedom to experience and express anxiety in the therapeutic hour. This expression is probably only possible if one is willing to bring his pathology to the interview. Intimacy necessitates a loss of pride, and most therapists are tempted by the adoration of their patients to build up more and more pride. It is not easy to say to the family, "We are in trouble," and then point out to them that it is partly your own fault. It is somewhat easier if you have already explained to them that any acting out is by implicit agreement. Further, it is difficult to limit the acting out that takes place outside the interview unless you are willing to formulate and present instructions that make the interview an isolated experience. The family's anxiety must be tied to the professional setting.

The breakup of acting out behavior is most easily accomplished when there is a continual imbalance between the therapist's acceptance of the parental role and the recurrent denial of it to the patient group. The therapist must be sure, however, that his affect to the patient has not become the center of his own world. He must always hold himself as his center. The breakup of acting-out behavior usually necessitates that the therapist lead in experimenting with the patient role. His humility may make him discover his own pathology and stimulate the patients to move toward similar insights. It is important that the therapist "confess" dishonesties which he uncovers. It is also helpful to present apparently irrelevant associations or fantasies which take place within the interview, or even fantasies which take place outside the interview.

It may not seem appropriate to bring a consultant into a situation this complex, but it is sometimes amazing what he can contribute. He may discover a split between the two therapists, so that one of them has become dependent and the other isolated. He may see some dynamic pattern in the family that is not apparent to the people who are by now so immersed that they cannot see the forest for the trees. Lastly, it seems to us increasingly clear that part of the freedom to grow will emerge in the patient when the therapeutic team is willing to "give up," that is, go beyond their delusion of grandeur. We are so tempted to assume that we can "do" therapy that whenever acting out takes place that we should suspect that this delusion is one of the dynamic features behind it.

CONCLUSION

Family psychotherapy seems to be almost the ultimate challenge for the therapist as well as his great opportunity to learn about people and to grow as a person. If being is becoming, then doing is a prize system to avoid being.

The awesome stress of this work creates a severe tendency to spill affect by acting it out. This avoidance of beingness by doing must be

countered in order that constructive anxiety can bring about the necessary change in the family and its members as well as in the therapists.

We have tried to describe patterns of acting out in the process of
family psychotherapy. We make apology for the fact that this formulation is incomplete since the subject matter is complex. Any discussion
of acting out in family psychotherapy resembles a discussion of the
dynamics of the therapeutic process. The dynamics of family psychotherapy are also incomplete.

THE SYMPTOMATIC ADOLESCENT— AN AWOL FAMILY MEMBER

This chapter demonstrates how far Whitaker had come in the 1970s toward a
family systems conceptualization of psychopathology. He uses the example
of the adolescent to demonstrate the importance of the family in the genesis
and amelioration of pathology, since the adolescent often seems little involved in the life of the family. The major point made herein is that a family
member's involvement in the family cannot be evaluated by knowing the
amount of time spent with family or by geographical proximity.

Family therapy offers the adolescent an opportunity to separate and
individuate from the family of origin rather than to merely physically escape
from it. For the parents it offers an opportunity to establish an adult-to-adult
relationship with their children as they separate. When an adolescent is
symptomatic, family therapy may be the only chance the family has to
successfully separate.

At the time of original publication, and even today, the treatment
offered to adolescents was most often individual psychotherapy. Although
Whitaker concedes that this therapy is often a fairly successful procedure, he
feels a more successful procedure would be to facilitate the adolescent's

Reprinted by permission from M. Sugar (Ed.), *The Adolescent in Group and Family
Therapy*. New York: Brunner/Mazel, 1975. Copyright © 1975 by Brunner/Mazel, Inc.

reentry into the family and then to develop a new autonomy from it. The symptomatic adolescent is considered a family dropout who needs first to rejoin the family.

Treatment of the adolescent is often considered to lie midway between play therapy for children and individual analytic treatment for adults. During the '50s adolescent psychotherapy was chaotic because we couldn't handle the adolescent's profound ambivalence: one moment he yearned to be dependent, and the next resented his dependence on the therapist. At a later moment, he'd fight for his independence and resent the therapist for not activating that freedom. However, by 1960, techniques of treating the adolescent with kid gloves had made individual treatment of the adolescent a fairly successful procedure. Therapists sophisticated in the use of psychotherapy could define the interpersonal distance the individual adolescent tolerated and thus leave him free to move closer as he needed intimacy and away as he needed separateness. Thus, neither the bind of all-out dependency nor the specter of rejection destroyed the therapeutic movement.

The transference–countertransference phenomena in the treatment of the 1970s adolescent, however, are uniquely complex. The contemporary therapist is stuck with not only the natural ambivalence but also the reality of the new cultural gap and its problems. The adolescent patient feels humiliated asking for help from an adult who belongs to the "establishment" and he is thereby uptight about being in therapy. He has also been conditioned by the peer group to believe that having any relationship to the older generation is disloyal to the group and denotes infantile hangups. However, his chance of getting help from his peers is also very restricted. Peers as social growth facilitators are empathetic only to a limited degree and only if the stress is in the direction of the accepted social role structure. Bitter anger at parents can be shared, but depression or strange behavior may be alienating. Creative therapists, however, have learned how to bridge the generation gap by their own therapeutic youth and by a capacity to hang loose in the therapeutic relationship. Some employ the music, the new language, and the mores of the teenage component of our society as a communication bridge.

During the World Congress of Psychiatry in Mexico in 1971, I was horrified to sit through a half-day of papers on treatment of adolescent patients with no consideration given to the use of family therapy. Transference resolution was apparently the only method accepted. May I suggest family therapy as a modality for the treatment of *every* adolescent patient?

Although the adolescent seeking treatment is obviously an individual and is clearly suffering from intrapsychic stress, that does not mean that the only methodology for treatment is individual therapy. Being a good physician does not mean putting salve on every wound and often individual treatment of the most concerned and expert quality is like a shot of morphine for the pain of appendicitis. It does not resolve the problem but makes the situation more serious by obscuring the systems component of the presenting symptom.

Freud's devotion to research on the adult and his intrapsychic stress has delayed our perception of the total context of individual stress. This is nowhere more evident than in treatment of the adolescent and his heartache. The usual symptomatic adolescent is an individual who has broken with his family in a precipitous, painful, and unsatisfactory manner. Both he and the family are bleeding from the wounds of this operation. Often dropping out at such an early emotional age results in a more profound dependence and unresolvable ambivalence in the escapee and in the family system as well. If you accept this conception, then the treatment of adolescents is really a reentry problem and a debriefing problem. The adolescent is really a family dropout who has not stayed through his senior year, the year in which he would gain preadult status and which is ended by a graduation ceremony. He needs to reenter the family system and separate to try life on his own. This then would not follow the divorce model referred to above, but make possible a group membership, free of enslavement on either side of the generation gap.

It has been hypothesized that one need not have stress during adolescence and that it is possible to leave the family in a ceremonial, constructive, and mutually satisfying manner. This was graphically expressed by an adult graduate student involved in couples therapy. She had spent a year in psychotherapy with her husband in an effort to prevent a legalized Siamese twin operation to divorce the two of them. The therapist remarked toward the end of therapy how good it would be to not have to see them anymore. She said, in surprise, "I wish to hell my father and mother had said that just once. I could have left without feeling so guilty." She did work through in the transference the reentry and graduation from this therapy family, but yearned to do the same with her family of origin. Needless to say, marital therapy is not a very economical system for reentering and graduating from the family of origin.

What are the indications and contraindications for family treatment? This author is convinced that there are no contraindications *if* the family is available and if the therapist is willing to struggle with the whole unit. This is probably true whether the identified patient is an adolescent or an adult but is certainly most obvious in the treatment of the adolescent. The family is *the* controlling agent in any adolescent's life—far out of proportion to time spent with them, and in spite of physical distance.

Although the family in treatment may include only adoptive or foster parents or may have only a mother in economic privation and battle fatigue from child-care, the family therapy must deal with the intrapsychic family who determines many of the dynamics of therapy. The alcoholic father who left 10 years before may be a most authentic ghost for the teenager and for his mother. The addition of the probation worker or the school counselor to the family therapy team may not only be helpful, but may also teach the parent figures a greater flexibility and the therapist new aspects of his professional job.

One adult of 45 years attempted suicide at the exact age his father did. A mother phones her married daughter in midweek and a single remark ruins the rest of the week. A daughter (of 35 years) acts out periodically in order to reconnect with her parents. These recurrent life stories emphasize the power of the family. Therapists, then, the cultural surrogates, must develop a method for filling the gap left by the decay of the traditional puberty rites that made the transition from childhood to adulthood a victory over dependence and an inauguration into the adult world (Flescher, 1968).

J. D. was a 19-year-old student who had been diagnosed as manic psychotic by a university inpatient service in a different city and put on Lithium and Stelazine. He had moved from city to city making repeated individual therapy contracts and then breaking them. He had stopped his Lithium, as well as other medications, and had stopped his psychotherapy. Finally one therapist asked for a conference with mother, father, and sister. In the middle of this 4-hour conference, he challenged the mother on her chaos and she then, for the first time, explained to her 19-year-old son about her 5 years of psychotherapy beginning when he was 3, and how she had lied to her own mother by saying that these appointments five times a week for 5 years were dental treatment. Father went on then to explain that it was not his life of pure scientific research that left no time or affect to relate to his son. It was really a life filled with nights of panic during those years when Mother was in psychotherapy and during J. D.'s recent mental hospital periods. Since J. D. was 8, Dad had been fighting to keep Mother's secret and to protect her from all stress, lest she become emotionally sick again. He was, of course, also trying to protect her from the shame of this confession. The son's response to this was startling. "So Dad, that's why you always raised hell with me whenever I tried to stand up for myself against Mother. I never knew before that you really gave a damn about me or Mother and I have never seen you cry before in my life. What a flip this is."

Episodes like this make one wonder whether there is much hope of resolving this kind of affective chaos by even long-term individual transference work. I am tempted to, but will not, quote Jim Framo, who says, "One hug from the mother is worth a thousand hugs from the therapist."

Bill's mother phoned from a nearby city. "It's my 18-year-old son. His therapist has given up after seeing him for 4 years and told me to call you." "Sorry, I only see families." "You mean you won't see him?" "I only see families." "All right, I'll come then." "What about Father?" "That's one of the problems. We're getting a divorce." "Sorry, better find somebody else." "Okay, I'll bring him." "Who do you live with now?" "My mother and father." "Bring them too." "That's crazy. They don't have anything to do with my son." "Sorry then, find somebody else." "Okay, I'll bring them." "How about your husband's parents?" "They live 500 miles away." "Well, have him call me if he can't get them to come." Everybody showed up except Father's mother who had a sudden attack of rheumatism. The conference was scheduled for 3 hours and as is my custom, I started asking Father's father my standard question, "What's going on in the family?" I then went to Mother's father, Mother's mother, than to Father, then to Mother. During a solid hour, I got nothing except the pseudomutual line, "All is fine. We're a close family. We don't understand why this boy became upset." Finally,

I got to the identified patient, "Listen, this whole family sounds crazy. Nobody can see past the end of his nose. Everybody thinks the family is perfect and yet you're accused of being crazy for 4 years." Bill, the diagnosed schizophrenic, then said, "Oh, I can tell you what's wrong. My father's father is the younger brother of my mother's mother and 'big sister' has been telling 'little brother' what to do ever since she was 5. I'm the victim of a three-generation family war, and all my life I have been trained to be a Hasidic scholar and I don't know how to get out of the corner I'm in."

Part of his difficulty was the usual child and adolescent dedication to helping the parents make a better life. It's hard to know how much of his emotional distress was psychological and how much familial, but it seems fairly clear that individual psychotherapy was not going to do much to this three-generational imprint. The identified patient was a victim of a war between forces much greater than he himself could control.

Sue was 20 and quite clearly suffering from a psychotic break. The family was called in, including three married siblings, all of whom lived in a neighboring state. Mother and Father gave the story of a close, friendly, warm family. Everybody got along well together and nobody had any idea why Sue was upset. After a half-hour of this one of the adult sisters said, "Dad, I don't understand why you go on like this. Sue doesn't know anything about her own family. Mother was in a mental hospital for 6 months, I've been in psychotherapy for 3 years. My sister's been in psychotherapy for 4 years and she's still in treatment. My brother has just begun. Why don't you tell the doctor?" With this type of programmed family secret, how could Sue expect to grow? The honesty of an intimate, loving family with open communication was unknown. The family consultation thus enabled Sue to get some sense that she was not the black sheep of the family and allowed Mother and Father to at least have the honor of facing life the way it was and of expressing their anxiety and concern in some better way than by hiding it.

The identified patient is many times only the top of the iceberg and the symptom that brings one patient to the therapist may well represent a state of family chaos which should be treated as a whole family pattern of pain and distress. The family symptom may be intrapsychic to one scapegoat or several. It may be concurrent in several family members or appear in a serial progression. The system controls the functions of its component members. Therapy often changes the components but still need not alter the system itself (Whitaker & Miller, 1969).

Bill brought his wife to the therapist because she was a serious alcoholic. It was revealed two interviews later that Bill also collects art prints. He has 35,000 prints piled in various places in their small house. Some weeks later their pompous, effeminate 10-year-old, who quite dominated the family, was discovered to be suffering from a school phobia. The school counselor was invited into the therapy then and 2 weeks later he discovered that, for the past 6 months, the 17-year-old son had been leaving as though for school each morning on schedule but had never shown up at school. The school had never registered him. The family seemed such a caricature that I suggested to the 15-year-old son that the least he could do would be to steal a car so he could belong to the family. That broke the family into a freedom to laugh at themselves. What if I had tried to treat the 10-year-old in individual therapy for the school phobia, or Mother for her alcoholism, or Father for his compulsive collecting? Any one of them could have been in individual therapy for years.

If an adolescent leaves his family in a self-induced puberty ceremony of rebellion, if he breaks with the family without some group resolution of the problems of the symbiosis among them, if he leaves without joining in an overt family effort to resolve his desertion— rather than by a therapeutic effort to relieve the individual and group stress—he is stuck with guilt and not free to instigate a new and creative life. He may then be compelled to reconstruct the old family again, to work out that senior year and that graduation ceremony at work, at play, or in his marriage.

Why does individual therapy work at all? Many times it seems individual therapy works because this patient and this therapist and their transference power are enough so that the patient can change the dynamics of his entire family. It may even be that the effects of individual therapy are only lasting if family change is possible. If one-to-one therapy is not powerful enough to change the family, then individual treatment fails to individuate the patient or to help him break with his family of origin. Such failure also establishes a wall between the patient and his family.

If the individual therapy transference relationship as a symbolic illusion becomes defined as the only acceptable pattern for parent–child relationships, then, of course, the actual family of origin can never live up to that all-loving delusion. The patient then tends to establish geographic or psychological distance and to maintain the illusion of adulthood while he carries on a covert effort to return to his momma for the graduation ceremony that never happened, or he develops other relationships which are substitutes for the family. The most conspicuous of these, of course, is marriage.

Family conferences may also serve as a basis for useful interaction with the disturbed teenagers. Not all that is useful is symbolic.

Mary, a 17-year-old freshman in college, was 3 months into family treatment after referral due to "loss of ego boundaries." Sunday at 7:00 A.M. she phoned the author. "Dr. W., my father won't let me do anything. Wouldn't let me do my thing. I wanted popcorn last night and I didn't have any at my apartment so I came home to make it. I stayed overnight and this morning they won't leave me alone. They keep coming after me." Therapist, "You came after them last night. Why don't you go back to your apartment?" "Hey, that's a good idea. I just will do that. Say, another thing, will you teach me how to be real?" "I'll try." "Okay, thanks. Goodbye."

It's pretty clear that the next time the family gets together there is going to be a pretty good-sized family fight. Since closeness and separation between adolescents and the family group increase point and counterpoint, the sense of we-ness and individuation for Mary and her family and its five individual members will increase slightly because Mary, first, ached for love enough to go home for popcorn and, then, dared her loneliness enough to leave the family next morning for her apartment. Could the same little jiggle from the therapist have had the same effect in individual therapy? Probably, but I'll bet the change would be more liable to neutralization by family interaction during the subsequent days. When Mary reentered the family scene on her own that night, she set up a rebirth prototype for that final freedom to establish a new family without living either a lifetime of hate for her parents or of triangular chaos between her spouse-to-be and her parents. The therapist had established a new triangle, so that Mary was not tied to her two parents as individuals, but to the new triangle of parents, Mary and therapist. The therapist thus could push Mary into the family and out of it. The new puberty ceremony could be repeated until it yielded mobility for both Mary and the parents (Zuk, 1969).

Jim was an 18-year-old who had attempted suicide—almost success-fully—by carbon monoxide in his closed garage. He was seen 3 days later with his parents, his older sister, and his younger brother in a family conference on the closed inpatient ward. The resident sum-marized current contacts: the boy had been aloof on the ward, obvi-ously not only very depressed, but also pretty disorganized in his thinking and quite unable to talk about his family relationships or the basis for his suicide attempt.

In the family interview, once Dad and Mother and two kids had tried to define the characteristic living pattern of the family, the patient was asked, "Who in the family wants you dead?" "Nobody." "There must be somebody. Nobody attempts suicide except as a two-person event." "Maybe my dad. He gets awfully mad at the way I treat Mother." "How about that, Dad? You think things would be better around the house if your son was dead?" The family, of course, was horrified. Father protested but after a bit the older sister said she could understand why I asked the question. She also expressed a feeling that maybe her brother's statement was partly true. Therapist to Jim, "Hey, what if you had succeeded? Suppose you had really made it. How long would Dad grieve?" He hesitated a moment and then said, "Two weeks." "How long would Mother grieve?" "Two months." "How about your brother?" "Quite a while." "How about your sister?" "As long as she lives." "What kind of a funeral would they give you?" "I don't know." "Would it be a fancy casket with lots of flowers and lots of people?" "I suppose so." "What would they do with your clothes?" "I don't know. Maybe they'd give them to my brother." "What about your girl's picture and the other things of your own?" "They'd prob-ably burn them all." "What about your room?" "I don't know." "Would you want to be buried in the family plot?" "I guess so." "Would your girlfriend come to the funeral?" "Probably not." "You mean she already has another boyfriend?" "I suppose so."

This kind of investigation into the family dynamics of hostility and the direct deliberate contamination of the intrapsychic fantasy of "they'll be sorry when I'm dead and gone" are techniques of family methodology which certainly would be hard to replicate in individual therapy. The fact that Mother and Father and siblings are present during the fantasy gives it a quality of reality and probably serves as a pretty good immunization against future suicide episodes. The activation of Jim's perception of Father's hostility and the direct presentation of his cynicism about Mother and one of the siblings will certainly change the overt, and maybe even the covert, dynamics in future family contacts. The therapist is making direct efforts to pull the son back into the family so that they can all work through the final separation process and he can leave constructively rather than by way of the graveyard.

The middle-class family may ask for help. The lower-class family is usually forced to seek help by society, that is, the school or the police. Such a family may not be available for insight therapy. The therapist may be able to reverse the motion toward a family dropout problem by direct manipulation of the family dynamic pattern.

Bill, 11, was adored by 9-year-old Mike. Father's indifference to the two of them was only equaled by mother's tearful whining. Mother, "Bill has been completely out of my control since he was 8. That was a terrible year. My mother died, you know—she did live with us." Therapist, "Dad, can you control Bill?" Father, "I leave the children to Mother. They never bother me." Therapist, "Mother, did you ever wonder if he's winking at the boys and sort of laughing at your suffering?" Mother, "Well, we've had a rough time too. Sometimes he acts like he hates me." Therapist, "Did he hate your mother?" Mother, "Yes, they fought all the time." Therapist, "And now you're the mother so he's fighting a cold war with you through the kids. Maybe if you decided to be the mother you could take over with the kids." Bill, "If she fights us Dad'll slap her face like he did Grandma's." Mother, "Shut up, Bill. Your father has never raised a hand to me and he'd better not either." Bill, "Shut your damned face, Maw." Suddenly Father's hand flipped. The back of it bounced off Bill's nose. "I don't like your talking to Maw that way." Tears flowed—of relief in mother's eyes—of consternation in Bill's. His moment of terror ended the interview. The flight into health was more gradual but the direction was set.

T.J., 35, decided to send his wife, also 35, to see a psychiatrist. The therapist insisted that he also come for the initial interview. The story of their 13 years of fight training was filled with ghosts of near-tragedy and bittersweet yen for revenge. When planning for the second meeting the therapist insisted that they bring the four children. This seemed senseless to the parents but they accepted the mandate. The children were a surprise—gentle, verbal, outgoing, and congenial with each other, the parents, and the two therapists. The parents opened up the third or report interview by demanding, "So what was the use of having the kids in?" The therapist replied, "That was the clincher in this evaluation. You folks can keep on talking about your pain but never again can you make us wonder if your pain is covering serious pathology." These parents in the initial contact appeared to be adults with serious pathology. Seeing the children made clear that the problem was a family problem. Subsequent three-generation conferences clarified the symbiotic quality of the tie between Mrs. T.J. and her parents which had been the undercover basis for their years of horror. Disruption of the adolescent rebellion between mother and grandmother enabled Mr. and Mrs. T.J. to develop a peer relationship that was nonsymbiotic.

These 35-year-old adolescents had never broken with the family feud of their parents. Yet, somehow the third generation seemed to have escaped without gross distortion. How could that be? Was the complementary character structure nourishing? Did the desperate dependence of the grandparents keep the parents from traumatizing the children? We can only theorize about what is taking place, but we do recognize the value of working with as much of the family system as can be pulled together into the reorganization process.

USING A PSEUDOFAMILY

Since the family is not always available, one may be forced to work with a pseudofamily. The peer mates many times offer a friendship network which has many similarities to the family of origin. Just as in marriage, there are both a projected intrapsychic family scene on the part of each person and a defined role.

Mike was referred by his parents from a distant city. They said he had come home after being sent by his colleagues following an attempt at suicide by carbon monoxide. The author saw the patient and his family for the initial interview. The family then went back 1000 miles to their home with the understanding that Mike would be seen with his "pad." The pad consisted of six boys and one girl; the girl seemed more directly related to Sam although all assumed she was really just one of the group. When it was pointed out that one of the members had attempted suicide and they were partially responsible for this near-tragedy, they showed considerable concern and some sense of responsibility. The evidence of their family quality included the fact that they had lived in the same rooms for 2½ years. Sam was the only one who did any cooking. He cooked two meals a week. He turned out to be bitterly angry at the fact that in the whole 2½ years, no one had ever offered to wash the dishes, even once.

It was clear to this group that Mike had drifted away from them and that they had been irritated by his walking through the group and going down to the cellar to play his guitar for 4 hours. It was equally clear that their bitterness with him was one of the things which precipitated his attempting to take his life. As a matter of fact, they were so angry at him and at each other that they were unwilling to go along with the offer to participate in family therapy. The author's failure to induce them to go on with family therapy made the subsequent individual treatment much less effective, since the dynamics of the group were partly responsible for the stress that precipitated the suicide attempt.

It may be possible to construct a surrogate family from living associates of the identified patient—a ghetto school class or the neighborhood primary interest group makes therapy a social group process. The addition of social workers or recreation workers may help expand the conference to include the disconnected family who will always be crucial to success.

Current psychotherapy of adolescents is frequently based on the concept that the family should be a resource for the adolescent. The therapist's problem then would be to increase the lovingness, increase the availability, increase the denial of self within the family group so that the adolescent can fill his emotional needs before he leaves. I contend that this effort is a mistake. The family members also have a right to their living process; they have a right to group loyalty, as well as individual initiative and liberation. There is no reason why they should be subjugated to the rebellious defiance of the teenager. The family needs the therapist's support to be hostile and to be loving.

They must demand the right to be a group and the right to be individuals. This should be the by-product of a good experience in family therapy. It helps the scapegoat reenter his family of origin, complete his individuation in coordination with other family members, and graduate with honors.

POWER POLITICS
OF FAMILY PSYCHOTHERAPY

In this chapter Whitaker examines the beginning of the psychotherapy process, a process that he describes as "political." Since the family therapist is not able to rely upon the minimal transference relationship established in family therapy, he must establish a therapeutic relationship through the use of what Whitaker terms "power tactics." Whitaker's early professional experience with the treatment of psychotic patients is the model he uses for the development of rules to guide the therapist's early moves in the therapeutic process.

It is postulated that the standard paradigm for psychotherapy, a cooperative transference neurosis, does not validly carry over to the successful psychotherapy of a two-generation family group. Just as the passive development of a transference neurosis does not function for the psychotherapy of the psychotic, so this model is not successful in the treatment of disturbed families. In the treatment of a psychotic individual a bilateral transference seems to emerge through a gradual, intensive, interpersonal give-and-take, which is similar to that between the mother and the very young child. It is postulated that in many disturbed families the necessary and sufficient dynamics for change must be initiated, controlled, and augmented by a group dynamic power play, precipitated by the psychotherapist. Indeed, the therapist, or better still, the therapeutic team, will be wise to regard the beginning of psychotherapy as a political process quite similar to that in the opening phase of a chess game. There is evidence that dominating the center of action, protecting the king at all costs, saving the all-powerful queen until midgame, and positioning the group members to protect each other are part of a valuable metaphor for understanding the success and failure of family psychotherapy.

ESTABLISHING A THERAPEUTIC RELATIONSHIP

There are three central patterns for establishing a therapeutic relationship—the neurotic pattern of transference neurosis described by Freud, for example.

"Doctor, I'm so glad you could see me; I've been so upset. I've been married for 5 years and I just became convinced yesterday that somewhere inside of me I hate my husband and he's the man I loved so much and have lived with all these years. How can I hate him?"

The patient comes with almost a free-form transference; her own doubt is pushing her to dependency and the therapist is obviously her symbolic parent almost on first touch.

The schizophrenic patient:

This patient does not establish an easy symbolic transference; his essential characteristic is to turn his back on people, to stay away from them, and be suspicious of them. Conversation could go like this:

PATIENT: (*says no word for the entire hour*)
DOCTOR: I intend to come back to your room every day, just like I came yesterday and the day before and, whether you like it or not, I intend to stay a whole hour. By the way, you just missed me that time; if you really spit in my face, I'll probably spit right back in yours. And if you slap me, I'll pull your hair just like I did yesterday, and I'll pound on your back anytime I want to, just like I did the day before. I thought that was good fun; I got some good exercise and I hope it made your muscles feel better. The way you sit there, silent like that all day long, just makes me want to push you around. Don't forget, if you slug me, I don't know what I'll do; I might turn you over my knee and paddle your behind, like I would any little 3-year-old who took a slug at me. And if you kick me, I don't know; I might just turn you over and

kick your behind. And I don't really know what I'll do if you kiss me. If you walk out on me, we're going to have a big problem; I probably won't let you go or I might start a fight with you so that you couldn't get out the door. And by the way, you don't snap your magic finger at me like that because if I snap mine back, it'll kill you just like that one killed me. And here I am, still alive.

PATIENT: (*still says nothing*)

Family psychotherapy is uniquely like the treatment of a psychotic; it is not possible to depend upon the minimal transference that the family announces by virtue of their arrival and their social chit chat. Even an honest family history does not mean that the family cares for you, trusts you, or will respond to you and your efforts to help them change. They are much more like the psychotic patient; their unity is reinforced by excluding the rest of the world and they can exclude you in the same way or if need be they can incorporate you just as easily.

Don Jackson found that the homeostasis of the disturbed family is greatly increased over even the normal family and, therefore, it's necessary for the therapist to mobilize great power in order to bring about any change in this situation. We call this early phase the battle for structure. The therapeutic team must become the new rule-maker in a family dedicated to confusion or the family will undermine his efforts to help them change. The first rule the therapist should make is that there is a generation gap between him and the family. He can model for the parents how to take control of a situation and construct a model in relating to the parents so that the children will sense the security of depending on a benign power.

EXAMPLE 1

"Jim, you and I have taken on a big problem working with this family. Dad's such a workhorse, he's apt to get an ulcer. Mother has herself become a nonperson in her devotion to the kids and the kids haven't any sense of their parents as people or really as parents other than as Mr. Pocketbook and Mrs. Cook. I'm also worried that things will get worse if we try to push them toward loving each other and being real persons."

He also models for that system a generation gap struggle, that is, the struggle that goes on between the therapist and the family. He may also model for the parents via the cooperation that takes place in their experience of the relating between him and his cotherapist.

Not only must the therapist take control of the situation in the real sense of deciding who shall come to the interview and who shall initiate the family history, but he must also structure the situation so that he shall be free to change those rules at any time. That is, the second rule shall be, "I will decide how things will go during this therapeutic hour."

EXAMPLE 2
"Dad, will you change seats with Mary," and, "Mother, I'd like you to listen. I want to hear John's story about your fight with Dad last night."

The third rule is, "The family must carry the initiative for the therapeutic group process." That is, the family must be the ones to decide how they can tolerate exposing and involving themselves, how much anxiety they can tolerate, and what areas they dare expose in the early stages of treatment. Once this initiative has been accepted the therapist may participate, but should be careful not to weaken it.

EXAMPLE 3
"Here it is, the third conference and nobody has gotten the courage to start us off. I'll bet I can wait longer than you can, especially since I've not really learned to care enough about you to worry lest we fail and the family repeats the old pattern again and again."

The fourth rule is that each family member must take an equal share in the family anxiety. The therapist should not tolerate the scapegoat carrying all the anxiety. The scapegoat must be relieved of his abnormal burden and each family member must share equally the anxiety and pain. The best plan may be to aid the formation of a rotating scapegoat paradigm.

EXAMPLE 4
"We started with Mother's alcoholism. She gets one point for that. Now we've uncovered Dad's gruesome collecting disease, so he gets two points; John's revealed his school phobia and bared Henry's delinquency. Mary, do you plan to destroy yourself by being the family heroine and the nurse to every patient in the entire hospital?"

The fifth rule is that the family shall live their outside life in any way they like; only the therapeutic process will be under the control of the therapist.

EXAMPLE 5

"Should you get a divorce? I plan to stay married, so why don't you do what you want to."

The sixth rule is that the therapist is free to separate himself at any time from the therapeutic anxiety and without any excuse.

EXAMPLE 6

"What do I think about what you were telling? I wasn't listening. I was having a fantasy about the genoa [a sail] for my sailboat."

The seventh rule is that the therapist is deliberately functioning to maximize the crisis and to augment the insecurity of the family group.

EXAMPLE 7

"Jim, if Mary tried to kill herself because she sensed you'd like her dead, do you suspect that if the gang of us help her, she might convert to trying to kill you?"

The therapist, of course, bears the responsibility for balancing the stress of this surgical move by the anesthesia of his own personal involvement and his personal caring about the family. But he must decide how much pain he is going to induce, how much bleeding he is going to create, and he should not use a democratic process for mobilizing the family's anxiety to force them to change.

EXAMPLE 8

"Folks, this is Dr. X. Dr. X., I asked you here because I'm bored with this family. Dad insists all is fine. Mother can't get beyond her depression and the children all take the fifth amendment, except Joe, who almost succeeded in killing himself 3 weeks ago. Maybe they think he has bad genes. Help me learn to care for them so I can be tougher."

Perhaps the most painful experiences of my professional life are those times when the rigidity and solidity of the family leave me utterly impotent. Inside I vary from an impulse to scream in rage at their mistreatment of the scapegoat or a terrible sadness often joined with some somatic symptom or a flight into goal-directed fantasy. One such family pushed me to dream up a people-sized disposal. Lately I've tried to develop the freedom to superimpose my emotionally loaded caring onto their shoulders. I try not to hide any of my despair and try to avoid at all costs that casual bedside manner support which leaves the family untouched and the therapist with a colder heart and less courage to care next time.

EXAMPLE 9

"Well, it's been a dismal hour. Your therapist has worked hard to help you change but to no avail. He even asked for this consultation to see if he was too blind or too feeble and failed you in that way. I'm convinced that I can't help either. It looks hopeless. I guess it'll just stay this way for 10 more years. Maybe this is the best you can do and that's all right, even though it is discouraging. I doubt if it will get worse and that's some consolation."

The backlash from such an encounter may ruin my day or my digestion or my sleep. I hope it will also give them bad dreams or the conviction that they have an enemy. Declaring war against me may pull the country together and a united family can do anything. I've had several follow-up reports where this has been effective. I assume that often it doesn't work but it helps to maintain my integrity which I regard as the essential tool in my growth and perhaps the most important catalyst for their unification.

SYMBOLIC SEX IN FAMILY THERAPY[13]

The process of all therapy, whether individual or family, has always been considered by Whitaker as a countercultural activity. One of the ways in which this is true is that it is free from the usual taboos of polite interaction. In particular, the therapist invades the family taboo structure in relation to violence and sexuality.

Reprinted by permission from P. Sholevar (Ed.), *Changing Sexual Values and the Family*. Springfield, Ill.: Charles C Thomas, 1977. Copyright © 1977 by Charles C Thomas Publisher.

Whitaker makes the point repeatedly in this chapter that the therapist can and should discuss—and initiate discussion—about all the unconscious fantasies of the family members *if* the therapist does so in a caring and personally concerned way. The therapist's openness and willingness to accept any and all feelings serves to increase the family members' flexibility in role function. Whitaker offers a style of therapist behavior that he uses to discuss sex and violence with children and families of all levels of openness.

In the process of family psychotherapy organized toward a flexibility in family role function and role expectations with the premise that the greatest flexibility of role structure defines a healthy family, the basic taboo in most families is that of violence. As a way to build toward work in the area of violence it is highly useful to wander around in the family dynamic patterns, hopefully, in your bare feet, so as to increase the sensual thermostat to make more feasible the warmth and sensual experience the family have with each other. This necessitates an implicit, or maybe an explicit, contract with the family that what happens in the therapeutic setting is free of the usual taboos and that in the exploration of sexual and sensual territory one is dealing in a kind of pilot plant or pilot project for the family's living with each other. The most obvious thing is to define early who in the family are heaters and who are coolers. In each family there are role structures which mean that certain people are assigned the role of warming the family and certain others the role of cooling it. Usually the most warmth is in the youngest and cooling process is frequently divided between father and mother. He bases his on reality and she bases hers on morality.

For the therapist to invade the taboo structure of the family he must first become personally related so that he has an understructure of caring and so that his movement within the family sculpturing and the family role assignments is received as either amusing or tender or experimental. It must be set so that it is not binding. If the therapist's movement becomes binding on the family there is no alternative but opposing it. Thus the therapist must be willing and able to withdraw all of his moods if it seems that they are too painful. One of the most obvious things is the use of a pattern of double-talk and this can move back and forth from double-talk about life to double-talk about the household to double-talk about sexual excitation, cuddling, playfulness, or childishness. It is important for the therapist and the family to see this as a valid structure, although awareness is not necessary and sometimes may be harmful. Nevertheless, the socializing process is exaggerated in the bosom of the family and further augmented by the incestuous taboos attached. It's important to recognize that as Esselin says, "Direct input frequently only produces recognition. Real learning comes from indirect communication." Therefore the therapist is well advised to not talk straight, to stay obtuse and overt. Double-talk is an asset, not a problem. Double-talk can be, of course, done in many different ways. One can use upside-down talk so he says the opposite of what he means and couches it in such a coy manner that everybody knows what's behind it, or he can express the other half by his disbelief either in tone or in the quality of the sentence structure. The tone of the voice can convey the message, "This is a put-on," so that the patient and family members recognize the tongue-in-cheek quality and with some families it's possible to set up an ongoing communication code with this double-talk.

It's important to state also that there is no danger in the chidren being part of family discussions of any character. It's my conviction that they can tolerate discussion of murder, suicide, divorce, infidelity, incest, and so forth with no traumatic repercussions *if* the therapist is caring and personally concerned with the set in the family and if he is trying to be helpful rather than pornographic.

It's perfectly possible to say to the wife of a husband who's been unfaithful, "Have you ever thought of competing with him? You might even go into the business and offer him a chance to be Number One customer at double rates." Such undercover talk escapes no one and yet fulfills the basic role that the therapist should not demand confirmation, agreement, or structure a war between himself and the family. The possibilities of "sexual symbolic carrying on" are almost infinite. For example, father sits by daughter Jane, who is 13; mother sits by son Jim, who is 16, and the therapist says part way along in the interview, "Jim, when did you get out of the double bed and did Jane replace you at once? Or was there a time when Mother and Father cuddled up to each other?" "I asked because I wanted to see if you'd ever let her out or would she have to stay home as an old maid for the rest of her life 'to keep you folks apart' or go crazy. After all, she's 13; it'll only be 3 or 4 years before she has her first affair or gets married or has a sex-change operation." One of the obvious ways to increase the sensual freedom and openness of the family is to carry on a tongue-in-cheek flirtation, sometimes with one of the little children, sometimes with grandmother, sometimes with mother or, more coyly, with dad or one of the boys. To make this even more useful, it's helpful to get permission from the spouse; for example, one can say, "Dad, do you mind if I have a little affair with your wife during this hour? I have the feeling she's been making eyes at me and it's good fun and I'd like to retaliate in kind but I don't want you beating me up." Father, in this way, is put in a corner. He can't say no and it does accentuate the triangular potential of the therapeutic situation in the same way that you can say to Mother, "I hope you don't mind us boys talking about fishing or about baseball. We really don't ask you to sit quietly too long." I remember one family in which the 70-year-old grandmother came with her hair fixed and I said at the end of the hour, "Grandma, you'd better not come back next time without the rest of the family. After all, abortions are still very expensive." In a strange way, this kind of innuendo is known to be silly and yet the fact that you thought of it makes it a compliment and makes it open the family for more fun with sex.

In the realm of double-talk and innuendo it's very possible either when you see a broken family in a "divorce setting" or a family in which father is dead, to deliberately train the kids to pimp for mother. One can start out by talking about how lonely it must be for her sleeping alone and counter the kids saying that they sleep with her by suggesting that that's not the same as Daddy and why don't they help her find a new daddy? The usual pattern of wife suffering no personal life for the sake of the children and the children trying to fulfil the role of the father in protection of their mother needs to be attacked and it can be done openly or with tongue in cheek.

Screwed-up families don't talk about screwing, but it's not difficult if you start the conversation to talk about sex using allusion rather than direct street talk. It's not hard to ask Mother if Daddy is warmer these days than he was before or has it cooled off between them. Was their life together fun last night? Do they dream of being married to somebody else? Do they believe that Daddy would like to be married to somebody else? Does he have someone in mind?—and so forth.

It's also possible to talk, again somewhat with tongue in cheek, of "Does anybody in the family have plans to be raped?" It looks as though one of the other entrees to a discussion of the affective component in marriage is to talk about the horrors of a husband and wife really falling in love with each other; being married and having children and sleeping together is bad enough, whereas if you fall in love you're vulnerable for the rest of your life. One of the other ways of getting at the process of sexual interaction in the family is to refer offhandedly to illegitimate pregnancy or allude to some covert sense on father or mother's part that one of their kids is being delinquent and flip the situation by saying, "So what's VD? A bad cold is a bad cold." It's also possible to get at the sexual component in the marriage by talking through one of the children. For example, we say to the 9-year-old when the whole family is assembled, "Have you ever thought that when Mother's so angry at Dad for being late 2 hours, she thinks he's dating his secretary?" The 9-year-old says no and you're free to back out, but mother and father are left with their fantasy and they come back later with some relevant discussion.

In discussing the pattern of the family structure one can get into the sensual or sexual thermostat, defining for the couple the fact that one of them has to be the heater and the other one the cooler but that it's very permissible to reverse roles, either gradually over a period of time or in a particular evening or even within the hour. This kind of role reversal can take place in the middle of a couple's fight so that one minute he's attacking and she's silent and a short time later the roles are reversed so that the roles can be reversed sexually and they should feel free to do this at a moment's notice.

One can take up with the family also the restructuring of the Oedipal pattern suggesting that the couple could plan to stay married by living close, that is, back to back, and all it takes is another cooperative couple to have sexual relations back to back, and of course if one doesn't include sex the cooperative couple can be the son or daughter or even, more appropriately and implicitly, his secretary can be his other mate and her children can be her other mate, or his mother can be his second spouse and her father can be her second spouse, or it can even be more coy; he can use his golf partners to form his second coupling process and she can use her bridge partners or her League of Women Voters group as her copartners.

At times one of them can use the psychotherapist of his individual therapy experiences as a second mate or he can have an affair with his love of money. The symbolic aspects of sex can be augmented in family discussion by converting the Oedipal triangle into the David and Goliath myth that in those families where the one spouse takes on the role of the Goliath, the other spouse, of course, can form a coalition with the child and gradually the child can learn to be the David that kills Goliath. This can be symbolic killing in the sense of the teenage daughter becoming a sexual delinquent as a way of punishing mother or father at the behest of the partner, of course, or it can be in much more realistic terms and one child can be brought up—a son for example—to hate his father with such bitterness that he eventually gets to the stage of physically beating up on father when father is mean to mother. One can expand the relationship of sex and aggression by getting into the problem of multiple affairs and the family expectations associated if a couple having sensed that their relationship is cooling decide to precipitate an affair, which is kind of an amateur way of getting into psychotherapy. Then they have to decide by multiple cues arising out of their conversation over a newspaper article or some rumor in the neighborhood which one is going to have the affair and then when that one capitulates, the other one, of course, will increase the temperature by having a fight about it. For example, if it's agreed that he will have the affair and that he will then find a way of exposing himself to her, then she feels free to hate him and he is guilty and then she can have the fun of forgiving him time after time, as a wife does to a chronic alcoholic. This may even go so far as O'Neill has demonstrated in *The Iceman Cometh* when the alcoholic comes back to the bar and says to his friends, "Well, I finally did it." They asked, "Did what?" "I killed my wife. She forgave me once too often."

The most important component in all of this discussion of the sexual aggressive combines in the marriage state is the recognition that the system is in control, that the plans are jointly laid by the couple and that the person who activates them is doing so under contract and by carefully agreed-upon plans. Fighting, like sex, is a gradually escalating contract with careful arrangements established between them on implicit and covert communication patterns. The best example of this, of course, is *Who's Afraid of Virginia Woolf*, as beautifully described and portrayed by Watzlawick, Beavin, and Jackson in *The Pragmatics of Human Communication*.[14]

PROCESS TECHNIQUES OF FAMILY THERAPY

with the collaboration of Augustus Y. Napier

This material, we feel, marks the beginning of a new phase in Whitaker's clinical maturity. Whereas in previous work he has dealt primarily with one or two facets of family psychotherapy, here he integrates most of his previous ideas into a single fabric. It is united by the idea of the unfolding process of clinical work with a family, an integration that Whitaker had conceptually made long before, but had not articulated clearly in his writings.

Whitaker discusses each phase of family process: pretreatment, battle for structure, battle for initiative, midphase or core phase, and termination, in terms of both family and therapist behavior. In addition, he offers the reader specific techniques for use during each phase and warns about the common pitfalls and resistances that can disrupt the treatment process. This is a chapter filled with the common sense approach of an experienced therapist rather than a theory-generated set of guidelines. Whitaker offers the reader a blueprint for guiding the therapist through the phases of family treatment. The techniques and strategies he suggests, however, are not so clearly described that they will obstruct a therapist's creativity.

He suggests strongly that family therapists utilize the "meta" techniques and structures of cotherapy, extended family sessions, and consultation. These procedures, he feels, maximize the power and impact of the therapy, increase the likelihood that the therapist will remain involved, and minimize the risks of countertransference.

INTRODUCTION

Family therapy is a fairly new field, although the study of the family and involvement with the family is probably older than the oldest profession. Discussion of techniques of family therapy at this stage of

Reprinted from *Interaction*, 1977, *1* (1), 4–19.

its development assumes a comprehensive understanding of the field and enough experience so that discussion of techniques is not a survey of gimmicks. It likewise implies a definition of techniques and a definition of family therapy. Otherwise, this chapter would resemble the man who asked his friend if he could play the violin. The friend replied, "I don't know. I've never tried." Family therapy techniques aim to activate change in the relationships within the family and between the family and the therapist or team of therapists. (I shall use the term therapist but assume that in family therapy, the presence of a cotherapist is preferable.)

I regard the "family" as that group of people who live together. It may mean the biological nuclear family but many times such a unit is not available or certain members are missing or replaced by say a stepmother or an adopted child. This may alter the process but is not crucial to our discussion of the subject at issue.

Since psychotherapy has as its objective change toward a different state of being-in-the-world, perhaps we should define a healthy family. A healthy family is one that maintains a high degree of inner unity and a high degree of individuation. It simultaneously fosters a freedom for regrouping and a relative freedom for the development of subgroups and triangles and teams and the functioning of mediators. This includes the freedom to leave and return without family dissension and a comfort in belonging to intimate subgroups outside the family and, on occasion, including outside intimates in the family. Involved in the definition also is the assumption that individuating in a healthy family makes possible such mobility that any member can function in any role. The 4-year-old son can "mother" his own father; the 40-year-old mother can be a little girl to her son or her daughter and this flexibility is available in response to a situation and the impulse or creative moment taking place within the family.

I also assume that the nuclear family is related to and dynamically involved with an extended family and a friendship network. I shall not discuss the techniques of working with these other units although I think of them both as valuable and the extended family as particularly helpful in family therapy.

Crucial to my freedom to discuss techniques is an assumption that just as love is not enough, even more obviously, techniques are not enough. A famous artist once was asked what was more important—

the expression of himself on canvas or his expertise in technical painting skills. He promptly blew his top. He yelled, "Neither and both!" Surely the objective of technique is the development of such a maturity that the therapist is beyond "using" techniques.

Soren Kierkegaard says there are three kinds of despair.

1. The despair of not being a person.
2. The despair of becoming a person.
3. The despair of being a person.

Just so, the therapist can do family therapy without being a person and while he is becoming a person. Then, as he continues growing through experience and the gradual development of new techniques, there will come a time when he will be a family therapist without having to use techniques. He does family therapy by being a person. I wonder if I'll even make it?

CONCEPTIONAL STANCE: A DIALECTIC

All psychotherapy is, to some degree, but family therapy is particularly responsive to the hidden agenda in the therapist's life. Is he growing as a person? Is he increasingly intimate within his own family? Such contaminants can be glossed over in individual therapy, but must be made explicit when therapists interact with a family. His agenda may include, for example, the following.

CRISIS INTERVENTION VERSUS THE GROWTH OF THE FAMILY

One can deal with the family on an administrative level by utilizing medication, by manipulative intervention in the social structure of the family and its environment, or by accelerating the family crisis into such a state of acting out that the family does resolve the stress and goes on living in the same old style. Therapists must decide for themselves and with each individual family whether they will work on the level of such intervention for symptom relief or whether they would prefer to invest the time and struggle to demand the maximal growth of the family in all the dimensions available.

THE THERAPIST AS A FUNCTION VERSUS THE GROWTH OF THE THERAPIST HIMSELF

Implicit in what happens in family therapy is the question of whether the therapist is simply doing a job, or whether he is *becoming* and dares to utilize his work with the family as a means to this end. The difference this philosophical stance makes is obviously profound. Studies have shown that therapists function best when they are between 30 and 40. I assume this describes the therapist who has dedicated himself to learning the job of being an MD, an MSW, or a PhD. Then in later years, like in sex, his technical expertise does less to excite his personal involvement with the family. In contrast to this, one old man I know assumes that if he maintains an orientation around his own growth, his psychotherapy will also become continually more exciting. He will not fade away like the old soldier, but will continue to expand. Thus, technique plus personal involvement makes for continuing growth: not technical, not professional, but personal. There is no steady state. One must either grow or shrivel!

PERSONAL INVOLVEMENT VERSUS COMMUNICATION TRAINING

It seems to this therapist that the process of communication training is a process of doing and as such may be valuable as a late stage fringe benefit in psychotherapy, but cannot be a substitute for the therapist being a person or for his being personally involved in the psychotherapy. As Plato so nicely put it when he talked to that father, "I cannot teach your son because after being with me for a year, he doesn't love me"; that is, Plato didn't love the son. I think the psychotherapist is in the same position. If there is no involvement on the part of the therapist, there is no real learning and when teaching is effective it comes late in therapy after a meaningful existential shift has taken place.

UNITY VERSUS INDIVIDUATION

The development of his intimacy with the family and the development of his separateness from the family is an essential process the therapist must negotiate. He must decide whether he is out for the joy of intimacy and the pain of separation and is willing to have the transference bilateral or whether he is going to stay outside the family group as a participant observer and commentator. Is he anxious to become part of the family and suffer the pain and vulnerability this demands?

Understanding versus Living or Essence versus Existence

The stance of the therapist negotiating a process of understanding or training seems particularly significant in family therapy and may stand in opposition to the effort for synthesis. The freedom to use a personal confrontation matches the freedom to use his own health as part of the therapeutic pressure. The therapist who reaches for understanding of the family is in the same bind as the therapist who believes communication training is the essence of psychotherapy. The symptom relief may reopen the process of growth yet not accelerate it nor extend its limits.

Finally, it seems important that the therapist sense that his usefulness is probably more related to his presence and the quality of his person than it is to the image that the patient perceives or one the therapist himself is striving to create. Psychotherapy does not begin in the first interview. It begins when the therapist himself has edged past his basic delusion that the patient is helped by an image of the helper person.

FAMILY TREATMENT: A TEAM VERSUS THE INDIVIDUAL THERAPIST

The model for employing a team is derived from the parents raising children in the home. One parent is hard put to do a good job raising the family of children. One therapist is in a difficult spot trying to treat a family. In the first interview or in the first few interviews his distance is maintained and he can be adequate, but as he becomes emotionally involved, and I think therapeutic change demands this, he is immediately in a one-down position. He is out-gunned as well as out-numbered and will be repeatedly out-maneuvered. If the family is fairly healthy and fairly adequate, this solo project may be tolerable for an experienced therapist but the less experienced therapist may well end up being entangled in the countertransference problem of extrusion or the countertransference problem of being absorbed. Thus he either will stay aloof from the family and be of little help or he will merge with the family and again be of little help. Even a team that is under stress, like a marriage under stress, is more useful than a distant psychotherapist or a dependent psychotherapist. The two-person therapeutic unit allows for creativity, for administrative freedom, for sharing of responsibility, for a greater degree of honesty about boredom, about anger, and about the therapist's own stress reaction. The strength of such a twosome is much greater than the summation of the two individuals.

I'm convinced there is no correct interpersonal distance for good psychotherapy. There must be freedom to move in and move out of the therapeutic unit without being locked in either position. Besides the existential qualities of such a setting, it offers the freedom to model for the family an honest peer relationship. Probably it is most important as an opportunity for the two therapists to grow as persons. If the therapist grows the patient can push his growing edge.

FAMILY THERAPY INITIATED AFTER
ONE-TO-ONE THERAPY

If a colleague has been working with a patient for some period of time and becomes convinced that the spouse should be involved, I suggest that he refer the spouse to me for a limited series of interviews and then the four of us sit down together to go on with the family therapy in a four-person framework, including the children either in the beginning or shortly thereafter. Those times when I foolishly assumed that I could move in and become aligned with the nonpatient spouse during the beginning phase of the four-way framework have not worked out well. My relationship to the therapist and his relationship to his patient makes the spouse feel profoundly isolated. This appears most graphic in the metaphor that any therapist is the mother-in-law to his patient's spouse. Therefore, when a therapist involved in one-to-one therapy becomes convinced that the process should be changed to include the spouse and just invites the spouse to become part of the ongoing relationship, he is asking for trouble.

Lest someone infer that I oppose one-to-one therapy, I should like to define my sense of when it is most valuable. The psychological treatment of an individual can be redefined as the treatment of the family scapegoat. Even though the family is all dead or are not available it seems to me that the symptom pattern in psychological illness is largely the result of the acceptance of a role. Mark Twain said, "The town drunk is an elected office." I think the psychological cripple is also an elected office. He not only has to run for election, but he also has to be voted on and elected. This premise nudges me to begin psychotherapy with all of the system that I can assemble. I have learned technically that many times when I thought it was not possible to get mama, papa, brother, sister, uncle, aunt, grandmother, and grandfather, I was wrong. If I say it's important and ask the "scapegoat" to bring it about, it takes place with amazing ease and amazing frequency. Furthermore, it has always yielded useful results. Once the system has been mobilized and involvement of the total unit has been established, the family rather than the scapegoat becomes the center of the problem. Many treatment variations are then possible.

Working with the system includes the resolution of major anxiety components in each of its members, the subgroups, the triangles, and the interpersonal relationships of the dyads. Then reconstructive intra-psychic surgery for each or any of the individual members is appropriate. The final stage in family therapy before the inauguration of such one-to-one therapy is usually the resolution of the relationship between the spouses. Deciding when to elect one-to-one therapy seems like, "How far should the music teacher go with a particular student?" Given talent and interest and willingness to work on it, some students can become concert pianists. Not everyone can go on to character reorganization by extensive individual therapy, but I believe the chance of its success is much enhanced by preliminary family therapy.

Technically, it does not seem wise for me to switch to individual therapy when family therapy has failed or been interrupted or disrupted. If members of that family want to go on, each should make that decision independent of the family therapist or any recommendation from him. Thus, if I fail with a family and subsequently take on one of the members, I open the family and the individuals to destructive fantasies and the treated individual will also suffer in isolation from his family.[15]

THE TECHNICAL PROCESS OF TREATMENT

At the risk of dealing off the bottom of the deck, I shall bypass the whole question of a family diagnosis or nosology and any effort to describe the development of pathology in the family and take up the techniques of family therapy as a process of treatment. First, three generalizations which may seem enigmatic, but to me they seem crucial, is the kind of freedom that the therapist (a team) must have to continue successfully with the treatment of family after family. First, the change seems to take place when the family team stops trying. I am referring to the situation where the current of the operation or transactional process moves from a teaming effort to a flowing, nondefinable state of being. Secondly, one must raise the crucial question, "What can the professional therapist add?" I shall take up details of this, but overall it is important to know that we are also most valuable in those moments when we are not straining to be helpful. Maybe the therapist's greatest contribution is his "animal faith." As Tom Malone said to one patient, "Don't be mad at me, I'm not trying to help you." The one-upmanship state of trying to help is by itself destructive. (I will make no note of how efficiently this has been proven by the United States government in its contribution to the joys of other national governments.) Furthermore, it is probably true, as Barbara Betz said many years ago, that "The dynamics of the therapeutic process are in the person of the therapist," or to quote the old Zen phrase, "You can't get there by trying but you can't not try." Thirdly it is also important that family therapy is really not a person-to-person relationship, but it is the relationship of a person—the therapist or the therapeutic team—to a system. One of the unique qualities of this difference is that family therapy is by its very nature much more a process of manipulation and political maneuvering than is one-to-one therapy. It is not possible to depend upon your altruistic good intentions, your sincerity, or your enjoyment of intimacy.

The simple implication of this is that the therapist must utilize power in his operation with the family. He must understand the ordinary dynamics of the family operation and he must be prepared to deliberately manipulate in order to keep the family moving in its growth.

Pretreatment Phase

The initial contact with the family in my setting is by a personal telephone call. For example, mother calls and says, "I'd like you to see my son" or "My husband is very depressed." I say on the phone, "Fine, why don't you bring him in and how many others are there in the family?" And, whatever the answer, I say, "Why don't you bring all of them?" Her protest may lead me to back down enough to either see father, mother, and the scapegoat, or father and mother without the children for the first interview, but I make it clear, even on the phone, that I assume the whole family will be in and that it is a bit of generosity if I don't insist on the whole family the first time. If the family has previously been in therapy, either family therapy or individual or couples therapy, I will be very insistent that everybody be there for the first time and may refuse to see them if they show up with one person missing, sending them home to make up their minds whether they really want help or whether only some of them want help and the others are going to fight any change. At that point I make it clear that I am not interested in starting therapy without all the chips on my side. Family therapy is a desperate process and I don't want to have any strikes against me in the beginning.

My first interview is to define the whole. Since general systems theory is applicable I utilize some of those concepts in the presentation. I usually employ a broad term—"What's with your family?"—address it to father first and then move around the family, usually to the younger children, being more specific about trying to speak in a broad framework so they can respond from many different angles. I start with father because he's farthest outside and because he is the one most apt to pull the family out of treatment if he is not given some kind of contact with the therapist in the early phase.[16] I try to defuse the scapegoat ploy by suggesting that we already know he is depressed or he is delinquent and let's find out about the rest of the family. Usually my initial moves to expose the family pathology are rejected and I increase the stress in my request to the next member for some help in getting a global picture. I follow the same model Virginia Satir does in trying to separate the generations by getting a picture of the parent's courtship or by suggesting that the life before the children is important to me. I have recently followed the pattern of a therapist I met who suggests that the grandparents or those who are not present be invited to send a tape either about the family or about their own life. I also try to describe as scapegoating those times when the other members of the family get physically ill, have temper tantrums or trouble sleeping. I endeavor to discover the subgroups within the family; who comforts mother when she cries? Who is on dad's side when mother and daddy have a fight? Who settles the fight between brothers and sisters or mother and her oldest daughter? And what happens if all the males gang up on all the females?

I also try during this first interview to blueprint the process of family therapy. I talk about the pain involved in the struggle, my deliberate intent to create confusion, my admiration for craziness, the fact that I believe in a team of therapists so that we can have enough power to push them around and my long-range intent to create a therapeutic community within the family so we won't be together forever.

BATTLE FOR STRUCTURE

I try to set up a treatment framework such that it is clear to me and to the family that this is my operating room and that I intend to be in charge. I call this the battle for structure, including my freedom to have consultants, to define how we go about the process, to decide who shall be present, to schedule the time and to be, in essence, the rule-maker for the interview setting. Dr. David Rubinstein calls this establishing the integrity of the therapist. It might also be in Murry Bowen's terms the establishments of my "I" position. I'm convinced that the therapist must maintain his freedom to move in and out of the therapeutic group and to some degree, in and out of the family as well. This battle for structure may also take place within the interview, not just administratively. For example, at one point in the second interview I was talking with a 19-year-old daughter when the sociopath father interrupted our very personal give-and-take. And at that point, I exploded at him, telling him he must never cross me when I'm involved personally with somebody in the family. If the therapist becomes one-down either on the telephone or in the first or second or even a subsequent interview, the therapeutic process is seriously impaired. No patient should trust a therapist who doesn't power-wise belong to an older generation, or one who isn't secure and comfortable in his role as a parent–person. This testing phase occurs with most families. It begins with the initial phone contact and may go on for some time. Families seem to actively search out the degree of the therapist's strength. If I lose the first battle, then it seems I must double the ante for the next struggle and be sure to win. If I had let father interrupt me in this personal give-and-take with his daughter, the whole family therapy process would have been jeopardized because I had become a "patsy" for the father.

BATTLE FOR INITIATIVE

Assuming the treatment has been structured, the initial treatment phase includes what I call the battle for initiative. Having set up my own integrity, my own realm here in my territory, I feel it crucially important to define the integrity of the family. You could call this the "I" position of the family. I demand that their life and their decisions are crucially theirs. For example, mother says in the second interview, "Do you think I ought to get a divorce from this man?" And I answer, "It's fine with me. I'm married and I don't expect to divorce my wife and you're free to have the same privilege of either living with him or divorcing him. I'm only concerned with whether you keep coming to the interview. However, if divorce means you aren't coming to the interview, then we better stop now." The battle for initiative includes also the fact that once we're past the initial history, the question of where we go should really be up to the family. I want to participate, but I don't want *them* to be passive. The ball is in their hands and although I can coach, I cannot carry the ball in their living and their efforts to make that living more successful. It's not only that I am unwilling to make decisions, I try to keep it clear that I am not interested in whether they get a divorce or not. I'm not interested in whether they call the police when the son misbehaves. That's their world and they have to live in it in their style. I don't think that my pattern of living is more valid than theirs and more important, they can't change their pattern of living unless first they are what they are. Imitating me is not the way to learn how to live.

THE FLIGHT INTO HEALTH

Once the family has moved into defining and struggling with some of its dynamic stress patterns such as mother and daddy's fighting with each other, the handling of Jimmy, the impudent one, or Mary, the withdrawn daughter, or the jealousy between the two boys, they may want to go it alone. They "feel" where they are in their stress and they sense that they can change it. The therapist should recognize that this step may well be the family's effort to unite by attempting their own resolution of the family stress. They say, "Things are better" or "We're very busy" or "This is expensive" or "Mary (the scapegoat) is doing nicely." I take all such statements as evidence that they would like to discontinue treatment and try it on their own. I take this very seriously, try not to block it, assume it will be successful yet make it clear that I am available in case they want to come back at any time: tomorrow, next week, or 5 years from now. I try to do this without the double bind, although it is a natural response for all us "mothers" when we fear the child will fail. It is amazing how many times these families make it on their own!

I should like to make it clear that this is different from crisis intervention therapy. I do not define a crisis, intervene in it, and then initiate the ending. I expose the growth effort of the family and accept their impulse to break away from me as a healthy move and one that I believe in. I assume they'll go on growing. I believe the family's flight into health is not just a defense. This covert effort to jointly resolve their stresses may be expressed in various ways. For example, they may describe how the children have been very helpful this week. The therapist can then activate this message so the family senses its readiness to terminate the treatment. They may then ask if the therapist is trying to kick them out or is bored with them. I encourage them, since in endeavoring to do it themselves, they may become unified as a family group. If they terminate, the family may get together for meetings or just go on living. If they later see themselves as a group of chaotically organized individuals or disrupting subgroups they may face a new kind of despair, the despair of *nonbeingness*, the despair of not being a family gestalt. At this time they may return. The necessity of coming back into therapy not only produces a kind of unity in the family group that was not present before, but it also produces a kind of unity in the therapeutic team that was not present before. It is like meeting with old friends. It is like the second date is different from the first date. The therapists are more ready to care because now the family as a whole is coming rather than one individual bringing the family.

The Children as Family Therapists

In the early stages of family therapy, the children frequently establish themselves as functional cotherapists for the parents. The parents, sometimes out of their guilt, many times out of their maturity, are more willing to listen to the children than to the therapists. And the children out of their anger and their lovingness are more free to "say it like it is." This results in a peculiar set such that the children become parents to their parents or as I sometimes tell them amusedly, their own grandparents. It's tempting for the therapist to forbid this since it interferes with his own functioning, or to protest it since it puts the children in an unnatural set. I should like to reassure the reader. As the parents become more adequate and have their own identity crisis they team with each other and promptly relegate the children to their proper generation. This establishment of the valid generation gap is rather a disconcerting but very happy event for the family. The children are suddenly free to be themselves and the parents are free to be in charge of the family generation gap. Furthermore, when this symbolic castration takes place, the parental subgroup is in a position to interact with each other in a very growthful and therapeutic pattern and the therapy moves into its final phase.

The Two Therapists as a Model

The initial phase of treatment many times is centered around the modeling by the two therapists of an honest adult couple. This can be highlighted by openly sharing with each other the affect of the present moment. "Hey, this gang is powerful. They not only got John set up to steal that car, but they also set mother up to a massive depression and it looks like she might even be suicidal" or "Gus, I wonder if we're riding for another fight" or "I enjoy these people so much I wonder if I shouldn't be suspicious of myself or you should check out my enjoyment of them." Secondly, the therapists can share their awareness of the family and their mistrust of the therapeutic collaboration. They can say for example, "You know, I don't see why they should trust us. I don't trust Dad. He looks as though he would fight dirty. He looks as though he is only here for the ride," and so forth.

It is important to me that during this initial phase the therapist try to remain a stranger, or a guest to the family as long as possible. It appears that our most abortive attitude is a make-believe friendliness or a professional bedside manner that leaves the family perpetually suspicious of where we are. Maybe it's my own insecurity, but I believe it is better not to show any imitation of caring. The therapists also should be free to share with each other openly, and in front of the family, their feelings of uselessness or despair or their fear of failure. Sometimes this is activated by discussing old battle scars or snapshots of the therapist's world. For example, I say to my cotherapist, "Gus, the way he talks about his daughter sounds like the way I sometimes feel about my daughter and those times really frighten me," or "This family has a lot of similarities to that family we failed with last spring. Do you agree or do you feel better about this family?" The therapists may also model for the family their own separateness or their unity. "Gus, this is going to be a hard interview. I'm still mad at you for the way you let me down yesterday afternoon," or "You know, it's interesting, this family must be boring me because I was just thinking what fun it would be for you and me to go canoeing Saturday." This open teaming often produces anxiety in the family, but also helps them depend on the strength of the twosome.

FAMILY EFFORT TO SPLIT THERAPISTS

Usually once their anxiety is minimized, the next step in family therapy is an effort on the part of the family to split the therapists: "Let's get Mother and Father to fight." The power dynamics of the therapeutic team are in fairly direct opposition to the power of the family group and one of the ways they can win is to separate the two therapists. Dad may say, "Gus, you seem friendlier than Carl. He scares me. If he can't come next week, would you see us alone?" This raises a technical question. It is probably not a good idea to split the two therapists in any way until the therapy is well along. If one can't be there, the therapy interview should be postponed until both are present. Later on it is possible to see subgroups of the family without disrupting the ongoing process but I always assume that the absent members are paranoid until proven otherwise.

MIDPHASE

DEVELOPMENT OF UNIT TEAM AND A CULTURE OF "CARING"

As therapy becomes established and moves into the more serious work of changing there are several problems that the therapist team must be aware of. Most important is the danger of being absorbed by the family. The therapist may become so comfortable and relaxed in the setting that he's like the parent who becomes one with the children. The therapy group is then a peer group rather than a two-generation unit and as such is dysfunctional. The second major danger is the danger of the therapist becoming aloof from, or indifferent to, the "patient" family like the parent who is never free to be childlike and to enjoy his children by playing with them. Such a family of "squares" is like the husband and wife who live back-to-back.

Once these two dangers have been avoided, it is necessary for the therapist to make some move toward the family so as to activate the caringness of the whole though he must risk being gobbled up by it. It is not fair to expect the family to expose itself while the therapists sit by as peeping Toms. Just as the therapist in the one-to-one relationship can prove his humanness by sharing his own free associations and the patient will be less terrified to expose himself, so it is important that the therapist in the family expose his own feelings and his own person to the family. He may do this by exposing his loneliness at the moment, his paranoia, his feeling of aggression or of identification. As soon as one of the therapists is free to unite with a member of the family or move into the family, then a family member joins the therapeutic team and shares his despair and his own individual problem with becoming a person. Sue says, "Dad, I agree with the doctor that when you raise your eyebrows like that it means you're extremely angry. I have the same kind of feeling about your anger and I know it is like that with me. When I get angry, I'm like you, I just hide my feelings." Strangely enough, when this happens one of the cotherapists may then withdraw from the therapeutic team and join the family for a time. He may move his chair over toward the family or he may suddenly have a sense of unity with the family. In essence, the members of the therapeutic team are modeling and testing out their own freedom to individuate from each other and make contact with a family member or with the whole family unit. Once this has taken place, it is more feasible for a second family member to join the therapeutic unit in a coalition.

It may well be that the two therapists and these two members from the family constitute a critical mass and at that point the whole family begins to move. The family system is forced to change in relation to this new suprasystem. The therapeutic team has become united with the family and at the same time is free to be separate from it. The family is united with the therapists and at the same time do not feel they have lost their own autonomy. One of the interesting side patterns in this is that very frequently the therapeutic team is pushed to change its own dynamics. For instance, the family says, "You two look as though you're mad at each other. I guess Carl thinks you're too soft, but I think he's too cool." In some way the family indicates their perception of the therapeutic team and their hope that it can be different. This kind of feedback, of course, should be taken seriously and may be very valuable to the therapeutic team and to the individuals who compose it.

TECHNIQUES IN DETAIL

During this midphase of family therapy there are some fairly specific techniques that can be useful. Some can be used to help shatter some of the family myths. One of the most specific is the *redefinition of symptoms as efforts for growth*. For example, mother accuses dad of infidelity. The team then carefully defines the fact that the two spouses had become desperate about the coolness of the marriage. They had then agreed implicitly and covertly that something had to be done to heat up the marriage and that one of them should go out and get help. Father was the one elected to help raise the thermostat of the family bed. When they then uncovered the infidelity the heat of anger was transmitted into a temperature elevation in the theramostat of their whole relationship. If they hadn't been ready for change, they wouldn't have dared the pain of exploding out of their impasse. Likewise, psychosis in one of the family members can be defined as an effort to be Christ-like: "I'll be a nobody so that you and father will be saved," or the desperation felt by one member of the family can be redefined as a hopeful sign since it means the family cares enough. Just a mild degree of tongue-in-cheek quality must be included with this technical ploy so the confrontation will not be too painful.

Technically, once the relationship is established and the supraunit team is operational, the therapist can add many practical bits of intervention which in one-to-one therapy would seem like inappropriate moves but in the context of the family is safe since the family will utilize what it wants and is perfectly competent in discarding what is not useful. For example, the husband whose wife is having headaches can be offhandedly offered the possibility that if he should spank her, the headaches might go away. Or the wife who is driven up the wall by her children's nagging or dad's aloofness can casually be offered in the presence of the whole family the idea that she could run away to her mother's for a week and let the family make their own meals. Another technical bit that works is *modeling fantasy alternatives to real-life stress.* For example, a woman who has attempted suicide can be pushed to a fantasy. "If you were going to murder your husband how would you do it?" or "Suppose when you got suicidal you decided you were going to kill me. How would you do it? Would you use a gun or a knife or cyanide?" These are merely examples of the kind of freedom possible within the family which is not very feasible in most one-to-one exchanges. Thus, teaching the use of fantasy permits expansion of the emotional life without the threat of real violence.

A fourth technique for intervention is *separating interpersonal stress and intrapersonal fantasy stress.* For example, the patient who has attempted suicide can be encouraged to talk with the group about who her husband would marry if she killed herself, how soon would he marry, how long would he be sad, how long would the children be sad, who would get the insurance, how would her mother-in-law feel, would he take the children to his mother, and so forth. This converting the intrapersonal fantasy stress to an interpersonal framework is valuable since it badly contaminates the fantasy. It also allows the family a new freedom in communication among themselves since they discover that such frightening words do not mean the end of the world. A fifth technique is *augmenting the despair of a family member* so that the family unites around him. This is usually most efficient when used with a scapegoat. For instance, I'll say to a schizophrenic son, "If you give up and become a nobody and spend the rest of your life in a state hospital, do you really think mother and father will be happy with each other 20 years from now or will they still be at each other's throats as they are now and you will have given your life away for nothing?" A sixth and very potent technique is to *highlight the family revolution.* For example, in one family, Bill, who had been away hitchhiking for a year, came back home to find his sister Mary was very disturbed. He decided to stay at home. In the interview, mother had a good bit of closeness with her son and we suggested that if he and Mary could get mother on their side the three might be able to defeat the four "squares" who made up the rest of the family. Father and his gang were keeping the family on the far right but mother and the two kids with our help might be able to break that up.

The family members also can be taught to share their dreams with each other. This is usually done most directly by the therapist sharing some of his own night dreams and asking for their help in interpretation, just as the family can be taught free association by the therapist sharing some of his own free associations. One useful technique we call "affect flip." This involves the therapist's sharing his sudden sense of absurdity of what's going on or his willingness to let his lovingness or his anger emerge impulsively and without the caution ordinarily maintained throughout our technical work day. This may lay a ground substance for the therapist to cultivate and utilize with effectiveness, a teasing playfulness with the family or members of the family. This may include some ridicule or teasing with a tongue-in-cheek double-bind quality. It is also possible for the therapist to allow his sense of humor full freedom, and although some impulsive jokes may not seem relevant, he will find that more and more of them are triggered by something significant in the family and that their value is much greater than would have been anticipated. I also think it very important for the therapist to cultivate this peer participation so that he will not become either technical or bored or hostile. If the therapist enjoys himself, the patient will grow.

It is very valuable in working with families to use some of the primitive modalities which are not easily available in the one-to-one methodology ordinarily used. These include the touching of the body, the use of vulgar language, and the use of "schizophrenese." All are valuable parts of the effort to communicate so that we get past the intellectual, social game playing or the doctor–patient game playing.

THE EXTENDED FAMILY REUNION

Whenever an opportunity arises or can be created for getting in members of the extended family or better yet, the total extended family, the therapy is certain to be speeded, broadened, and made more creative. There are several functions served by this consultation visit. The visit activates the perception on the part of the family that they are a whole, that even the more removed members are an organic part of the family unit, are of necessity involved, concerned, and have an effect on each of the other members and on the group as a whole and on its subgroups. This interaction tends to bring about the kind of growth experience that made the family reunions so cherished in the good old days. Under the stress of the therapeutic objective, the contributions of Aunt Minnie, Uncle Henry, Cousin Bill, and Grandma take on a significance, a pertinence, and an incisiveness which is not apparent until you see it happen. Such an extended family interview is not set up with the purpose of treating the noncentral members; it's not expected that Grandma and Grandpa shall change, but that they shall contribute to the change process going on within the family who are in treatment. That contribution is frequently better accomplished if the meeting does not have an explicit purpose. It's not necessary to learn about the early life of mother or father. Given a nonstructured pattern, the family will interact according to their tolerance of anxiety and their intuitive perception of what will be most valuable. It is also unnecessary to expose to the extended family any of the data involved in the family's treatment process. The objective is an affect contribution to the treatment, not a confessional ceremony within the family. It is also unnecessary to have a family fight. Although such confrontations are frequent, they contain their own constraints and ordinarily do not necessitate the therapist's intervention, merely his presence and his being the symbol for the meeting. The dynamics of such a meeting are very complex, but the most significant one is that the therapist takes over the function of mediator, which had been passed from hand to hand within the family or had been established in some crucial member. Without their elected mediator, the family's experience of itself may open in a new sense. It is also possible that the family's cohesion is partly based upon the therapeutic team as a personification of the "they." In the face of such danger, the family gets together.

The value of the extended family conference may be augmented by the presence of the therapists as opponents. The family perceives its individual members in their current age of maturity in contrast with their antique childlike introjects. The parents may also see the children as grown to their actual age. This kind of rearrangement of perception may be quite constructive.

CONSULTATION FOR IMPASSE

The use of consultation as a technique in family therapy is little understood. It is probable that any foreign move is valuable in adding to the total treatment set and that if family treatment is at an impasse, a consultation is valuable. The consultant should be an intimate or respected colleague. He may be a person to whom the therapist and the family tell their story and why things seem bad, or it may be a video-tape with playback or even an audiotape with playback. It is important at any stage that the therapists faced with an impasse take the responsibility for confessing their failure to the family first and if that is not enough to make for movement, they then should take the responsibility for confessing this failure to an esteemed colleague who is in a position to castigate them or at least reprove them and thus augment the union between the two therapists and the family. The consultant is like a stepmother—an invader who has enough of the parent's affect to be a real emotional threat. Part of the resolution of the impasse is also involved with openly admitting the failure. I sometimes call this the "impotence ploy." I say to patients, "I have gotten as far as I can go; I am afraid you are going to lose my affect, and if you do, then there is no more I can do about it than you can, in bringing your affect here."

LATE PHASE

As the therapy moves into a phase of ongoing steady change, the family unity becomes established, the subgroups get mobilized, triangles become flexible enough so they are not too painful, the mediators give up their role of saviors, and the family becomes a rather flexible, fluid group. The late phase of the treatment process may become such that the interview seems like a time and space setting. The family begins to have its own interviews and the therapist, like the parents of a late adolescent, feel incidental.

The family has in essence become a milieu therapy unit. The interview hour is the time for them to work on each other and the therapists have an increasing feeling that they're just along for the ride. Indeed, at times the whole interview will be carried on and no one will notice the therapists. They feel very much on the sideline and the family has begun to move out of the comforting arms of the therapeutic unit. The family may even begin to push some members and subgroups in a fairly massive way. A delicate balance exists if one can be helpful and yet secure enough in himself so that he doesn't have to take over or demand an involvement that is not required or needed by the patient group, the ending is easy.

SEPARATION STAGE

The ending of family therapy is still little understood. It seems as though families end their treatment in very diverse manners. Usually the typical rejection of the parent takes place. The family begins to reject the therapist's value system or as children do in play therapy, refer in another family as replacement. It is important that the separation anxiety characteristic of this situation be dealt with. One simple way is for the therapist to talk about his own grieving. The chance to get help from the family is also very opportune. It is important that the therapist not try to polish his "graven image" of himself by making believe he is doing psychotherapy out of altruism. If the family can offer feedback to the professional team, they build self-esteem and reduce the guilt about the poor old therapist who worked his fingers to the bone.

If the ending phase seems to be at an impasse or if the therapy seems to be harmful, the therapist should take the initiative. He may

1. Refuse to extend the therapy by seeing the parents alone and instead advise the family to try living out their gains.

2. Refuse to permit the healthy members to end; thus they will precipitate the family cut-off.

3. Invite a professional consultant to intervene or invite others of the extended family to act as consultants.

4. Initiate multiple family sessions so two or more families can interact with each other.

5. Face with the family his fear that he keep them dependent and therefore his decision to stop the interviews lest that process be harmful.

It's at times valuable for the therapist to include in this final phase a promissory note of future adult-to-adult relationships and to clarify for the family that the therapists can get along alone, either because there is another family (a new baby) or that they can have fun with each other.

CONCLUSION

I insist that the best model of family therapy is the model of family growth and, therefore, the two therapists need to stay with the primal scene that they represent for the most efficient and successful separation. Sex education is useful and important with anyone you love. If you don't grow to love the family you work with, you've not only missed a golden opportunity, you're probably making believe something hasn't happened when indeed, it has. A family that is worth treating is worth loving, and parting is bittersweet sorrow.

A FAMILY IS A
FOUR-DIMENSIONAL RELATIONSHIP

In this chapter Whitaker picks up and enlarges on a single idea mentioned previously: his increasing need for a third generation in his family work. He suggests that this need is both his, to push his own growth, and the family's, to come to grips with their continuity over time. At the time of this writing,

Reprinted by permission from P.J. Guerin (Ed.), *Family Therapy: Theory and Practice.* New York: Gardner Press, 1976. Copyright © 1976 by Gardner Press, Inc.

Whitaker required that all family therapy include some contact with the grandparental generation.

Whitaker's move to three-generation treatment was frequently fore-shadowed in his early work. It was as if he knew that he should involve all available generations, but felt that the practical problems made such a demand impossible. What appears to have forced him to begin demanding this involvement was his sense that he was becoming sterile and stereotyped in his two-generational work. As was true of previous major changes in his therapy style, Whitaker followed his own needs for a growth experience rather than a theoretical conception of what psychotherapy should be about.

Twenty years of play therapy with children, relationship therapy with delinquents, mothering of neurotic self-doubters, and depth therapy with chronic schizophrenics was coming to a grinding halt. Couples therapy became more and more boring. How could one aging therapist stay alive? Even cotherapy, the 20-year model for patient parenting, felt sterile and stereotyped. It became clear that my personal growing edge must become my central objective in every relationship—if experiential therapy was for my experience, then patient modeling could be for real. If I could change, they might try to. I am time-limited; my marriage is deep, long, and wide-coursing; but the family lives, and has a forever-extended time dimension.

THE NECESSITY OF THREE GENERATIONS

M.J., a man of 40, with three children, left his wife to live with another woman and her two sons. He'd always done "whatever gave him fun." Marriage didn't make any difference in his sexual life. He had lived for a year in a European village with his girlfriend—a hooker with two children, whose husband "hadn't supported her in 4 years." When her boyfriend had doublecrossed her, M.J. took her on to help her "get herself back together." The endless struggle to keep the two women in his life happy required lies and all sorts of cheating, although he always stayed inside the law. Jealous of each woman, he kept convincing each that he was faithful. M.J. had occasional fantasies of suicide: he'd tried hypnotherapy and marital counseling, but he still felt "terribly insecure."

He has a brother and two sisters, all much older than he; his parents are still together. They are "good people," and he reports that life with father was "rugged." His wife is not exciting sexually. His girlfriend always has 20 ways to increase his sexual excitement, while his wife can't think of any way to satisfy. However, when he told her to go off on her own, she made a life for herself without him, which threw him into an acute panic.

THE PLAN FOR TREATMENT

"Those two women you're sleeping with are catching on to you. They should both come into the interviews. I'll need a cotherapist. We would try to help solve the problem all three of you share. Each of them is suffering like you're suffering. Each is as dishonest with you as you are with them. Read the *Mast of Sanity* by Hervey Cleckly; listen to the record of George Bernard Shaw's *Don Juan in Hell*. Don Juan thought *all* those women loved him. Call me when you've thought about it!"

If M.J. does bring in his two women and all five children, my cotherapist and I will then insist on at least one consultation with his parents and his siblings. Without the additional stress of facing his family of origin, he might still avoid an integrating experience, continuing to wear this mask of sanity that enables him to make believe he's two separate people in two separate places. The third generation would escalate the pressure, and therefore might evoke the psychotic-like episode needed to put him together into a single person who is not self-destructive one minute and pseudostimulated the next.

My engagement with two-generation families began in 1945. I decided I didn't believe in individuals. They seemed more and more like fragments of a family. Then, as time went on, I heard the ghost of grandmother knocking on the door. Each dad was apparently trying to restructure his own family of origin, using his wife and children as puppets. Each mom was also pushing to rekindle her at-home security by using the same nuclear family group. Why not get the three-generation system together and at least begin an accommodation to the introjected reality of the entire two-family system? Homogenizing that dual set of family myths might make the nuclear family myths less enslaving to the grandchildren. It might even allow the grandparents to dump their 30-year child-raising hang-up, and begin to live. I don't believe in the individual or free will at all any more. I'm tempted to say over the phone before the first visit, "Bring three generations or don't bother to start."

Many people question the grandparental visits to the interview and the purpose it serves. Should they be patients? Should there be a place for the identified patient or spouse to express affect or confront old myths? The most basic reason for having the parents in is to get their implicit permission for the therapist to become the object of transference.

In individual therapy, transference takes place in the framework of an implicit and sometimes explicit disloyalty to the parents. Psychotherapy is basically countercultural, and as such involves breaking with the parental model. If we get the parents in for the first interview, it helps the patient feel less disloyal and the therapist feel less responsible for moving in a direction antagonistic to the parental model. The content of that interview may be purely social, or merely supportive: it certainly need not involve content of any significance. It need not, for example, results in the parents' discovering that the patient is homosexual, or has had an affair, or is suicidal.[17] It merely serves as a time when the parents meet this man who's going to replace them, and develop some willingness to turn over to him the care and nurturing of their child.

Jim and Mary came about two things, the question of a divorce, and how to discipline their 3-year-old. Mary wanted the divorce because Jim had a terrible mother. She said mother still kept the blue-chip stock left him by his father, and also kept Jim's Army savings from the 2 years before they married. Her fury had grown during the last 3 years because mother had sent such chintzy Christmas and birthday gifts to their child. After several years of listening to this, I insisted they bring mother from a distant city for a consultation visit.

As the consultation got going, Mary confronted her mother-in-law about the chintzy gifts. Mother said she thought the gifts were merely symbolic, since she also sent a $100 check each time. She also had sent money for the new piano they had asked for, after rejecting her offer to rent one for a year.

The values of this consultation were that I was able to rectify my image of that mean old mother-in-law who sent chintzy gifts and kept the husband's savings account; Jim developed the courage to stand up to his wife's attack on his mother; I was free to tease the wife about the

projected bitterness she carried toward her own mother; the grandmother and her son resolved the bank account remnant of their premarital affair; and the grandmother achieved a new freedom, released
from the triangular war that had been heating up within the group.

The family ended treatment soon after and a 5-year follow-up
indicates that all goes well.

Mrs. W.M. divorced her husband 1 year after marriage because he
beat her up. She was then 6 months pregnant. Subsequently she had
several years of good psychotherapy, and was referred to me by her
therapist so that I could monitor the relationship between her and her
10-year-old son. I had from between one and five triangle interviews
each summer for the next 6 years. These interviews helped maintain the
separation between the generations—that is, the identity of mother and
son as two separate persons, and a two-generation, one-parent unit.

When her son was 17, the mother asked to bring in her own
parents, so she could work on that relationship. She arrived with her
mother, but without her father. When asked why her father hadn't
come, she said he wasn't needed, and anyway he didn't want to come.
She was refused the interview; she came back a week later with son and
both parents, and within 20 minutes she and her father were in a
physical fight. After this had been resolved, father explained to the
therapist that he thought her assault was a fake. I suggested that it
looked like a husband–wife fight. The identified patient immediately
flared into a blistering attack on the missing husband, whom she
hadn't seen in 18 years, as "a horrible person" for beating her. I insisted
that it was necessary for her to get him and bring him in. She called
him. He arrived from across the continent 3 days before the next
interview; they met, and she beat him up within 36 hours. We had three
subsequent good appointments, and did a great deal to resolve all three
generations of chaos. Oh, if only I'd done this 6 years earlier.

This reactivation of the bilateral paranoia between the patient and
her ex-husband resolved the identification of father and ex-husband. It
also helped rectify the disorganized family introject in the 17-year-old
son. He finally knew how it was with his mother and her parents, and
with "that man who had once been his father."

Looking back to individual therapy, I wonder how and if I really
changed anybody. Did couples therapy change the relationship or the
people? Or was it time that healed, and role expectations that shifted?
Is therapy any different with three generations on the first visit? Why
try it? And, how does it help?

Sixteen-year-old Sue had failed school, had been out all night and now was surly and bitter. Her little brother was withdrawn, mother was depressed, and father was furious, tight-lipped. He demanded that Sue conform with school, and also with home rules. Since grandmother was visiting at the time, she was invited to the interview. Asked about the family, she said, "I never put my nose into my daughter's family life." Asked about grandfather, she said, "He died 8 years ago." "How?" "A motorcycle accident." "Had he been suicidal?" "Well, now that you speak of it—I hadn't thought of it, but he'd had lots of motorcycle accidents." "Were you afraid of him?" "Oh, yes. He beat me several times."

From there it was easy to help the father see how his wife expected him to beat her. He agreed that he was afraid of his temper, and then recalled a violent fight in high school when he almost killed a classmate. That led to the daughter's getting family credit for teaching mother how to fight with dad, and helping dad enjoy his temper without becoming suicidal or beating his wife.

THE HIDDEN AGENDA

Twenty-four-year-old Ezra had been referred after 5 years of psychotherapy that hadn't helped his "schizophrenia." Mother phoned asking an appointment for son, and was told, "I don't see patients, I just see families." She said, "Well, I'll come." "How about your husband?" "Well, we're getting a divorce." I explained to her that I would not see them without the father, and she said, "OK, I'll bring him." "Who do you live with?" "My parents." "Well, let's bring them." "They aren't related to my son's problem." "OK, go see someone else." "But I want to see you." "So bring your parents." "OK, I'll bring them." "How about your husband's parents?" "Well, they live in Montreal." "That's okay. Just have him call me if they won't come."

All arrived for the 3-hour consultation except father's mother, who had suddenly developed arthritis. I took a history about the family's life together, first from father's father, then mother's father, then mother's mother, then father, and finally from mother. The whole story was pseudomutual sweetness. There was nothing wrong with this family. Exhausted, I turned to the "schizophrenic." "Listen, they're all nuts. You're a crazy grandson in the middle of all this family who are so ideal. It's impossible." He answered, "I'll tell you the story in 5 minutes. Mother's mother is father's father's big sister. And she made her little brother force my father to be a rabbi, and now they're all forcing me to be a Hasidic scholar." Without this third generation, I could have spent 4 years treating the nuclear family, and still never discovered the problem in the grandparents.

We all realize that in a large percentage of marriages the family of the bride and the family of the groom stay covertly or overtly hostile for years. Those mother-in-law jokes are not funny. They're real. "There's something eerie about that guy who stole our daughter." "Mother, don't you think Edna is awful snooty to Jim?"

The initial therapy visit of a three-generation system resolves several issues. It establishes the fact that this is a network, and that it is concerned with the problem at hand, even if it's just the nuclear couple's effort to grow. There is a group that each person belongs to, and that whole group is involved. Secondly, the implicit contract in the visit does settle a mantle on the therapist. The responsibility for the pain and the operation has been transferred to him. If the hour goes well, and first one and then another tries to express doubts, fears, and hopes, there may even be a new warmth between the two sets of grandparents. However, if the isolation walls are left intact, the members of the nuclear family are able to see quite clearly that they are truly responsible for their own destiny.

Mary was just out of a state hospital after 4 months of serious psychotic behavior. The husband was a profound square, and the three children, 6, 8, and 10, were having great difficulty readapting after their mother's long absence. The two sets of grandparents had not seen each other or talked to each other since the marriage 11 years before. Each set had been unhappy about their child's choice. The 2 hours of consultation seemed to be quite superficial—chitchat about the usual family tension systems, but without the courage to get into serious matters. Nobody was able to face the fear of another psychotic break, and the consultation as a whole seemed like a fairly inadequate experience. At the next interview, however, Mary said almost immediately, "Now I know why my husband is such a compulsive. I'd never met his mother. She's just like him. She even made me be careful about my behavior. I had thought he was just an old maid."

As a result of the consult, the wife forgave her husband some of his covert hostility and pathological "sanity"; his parents, who had not come to the wedding, became friendly with her parents; the husband–

wife war about which family of origin system would be copied in this new family system was resolved in a relative compromise; the children were less constrained by stress about which set of grandparents they should be loyal to. They did not have to choose either father or mother; both sets of grandparents could back away from their parental responsibilities and enjoy the relaxed play quality possible between grandparents and grandchildren; and finally, hope of preventing another psychotic break was increased, because there were two sets of grandparents ready to support the nuclear family's effort to build a healthy family system.

Does it make any difference if you have already started with a two-generation unit? I think it's wise to establish the symbolic significance of the third generation on that first visit. Then a visit from one or the other, or even both sets together, can serve as a consultation. The therapist need not reveal secrets nor even ask for data about childhood problems. The fact that this family reunion has a purpose, plus "that family therapist and his X-ray eyes" make the meeting significant. Even a casual history of the early relationship of grandma and grandpa will turn up loaded topics for the parents, and often for the grandchildren as well. Let the group carry the ball. They know how much they can stand, and what topics are poison.

What if there has been a divorce or two? Invite 'em all! Reopening old doors with the idea that parenthood is forever always seems useful, and I have never seen it harmful. What if they refuse? Keep pushing, and ask the symptom-bearer to urge them to come as consultants to the therapist. "I don't want more patients. I don't want to be a judge. I'd just like help with my therapy job." What about the aunts and uncles and cousins? The more the merrier. I've worked wtih a family of 30 for 3 full days together; many times I've worked with 15 to 20. A large group demands much less of the therapist. Such a family system needs none of the leadership that makes network therapy or group therapy so arduous. One spark in the extended family usually strikes tinder; and it's a rare family that doesn't have flint and steel available, just waiting to strike each other.

When family therapy has reached an impasse, and the therapist decides to increase the therapeutic power either by adding another member or inviting a consultant, it's equally helpful to add one or many team members from the extended family. They should be invited as assistants to the therapist, not as patients. Otherwise, if it is the grandparents, for example, who are invited in, they assume they're going to be assaulted, made guilty, made responsible for what's gone wrong. But if the cotherapists, in setting the stage for this consultation, tell the couple or the family, "We want your grandparents in to help us; we are failing," then the grandparents can come in as assistants to the therapist. Once in the interview, it's explained to them that the therapy *is* failing. "We're not doing our job in helping these people become more satisfied and more alive to their own living process, and therefore we'd like any help we can get." If this does not start anything going, the therapist can ask if they're willing to share any of their perceptions of the family, either about the past or the present, and maybe their fears or hopes for the future. If this does not succeed, the therapist can ask if they would reveal some of *their* problems in marriage, or their successes, and tell what caused them in hopes that this information might be helpful in the current family struggle. Should they come back once this consultation hour is completed? I usually invite them to visit if and whenever they like; I also offer them a chance to come every week if they feel they would like to.

This kind of consultation interview serves many symbolic purposes. The therapist does not see the grandparents as ogres. This may be a surprise to the parents. The grandparents are able to agree that their children are adults. The parents usually discover in this real-life confrontation that the grandparents are much different from their introject of 20 or 30 years earlier, which may enfeeble the control residing in that introject. The parents may discover that the grandparents are capable of running their own life. Thereby they are freed of that reverse parental responsibility they've been carrying. The couple may discover their grandparents don't object to their independence, don't object to their belonging to the younger generation, and will allow them to discipline their own children. Thus both the parents and the grandparents become freer to live their own lives in their own way. The two families become free to separate and thus free to belong.

I must stress here that in many years of utilizing this extended family consultation I have never seen it harmful, although occasionally grandparents are angry afterwards. Also, I've never seen it fail to be useful. Many times I can't understand why, but I grow more and more convinced that it's always helpful.

Jim, the father, had been in personal psychotherapy for 4 years, without losing his retiring shyness. His wife, a schoolteacher, then began psychotherapy because of psychotic episodes related to stress over her four adopted children. After a year of treatment her psychiatrist turned gay and left town. She was referred to me, and I asked the father's therapist to be cotherapist and help treat the family. Mother had three psychotic episodes in the next year. In one of them, she jumped in front of a car, breaking several bones, and was in the hospital for weeks. During this time the cotherapist forced the father's father and the mother's mother into psychotherapy, as well as father's sister. For the next 2 years treatment included husband, wife, four children, two grandparents, and one adult sibling. No interview was allowed unless all were present.

The essence of this therapeutic process was the gradual emergence of the grandparents out of their isolated retreat from life. The father's psychotic understructure also surfaced and was integrated. The children matured from belligerent, chaotic little animals to creative human beings, and the extended family group interaction became alive and vivid. Mother had more psychotic episodes, progressively less serious, and the entire three-generation system became more cohesive.

Including the third generation increased the power of our intervention in resolving the identified patient's symptom, as well as helping with the multiple family problems. Having the three generations present also allowed the therapists operational freedom to move in and out of the family structure. This was vital, since if the cotherapists ever become enmeshed, the game is lost. The three-generational process brought about the rehabilitation of all the individuals in the family: four children, two parents, a sibling of one parent, and two grandparents. Three-generation therapy also prevented the total failure of the previous treatment of the two individuals, the couple, and their children.

How does one start such a three-generation group cooking? I usually begin by defining my impotence in detail. "Family systems are powerful groups. Like the Green Bay Packers, any change must be a group decision. This family seems to be losing games; I'd like to coach them to victory, but I feel pretty feeble. I'm not even on the field of play—just a new coach. How can I help you most? What did you grandparents do when you had similar problems in your younger days? Did you see this trouble coming on?" I always invite them back at any time they can come, and every week if it's feasible. Sometimes they keep coming, and it becomes a revolution *in situ*. If they cannot come in regularly, I ask for the right to use them as consultants at a later period, either as a group or as subgroups at their convenience or my need.

Much of the progress in psychotherapy has been serendipitous. Professionals tend *not* to be innovative until they are pushed into it by their caring and the creativity of their patients. I moved into couples because of my insecurity in working with individuals, and then into families as a way of breaking out of impasses with couples. I'm now discovering what one patient can do to bring about the reunion of an entire family. One symptom-carrier instigated a massive number of telephone calls that resulted in 35 out of 45 available family members arriving to meet with a psychotherapist for a 3-day family war. Objective—the cauterization of family bleeding.

One of the characteristics of family network therapy is that the more people who are present, the less pressure there is on the professional therapist. His function is mainly to be a time and a place; it's not even necessary for him to be a moderator. The anxiety and the preplanning that have already occurred in each person's head, as well as between members of the group, guarantee a meeting loaded with secret agendas. The only question is, who will have the courage to start? The therapist may structure the situation by giving them some idea of systems theory; he may also destructure their fantasies about what he will contribute. But once the reunion has begun to move, usually with the senior people firing the first guns, the battle is on; the therapist need only sit still and watch. Many times there is so much stress that he will not be able to even add perspective because things are too hot for him to touch. The traditional multiple-impact approach, or recurrent meetings, are generally not necessary, since the family reunion has its own dynamics; another meeting may also be difficult to arrange because of time and space. It is possible, however, to use 1, 2, or 3 days of full-time meeting, and accomplish a remarkable release of affect, discovery of new realities, detriangulation of some of the family structurings, remobilization of groups that were previously intimate, and cooling off some of the wars.

The objective of such a conference is to resolve rifts in the family subgroups, and, almost as important, the discovery of who the other family members are, how they live, and the way they operate. Like resolving intrapsychic ambivalence, it's an integrative process. If you ask me whether this effort is supposed to reorganize the entire family, my answer is, I have no intention of trying for that. However, the discovery that one belongs to a family, and can call on blood connections makes a great deal of difference to people who feel isolated in a socially manipulative, cold, urban community.

When the family group becomes convinced that I really do believe that people know more than anybody, a kind of serendipity may develop. The group may bring the minister who was their first counselor; or they may recall what the family physician said during that last asthmatic attack. One family brought mother's newly acquired stepfather, who had been accused of killing the father in a brawl. Still another extended family brought a neighbor who was invited by the family to spread the dirty linen on the table, and did so to everyone's benefit.

Many times the therapist is well advised to keep a low profile, except to ask forgiveness for his own personal circumstances: "Sorry, I'm not Catholic," or "Wish I could speak Dutch."

One almost universal fallout residue of the three-generation approach is a sense of dignity in the family as a whole—a sense that "We are the John W. Does." This perspective and historical awareness makes possible a feeling of continuity which is not present at the ordinary family parties, weddings, or funerals. Often the discovery of the grandparents by the grandchildren may evoke forgiveness and a group esprit, which have the long-range effect of healing that kind of stir-crazy stress so usual in the isolated nuclear family. A suburban mother's battle fatigue, or the workaholic addiction of a successful father are really massive problems; they are difficult to resolve with the limited facilities of the nuclear group and their therapist.

One further spin-off from the use of the family as consultant is an emphathic sense of wholeness which serves as an excellent counterforce to the cultural alienation so neatly defined by Kaiser[18] as the "delusion of fusion," and which also increases each individual's readiness to face his own aloneness and his time-measured finiteness.

Interaction within the three-generation group may neatly define and lubricate the interface between the generations. The therapist can easily stimulate them to talk about the good old days, which allows the grandchildren to picture family rituals and enjoy biographical tidbits. Each generation group may come to admit that it is only possible to belong to one's own generation, so that role expectations are eased, and new roles are developed. The interface between the sexes—flirtation between grandma and grandson, between grandfather and granddaughter—may often serve to relieve much Oedipal guilt in the nuclear family, and turn love and sexuality into an integrated, rather than a dissociated, recreation.

The interface between the two families of origin is especially benefited. Each family of origin secretly claims all the adapted offspring, and parenthetically attributes to the other family all misfits, either real or imagined. The jealousy thus induced may escalate and spread. A family conference often burns away this dissonance by the warmth of visual introjection. This recognition of otherness further induces in the individuals a sense of self-esteem unrelated to the self-respect derived from the drive for success. Every individual has his own I position in his family of origin, and it's given a third dimension by increased belonging to the three-generation group.

Covertly, and at times overtly, the individual sees himself 25 years ago and 25 years from now, and this sense of projected time redefines the present in right-brain wholeness in a way not possible by any episode of therapeutic working-through. Some members may even begin to make tentative forays into a new adulthood. Roles become flexible. Teenagers can contribute wisdom, oldsters can dare to be irresponsibly childlike, men can be tender, and couples freshly loving. Grandparents may become fun playmates for the first time.

When the three-generation system has been assembled, whether as a preventive experience, a healing force, as consultant to the frustrated therapist, or to mediate a three-generation civil war, the long-range benefits may outweigh the immediate ones. Increased flexibility in role demands are almost automatic; frequently loyalty debts and covert collusions are altered. Involvement in the metagame of change allows new visual introjections of individuals and subgroups, thus altering each person's intrapsychic family. Discovering that one belongs to a whole, and that the bond cannot be denied, often makes possible a new freedom to belong, and of course thereby a new ability to individuate.

THE HINDRANCE OF THEORY IN CLINICAL WORK

This chapter represents Whitaker's clearest statement about the need of the therapist to be a person in therapy rather than a theoretician or technician. Theory, he warns, destroys creativity and intuition and eventually destroys the therapist. Whitaker suggests that the therapist must deny himself the anxiety reduction that comes with adherence to a theory, in order to encourage the family to increase their tolerance of anxiety.

Belief in a theory leads, Whitaker feels, to a reliance on techniques and a tendency for the therapist to attempt to manipulate the family toward a particular goal. The nontechnical therapist is willing to just be with the family and allow them to develop the family they want. The therapist refuses to play a constant role in the family and thus encourages the other family members to develop role flexibility. Above all he models integrity and growth for the family.

This presentation, perhaps more than any other, states Whitaker's primary message to psychotherapists. It is a message, however, that most psychotherapists do not want to hear or accept. The fear it generates is that therapists will behave chaotically and will be destructive to those treated. As Whitaker sees it, however, the danger is in the other direction, on an overreliance on theory, not on an underreliance on it. The psychotherapist is taught theory for years, and Whitaker's work is an attempt to provide an antidote to that indoctrination. The therapist is urged to transcend technique as much as possible, but it is an urging predicated on the assumption that the therapist has a theory and technique to transcend.

I have a theory that theories are destructive—and I *know* that intuition is destructive. Isn't it sad? And no excuses will be accepted. Bert Schienbeck says,

Reprinted by permission from P.J. Guerin (Ed.), *Family Therapy: Theory and Practice.* New York: Gardner Press, 1976. Copyright © 1976 by Gardner Press, Inc.

Kyk.
('t is vell erger)
(dan je denkt)
als je denkt
is 't nog erger

Look. It's worse than you think. And if you think, it's much worse.

THEORIES

Theory is the effort to make the unknowable knowable. It's trying to work out a method for forcing the left brain to control the right brain. The process was defined many, many years ago: "It's not given to man to see the face of God except through a glass darkly." Theory is also, of course, one of the ways of trying to understand the impossible. It's been theorized, for instance, that we are all conceived in sin. It has also been hypothesized that we are all born innocent. Tillich says being is becoming, and that we avoid being by trying. We keep doing to avoid being. My theory is that all theories are bad except for the beginner's game playing, until he gets the courage to give up theories and just live, because it has been known for many generations that any addiction, any indoctrination, tends to be constrictive and constipating.

Success in psychotherapy with neurotic patients leads to a theory that developing the capacity to "comment upon" the double binds we use to entrap ourselves is curative. This escape hatch is not often available in psychotherapy with seriously disturbed persons, and is probably never available in working with families. However, psychotherapists are very susceptible to the disease of metacommunication. We talk about talking so successfully or think about thinking so effectively that we are in danger of losing our freedom to talk or think.

Furthermore, the combination of metacommunication and professional objectivity tends to bring about a loss of caring. We talk about the "love object," or the development of techniques for "social manipulation." It's like talking about "body counts." Dependency on theory is often increased by the discovery that many patients get well. Some neurotics get well from even a research investigation of their etiology and psychopathology. (The fact that psychotics do not get well from this kind of research is merely viewed as a matter of unresolved additional data.) But technical approaches do not seem to succeed for second-generation therapists. Rogerian theory, which worked so well for Carl Rogers, did not work as well for those people who learned to follow him; eventually many of them gave up Rogers' theory and became themselves, rather than carbon copies of the master. This same thing occurred with Lazarus, who moved from copying Wolpe's theoretical structure to being a real person, and even wrote a book called *Beyond Behavior Therapy*.

THE SYMPTOM THEORY

Medical practice teaches the serious danger of relieving symptoms as though they were the disease to be treated. Every medical student is warned not to treat a lower right-quadrant abdominal pain as a sui generis problem. Doing so may lead to a ruptured appendix. Yet in psychotherapy much effort is expended to relieve the symptom as such. Success at this maneuver may indeed be of great relief—but what if the symptoms arise because of an adaptation to a pathological cultural and family situation? Aiding the patient to adapt may be at least a disservice and at most an abortion of the central striving for growth and integration. The symptom may be an exquisite experience of regression in the service of the ego, and if it is, a comforting therapist may reverse an existential shift (Eisenberg) that would not only yield a 2-week "peak experience" (Maslow), but change the person as both person and teammate. Mayhap relieving the pain will prevent the formation of a pearl.

The chilling effect theory has on intuition and creativity in general is highlighted by the fact that it tends to make symptom relief the objective of psychotherapy—adaptation to culture, to family, to situational stress. Psychiatric symptoms, like abdominal pain in the lower right quadrant, must not be relieved, lest it disguise the appendicitis so that the patient dies from generalized peritonitis. The patient whose symptom is relieved while his effort to integrate the conflicting forces in his own life experience is destroyed is an example of an operation being successful, although the patient dies.

An example? Joe went psychotic. His Christ-like efforts to show his terrified mother that her fearful nightmares should be suppressed worked. She became comfortable again, although, of course, worried about his terrible problem.

One of the objectives of psychotherapy of the family is to counter the culture bind. One demand made by our culture is like the demand of mother—that we feel a symbiotic belongingness, addiction, and enslavement to the culture pattern. This is enforced, like mother, by making it hypnotically important to not know that you're symbiotically enslaved. The family also uses the culture's demands that we be different from each other as substitute for being a self. If I am indoctrinated with the clear conviction that I'm not like you, I can believe that therefore, I must be me. Self-discovery by denial is, of course, one of the basic understructures of attempted divorce. If I'm not part of that other person, then I must be myself—a very neat delusion to induce isolationism.

Zoroaster is supposed to have instigated the Western world's addiction to the god–devil dichotomy. People are labeled as good or bad; behavior becomes the basis for judgmental decisions even about life and death. Theory is used by its devotees to dichotomize patient and therapist patterns of interaction. Interpretations carry endless judgments; the freedom to interact exists only beyond the borders of the system, away from the tyranny of a right–wrong polarization.

One of the effects of a therapeutic orientation based on theory is that the therapist becomes an observer. In doing so, he not only avoids his chance of being a person, but he also tends to help the family avoid their courage to be. The resolution of Tillich's koan, "Being is becoming," turns into "Doing is to keep from being." Many families who are very busy use their busyness as a kind of reciprocal contract to be functional and thus avoid anxiety, and also to produce a paralysis of the integration that is wholeness. Each becomes an observer and presents a performance demand; each becomes distanced thereby and afraid of the performance failure. The pathology is a static, nonevolving groupness.

Young physicians very often find the anxiety-provoking experience of sharing a patient's life stress very hard to tolerate. Their failures leave a residue of impotence; their successes induce a euphoria which covers the phobic concerns about the next patient. Any shorthand label helps them neutralize some of these effects. At first their theories are simple—her mother was unloving, his father was cruel, the parents didn't want this third baby. As their three training years unfold, so do the concepts: play therapy should be designed to release aggression; physical touching is effective in resolving the affect hunger of the orphan syndrome; all women over 30 are neurotic, and all men over 30 are indifferent. They need to devise reasons why for their experiences.

The faculty of course are much more sophisticated, so that we can and do give them complex, all-inclusive explanations for why the patients are distressed. Courses in child development offer an endless series of parenting distortions, and failures are explained as due to excess permissiveness, the lack or excess of a generation gap, an authoritarian atmosphere, or lack of intimacy between the parents' unwanted children.

There must be a way. The poor resident is himself haunted. Is the answer Freudianism, Jungianism, or Rogerianism? Who is right? Adler seems to have something, but so do Rank and Reich. Maybe all psychology should be thrown out—isn't biology gradually taking over? If one drug won't solve it, two or three might. Or "they"—*Who are these they?*—will find a new drug to relieve their anxiety. As experience with patients grows, theories expand and become both more global and protected by subtheories: the patient wasn't ready for therapy; or, the etiology was Oedipal, but father's death made resolution impossible. Sometimes the explanations are as tortuous as those of a theologian who has resolved his anxiety about the way with a theory, or two, or five.

There are three usual resolutions of this dilemma of psychotherapy training. Each resident either gives up on psychotherapy, becomes a convert to one system of thought, or espouses a life-style of endless searching. The half-life of his transference to each new theory varies, but in general their usefulness decreases as he is forced to recognize that there are as many spontaneous recoveries as there are theoretical. Part of the problem is the theoretical delusion that science is curative—that enough knowledge, enough information, the right kind of facts will bring about the resolution of life's doubts, the resolution of all distress. This point of view differs, of course, from most philosophical and therapeutic efforts in the East. Yoga is not really a method of therapy. It assumes that the individual's therapy takes place within the culture; yoga is then utilized for expansion of the person after he has become a well-adapted individual who knows how to utilize himself, and after he has lived through many of his growth struggles.

And in the West, too, therapy takes place in the culture, despite the fact that books on psychotherapy may assume that nonprofessional helpfulness is inadequate, nonexistent, or a mistake. There is no question but that a great many children headed for schizophrenia in their infancy happen to make contact with a loving-hearted lady next door, or even maybe with a friendly dog next door, and so learn how to love, learn how to be personal and intimate. This context is ordinarily just called friendship, but more honestly should be called social therapy. The grandmother who gives some little girl cookies whenever she comes to visit, the old carpenter who takes a neighbor's boy fishing, the boss who calls an employee in and rakes him over the coals, the supervisor who sits down to be straight with one of his workers may each be therapeutic. Our culture itself, however, seems to have grown less therapeutic over the recent decades. Family reunions used to bring people together for a Sunday celebration at grandma's house, but this kind of community psychotherapy is not as common today.

Without theory, though, how is the young therapist to make decisions? Psychotherapy is an art. The development of that right-brain intuitive gestalt process not easy; the techniques emerge painfully from under the compulsive dominance of the anxiety-binding, verbalizing authority of the left brain. Good supervision, and protection from the excess grief of raising one or more specially crippled children may help to develop sensitivity to the pain of caring. Gradually the toughness needed for the separation and the recurring empty nest syndrome will develop. If that toughness is not achieved, the young therapist will inevitably withdraw to a safe distance with almost every patient. The new mother needs the tender care of her husband and of her mother as she learns to feed and love her new baby; the new therapist needs a teammate and a nurturing elder statesman.

Nontechnical or nontheoretical family therapy has various components. One of the most valid is borrowed from Zen, which is structured around the effort to break the computer programming of the past by posing an impossible problem. Zen does not teach adaptation; it teaches increased courage and how to face impossible problems. It aims at helping or pushing the student to break through into a new integration by separating him from all logical, theoretical, disciplined patterns of understanding. It asks the student to answer an unanswerable question, a koan. The best known koan is, "If two hands clapped together makes a loud noise, what is the sound of one hand clapping?" To answer this may take many months of struggle and necessitate moving out of the ordinary framework of thought. One of the possible answers is that the sound of one hand clapping is *om*, the sound of the universe.

The process of nontechnical or nontheoretical family psychother-apy also uses a deliberate effort to increase anxiety. The therapy team establishes a pattern of caringness, so the family dares to be more anxious instead of escaping into protective, defensive patterns. The therapist models, with some member of the family, an I–thou relation-ship characterized by caring and flexibility, with the aim of pressur-ing the family into tolerating more anxiety. Much of the modeling is the freedom to share with the family the secret language that the therapist uses with himself, including metaphorical allegories, free association, and fantasies. Once, for example, a picture came into my mind of a fishing line that went through the lobe of each ear of a family's scapegoat and then around the room through each earlobe of the other family members. Sharing this bit of fantasy with the family helped them to move toward a kind of togetherness that they had dreamed of but had become hopeless about.

The initial phase of family therapy is a struggle to see whether the family can depend upon this foreign person to maintain their stability while they reorganize their system to cure the scapegoat or make for better individuation. Once the battle for structure or the battle to establish the generation gap between the patient and the therapist is settled, the subsequent tendency is to demand that the therapist give rules for life, take over the family, say what's right and what's wrong. If the therapist is dedicated to a theory, or even if he himself believes a theory of psychotherapy, he tends to make it into a theory for change and a theory for growth, or even a theory for living. And once that is imposed, no matter how subtly and no matter how carefully, the patient or family becomes dependent and rebellious, and the genera-tion gap ends with less than ideal results.

Ideally then, there should be a reversal of roles so that once the therapist has been established, he denies all theory and forces the family to establish its own theoretical or systematic organizational way of living. He insists that just as his life is inexplicable to him, their life must be inexplicable to them, but it is nonetheless something they must make decisions with, for, and about. This reversal of roles, which may look like paradoxical intention, is really an active parenting with a reverence for the identity of the individual and the unique identity of this family. Just as one person is intrapsychically unique, the family is interpersonally unique. Once this fact has been settled and the family is clear that they have their own structure and the therapist does not know what is best for them, he becomes able to join the family as the consultant, to move into and to individuate from the family. By making it clear that his living is his own affair and must be handled in his own way, he moves out of the family.

The therapist thus becomes a model. The modeling may be done using a purely technical style. Typical is the good mother whose breast is always available. At its worst, this induces symbiosis; at its best it results in increasing dependency and a psychopathic manipulation for more milk at less need. It is, in essence, a kind of addiction, in which the patient or family becomes addicted to the therapist. In this kind of all-giving approach, in which the therapist forces the patient into dependence, the therapist himself becomes mechanical and bored, someone who is living in the world of metacommunication and doesn't communicate. The performance demand from the family is also massive, for they must conform or leave.

Mastery of a theoretical approach often results in an effective technique that is able to induce the family into therapy. When the process is not successful and the family stays dependent, or becomes rebellious and breaks out of therapy, the therapist's fear of failure may lead him to take up the observer role. He's then stuck with a loss of intimacy, and co-opts the patient by his own self-denial. That is, he becomes a kind of technical prostitute.

The nontechnical psychotherapist or the therapist who is not addicted to a theory operates in a much less rigid manner.[19] He demythologizes himself to the family by modeling his own unpredictability. This modeling takes the form of uniting with the family at one moment, and separating from them at another moment. His caring for them is clear both when he's joined and when he's separated; but he also exposes the fact that he cares more for himself than he does for them. They sense that his reason for working with them is to expand his own capacity to care and to expand his own person. In defining with them the usefulness of craziness—that is, compulsive noncompulsiveness—he teaches them to individuate and be creative as individuals, as subgroups, and as a whole. He extols the group craziness of the family who go off on a cross-country automobile trip together, or the individual craziness of the psychiatric resident who 1 day a month puts on a clown costume and wanders around the city playing silly tricks and being somebody else, or the group of teenagers who go off on their own as a whole group leaving the parents to struggle with their twoness. In modeling playfulness, the therapist by his own regression induces the family to regress in the interview. They may have a whole interview which has no purpose.

One of the other functions of the therapeutic modeling role is to break the cultural mythology of psychotherapy. When therapy has been well structured, the therapist can bring in a cotherapist, a consultant, or one of his own children. He can become the patient and struggle with one of his own problems, or bring in other patients or even another family. The sharing of his own slivers of pathology, remnants and fragments of his undisciplined, unintegrated person, or vignettes from his family of origin are all grist for this midphase stage of family therapy, which should be free of any theoretical structure and intensely involved in the process of disrupting all ingrained, imprinted patterns.

One of the most useful aspects of this kind of nontheoretical approach is the therapist's freedom to not demand or even push for progress. The freedom to be involved in the current "beingness" of the family, the freedom to invite the family to be involved in his current "beingness," help establish a break with their theory of change, as well as with their theory of hope for the future or threat of the past. Finally, the therapist should be able to reverse roles in such a way that he exposes his own hunger and thereby allows himself to be co-opted by the family system as its new scapegoat; he can then prove that he can break his way out, as the individual family members are hoping to do. They don't really want to stay out of the family. They do want to be free to go in and out as they choose.

We have to have some way to decide what the object of psychotherapy is in order to talk about it. We presume that families come because of their inability to be close and the resulting inability to individuate. They come to recover their capacity to care, to discover that people can be symbiotically close without being bound, vulnerable, or victimized. We assume that they're also coming in hopes of getting their anger resolved so that they can be more free to care.

The objective of family therapy is to become part of a group which has such role flexibility that anyone can take any role under the proper circumstances. We assume the normal family grants a freedom to subgroups in any way—that is, father–daughter and mother–son can play at being partners without evoking jealousy in the other parent or in the other children. Mother and father can each become a child in the family set without disrupting the group belongingness. Father can come home with a headache from work and feel comfortable in asking his little son or daughter to be his mama; and mother can come home from a hard day and comfortably be a little girl to her own child.

However, any family must also establish a clear generation gap. Although the parents are a subgroup of the family as a whole, their role is differentiated by their generation. We assume the triangles within the family are comfortable and mobile, and that if father and daughter gang up against mother, or mother and daughter gang up against father, this is temporary and exciting, not static and painful. The normal family casually revels in the present. The ghosts of the past and the hopes of the future do not bedevil the present. Each person has an I position and is an integrated, that is, focused, unidirectional person. All members are clear that the center of each person's life is in himself even though the family is part of his expanded self. It's enriching that the nuclear family has an intimate connection with mother's family of origin and father's family of origin. In essence, then, the normal family is a genuinely mutual and loving family; struggles for individuation and separateness are acceptable and exciting, and despair is not the affective undercurrent. Their freedom to regress in the service of individual egos is exciting, and their fun as a group is childlike, open, and free of the metacommunicational heaviness of an intellectual orientation to life.

Masters and Johnson have reduced sexual problems to two basic patterns: the fear of performance, and the distancing process of the spectator role. This simple formulation may be an excellent place to start an effort to move away from 50 years of evolving theories, each of which has had some serendipitous therapeutic success. Is it possible that our theoretical efforts are a head trip to avoid our fear of impotence?

The objective evaluation of pathology and the deliberate effort to correct deviation cannot be applied to the family. Theories about the etiology of psychopathology are abstractions relating to infantile character and personality development: they cannot be superimposed on the development of a family system and its pathology.

Family pathology requires an operational theory that includes family myths and cultural myths. Indeed, the therapist lives by his unconscious operational theory based on the family myths and cultural myths of his own upbringing. Whereas research into the pathology of an individual patient with neurotic problems can many times result in the correction of the pathology, it's very clear that in family therapy this process is not sufficient. The essential therapeutic defect seems to be a lack of power in the therapist. He is impotent. One of the bases for this impotence is that he has been trained in linear causology, whereas study of the family system shows very clearly that causology is circular. There's no way of saying where the pathology is in a family, just like there's no way of saying what caused World War I. Although theories are valuable in explaining processes and are important as a preliminary to work of any kind, a good blueprint does not guarantee a good house.

Good therapy must include the therapist's physiological, psychosomatic, psychotic, and endocrine reactions to a deeply personal interaction system. The freedom to move in shamanlike primary process responses must be defended by a professional cotherapist or a professional cuddle group. Psychotherapy is a counterculture process, and if the therapist is not protected, the community will wither him.

Dedication to theory in family therapy work is essentially a cop-out, a disguise that will eventually conceal even the process of therapy. It's an emergency escape hatch from the powerful stress that exists between the therapeutic team and the family itself. It is assumed by many that the intellect provides a structure that makes involvement possible without abnormal entanglements. I do not believe this is true. Theory is a left-brain abstraction of a two-brained operation. Theory supports an objectivity in order to prevent countertransference—more truly, transference—and as such it's as fallacious as the theory of unconditional positive regard, which is to say that love conquers all.

Exactly how little effect theory may have on the actual practice of psychotherapy is well illustrated by the story of group therapy done with members of the 8th Air Force during World War II. The group therapist in charge had 30 group therapists under him. They were struggling to keep the bomber pilots who flew each day to bomb Germany from becoming psychotic. More particularly, they were trying to keep the navigators sane, since with nothing to do on the missions except sit, they went crazy at a much higher rate. Among these therapists were people who were trained—Freudians, Sullivanians, Kleinians; therapists who were pediatricians who'd been given a 90-day emergency course; and doctors who had only taught. During the 2 years he ran this intense group therapy, he observed that success and failure seemed related exclusively to the person of the psychotherapist. That is, people who were expertly trained, people who had had long group therapy experience, and people who had no group therapy experience all seemed to succeed or fail largely to the degree to which they were human beings with their groups. Effectiveness, in other words, seemed to be independent of technical expertise. He also decided that the inexperienced people could be used provided that supervision was available to protect them against recurrent countertransference problems.

What can we use as a substitute for theory—the accumulated and organized residue of experience, plus the freedom to allow the relationship to happen, to be who you are with the minimum of anticipatory set and maximum responsiveness to authenticity and to our own growth impulses. We must also recognize that the integrity of the family must be respected. They must write their own destiny. In the same sense that the individual has a right to suicide, the family has the right to self-destruct. The therapist may not, and does not, have the power to mold their system to his will. He's their coach, but he's not playing on the team.

The fact that patients—and especially a family—declare themselves impotent by asking for help does not imply weakness. The weakness that becomes apparent early in therapy is a transference syndrome; in no way does it indicate any need for the kind of tender, passive listening. Instead, the caring therapist can trust his own empathy and the strength of the family to make direct interchange useful and valuable.

The therapist must develop the kind of power necessary to invade the family, and do battle with them. Simultaneously, he must develop the courage to be himself, and to share his own irrelevancies and free associations. He must expand his own person, thus modeling for the family their own growth. Family therapy is like psychotherapy with the psychotic—long-circuited thought processes will activate the "it's phony" switch, which is as sensitive in the family as in the psychotic. Breaching the programmed family mind must be induced by the therapist's deprogramming himself, and advancing his own growing edge. The only personal response to primary process communication is primary process—that is, free association—by the therapist. Free association has an instantaneous response time that forces an intimacy in the relationship very difficult for even the hypermanic or sophisticated paranoid schiz to parry or repress. Sharing intrapsychic responses induces first a symbiotic sane–crazy weness, and soon thereafter a reversible role teaming. This role switch leads to individuation of the therapist and the patient, after which the step to independent loving-ness completes the repair cycle. Crucial to the intimacy is a freedom to be vulnerable—the exposure of personal value systems, codes, and even slivers of the therapist's pathology. As Barbara Betz said, many years ago, "The dynamics of psychotherapy is in the person of the therapist." Why should the family expose their tender underbelly if the therapist plays coy and self-protective?

The medical ethos insists that the physician's unswerving devo-tion to science and humanity is enough reason for being. Those who choose to be physicians therefore very often become workaholics and coronary victims; psychotherapists seem to elect suicide as their early resolution. My personal opinion is that either a coronary or suicide is better than drying up. But there is an alternative—a set of rules that will help to keep the therapist alive.

1. Relegate every significant other to second place.

2. Learn how to love. Flirt with any infant available. Uncondi-tional positive regard probably isn't present after the baby is 3 years old.

3. Develop a reverence for your own impulses, and be suspicious of your behavior sequences.

4. Enjoy your mate more than your kids, and be childish with your mate.

5. Fracture role structures at will and repeatedly.

6. Learn to retreat and advance from every position you take.

7. Guard your impotence as one of your most valuable weapons.

8. Build long-term relations so you can be free to hate safely.

9. Face the fact that you must grow until you die. Develop a sense of the benign absurdity of life—yours and those around you—and thus learn to transcend the world of experience. If we can abandon our missionary zeal we have less chance of being eaten by cannibals.

10. Develop your primary process living. Evolve a joint craziness with someone you are safe with. Structure a professional cuddle group so you won't abuse your mate with the garbage left over from the day's work.

11. As Plato said, "Practice dying."

SYMBOLIC–EXPERIENTIAL
FAMILY THERAPY

with David V. Keith

This section of a much longer work includes Whitaker's most exhaustive discussion of family therapy techniques and process. It should be read with the previous chapter in mind, however, which warns the therapist about the hindrance that theory and technique may have on therapy. As usual, Whitaker, at a "meta" level, makes the point that neither technique nor art is sufficient alone; in fact, they may both be destructive. As Whitaker puts it, "It's worse than you think. And if you think, it's much worse."

With these warnings in mind, this chapter offers specific lists of techniques Whitaker and Keith find frequently useful and common technical errors in therapy. In addition, Whitaker and Keith discuss in detail the factors in their therapy that they feel are curative. Throughout the chapter the authors differentiate between real and symbolic curative factors in therapy. Both are considered important, although to varying degrees at different points in therapy. In this discussion they summarize and encapsulate many of the ideas Whitaker has advanced over his long career.

TREATMENT APPLICABILITY

The main contraindication to family therapy is the absence of a family therapist. There is also a relative contraindication, the absence of a family, that is, the absence of relatives. Our method of clinical practice is family therapy. *We do not simply do family therapy: we are family therapists.* Any psychotherapy venture ought to begin with a family interview. If the whole family is not available, then someone from the

Reprinted by permission from A. Gurman and D. Kniskern (Eds.), *The Handbook of Family Therapy.* New York: Brunner/Mazel, 1981. Copyright © 1981 by Brunner/Mazel, Inc.

patient's world should be there for at least the first interview. The presenting problem is not what determines the suitability for family treatment. Suitability depends upon the extent to which they share our culture's implicit belief about how the world works. It works best with people who believe in families. It works less well with people who do not believe in the family.

Families Most Likely to Have a Therapeutic Experience with This Approach

These families are most likely to find this approach therapeutic.

1. Crazy families who are in for fun and/or involved in a dilemma which is multifaceted and multipersonal.
2. Therapists who would like a family therapy experience or families with psychological sophistication.
3. Nonsubjective families with psychological problems. Again, the system is not based upon intellectual understanding but rather upon an interactive process, metaphorical language, and personal interaction.
4. Families in crisis.
5. Families with a serious scapegoat, for example, with a schizophrenic in the family (pre-, acute, or chronic).
6. Families with young children seem to get more from working with us. We become parents to these new families.
7. Families with multiple-level problems.
8. High-powered or VIP families.
9. Families who are disorganized by the culture (i.e., a family who has a probation officer, a social worker, or an alcohol counselor overattached to them). Our effort is to increase the family's unity so that they can get rid of intruders.

Families Who Are Immune to Infection by Family Therapy

The families for whom there is no "take" in experiential–symbolic therapy are idiosyncratic. We have no way of predicting a priori what families will and will not work well. The approach has developed in work with biologically intact families. It works better when all three generations are available. It works less well when members are not available by reason of death or distance or simply refuse to come. We assume this referral to be a family ploy. We do adapt our work to all sorts of situations, but the likelihood of a "take" is reduced. We work with extended families, social networks, divorcing couples with simultaneous affairs, divorced couples with a child in crisis, and lesbian and homosexual couples. Still, families who seem immune to infection by this method of family therapy are

1. Those that are panicked by spontaneous feelings, for example, postdivorce situations where wounds are still healing and are too tender for reexploration.
2. Those with long-standing pathology and no strong inducement to change.
3. Those in which the scapegoat is an adopted child.
4. While we often work with acutely psychotic schizophrenics outside the hospital and without drugs, we are less successful with manic psychotics who are new to us.

DECIDING ABOUT REFERRALS

It is unusual for us to make a referral to someone else once we have started with a family. If the family members decide they don't care to see us, we counsel them to do their own referral. We have a substitute system: the use of cotherapists and consultants can abrogate the need for referral.

CASE EXAMPLES

A wealthy WASP family was at war about daughter's engagement to a black high school teacher. The therapist brought in a black cotherapist.

A pediatrician referred a family with a child who he thought was autistic. The therapist asked a child psychiatry fellow to work as cotherapist. After a therapeutic alliance was established with the family, they were referred for a more extensive assessment of the child's educational needs. The family continued in treatment.

Two male cotherapists worked with a family with a schizophrenic adolescent. The mother was put off by the uneven sex ratio. A woman was brought in as a consultant for three visits.

We refer for individual therapy when the family therapy experience is completed. When there is a question of neurological difficulty, we refer to a neurologist. In the case of a manic attack, we refer the patient for Lithium. We do not want to supersede the family therapy. Two schizophrenics were in marital treatment. The wife was experiencing anxiety which was painful to her. She requested medication. The therapist told her that he did not believe in medication and would not give medication to her. However, he did not feel it appropriate for him to make a final decision about it and told her that, if she wanted medication, he could suggest another physician whom she might see. The family treatment continued; however, it lost some of its excitement for the therapist.

Situations in Which No Treatment Is Recommended

No treatment is recommended in certain instances.

1. When there has been a completed treatment case, the family has had a therapeutic experience and ended. When a new symptom emerges or an old one reemerges, we have the family come back for a single-visit consultation. If there is excitement in the whole family and they are handling the symptom well, then it is not useful to reactivate treatment. These situations are like fire drills. The family is testing its ability to respond to a crisis and checking out our availability.

2. Families who have had too much therapy (i.e., professional patients) are advised that they should stop looking for treatment. They are to come in if a crisis arises.

3. Families who are seeing a good therapist and come to us out of a negative transference response. We send them back with the suggestion that we would be glad to act as consultants if the therapist so desired.

There are some situations where we are not likely to continue or to begin treatment, but it is not because treatment is not indicated. If the family is only willing to send a segment, that is, the husband, one child, or husband and wife, or husband, wife, and one child only, then we suggest they find someone else. If the father is against psychotherapy, we would rather not be involved. The family members are free to do whatever they want with our refusal. We leave the opportunity open to return to family therapy at any time father may decide that he is willing. The same is true if there is not enough anxiety in the family to make psychotherapy worthwhile. Then it is our preference to decline the referral rather than trying to carry their part of the anxiety load.

THE STRUCTURE OF THE THERAPY PROCESS

It is critical to begin the treatment process with the whole family. In this way the therapy team gets permission from the whole system to change components of the system. If it is not possible in the beginning to have the whole group, we set it up so that the extended family comes in as soon as possible. Once they have been in and the intrapsychic projections of the different generations onto each other have been contaminated, modified, and weakened, they can return whenever possible, but they are not necessary. It is best, however, if all those people who are living together join the interviews.

Our demand to have the whole family in is the beginning of the "battle for structure." It begins with the first phone call. It has to do with when we meet and who will be there. We never split a marital pair for the first interview, but we may accommodate by splitting the generations. If the parents are in a panic about impending divorce or father's newly discovered affair and they do not want to bring the children, we tell them that it is all right the first time, but they must plan to bring the children for the second interview. An internist referred a policeman who was having severe work-related anxiety attacks. Neither the man nor his wife had had previous psychotherapy. He did not feel that he could talk about some of his feelings with his wife present. Keith set up the initial interview structure so that we would balance. There were 20 minutes with him alone, 20 minutes with her alone, and 20 minutes with the couple. We followed this pattern for three interviews and then met conjointly thereafter. A second example with a different flavor involved a minor-league VIP from Los Angeles. He was planning to move to our area with his daughter. He was divorced from his wife, who lived near our medical center. He was concerned about his daughter, who had had extensive psychological and medical evaluations in Los Angeles. The evaluation produced an indeterminant diagnosis somewhere between schizophrenic reaction and hysterical personality. Family therapy with himself and his daughter had been initiated and in his eyes it had been a failure. Father decided to move back closer to his ex-wife. He was referred to one of us. "Would you see my daughter?" Keith said, "I would be delighted to see her as long as you and your ex-wife come along." "Oh, but we wanted her to be seen individually in addition to the family treatment." "Sorry, I do not work that way." "Would you see me and her alone?" "Oh, no, I would need to have both you and mother in. And, by the way, both grandmothers would have to come for the first sessions." The family never called back. Keith set up this structure because of the father's attempt to prescribe the type of therapy necessary. They were not psychotherapeutic virgins and had already had a family therapy failure. Keith needed all the power possible on his side in the beginning. It is better to fail to start than to start and fail.

As the therapy goes on, we push to get the entire family at each meeting. We also suggest "consultation" visits by three or four generations, as well as related network people, including boyfriends, girlfriends, sexual partners, neighbors, or previous therapists. This effort is to help evolve a large system anxiety. We at times schedule conjoint play therapy with small children, or occasionally with subgroups of the family. We discover and rediscover that the power to change anything in the family, whether schizophrenia, divorce, or internecine fighting, requires a voltage amplification in the suprasystem. Subgroup or individual therapy tends to develop massive covert paranoia among the people who are in and the people who are out and is much less functional than small changes arising in the large group. Our intent is to infiltrate the largest system possible and get permission for change. The permission can be overt, although it is usually implicit in any meeting of the larger group. We strive not to allow any favoritism, such as individual interviews with the family scapegoat, whether it's the black sheep or the white knight hero.

Combining treatments is not a favorite method, but, again, there is not a hard-and-fast rule against concurrent therapy. The chance of being ineffective is increased when several unconnected therapists are involved. Patients need all of their emotional energy available in one place for treatment to be effective. Sometimes we functionally divide our effort. In our work with anorexia nervosa, the pediatrician monitors the weight and physical effects, while the psychiatrists do family therapy. Occasionally, at referral, one of the family is on psychotropic medication. Then we have another psychiatrist monitor the medication to avoid seeming like a magician. We use very little medication in our practice. While we rarely start medication, we do not take people off medications prescribed by another.

Family therapy is the best way to start any psychotherapy process. The family members need to be implicated in one another's living. Individualism without individuation (i.e., the absent-without-leave family member) is a common psychiatric illness in our culture. Therapeutic experiences are most valuable when they occur with significant others. By this process, the experiences are built into one's living rather than "in the head" insights.

If causation is circular, change is circular. Everybody in the family is altered by change at any level. A cross-generational group carries the most power for change. Grandparents have amazing symbolic power and it is amplified when they remain separate from the treatment process. By bringing them into the interviews, the grandparents' homeostatic power may be modified or adapted to catalyze change in the family system.

It is difficult to do process-focused family therapy without the children. They are more flexible, more honest, and more affectively available than the parents. The therapist may use them as a lever to invade the family's boundary. With children, he can model for parents the methods and freedom to individuate and reunite. The therapist moves in and out, the children soon learn to move in and out, thus defeating the parents' attempt at embedded consistency. When the children are not present, the sacred component of their role in the family is ritualized and keeps the system from changing.

Thus, the experiential quality of family therapy requires the children's presence. Frequently, change is ignited by the therapist's playing with the children and teasing by his parent–child fun. It tips the parents to be childlike and drop their prideful, adult status role. It is particularly useful to help father avoid the isolation that the culture dictates. Mother may get some sense that she doesn't have to endure battle fatigue but may fight for her personal individuation. Play with the kids includes taking them on our lap for cuddling, rubbing shoulders and backs, or play fighting. Parents enjoy this physical contact personally. When the 11-year-old son's shoulders are massaged, mother often rolls her shoulders perceptibly. Children usually grow in the family therapy. We do not see situations where they are injured by their presence in the therapy. Usually, their anxiety about the family whole is somewhat alleviated. The children's dreams and nightmares are more distressing than any reality component.

COTHERAPY

Cotherapy is a regular component of our work. Mostly, two therapists join together in a professional marriage for ongoing treatment; however, we use alternatives. A therapist may work alone, but use a colleague as consultant along the way. The consultant comes into interviews on call. We also get together as therapists to share case fragments and problems.

There are a number of reasons for operating as a team. (1) Teaming allows more creativity and variability in functioning. At root this gives more power to the cotherapy team. (2) Psychotherapy is anti-cultural and it is important to have a close colleague in order to not pay the price of being depersonalized. When two professionals are present in the name of therapeutic change, the spiritual power increases exponentially. When subjective perceptions are shared by two members, they are less easily disregarded. (3) The therapist's pathology intrudes less. This component may be less important if the therapist uses a structured method of working. In cotherapy each therapist may use himself and his subjectivity with a colleague there to counterbalance. (4) Cotherapy offers the freedom to think. While one therapist is working actively with the family, the second therapist may sit back, look at what is happening from a distance, think over what is said, and arrive at some differing conceptions. (5) Cotherapy helps prevent the therapist from stealing one family member for a therapeutic helper. Either the black sheep or the white knight, when used in this way, distorts the process of family unity and further isolates the scapegoat of the family. (6) It is our belief that cotherapy reduces affect spilling outside the interview. There is less chance of the therapist's holding himself aloof during the interview and taking his affect out in a supervisory or curbstone consultation with another therapist, his spouse, or some unrelated person. (7) Cotherapy decreases the sense of loss at the family's leave-taking. Protective withdrawal of the individual therapist from his next patient and the grieving which might distort the family's leave-taking are minimized. When the family ends, the therapists have each other. Thereby, the therapist augments his professional development, his increasing competence, and his increasing enjoyment of family therapy. More simply, it is much easier for two therapists to avoid compromising their integrity or their goals because of the impending departure of the family. (8) Finally, it is possible in the cotherapy setting for one therapist and one patient to have an extended experience in a one-to-one relationship while the family is present but not feeling extruded. This may take place either in a single interview or over a period of interviews. Such special empathy and interaction between one member of a team and one member of the family will not distort the therapeutic process as it does when one therapist wears several hats.

There are obvious disadvantages in working as cotherapists. It costs the patients more, there are more scheduling problems with a whole family, it reduces each one's grandiosity, and interpersonal complications between the therapists can arise. We use marriage as a metaphor to guide our work as cotherapists. At the heart of a growthful marriage is the struggle between the two spouses to remain autonomous "I's" and at the same time to join in a dependent "we." This same struggle is at issue for both the family and the cotherapy teams.

We do most of our work in our offices. However, we do not exclude working in other settings by any means. The spatial arrangement in the therapy room is simple, yet it is a significant factor in the therapeutic process. The family who comes to our office for help is dependent and one-down. The therapeutic team should be physically grouped rather than invading the family's seating arrangement. The bilateral transference relationship between the team and the family develops a suprafamily, or a surrogate extended family. A subsequent extended family conference occurs against the background of this transference and allows more fluidity in structure for the family itself. The flux of closeness and separation between the treatment team and the family is clearer when there are physically established boundaries. We preserve playing space in the middle of the family room for children or for adults since the process usually involves physical interactions (e.g., arm wrestling, seating changes, or play therapy on the floor).

Ordinarily, our therapy is unlimited in time. Time-limited therapy is invoked when there are reality reasons: the family moving out of the state, not having insurance, or being concerned about the financial aspects of treatment. Time-limited therapy is also useful for people who don't know whether they want psychotherapy, or are just interested in having the experience of being in a therapeutic state. For example, a psychiatric resident and his wife may want therapy with their baby so they can get as much as possible in the way of growth input, but they are not interested in extended probing.

We try to pick up any evidence of the family's desire to take on fuller responsibility for itself and for the therapy. If the therapy is working well, the therapeutic team says, "We'd better quit while we are ahead." If the therapy is not proceeding in a useful way, we suggest, "Why don't we give the whole thing up? Maybe it really isn't worth the stress."

Unlimited time allows the family's objectives to change as time goes along, just as a piano teacher may have one pupil who starts out with little enthusiasm but becomes intrigued and ends up 5 years later playing Beethoven. If the family is intent on expanding its flexibility and increasing its creativity, we see no reason to stop at the originally defined goal or goals. It seems to take a year for creativity to blossom and interest in Beethoven to bear fruit. In the reality of practice, there are many variations in time. The average family comes 10 to 15 times consecutively and then terminates for good. Some make several later follow-up visits. A large percentage of families come in for a consultation or crisis intervention. These families may come to the clinic only one to three times and not return.

Sessions are usually offered once a week, although if only a minimum of anxiety is present or if the family is unusually rigid and with low anxiety tolerance, we may spread out to 2 or more weeks. In contrast, appointments might occur every day if anxiety is high.

In the early part of therapy, decisions about the therapeutic time and structure are made by the therapeutic team. It is the way that all psychotherapy begins. The family starts like a small infant, taking only limited responsibility for themselves. They require structure. We often repeat in our workshops and residency training that the therapist always has the right to make unilateral decisions. The nature of the unilateral decisions is variable from family to family. The freedom to make them decreases as one becomes closer to the family. At the beginning, they are made arbitrarily; later on in therapy they are often made more out of frustration.

Some critics fear we drive people away by being too structured or making too many demands early in treatment. This has not been our experience. We do not bribe people into therapy by agreeing to do whatever they want. We, in fact, challenge their motivation with the result that they push for therapy or go away if they are hesitant. Once we have managed to win this battle for control, however, we soften considerably. This same model applies to rearing children. If the children are in control, the flow of love between parent and child is much inhibited. And in the long run, both parent and child are cheated.

In the midphase, decisions about treatment are made by common agreement. Later in therapy, the decisions are usually made by the family alone. As the therapy becomes more a suprasystem, the family takes more and more responsibility for making their own out-of-therapy decisions and the therapist is given the opportunity to back out of being the parental figure in a parent–infant relationship. Finally, the family becomes better integrated in changing themselves so they do not need an outside person. The model for this process is once again the evolving parent–child relationship. It begins with infancy and goes to late adolescence, where the initiative is with the kids, who then bear responsibility for their own living.

ROLE OF THE THERAPIST

The therapist is like a coach or a surrogate grandparent. Both roles demand structure, discipline, and creativity, as well as caring and personal availability. Balance between these components is established through experience. Our availability is different from the biological parent in that it does not involve the whole self of the therapist.

We are very active as therapists. We don't exclude being directive and may use silence as one unusual activity which is used to increase anxiety. The therapist overtly controls the first few sessions of family therapy. He is very active, both in infiltrating the family and exposing anxiety-laden territory, but usually without being directive. We expect to be part of the family's interaction. Although we do not forbid family members from talking to each other, we assume the main process to come from the family's interacting with the therapeutic team.

We always prefer to work as cotherapists. The therapeutic team is modeled after a marriage with children. The family is seen as a new baby who, with luck, grows to be a child, an adolescent, and finally leaves home. The two "parents" ordinarily assume the roles described in the small group literature as executive or educational director and the supportive or nurturant individual. These roles with the family can be stabilized, but, ordinarily, they move back and forth in a single interview or from the early part of therapy to the later part. The third therapist, the cotherapy "we" (or, from the other side, the paranoid "they") functions as a decision-making discussion center.

The evolving role of the therapy team moves through several stages. In the early part of therapy, the parental cotherapy team is all-powerful, but it quickly defines itself as impotent, unable to push the whole family around. The cotherapists depend upon the family to lead the suprafamily. The therapeutic team declines all efforts to be regarded as magic or possessing supraknowledge of how that family should conduct its life. We assume that each family culture has a style all its own and that our function is to help perfect it and give it more explicit and specific direction defined by its own function patterning. It is like teaching tennis to an advanced player. The entire game cannot be made over; rather, the player's strong points are consolidated and emphasized and weak points corrected.

In the second interview, the family says, "What should we talk about?" The therapist replies, "I don't know. What do you want to change?" "Well, we told you last time." "I know, but that has probably altered since then. You carry the ball and we'll be glad to try to help."

In the midphase of therapy, the parental therapeutic team functions as a stress activator, a growth expander, and a creativity stimulator. In this phase, when the family is secure, the therapist may say, "By the way, Mother, when you spoke like that to your husband you sounded like you were talking to your mother or your father. I wonder if you really want to let him get away with that." This implies that it is a joint arrangement between the two spouses. She is being infantile not only because she wants to be, but also because he needs her to be infantile. The difference between the early and midphase is often best seen when the grandparents are brought into ongoing therapy. Two things commonly happen. First, the whole family reverts back to first-interview behavior. It is like a sociable family reunion. The therapist asks questions. The second possibility is that the subsystem of the family that has been having interviews pushes ahead with their work, bringing the grandparents right into the middle phase therapy. In a subsequent interview, we hear reports that the older generation reports that they didn't think anything happened and it wasn't very useful. Too much was being made of too little is their frequent comment.

In the adolescent or late phase, the team has no functions except to be there and to watch. The cotherapists provide a time and place for the family to get together. Of course, they are available. The therapists depend upon the family to carry all of the initiative and should not try to interfere even if they see they can contribute. In this later phase, the therapeutic team functions as a proud parent, watching the family yet mitigating its own role. This follows the patterning of the parent relationship to a late adolescent who is about ready to leave home. Parents who try to continue educating their children at this late stage are making a serious mistake. The adolescent's independent functioning should be more than respected: it should be revered. The therapeutic team needs to do this with a late-stage family. For example, mother says to father, "I think I may end up divorcing you." It is tempting for the therapist to say, "You've never done it all these 18 years. I don't see why you think you could do it now." Or, contrariwise, "It looks like you two are more loving. I cannot see why you talk about divorce." These are a contribution in the early or midphase of therapy, but are certainly not pertinent in the late phase.

We often use self-disclosure, sharing minutiae in a metaphorical manner, imposing upon ourselves the limits of our own role models. We use it in specific ways, usually sharing fragments or facets of our lives which we have worked over in our own therapy or through our living (Fellner, 1976). Going beyond the role model must be carefully monitored so that there is not a role reversal where the therapist becomes an organizing educator while the family is not allowed full opportunity for its own initiative. *Like humor, personal disclosure is used to increase the interpersonal focus, to shatter a gestalt which is becoming too set—never to diminish anxiety.*

Later in therapy, the therapist's participation can at times be increased, moving toward fragments of his fantasy as they occur during the interview, or bits of his personal history. As the family becomes more secure in handling his input, he can feel free to be increasingly nonrational, free-associative, fantasy-organized, confronting, or paradoxical in any one of many different models. For example, "Dad, I don't think you have to worry about the family getting along so much better. It's not going to last anyway. They'll go back to isolating you and beating on mother by next week or at least the week after." Or, on another occasion, "Mother, I'm certainly glad I'm not married to you the way you take off after your husband. I think I would run for the hills if you were my wife." Or, to one of the kids, "Hey, you know the way your father looks at you when he tells you to either clean up your room or he's going to paddle your behind? I would be tempted to head for San Francisco and probalby get on drugs just to get back at him." Noting physical responses to interactions can be extremely powerful. "The way you glared at me just then gave me a prickly feeling in the back of my neck."

Another method of self-disclosure which we use is interaction between the cotherapists. It may be in the form of a private joke or a comment about our outside life. We may share a childhood recollection with our cotherapist. Or we may ask if he thinks we are too judgmental about the mother. The therapist is sharing fragments of himself and not really asking for help. It is important to note that the therapist is not raising questions for the family to answer, but is making statements about his own set for which he can be fully responsive. He is not imputing to them anything that they have to face, reject, rebel against, or become dependent about.

Therapists do not have a choice about joining the family. If the family continues to come to the clinic, they do so because they have given the therapist some role. We actively join the family. Our transference to them we assume to be the anesthesia for their tolerating the anxiety precipitated later in the middle phase. Ongoing therapy demands both joining and distancing sequences. That is, the therapist must be able to leave the role by his own initiative and later reenter it. It's as though the cotherapists take turns jumping over Wynne, Ryckoff, Day, and Hirsch's (1958) "rubber fence" into the family, holding hands with the partner and jumping back. They thus take turns being "in" and "out." They model the basic problem in family growth. The process of uniting and individuating is both a group stress and the fluctuating experience of individual members as well as family subsystems. The cotherapy team joins the family and in so doing forms a therapeutic suprafamily of which it is a subgroup.

The sequence of joining and distancing is important. It is a lot like being with children. A father can get furious with his kids one minute, then be loving the next. We take the same stance with families. If Keith gets angry, he does not hold onto it. If Keith is joking with the son about his flirtation with mother, he retains the freedom to empathize with father's sadness about being left out. A model is Don Juan, Carlos Castaneda's (1975) teacher. He describes a number of quasi-real, quasi-metaphorical situations where the teacher moves close and then away, and then disappears and suddenly reappears. This is a nice model for the family therapist. It is a difficult, advanced technique for the therapist to master. Less experienced therapists oftentimes do not have a sense of when they are in and when they can afford to withdraw. There is a difference in the way that we handle this. Whitaker can allow himself to be disinterested, suddenly become involved deeply with a family member, then just as suddenly change the topic or dissociate himself. Keith operates more cautiously. He is apt to lead gradually toward a confrontation, engage in the interaction, and then move back more slowly.

The therapist's role changes throughout therapy. In the beginning, the therapist is a kindergarten teacher–shepherd. Within the therapy he moves from being this dominant, all-giving parent of the infant to being the "as-if" pal, an agemate of the young child, then to be the advisor and resource person of the older child, and eventually the retired parent of an adult. As the family becomes more independent, the therapist team can become more personal, more educational, and more outside the family as such. When a family moves toward termination, we respect it as a real initiative, not a symbolic one. We always stand ready to end with them. We do not "look" at reasons why the family wants to leave, but begin to help planning the termination as soon as it is mentioned.

TECHNIQUES OF MARITAL–FAMILY THERAPY

Earlier we noted that structuring in our therapy sessions is implicit. The first interview includes a systems history of the family. We actively attempt to learn about the family emotional system: Where are the stresses located, who has had symptoms, what are the individual character structures, and what about past stress episodes? We try to expose the personality style of each individual, as well as the personality of the total family and its subgroups. We ask about grandparents from each family of origin. Where are they? How are they? What do they think about the situation? We propose an extended family interview. When can they come?

We follow a pattern in our first interview. The family is told that we will talk with each member singly to get a multiple view of what is going on with the family. We start with the member who is psychologically most distant, most often the father. After father, we go around to the different siblings, saving the mother for last. In most cases, the mother knows what is going on and is most available to be a symptom-bearer. This style of interviewing may seem awkward and may go against the instincts of many therapists, but the interactions that develop around it and the messages that are sent result in a big therapeutic payoff.

If one or another of the family members interrupts the talking person, we politely ask him to wait his turn and reiterate that each will have a chance. If an argument breaks out which sounds like one that has been ongoing, we ask them to hold it, because we are not trying to cause trouble but to find out what is up with the family. While we get the history, we are continually restructuring what they say by deciding who talks, minimizing some information, and highlighting other areas.

Joining the Family

The family therapist must develop a basic empathy with the family. We hope his transference feelings will include an identification, a feeling of pain, and a sense of the family's desperate efforts to self-heal.

We work hard to capture the family in the first interviews. If the therapist can develop a liaison with father, there is a good chance that the family will continue in therapy. If not, the chances are they will drop out. Additionally, the chance of losing the family is increased if the therapist gets overinvolved with the mother too soon. The over-involvement can happen in several ways: (1) sexually tinged seduction; (2) taking her on as the identified patient too soon, thus stealing her from the family; and (3) making her angry.

Another way the therapist gains membership in the family is by the bilateral transference. We adopt some of their language, softer accent, or rhythm. The therapist's posture may be the same as that of someone in the family. We listen for their metaphorical set and attempt to make use of it.

Playing with the children is one important way to join the family. It need not be explicitly significant, but often is by surprise. We described earlier our techniques for this.

SPECIFIC TECHNIQUES

One of our standard early techniques is to precipitate in the family a taboo against the bilateral pseudotherapy which develops in every marriage. We give the parents full credit for what they have accomplished in straightening each other out. We declare the end of that therapy, its failure, and demand they turn that therapeutic function over to us. They are to allow no further crying on shoulders, no further talking about illness, symptoms, or their relationship except during the interview. Isolating the metacommunication to the interview setting induces a great reality to the home-edited interpersonal communication. It interrupts the parentification typical of the ordinary marriage. It undercuts the secondary gain they had accrued as each took a turn at being infantile to precipitate the parental (therapeutic) function in the spouse. The technique is most ably activated in the middle of the first interview, when father says, "You see, Mary, that's exactly what I was saying to you." The therapist may say, "Shut up! This is my project. I don't want you helping. You'll just make things worse and think of the joy of not having to listen to her whining anymore." This kind of specific interdiction is a modeling of what we hope will happen outside the interview.

Changes in the family structure many times result from the therapist's invading the family dynamic operation. We tend to emphasize noneducational, noninsightful patterns, such as paradoxical intention, the posing of dissonant models, teasing, deriding or reversing a family's statements, or presenting arguments which are ego-syntonic. For example, mother says, "I am unhappy with my husband." The therapist suggests that the next time she should get a younger man since she looks more energetic. Maybe she could pick a professional athlete who likes a lot of exercise. She could consider taking all this husband's money and going to San Francisco where life is very exciting and the possibility of happiness much greater.

We like to use personal confrontations, even presenting our own boredom. "Mrs. Zilch, the way you responded to your husband just then made me have the nicest feeling that I was not married to you. I don't know whether I would cringe and leave the house or move to counterattack, but it certainly was upsetting to me and I'm just a visitor here." In like manner, if mother, for example, is talking about how weak she feels in the family, we tease her by presenting contrary evidence. She has raised five children who were born 1 year apart, her husband was absent during that time, and it is a wonder that she is not flat on her back with battle fatigue or maybe psychotic.

Our intent with these techniques is to produce transcendent experiences, that is, to help the individual members or even the family as a whole to move above the pain and stress to savor the laughable situations the therapist verbalizes, or to indeed enjoy the experience of looking from a completely different frame. We hope to attain the kind of existential shift that Ehrenwald (1966) presents. In like manner, we confront patients on praxis, that is, the accommodation he makes to her projection. For example, she wants a mother and looks up to him and he very obligingly agrees to play the mother game, even though they both agree it is a pseudomothering she gets.

With our emphasis on the power of the experience in the therapy hour itself, it is not surprising that homework is rarely used, except to interdict the generation flip as described previously. We try to end their pseudotherapy work on each other. We also advise getting the extended family in and pressure until this is accomplished. We may suggest that each person visit his home of origin without the other so as to regress in the service of that family's ego. If the extended family cannot come in and a home visit is not possible, we suggest that the members of the marriage send empty audio cassettes to their families. The instructions are for the parent to dictate a tape describing their lives up until the kids were born.

These techniques are used gently and early in therapy to test out the family's tolerance. Later on, we push them more specifically. The techniques we consider most important follow.

1. *Symptoms are redefined as efforts for growth.* We then increase the pathology and implicate the whole family. The family seen is converted into an absurd one. Our effort is to depathologize human experience. The wife was complaining that her husband was trying to get rid of her. "He's never loved me, you know," she said. "He said once that he would cut me up. Another time he threatened me with a gun." The therapist replies, "How can you say he doesn't love you? Why else would he want to kill you?" Psychosis in one of the family members can be defined as an effort to be Christ-like: "I'll be a nobody so that you and father will be saved." Or the desperation felt by one member of the family can be redefined as a hopeful sign since it means the family cares enough. Just a mild degree of tongue-in-cheek quality

must be included with this technical play so that the confrontation will not be too painful.

2. *Modeling fantasy alternatives to real-life stress.* A woman who has attempted suicide can be pushed to a fantasy. "If you were going to murder your husband, how would you do it?" Or, "Suppose when you got suicidal you decided you were going to kill me. How would you do it? Would you use a gun or a knife or cyanide?" In a family with a schizophrenic son, the daughter's conversation with her father was understood by the therapist as a sexual pass. The family was embarrassed and perplexed by that. At the end of the hour, however, the father tenderly held his daughter and rocked her in his arms. Thus, teaching the use of fantasy permits expansion of the emotional life without the treat of real violence or real sexual acting out.

3. *Separating interpersonal stress and intrapersonal fantasy stress.* For example, the patient who has attempted suicide can be encouraged to talk with the group about whom her husband would marry if she killed herself, how soon he would marry, how long he would be sad, how long the children would be sad, who would get the insurance, how her mother-in-law would feel, what they would do with her personal belongings, and the like. This conversion of intrapersonal fantasy stress to an interpersonal framework is valuable since it contaminates the fantasy. It allows the family a new freedom in communication among themselves since they discover that such frightening words do not mean the end of the world.

4. Technically, once the relationship is established and the supra-unit team is operational, the therapist can *add many practical bits of intervention which in one-to-one therapy would seem like inappropriate moves,* but in the context of the family are safe since the family will utilize what it wants and is perfectly competent in discarding what is not useful. For example, the husband whose wife is having headaches can be offhandedly offered the possibility that if he should spank her, the headaches might go away. Or the wife who is driven up the wall by her children's nagging or dad's aloofness can casually be offered in the presence of the whole family the idea that she could run away to her mother's for a week and let the family make its own meals.

This brings us to the question of homework. We underplay it in our effort to bring all the experience into the therapy. Keith favors positive feedback absurdity assignments like suggesting the couple take turns being in charge and change roles next Wednesday, or suggesting to the juvenile delinquent daughter that she and her mother change bedrooms. *Our most important homework assignment is to avoid discussing the interviews between sessions.*

5. *Augmenting the despair of a family member* so the family will unite around him. This is usually most efficient when used with a scapegoat. For instance, we might say to a schizophrenic son, "If you give up and become a nobody and spend the rest of your life in a state hospital, do you really think mother and father will be happy with each other 20 years from now or will they still be at each other's throats as they are now and you will have given up your life for nothing?"

6. *Affective confrontation.* This is the kind of event that takes place vis-à-vis the parents, most often in defense of the children. It is the change in tone that occurs when the child in play therapy goes from knocking over a pile of blocks to throwing a block at a window pane. An 8-year-old boy and the therapist were mock fighting during a family interview. The parents viewed it as a distraction and continually interrupted, as though the boy were the initiator, although it was clearly the therapist. After several minutes of the parents' complaining to the boy, the therapist got angry and told them to bug off. He said he was playing with their son and he did not want to be interrupted by them.

7. *Treating children like children and not like peers.* Younger children, at times, like to tease us or to fight us physically. We enjoy taking them on and always overpower them. We are willing to be supportive and understanding of teenagers but we also set strong limits with them. Despite our usual openness and acceptance, we can be very moralistic when chewing out a teenager for pushing us around.

Choice of Technique

Decisions to use a particular technique at a particular time are based on clinical experience. Each therapist, out of his own style, develops a set of opening game procedures. It is in the beginning that any therapy process is most structured and therapy is professional, not personal. However, midphase or late-phase participation on the part of the therapist should arise out of his creativity and his aliveness at the moment rather than out of preplanning or some set decision making at an intellectual level. The best interventions to those ends are the therapist's free associations or fantasies. Paradoxical patterns that we use with great frequency usually result from frustration at simple relationship therapy, or a metaproduct of the absurdity offered by the family. The dream of a magical cure, the conviction that all pathology is in one person, the inability to conceptualize or even accept other options than the one they have decided upon—all indicate an absurd, reality-narrowing life-style. It is absurd to argue about absurdities. Our usual response is to be absurd ourselves, to play in such a way that we counterbalance the squares in the family. Many times we use disconfirmation of the whole situation or the family or the individuals as a way to avoid being co-opted and to disrupt their preset opinions. We repeatedly use non sequiturs to derail a train of rationalizations or excuse-making which feels pointless, empty, or repetitive. We utilize silence as a deliberate effort to stop the "blahs" or the pathology of reason and may move out of the situation physically as a way of expressing our inability to be part of it. One response to frustration is the impotence ploy, really a direct statement of the therapist's impotence. "I see no way we can be useful to you folks; your fight is so important to you and your capacity to blame each other is so well established that I see no way to help you get rid of it and it's very possible that this is the best life you can make for yourselves. We suggest you go ahead this way until something further develops or maybe this will become more enjoyable."

In reference to the family as a whole, our basic objective is to induce regression by way of confusion. Regression may be precipitated by two-level messages or three-level messages (e.g., a symbolic statement which is verbal but in contrast to a nonverbal message). The therapist says warmly, "Have you ever thought that killing yourself might make the family happy." Many a double message includes a pseudodisconfirmation. "If you were my wife, I would probably try to increase your interest in me by doubling your allowance." Similarly induced regression can be brought about by non sequitur statements, or statements which have only a very tangential and metaphorical relationship to the things that are going on in the family at the moment. These may come out of fantasies or errant thoughts that arrive in the therapist's head or may be the result of putting together signals given by the family which are in direct contrast or not related to the subject at hand. The same induced regression may be brought about by nonrational participation or even by quite irrational presentations, such as teasing, play, or jokes. We feel no obligation to make sense and we enjoy our inconsistencies. One may pay attention to the story that mother is telling while at the same time rubbing father's neck or cuddling the baby. Similarly, the therapist may deliberately mishear a delinquent's cursing as his physical offer to play with the baby or as an expression of love for the mother. "Fuck you" may be translated into "I love you." Similarly, the mother's request that junior stop watching so much TV may be interpreted to mean "I'm jealous of your intimate relationship with our TV set."

Dealing with Resistance

We have trouble with the concept of resistance. It implies that the therapist must do something about it. Perhaps it could be better thought of as differential motivation for change, or the absence of desperation. In family therapy, resistant, differential motivation or ambivalence about therapy is a problem for the whole system. One member of the family may express it for the rest of the family, but we assume that everyone shares in it. After several visits, the adolescent scapegoat says he thinks that the family therapy is a waste of time and that they ought to quit. Usually the kid is expressing the family's ambivalence. The family looks on to see how the adolescent is handled and then factions in the family begin to express their ambivalence. We don't simply regard the resistance as being individual; we always regard it as the family's conviction that their present solution is the best available. One way to induce desperation is to move to the negative side of the ambivalence and offer to end the therapy so that the family can reunite after they get rid of the therapist. Another move is to augment the differences and suggest that the family members cannot really get together as long as they are clearly fighting each other. One can devise a high-level drama by getting the family to vote about how many would like to kill big brother. Or, a mother who wants to drop out of therapy because of father's infidelity can be confronted with other options. Divorce would be a possibility, staying home to nag him is a possibility, or she could get a boyfriend or tell his mother and the people around town that he is homosexual.

No one in a family system is untouched by a major therapeutic change in the system. These changes are usually nonvoluntary and are most often behavioral in the broadest sense. On the other hand, everyone in the family does not have to make a decision to change behaviors. We want everyone in the family to be at the interview, but everyone does not have to be a patient. In fact, when another patient emerges to replace the one identified by the family, it often produces a good outcome. Each family member is encouraged to change out of his own initiative. If someone wants individual therapy, we can provide it while the rest of the family watches. We defend everyone's right to remain the same. We defend each one's right to be who he is and not to change just because someone else wants him to. Early on we insist that each member give up trying to get something from the family. If the family as a whole fights against us, we usually give up and send the family off on its own, assuming that its winning may be as effective as intervention.

TECHNICAL ERRORS

What are the most common and most serious technical errors the therapist can make with this approach? An important part of our method is the use of our own affect and intuition. The method is regarded by some as dangerous and unteachable. It may be dangerous, but it is teachable. The teaching of it is difficult because it requires apprenticeship, as well as some interest in changing oneself and growing more in relating to one's own family. Psychotherapy is powerful and therefore dangerous. However, in our estimation it is important to teach people how to be effective, not just safe. Surgery is a dangerous business, but that is not to say that it should not be practiced.

Common technical errors occur on two levels. The first is a meta-level which has to do with being a therapist. Errors on the second level are more specific and have to do with doing therapy. Let us start with a list of the metaerrors.

1. It is an error to be co-opted by the family. The therapist enjoys seeing the family and is warm and friendly with them. He becomes so much a part of the family that he cannot help it change.

2. Another serious error is to be so professional or so inimicable to the family that one stays aloof from it, using only technical processes of communication training or interpretive work, both of which have little power to produce the kind of change we aim for. The therapist's anesthesia for his operating to bring about change is his own affective empathy with the family. This may be either a positive concern for the family members' pain or a negative response to them within himself, but in either case he is emotionally invested in them and that enables his participation to be authentic. In truth, his own affect is

anesthesia for doing whatever he feels right in doing. The game of playing at being concerned or playing at changing the family may be useful in sensitivity training groups or in Gestalt groups that have to do with the early experience of a family or an individual, but is so distancing and so chilling that it weakens the affect and induces the family to reconstruct its rubber fence so that the therapist gets only as far in as they want him to and then they thrust him out again. Control of change is in the hands of the family and they won't be any closer to the therapist than he to them.

3. Another error is to make believe the therapist feels no stress and no inadequacy. For example, a white therapist treating a black family is playing a trick on himself. He cannot be consonant with that kind of family. He can try to be closer by having a black cotherapist. The same problem exists where there are strong religious differences or other cultural differences. The therapist is less adequate when he works with natives of other countries because the nonverbal behavior signals given in any one culture make good psychotherapy most effective to someone who belongs to that culture.

4. Family therapists develop methods for pulling the family out of its chosen anxiety-binding system. That is implicit in our way of working. We deliberately manipulate the family, so that the scapegoat cannot function in his usual way, or so that the family is forced into a different kind of behavior. Such tricks can explode the immediate setting and/or precipitate serious stresses outside. For example, in one family, the father, a physician, had recurrent manic attacks and was brought into family therapy, whereupon mother immediately flipped into an acute paranoid psychosis. The family wisely discontinued therapy and a serious failure was prevented.

5. Another problem develops when the therapist plays insight games. He assumes that the family is able to take intellectual input and convert it to a family change process. We don't believe that this can happen.

6. Another error occurs when the therapist makes believe that the family lives in his value system and tries to treat the family as though they were from the same family that he grew up in. Good examples are when the therapist confuses psychological investigation with psychotherapy, or when a Protestant tries to treat a Catholic family while assuming they have the same emotional culture bond.

Next are specific problems in methods. The problem is not, however, that they are apt to do damage to families, but rather that they will just be ineffective.

1. The therapist moves too fast for the family without reading their responses. It is possible to intervene in a way comparable to early interpretations in individual therapy.

2. Failure to treat intuition as intuition. The therapist has an idea which comes out of his own free associations and the family does not hear it or they reject it. The therapist needs to remember that his intuition is his own subjective perception. It may not correspond with the family's view of things. When they resist, it is best to back off very quickly.

3. Failure to know when the therapist is in with a family. The therapist may maintain a first interview posture too long. He dares not use his own affect and is afraid to withdraw from the family lest they view it as rejection.

4. Scapegoating someone else in the family. That is, the therapist may identify with the scapegoat and then scapegoat mother, father, or the marriage. The scapegoat must become the whole family, all three generations of it.

5. Another mistake is to select an emotional or ego set and retain it. It is important to use a lot of variability in work with families. For example, the therapist is sociable when the family arrives, as they talk about the weather or the road conditions, and then starts to gradually switch the content to symbolic by either going silent or by making a symbolic inference.

6. A final problem is the failure to recognize the utility of not treating someone. See our earlier discussion of treatment applicability.

TERMINATION

The ending of family therapy is usually based on a lessening of stress. The family members gradually stop pushing each other, their living together becomes more enjoyable, and talking about life becomes quite empty. They spread out appointments or set up some preliminary subgroup appointments. Usually the therapist picks up symbolic symptoms of his diminishing affect for the interviews and raises the question of how much more is needed. The family is invited to return if it wants to. Individual therapy may be offered if requested. An extended family conference may also precipitate an ending point.

The disengagement of the therapist is a very limited problem in cotherapy, since the "parents" have each other and do not need to use the children. The children recognize a deeper involvement with their live-in parents than with the therapists. The therapist had begun to disengage from the family in the first interview and maintains his freedom to move in and out throughout the entire process. The initial contact is based on the therapist's concern for the family, but the therapist must turn away any effort to make inroads into his personal life or his decision making. The therapist maintains his functional separation in the same way a parent does. With freedom to disengage and reengage, the eventual termination is fairly simple. The therapist has shared those times when he is bored, the patients are experiencing less and less dependence on the therapist, the symptomatic relief has taken place, and the family members are more and more involved with their real living.

Usually, the therapist makes efforts to reinterpret symbolic signals the family gives about ending. Junior talks about the fact that football is going to begin. Mother talks about the fact that she almost forgot the appointment because she had a bridge game. Daddy complains that coming down here is making it more and more difficult for him to earn his full salary, or one of the family members starts talking about somebody else's problems. Any of these events symbolically indicates the family's decreasing interest in working on themselves; if a therapeutic experience has occurred, these can only be construed as evidence that the therapy is nearly ended.

There are other indications. One patient does not show or everyone is late. These symbolic expressions of the readiness for ending may also come from the therapist. He may forget the appointment time, double-schedule another family at the same hour, fall asleep in the middle of the hour, discover himself being noncreative or educational with the family, thus indicating that they are in a stage of late adolescence and ready to leave home.

The wish to terminate by the family is never viewed as a symbolic wish. If they suggest stopping, we agree with them. Our rationale is that if we try to get them to metacommunicate about why they wish to quit and turn that into a therapeutic issue, we all become locked into a pseudotherapeutic relationship. The model is the teenager who decides to leave home, but then keeps postponing it. At some point, the parent must decide that he has done what he could and, although the offspring is never a finished product, he has to let go so the kid can finish growing up on his own.

CURATIVE FACTORS IN SYMBOLIC–EXPERIENTIAL FAMILY THERAPY

It is assumed that, preliminary to a curative process, the family must develop a sense of its wholeness. "We are all in this together and something has gone wrong which has made the first baseman goof up, or something has gone wrong that we're losing one baseball game after another, or something's gone wrong that the pitcher and catcher are fighting with each other." This offer of change is ordinarily set up so that change is induced and carried out on a covert implicit level and a general attack on the symptoms is minimal. Families that do not achieve a sense of the whole seldom stay in therapy.

We do not believe that insight is necessary to change, although it is a frequent by-product of change. Historical and genetic insight brings recognition and change may follow. The important thing is that insight not be overvalued, because recognition can easily occur without learning. Real learning is based upon experience plus evaluation. Learning most often takes place after change has occurred. We push for insight to recalibrate the family's self-image and the individuals' sense of themselves. When families are intellectually sophisticated, it is difficult to shift their intellectual system by interpretation or educational processes of a simple, direct nature. Interpretations are most valuable if they are metaphorical.

Interactional insight is most valued. At best it involves an interactional experience inside the therapy room. The most common interactional insight is the one which involves joint participation in the family complaint. For example, husband complains of the wife's sexual unavailability. We assume that she remains unavailable because he is impotent when she is too eager. These interactional insights break up the web of relationships in the family so that the individual can feel less inhibited by the system.

Interpretations are not essential. Sometimes history is important and must be taken into account. However, interpretation, insight, or history can become an obstruction to therapeutic experience. It is our inclination to save these components of therapy for the later phase. For example, in work with autistic children, Keith avoids a child evaluation early in the treatment. His main emphasis is on developing a therapeutic alliance with the family as a whole. This gives the family a symbolic experience without reifying its distress. Later on, they can be referred for evaluation and a more specific educational process. We cite this as an example of the underlying family change focus we give priority in our work, regardless of the presenting problem.

We do not struggle to teach new skills in any didactic fashion. We may offer to expand the options they fix on. For example, the wife says, "I want a divorce." The therapist replies, "Where will you go? Will you go home to mother? Do you think you'll get your old room back? Do you think Fred will remarry or will he be too bitter about this first marriage?" In the later stages of therapy, the family may ask for certain educational bits and pieces and these are offered, but in an after-the-fact, casual manner. For example, if the family asks for help in understanding the psychodynamics that brought them into therapy, if they want to talk about their relationship to previous generations, if they want to discuss the relationship of the family to the community or alter their family boundaries, whether individual or group, the therapist can be explicit, supported by the affect that has been accumulated in the earlier part of therapy. He is free to express his opinion without dominating or subjecting the family to something extraneous and irrelevant. The family is by then capable of taking his educational input and insightful additions into the framework of their experience. They can freely modify the therapist's advice, discard it, or utilize it, depending upon its value to them. In the early stage, however, such information would be taken symbolically and thus be highly dangerous.

The therapist's personality and psychological health yield the greatest rewards in treatment. Where the therapist is in his own personal development (personal adequacy and place in the life cycle) intermeshes with the kind of helpfulness he can provide to the family. If the therapist does not get therapeutic input from his work, chances are the patients will not get much from therapy. The difference between the patient and therapist in this regard is that the patient brings his whole self into the experience while the therapist must restrict himself as a function. Another way of saying it is that, in effect, the dynamics of therapy are in the person of the therapist (Betz & Whitehorn, 1975).

The presence of two therapists offers not only the differential adequacy of the two individuals but also a separate experience with the quality of the cotherapy relationship. We think the cotherapy treatment model provides a very valuable metaexperience for the family. The intimacy achievable in the family during therapy may even be limited by the intimacy available between the cotherapists. Therapist factors which we value include personal adequacy, the ability to be caring, the ability to combine lovingness with toughness, the ability to combine craziness with structure, the willingness to let patients go, and the ability to be inconsistent.

Two ideas which we use frequently cause trouble with some other therapists. The first is *craziness*; the other is *the importance of being inconsistent*. The word craziness sometimes implies immaturity and a symbiotic lock-in to another. The craziness that the therapist should have available is the craziness which is not symbiotically locked in to anything, but is available to him as another component of his personhood. It is not necessary to be immature in order to think nonrationally. It is not necessary to be immature in order to have irrelevant, free-associative fantasy components. It is not necessary to be immature to talk wartzlot or schizophreneze. All of these are available to the healthy, free person who has broken with the culture bond, who has broken with his parental transference struggles, who is free to be infantile; as Rioch (1944) said many years ago, "Maturity is the capacity to be immature." That is, maturity is the capacity to function on a regressed level in the service of the therapeutic process, just as many patients regress in the service of the family ego or as neurotic patients regress in the service of the individual ego. A deliberate functional regression often takes place in us in relationship to the therapy setting. The patient family is forced to take over the function of being the "sane" component of this suprafamily "we." While the therapists enjoy the crazy component of the "we," they simultaneously give the patient (family) permission to stay crazy in the right time, in the right place, with the right people, and to be unbound from his symbiotic bind to his mother's phobia about psychosis (Whitaker, 1978).

It is, of course, true that we are more mature in our functional relationship to patients than we are in the outside world of our own families and our work. It seems as though we have more of both our rational and irrational selves available when we have the security of the other therapist. We have the security of the cotherapy as a subculture: a "we" which gives us a sense of belonging while rebelling against the outside culture which wants us to be sane, rational, reasonable, and altruistic.

In order to be an effective change agent, we believe therapists need to learn to be inconsistent and to live with their inconsistency. A model for this is the parent who must admit to and live with his inconsistency in parenting. The parent who perceives himself as consistent is either delusional or being consistent with his kids at the expense of being personal. The therapist's inconsistency helps to undermine the family's attempt to maintain a rigid pattern of living.

Techniques are important for the inexperienced therapist and for the early stages of all family therapy. Techniques, once developed, however, become mechanical and then should be discarded. It is important that techniques be incorporated into a game plan. It is like the young football quarterback who can throw long passes well. He is not as valuable as the quarterback who can develop a good game plan and get together a series of plays in order to make a touchdown. More important than explicit techniques are the metatechniques, such as timing, application of emphasis, how and when to apply pressure, when to back off, or when to be cautious.

Techniques, once developed, become mechanical and then fade out. The objective of all techniques is to eliminate techniques, to get beyond technique in the same way that the experience of loving transcends the experience of sexual intercourse techniques.

In our frame of reference, psychotherapy does not occur without transference, but transference does not work unless it is bilateral. In family therapy, transference is more complicated by the number of subgroups and people present and the fluctuations in ego states which continually go on. We make little attempt to keep the field sterile, except in specific situations where the voltage has increased and there is some obvious therapeutic gain immanent. The transference between the therapists is also assumed to be apparent and a valid part of the interaction within the suprafamily.

Countertransference is dangerous in family therapy when it blocks the transference relationship, that is, goes counter to the transference. One way to think of countertransference is as a consistent pattern of operating which has no built-in alternative. For example, Keith frequently got into fights with mothers in his early years of therapy. The fights were not harmful to the family, but oftentimes ended the treatment. He has learned now to sidestep these wars and save them for later. The result has been an increase in effectiveness and in satisfaction with his work. Countertransference is not seen as a major risk when it is exposed and made part of the ongoing process. Most of the affect available is transference affect in all directions. The transference that mother has toward her oldest son from her husband is just like the transference she has to her husband from her father, and the transference that the youngest daughter has to the female cotherapist from her mother. All of these are responded to and utilized as a valid part of the family therapy experience.

When Keith started working with families, he felt like a failure unless every family member showed change. A few years' experience has made it clear that every family member does not change overtly. The likelihood of a useful experience for the family is diminished when some members do not accept any change. Each member of the family ought to become involved with his own personhood and must bring to the therapeutic process his anxiety about himself, about the subgroups, and about the family as a whole. We believe that men are hopeless because they are so fact- and time-oriented that it is almost impossible for them to be intimate or to think esthetically. Oftentimes father does not appear to change but the other family members lose their terror about him. They love him and regard his unavailability as his form of craziness.

Oftentimes the scapegoats appear beyond change. Sometimes by the time we get to them their character structure is very well established. The scapegoat may not appear to change, but he may take up less space in the family unconscious. It is not, therefore, uncommon for the scapegoat to still have symptoms when the therapy ends and the family has changed.

The so-called healthy member of the family is usually pathological in the same sense that we psychotherapists are. He is preoccupied with doing good, helping others, and may become a nonperson in the process.

The likelihood of the family problem being resolved is reduced when everyone does not change. We insist that even if the family member does not wish to become a patient, he still must attend all the therapy sessions. The family problem is not only a systems problem of its own, but it is augmented and reinforced by each family problem that the individual members carry.

The most powerful factor limiting or enhancing success is the pressure from the family as a whole. If the entire extended family is convinced that "something has to be done about us," psychotherapy is at a very good place. A difficult factor is the nonbiological groups within the family, for example, the adopted child, the second marriage, the nonmarriage combination, the triangulation with father's girlfriend or mother's boyfriend. Secondly, there is greater stress and less pressure for change if the individuals in therapy do not live together. The chance of working things out well is much reduced if there has been a good bit of previous treatment, either individual or, even worse, family treatment which has not been successful. Growing cynicism, lack of hope, and a facility with psychological terminology are vectors which frustrate therapy.

Rigid, socialized paranoids are troublesome in family therapy; they have too much belief in individuals and individuality and frequently too much support from the community. Long-standing, well-stabilized pathology decreases the possibility of much change. Psychosomatic families are frequently seen as difficult to work with in family therapy. In the psychosomatic area, there are two components. First is the attempt to translate the family search for help from the pediatrician or internist to the psychiatrist, and second is the therapist's demand that they switch from body language to psychological language. It is important not to force the leap with these families and to treat them either with administrative effort or metaphorical pressure.

Some other components that make change difficult include the family who is not very concerned, or where one or two are concerned and the others are on the opposite side and think things are fine. As noted above, symptoms present for many years have been adapted to by the family and any attempt to get treatment will be a pseudoeffort. Success with families is greatly inhibited by the withdrawal of any family member from treatment. The more family members withdraw, the less chance there is of success. It usually behooves the therapist to give up if one or more members have decided to drop out. Even if these are the healthy members, it is many times true that, although the therapist may be tempted to let them go on with their lives since they're working well, the family then tends to change less by having lost its hero or heroine. The family without initiative is almost a family without potential for change. The therapist must face the fact that he usually cannot induce real change in such a family. If family members want to change, he may be able to stimulate them with his effort to help and the result may be useful, but without their initiative, little can be done.

In the final analysis, the most important family factor which relates to change or failure to change is desperation. When family members are desperate, they change; when they are not desperate, they remain the same. Some factors which help to move the project along are the self-interests of family members and the tolerance for ambiguity (love–hate, body–mind, the open gestalt).

Good successful termination is like the adolescent's individuation. Sometimes it works out peacefully and gradually and other times the adolescent leaves in an angry rebellion. Most of our terminations with families tend to be abrupt. At a given interview we note that they are living in the here and now and suggest that they go off on their own. Some families take up our offer and do so; others resist and the termination occurs more slowly and on their terms. Like adolescents, some leave, promising to come home for Christmas, then cannot make it or they forget their promise, go off, and live their lives.

A good termination is characterized by increasing here-and-now living, increasing here-and-now therapeutic process in the interview, the freedom to make family decisions without consultation with the therapist, the freedom of the family to correct the therapist and be therapeutic to him, the greater freedom of the family to be silly, comfortable, separate, close, and quite physical with the therapeutic team.

Another kind of success occurs with the family which terminates early. We believe that the flight into health in family treatment is always useful. It means that the family has decided, whether on the basis of negative anger or positive success, that they will reorganize its life-style. The therapeutic experience, even if it is only one interview, contributes to the decision making and may even be more useful than a longer period of psychotherapy. Learning to pick up this symbolic effort to withdraw from therapy or to recapture the family territory is very important in the training of any therapist.

A bad (unsuccessful) termination is the one where the family stops unilaterally and goes to another therapist who takes them on within 4 weeks. A failed therapy followed by a rebound is the same as rebound marriage after divorce. The whole self is not available.

The dynamics of ending in family therapy are not well understood. The therapy process is certainly not like a bus ride out to the end of the terminal. We dispel the idea that we direct ourselves toward a nirvana-type endpoint. We attempt to add 10 percent to the family's living. Such a partial success is seen in a family with four children where the parents are 2 months away from finalization of the divorce. The pediatrician asked for assistance from one of us because the 14-year-old son was depressed. There were three interviews with the whole family and it seemed like a useless cause. Two weeks after the last interview, the father called the pediatrician to apologize for being uncooperative. He was glad they had come because his kids were no longer isolating him. He was back in touch with them and said he had not realized before how much he missed them.

Families end their treatment in diverse ways. Usually, the typical rejection of the parent takes place in some form. One sign is the forgotten interview. The family may begin to reject the therapist's value system or, as children do in play therapy, refer another family as a replacement.

PART SIX

GATHERINGS

One should always start out on the wrong foot.

The body is the temple of God; the bodily sensations are probably the closest to God, the unconscious, than any part of our experience, closer than the interpersonal experience, probably closer than the fantasy experience, since they are more direct. Therefore, the child's competitive athletic work is work with his hands; his experiencing of his body sensations, whether it is with masturbation or physical illness, probably informs him best about potentials and the possibilities of his own unconscious self, his own God.

Your divorce is really an effort to find the person of yourself.

Question: Do I want children? Only answer: Did my mother feel good about her children, especially me?

The postmenopausal peacefulness of a couple is evidence of no residual jealousy about the mother's intimacy with the baby.

Question: Am I a good father? The only answer: Are my sons good fathers as evidenced in their children?

How to stay dead: Just keep telling anyone who will listen about the good old days.

If carrying a burden for others would really help convert us to being grown up, many of us would be real people.

The greatest ordeal in life is marriage—it is the central focus for enlightenment and the natural therapeutic process in the culture.

Beauty in a woman is long, red fingernails and the ability to scratch your eyes out. The naive can only see a marriage by superimposing the picture of their parents' marriage on what they see.

The anatomy of marriage includes an adaptation to the ways of the other, being equal on both sides, the therapeutic value of each to the other being equal on both sides, the historical data available for contact being equal. But there is no oneness in marriage. Each is along and each uses the other to complete his own biological self—no man is a complete biological unit without a woman; no woman is a complete biological unit without a man. The bilateral use of each other produces a bilateral experience of completeness and results in growth as a joint process.

Insight is a by-product of growth or change rather than a precursor or a cause of growth or change.

How to be all alone: Handle all your friends with kid gloves or dedicate yourself to helping others ("Don't be mad at me, I'm not trying to help you").

The only reason I got here at 2:30 is because I thought the meeting started at 2:00.

Professionalism can be a serious problem.

The secret of being a good parent is in the enjoyment of being hated.

Mother Nature always comes through.

I'm ashamed to have fun or enjoy myself, but I'm getting over it.

Interrupted therapy: If the therapist is surprised that the patient did not return, he has the responsibility for conveying it to the patient. He may say in effect, "I was surprised and disappointed that you did not come back. I recognize your right to stay away, but I'm concerned lest somehow I have double-crossed you or you felt I was not competent to go further into your personal struggle. If you have decided that you want no more of me, you certainly have the right to stay away, but if you feel I have let you down, I hope you'll come back and fight it out with me even if we separate. I would much prefer to have it out with you and discover that I am inadequate than to be left up in the air feeling that you ran out on me, that I must have failed you, but not knowing how." If the therapist writes to the patient, the therapist confronts the patient with a reality factor. He should not let the patient leave without trying to participate in a separation fantasy, at least by letter.

My theory is that all theories are bad except for preliminary game playing with ourselves until we get the courage to give up theories and just live.

You know the story of the scarecrow? The traveler went by a field on his way south. He saw a scarecrow out in a field and stopped to talk to it. "Don't you get lonely being out here in the field all the time?" he asked. "No, not really," said the scarecrow. "I enjoy scaring the crows." So they talked a while and the traveler went on. On the way back in spring he stopped again. This time the crows were nesting in the scarecrow's hair, and he had become a philosopher: "I'm convinced that a lot of what I do that turns out well is because I can enjoy my own sadism."[1]

Cotherapy: I had a psychopath once who said, "Well, I can see you, but I could never handle two people at once. That's just like having the whole world in here." And I think that's what it amounts to. As soon as there are two therapists, it becomes a cultural thing. It amalgamates the one-to-one intimacy and the social adaptability.[2]

You don't really know somebody until you know their parents.[3]

The love that sets you free: The patient thinks that the childlike dependence in psychotherapy that we call transference is dangerous. He is right if the therapist needs this for his own personal reinforcement. But if the therapist really loves his spouse or professional colleague then the child is free.

The mature therapist is constantly parental.

We put people in the hospital because they have delusions. If I have a delusion they call it a theory.

You can fall in love but you can't fall out.

I don't believe in marriage either. . . . It's really just two scapegoats sent out by two families to reproduce each other. . . . The battle is which one will it be.

The arrival of the consultant in an ongoing therapeutic relationship can be understood more easily if it's assumed that this consultant is a stepmother to the patient.

The hidden factor in therapy that is many times neglected or never understood is that there can be no Garden of Eden unless the therapist entertains the fantasy that his patient is his real child. In effect, he participates in this and this is what makes the cure come about.

Gossip is the clinical case conference of amateur psychotherapists.

Psychotherapy is like learning to play the piano. How much, how long, how deeply depoends on what you want as an experience—to play hymns or to play Bach and Beethoven.

Infidelity is always known by the "cuckolded" ones, both spouse and children. Usually one spouse unconsciously wants the affair to go on and the other spouse senses it and responds negatively.

Homesickness is a symptom of health; it's the period of integration: aloneness and the hiatus between the family that was and the family that will be.

Psychotherapy must proceed at its own pace and any effort to speed it or slow it because of the character of the therapist can only be destructive.

God protect me from the person who makes believe they're not vulgar.

The identification of an individual with his peers is always ambivalent. Each person alternates between the desire to emulate and the desire to destroy the other and maintain his own omnipotence.[4]

Whenever the therapist steps off his throne he is apt to grow.[5]

Any triumph is inherent self-destruction.

Psychotherapy is a time for not doing anything; yet trying to not do anything is doing something, and not getting anywhere is not the same as not doing anything, since it may be just deliberate effort to keep from getting anywhere.

The awful truth: There is no Santa Claus; the sexiest looking girls are the coldest; the one you love the most is the one you can help the least. Aloneness is based on the delusional hope of togetherness.

An endless series of rapes still leaves the victim a virgin. An endless series of seductions still leaves the man a child (nobody is "made"). If you ever end the virginity state, it is by getting "it" for yourself instead of making somebody else give it to you. Nobody has ever lifted himself up by his boot straps.

The battle between husband and wife is part of marriage but talking about (around) the relationship by the husband and wife is being psychotherapist or parent each to the other.

Marriage is a horrible state, and the only thing that's any worse is being single.

A delinquent is a person who has his feelings in a low-voltage situation, for example, in the community rather than at home.

He who touches many people may do it to keep from being intimate with anyone.

A dead mother is more demanding than a live one.

The passion (sex or anger) in the family belongs between the husband and wife, not between one of them and the kids.

The secret of growth in marriage is access to silly or vulgar sex.

Bad fathers make it easier for the kids to leave home and family.

If you're free to hate, you'll love more.

Every expression of the psychiatric patient, even his most complex psychopathology, seems to reflect directly his effort toward growth.[6]

Learn how to be crazy, but learn also to be smart.[7]

When he can't feel her love, it's because she can't feel his hate.

Question: Whom to trust? Answer: The man who openly loves himself more than he does you.   .

There is nothing more helpful than deceiving oneself, since both parties to the deception stand to gain from it.

The therapist is like Christ in that he says to each patient, "Give up that which you love most," (pride, hope, projection on mother), "and follow me." If you intend to be born again, I can be the obstetrician but I can't be the mother.

To find yourself, keep from saying what you've ever said before.

Just as the 3-year-old played at being mama with dolls, the 4-year-old plays at being sexy with papa. If papa can play in turn, instead of being adult sexy, the child will know what love is and never confuse it with sex.

You are what you worship—what you wish is a graven image.

The sociopath isn't blessed with no conscience, he's cursed with too much conscience.

Repression is not one of the cardinal sins.

The mystery of truth is its paradoxical quality.

Selfishness increased to the ultimate becomes unselfish.

Life isn't mind over matter, it's present over past, and present over future.

I hate my husband's psychiatrist worse than I hate my mother-in-law.

Love can only increase in proportion to hatred, sensitivity in proportion to toughness, togetherness in proportion to separateness, depth in proportion to humility.

In order to be hot from time to time, a couple must learn to be cold between times. It is only possible to say yes after one has thoroughly been convinced of his right and capacity to say no.

I'm the only person who'll never leave me—I may hide from myself, I may turn my back, I may hurt myself. Every other love is time-limited and is person-limited by that person and by me and by us.

When motherhood as a function takes over the person of the mother, there is no person; she is an amateur caretaker, expecting to be paid with love for a professional job. If she sees her role as secondary to her person and as a time-bound process, then she, as a person, can stay emerged or alive.

Advice to a young woman: Never move out of one man's nest into another man's nest—learning to fly can only be done on the wing.

The reason marriage is so destructive is because one uses it to destroy (avoid) oneself.

Mother and father are part of the graven image you worship. Mother helped design it so that you would be like her father in this image. It makes no difference whether she hated her father or loved him, except that when you live up to the image, she then hates you or loves you or both, as she did her father, but it's not you, it's the image.

The best way to avoid psychotherapy is to have regular interviews with a therapist.

Parents usually discover that their children are people about the time when it's too late to enjoy them as people.

What you say is, first of all, a communication to yourself, and only secondarily an effort to communicate with another.

The best cure for insomnia is insomnia.

Depression in its psychopathic stage is enjoying the hatred of self for the effect it has.

Real hatred is probably never destructive—we don't want to lose the object of our hatred; hatred has a unifying effect.

The greater the prudishness, the greater the undercurrent of vulgarity.

Cultural delusion: "Sexy" is identical to sexual. Factually, the teaser is also the castrater, and the greater the "sexiness," the greater the frigidity.

Cultural delusion: One is supposed to do his duty for other people, not for himself. If he keeps working all the time, then his self-esteem will be increased. In essence this means the wife should go to bed with her husband to make him a Christian.

Each of us is a missionary trying to find a heathen to save so we can bribe our way into heaven.

A person, by definition, is one who is alone.

"I'm having trouble with my husband" means "I'm having trouble with being in charge of our marriage." Whenever one member talks about the relationship in the first person and the third person, they are denying the first person plural, we. For the isolate person, the sense of loneliness is a step toward better health. The last remaining symptom is a goad to maintain growth, a push to keep life moving.

Every parent fails at bringing up children. No child grows up to be what the parent wants. If the parents give up the child, he will evolve as nature would have it. No matter what they think they are teaching, the child will grow up to be like the parents in his life-style.

The maneuvering person is one who is convinced that there is no way to have access to his unconscious, that is, to the face of God, so he must look at man, not himself, for all the answers.

It may be that frigidity, which we can call repression, is more related to the fear of craziness as expressed by the orgasm than the fear or avoidance of sex. It is not sex that is frightening, but the loss of control, which means insanity, not relaxation.

I believe craziness is where life is.[8]

I can't imagine coaching a football team and telling them, "If you get tired don't exercise anymore. It might hurt you." I feel the same way in psychotherapy.[9]

I've always been scared at the hazards of the profession: would I go crazy, would I commit suicide in my despair? Later in life it changed. Would I get calluses? Would it progress until when asked "How are you," I would routinely answer, "Oh, keeping cool"?[10]

ENVOI

Old age is a joy. In the past 6 months I've been invited three times to be exhibit "A" for psychiatric residents studying the affects associated with geriatric mind set and the dilemmas of retirement! Five years ago I phoned my guru and said I was making retirement plans. She said, "You can't retire." Was that a paradox or a transference taboo?

Youth is a nightmare of doubt; middle age a sweaty, rock-breaking marathon; while old age is the graceful enjoyment of a well-choreographed dance. Maybe a little stiff in the joints, but the timing and the finesse are automatic, not studied. Old age knows more than it can say and, best of all, has little need to say it. More and more life is for living. My wife and I know each other. Life with her is like the joy of walking around inside the house with all the lights out, and every step is filled with the welcome security of belonging. Those six who were our children are our deepest friends; the eight grandchildren a flower garden to walk in and to sniff the fragrance of.

As I watch the talented and dedicated young therapists try to find the next rung on the ladder, I often wonder, how can they prevent burn out? One asked me sadly, "What can I do? I'm already burned out." I wonder, how did I avoid burn out? Was it the luck of switching from an ob–gyn residency to psychiatry on an uncritiqued impulse? Was it the luck of a full year of play therapy, and 3 more years of psychotherapy with delinquents (they're like Cadillacs with broken steering gears)? Was it the chance of teaching medical students before I knew anything about psychiatry? Was it never being exposed to "hard" psychiatry? Everybody who should have been teaching in 1941 was overseas. You can't be an alcoholic if you don't go to the AA meetings— you're just an ordinary drunk. The next ironic twist flipped us to Oak Ridge. That atomic-energy, secret city was an adrenalin high, a total push to save the world—burn out was unthinkable.

The next turn of life's screw left us originating a 4-year crash training program in the psychotherapy of medical students. I was too inexperienced to know that all medical students shouldn't be forced to take 2 years of group therapy. The Dean was too new to know that they should have been forced to learn the facts of psychodynamics, not the humanism of a good listener. It worked for 10 years before "they" (Who is "they"?) realized that psychotherapy was not a science. They had my head! It was a bloody scene, but a profound learning experience. I wonder, is defeat the only good teacher and change the only antidote to burn out?

Cotherapy for individual schizophrenics was successful—until they went back to the original family. That defeat took more than a pound of flesh, but fueled the next twist—my move into family therapy. Will that be the final touch that produces a burn out? I defy it, not in this life!

CARL WHITAKER

EDITORS' NOTES AND REFERENCES

PART ONE

1. Chapman, A. H. *Harry Stack Sullivan, the man and his work.* New York: Putnam's, 1976.
2. Published in revised form as Whitaker, C. A., & Davidoff, E. Without psychosis—Chronic alcoholism. *Psychiatric Quarterly,* 1942, *16,* 373–392.
3. Rank, O. *Will therapy, truth and reality.* New York: Knopf, 1947, p. 21.
4. *Ibid.,* p. 98.
5. *Ibid.,* p. 206.
6. *Ibid.,* p. 28.
7. Federn, E. The therapeutic personality, as illustrated by Paul Federn and August Aichhorn. *Psychiatric Quarterly,* 1962, *36,* 29–43.
8. Whitaker, C. A. Ormsby Village: An experiment with forced psychotherapy in the rehabilitation of the delinquent adolescent. *Psychiatry* 1946, *9,* 242.
9. *Ibid.*
10. Clarke, E. K. Psychiatric problems at Oak Ridge. *American Journal of Psychiatry,* 1945, *102,* 437–444.
11. Whitaker, C. A., & Malone, T. *The roots of psychotherapy.* New York: Blakiston, 1953.
12. Whitaker, C. A. (Ed.). *Psychotherapy of chronic schizophrenic patients.* New York: Little, Brown, 1958.
13. See, for example, Schwartz, E. K., & Wolf, A. Irrational trends in contemporary psychotherapy. *Psychoanalytic Review,* 1958–1959, *45,* 65–82.
14. Rosen, J. A method of resolving acute catatonic excitement. *Psychiatric Quarterly,* 1946, *20,* 183–189.
15. See Brodey, M. W. *Observations on direct analysis: The therapeutic techniques of John Rosen.* New York: Vantage Press, 1959.
16. Segal, H. Melanie Klein's technique. In B. B. Wolman (Ed.), *Psychoanalytic techniques.* New York: Basic Books, 1967, pp. 168–190.
17. Whitaker, C. A., & Malone, T. *Op. cit.,* p. 58.
18. It is interesting to compare this group self-criticism to that practiced in certain Utopian communities. See, for example, Noyes, J. H. *Mutual criticism* (M. Levine & B. B. Bunker, Eds.). Syracuse: Syracuse University Press, 1975.

19. Whitaker, C. A., & Malone, T. *Op. cit.*, p. 66.

20. See Whitaker, C., & Olsen, E. The staff team and the family square off. In G. Abroms & N. S. Greenfield (Eds.), *The new hospital psychiatry*. New York: Academic Press, 1971.

21. Whitaker, C. A family is a four-dimensional relationship, p. 305, this volume.

22. Whitaker, C. Out of Janet's magic into limbo. *Voices*, 1973, *9*, 50.

23. From Eliot, T. S. Little gidding. In *Four quartets*. New York: Harcourt Brace Jovanovich, 1943.

PART TWO

1. Whitaker, C. A., & Malone, T. *The roots of psychotherapy*. Philadelphia: Blakiston, 1953, p. 105.

2. Conversation with C. A. Whitaker.

3. Whitaker, C. A., & Malone, T. *Op. cit.*, pp. 188–189.

4. Harper, R. A. *Psychoanalysis and psychotherapy: 36 systems*. Englewood Cliffs, N.J.: Prentice-Hall, 1959, p. 103.

5. The reader is referred to the discussion of object relations theory in Guntrip, H. *Psychoanalytic theory, therapy and the self*. New York: Basic Books, 1979.

6. This, as well as other paradoxes of this genre, is considered in Haley, J. *Strategies of psychotherapy*. New York: Grune & Stratton, 1963, pp. 179–191.

7. For more on Rank's influence on Whitaker's work, see Part One.

8. David Levy was a child psychiatrist whose work influenced Whitaker.

9. See Whitaker, C. A. Group encounter: The now self of me, pp. 155–160, this volume.

10. Jennifers, reference is lost.

11. Barbara J. Betz. Personal communication. Dr. Betz was an early researcher into the question of the personality of the therapist and development, at Johns Hopkins, of the "A–B" therapist typology. See Betz, B. J. A study of tactics for resolving the autistic barrier in the psychotherapy of the schizophrenic personality, *American Journal of Psychiatry*, 1947, *104*, 267–273 for her emphasis on the person of the therapist.

12. See Ruesch, J. *Therapeutic communication*. New York: Norton, 1961.

13. Martin Grotjahn, M.D., a psychoanalyst. This is apparently a personal communication.

14. Note that the therapist is a full experiential participant, not a Sullivanian participant observer. Also, he is not a "director" of the process the way a Gestalt therapist might be.

15. This is another example of the "extended" or "joint" fantasy. See Whitaker, C. A. Training for the unreality experience, pp. 70–74, this volume.

16. That is, the Atlanta Psychiatric Clinic; principally, T. Malone, J. Warkentin, and R. Felder.

17. These are therapists who put greater emphasis on verbalizing interpretation of primary process material to schizophrenic patients. See Rosen, J. *Direct analysis*. New York: Grune & Stratton, 1953.

18. Charles Kettering, the industrialist.

PART THREE

1. See Eliade, M. *Shamanism*. New York: Bollinger Press, 1964.

2. Whitaker's idea of a therapist's vocation is confirmed by the study of the lives of some prominent therapists. See Burton, A. *Twelve therapists: How they live and actualize themselves*. San Francisco: Jossey-Bass, 1972.

3. Whitaker, C. A. Comment: Live supervision in psychotherapy. *Voices*, 1976, *12*, 26.

4. *Ibid.*, pp. 24–25.

5. Whitaker, C. A., & Abroms, G. New approaches to residency training in psychiatry. In G. Farwell, N. Gamsky, & P. Mathieu-Coughlan (Eds.), *The counselor's handbook*. New York: Intext-International, 1974.

6. Whitaker, C. A. Unpublished manuscript.

7. Ferber, A., Mendelsohn, M., & Napier, A. *The book of family therapy*. New York: Science House, 1973.

8. Whitaker, C. A. Unpublished manuscript.

9. Dr. Ackerly was the chairman of the Department of Psychiatry at the University of Louisville when Whitaker was there.

10. Dreikurs was a student of Alfred Adler. See Dreikurs, R. Techniques and dynamics of multiple therapy. *Psychiatric Quarterly*, 1950, *24*, 788–799.

11. Here multiple psychotherapy is synonymous with cotherapy.

12. This was the format for the teaching of psychiatry to his medical students when Whitaker was at Emory University as chairman of the Psychiatry Department.

13. Albert Scheflen, PhD. Scheflen was the head of a team at Temple University in Philadelphia studying nonverbal communication patterns in psychotherapeutic interviewing. His study of Whitaker and Malone, undertaken in 1956, is the substance of his book, *Communicational structure: Analysis of a psychotherapy transaction*. Bloomington: Indiana University Press, 1973.

14. That is, a model for a mature relationship. See also Whitaker, C. A., & Warkentin, J. The therapist as prototype. In J. F. T. Bugental (Ed.), *The challenges of humanistic psychology*. New York: McGraw-Hill, 1967. The idea originated with Alfred Adler.

15. Speck, R., & Attneave, C. *Family networks*. New York: Pantheon Books, 1973.

16. See Ferber, A., Mendelsohn, M., & Napier, A. *Op. cit.*, pp. 496–498.

17. At other times, Whitaker has stipulated only that one be able to respect his cotherapist as a person.

18. Whitaker has worked in several extended cotherapy relationships, notably with John Warkentin, Augustus Napier (in Madison, Wisconsin), and David Keith (also in Madison). For a cotherapist's eye view of working with Whitaker, see Napier, A., & Whitaker, C. A. *The family crucible.* New York: Harper & Row, 1978. A multiple-therapy case study, with transcript material, is presented in edited form as Whitaker, C. A., Warkentin, J., & Malone, T. The involvement of the professional therapist. In A. Burton (Ed.), *Case studies in counseling and psychotherapy.* Englewood Cliffs, N.J.: Prentice-Hall, 1959, pp. 218–256.

19. This turns on the distinction between the professional therapist and the social therapist. See the introduction to Part Three.

20. Commitment is an either–or decision, just as one cannot be "a little bit pregnant."

21. The "battle for structure" is the first task of therapy. See the introduction to Part Five.

22. That is, acting as a social therapist or acting administratively.

23. That is, the therapist becomes the patient.

24. It is the *sharing* of the affect that is important, not so much *explaining why* the therapist feels as he does. Thus the patient is clearly not responsible for "fixing" the therapist.

PART FOUR

1. The connection in Whitaker's mind between life and craziness and between craziness and intimacy is brought home in this section. For Whitaker a rational, polite marriage is a dead marriage.

2. Implicit in this description, although not developed until later, is the notion that people select partners who are able to tolerate the same level of intimacy.

3. Bierce, A. *The devil's dictionary.* New York: Sagamore Press, 1957. (Originally published, 1911.)

4. Eisenstein, V. W. *Neurotic interaction in marriage.* New York: Basic Books, 1956.

5. The research reported on in this chapter represents one of the earliest attempts at assessing the efficacy of marital therapy. It is methodologically crude, but helped stimulate researchers toward more sophisticated research.

6. Whitaker's focus on mothers to the neglect of fathers is reflective of thinking in the field in the 1950s and 1960s. It seems clear from later work that he would view the child's behavior as expressing family pathology rather than mother's pathology.

7. Bierce, A. *Op. cit.*

8. Whitaker would say, completing the parallel between cotherapy (i.e., multiple therapy) and marriage, that the cotherapy team is also greater than the sum of the individual therapists.

9. The implication of these comments is somewhat paradoxical. The couple seeks psychotherapy at a time of instability, that is, at a time when they are more healthy than during times of homeostatic stability. The therapist's goal then should be to increase the couple's tolerance for the instability they are experiencing and not to reduce the intensity of the problems they are experiencing. Crisis intervention is thus antithetical to psychotherapy.

10. The term "in the round" means simply that couples were always seen for therapy together, that is, jointly.

11. This section exemplifies the difference between Whitaker's experiential therapy and the communication approach to marital therapy. Whitaker stays between the couple during the period of therapy and attempts to disrupt and limit direct communication between spouses.

12. At this point in the history of marital therapy this position was controversial in that marital therapy was seen by most therapists as a treatment solely for interactional problems.

13. Recent research supports this observationally derived hypothesis. Gurman and Kniskern, in their recent review of the research literature on family therapy, conclude that individual therapy for marital problems is less frequently successful and more often deteriorative than is joint therapy. See Gurman, A. S., & Kniskern, D. P. Research on marital and family therapy: Progress, perspective and prospect. In S. Garfield & A. Bergin (Eds.), *Handbook of psychotherapy and behavior change* (2nd ed.). New York: Wiley, 1978.

PART FIVE

1. Group for the Advancement of Psychiatry. *Treatment of families in conflict.* New York: Science House, 1970.

2. Whitaker, C. A., & Keith, D. V. Symbolic–experiential family therapy. In A. Gurman & D. Kniskern (Eds.), *The handbook of family therapy.* New York: Brunner/Mazel, p. 200.

3. This anecdote may be confusing to the reader. As is typical of many of Whitaker's "therapy stories," it is ambiguous and somewhat opaque. One of the "messages" seems to us to be that the therapist must assume wholeness in the family regardless of how the family experiences themselves. As Whitaker frequently says, "Facts are stronger than feelings."

4. The "rules" Whitaker is referring to are related to the family's participation in therapy, the who, what, when, how of psychotherapy structure. He does not refer to rules about the family life outside of therapy.

5. Whitaker's confidence in the family's ability to make things better if the current pattern is disrupted is a direct outgrowth of his notion of the biological push toward growth in the individual.

6. This statement reflects Whitaker at the midpoint in his development of the notion of the family. He began with a focus on the marriage and has now evolved to a focus on at least three generations.

7. The idea of chaos as a family defense has never been discussed as much as rigidity. The implication, however, is that "health" is an intermediate state between fluidity and rigidity.

8. As Whitaker points out, at times the missionary often gets eaten by natives.

9. In later writings Whitaker also suggests that countertransference can, at times, be managed with a consultation with another therapist or by increasing the number of family members present at the interview.

10. See the report included in Whitaker, C. A. Ormsby Village: An experiment with forced psychotherapy in the rehabilitation of the delinquent adolescent. *Psychiatry*, 1946, *9*, 239–250.

11. Surprisingly, this could still be said of family therapy today, even though 17 years have passed.

12. The common experience of inexperienced therapists is that of being overwhelmed by the quantity of individual problems in a family. Seldom is this perceived as a family defense against change, as Whitaker here suggests.

13. It is important to remember that, as Whitaker stated earlier, the non-sexual family is a perverted family.

14. Watzlawick, P., Beavin, J. H., & Jackson, D. *The pragmatics of human communication*. New York: Norton, 1967.

15. It is worth emphasizing that for Whitaker the failure or impasse in family psychotherapy is reason to increase the number of people involved in the treatment process. "Success" with a family can be a signal for reducing the number of involved family members.

16. Whitaker's intuition has been borne out by research that confirms the father's importance in preventing "early treatment dropouts." Compare Gurman, A. S., & Kniskern, D. P. Research on marital and family therapy: Progress, perspective and prospect. In S. Garfield & A. Bergin (Eds.), *Handbook of psychotherapy and behavior change* (2nd ed.). New York: Wiley, 1978.

17. Therapists and patients often conspire to avoid involvement of other family members by using these content issues as reasons, as if they need to be disclosed if the extended family is present.

18. Kaiser, H. *Effective psychotherapy*. London: Free Press, 1965.

19. Whitaker stresses the relationship between theory and technique. The theory-oriented therapist is the technique-oriented therapist.

PART SIX

1. Ferber, A., Mendelsohn, M., & Napier, A. *The book of family therapy*. New York: Science House, 1972, pp. 483–484.

2. *Ibid.*, pp. 491–492.

3. *Ibid.*, p. 490.

4. Whitaker, C. A. The ongoing training of the psychotherapist, p. 135, this volume.

5. *Ibid.*, p. 128.

6. Whitaker, C. A., & Malone, T. *The roots of psychotherapy.* New York: Blakiston, 1953, p. 56.

7. Whitaker, C. A. The technique of family therapy, p. 229, this volume.

8. Whitaker, C. A. My philosophy of psychotherapy, p. 34, this volume.

9. *Ibid.,* p. 34.

10. *Ibid.,* p. 35.

AUTHOR'S REFERENCES

Auerbach, A. H. Application of Strupp's method of content analysis to psycho-therapy. *Journal of Psychiatry*, 1963, *26*, 137–148.

Betz, B., & Whitehorn, J. C. *Effective psychotherapy with the schizophrenic patient.* New York: Aronson, 1975.

Bion, W., & Richman, J. Intragroup tensions in therapy: Their study as a task for the group. *Lancet*, 1943, *2*, 678–681.

Castaneda, C. *Tales of power.* New York: Simon & Schuster, 1975.

Ehrenwald, J. *Psychotherapy: Myth and method: An integrative approach.* New York: Grune & Stratton, 1966.

Fellner, C. The use of teaching stories in conjoint family therapy. *Family Process*, 1976, *15*, 427–433.

Flescher, J. Dual analysis. In J. H. Masserman (Ed.), *Current psychiatric therapies* (Vol. 8). New York: Grune & Stratton, 1968.

Lindner, R. The jet-propelled couch. In *The fifty-minute hour*. New York: Bantam Books, 1956.

Luener, H. The use of initiated catathymic imagery in psychotherapy. *Zeit-schrift fuer Psychotherapie und Medizinische Psychologie*, 1955, *5*, 186–233.

Malone, T. P. *Experimental encounters in family therapy of schizophrenia.* Read at the American Psychological Association Meeting, September 1961.

Malone, T., Whitaker, C. A., & Warkentin, J. *Effectiveness of medical students as psychotherapists.* Unpublished manuscript, undated.

Malone, T. P., Whitaker, C. A., Warkentin, J., & Felder, R. E. Rational and nonrational psychotherapy. *American Journal of Psychotherapy*, 1961, *15*, 212–220. (a)

Malone, T. P., Whitaker, C. A., Warkentin, J., & Felder, R. E. Operational definition of schizophrenia. In J. G. Dawson, H. K. Stone, & N. P. Dellis (Eds.), *Psychotherapy with schizophrenics*. Baton Rouge: Louisiana State University Press, 1961, pp. 123–135. (b)

May, R. *Existence.* New York: Basic Books, 1958.

Meerloo, J. A. M. *The two faces of man.* New York: International Universities Press, 1954.

Potter, H. W., Klein, H. R., & Goodenaugh, D. R. Problems related to the personal costs of psychiatric and psychoanalytic training. *American Journal of Psychiatry*, 1957, *113*, 1013–1019.

Rioch, M. Personal communication, 1944.

Rosen, J. *Direct analysis.* New York: Grune & Stratton, 1953.

Srole, L., Langner, T. S., Michael, S. T., Opler, M. K., & Rennie, T. A. C. *Mental health in the metropolis: The midtown Manhattan study.* New York: McGraw-Hill, 1962.

Warkentin, J., Felder, R. E., Malone, T. P., & Whitaker, C. A. The usefulness of craziness. *Medical Times*, 1961, *89*, 587–590.

Warkentin, J., & Taylor, J. E. *Case fragments: The experimental physical contact in multiple therapy with schizophrenic patients* (Vol. 3). Zurich: Report to 2nd International Congress for Psychiatrists, 1957.

Whitaker, C. A. (Ed.). *Psychotherapy of chronic schizophrenic patients.* Boston: Little, Brown, 1958.

Whitaker, C. A. Cotherapy of chronic schizophrenia. In M. Berger (Ed.), *Beyond the double bind: Communication and family systems, theories and techniques with schizophrenics.* New York: Brunner/Mazel, 1978.

Whitaker, C. A., Felder, R. E., Malone, T. P., & Warkentin, J. First-stage techniques in the experiential psychotherapy of chronic schizophrenic patients. In J. H. Masserman (Ed.), *Current psychiatric therapies* (Vol. 2). New York: Grune & Stratton, 1962, pp. 147–157.

Whitaker, C. A., & Malone, T. P. *The roots of psychotherapy.* New York: Blakiston, 1953.

Whitaker, C. A., & Malone, T. P. The psychotherapy of the acting-out schizophrenic. *American Journal of Psychotherapy*, 1963, *17* (3), 417–426.

Whitaker, C. A., Malone, T. P., & Warkentin, J. Multiple therapy and psychotherapy. In F. Fromm-Reichmann & J. L. Moreno (Eds.), *Progress in psychotherapy.* New York: Grune & Stratton, 1956, pp. 210–216.

Whitaker, C. A., & Miller, M. H. A reevaluation of psychiatric help when divorce impends. *American Journal of Psychiatry*, 1969, *126*, 611–618.

Whitaker, C. A., Warkentin, J., & Johnson, M. The psychotherapeutic impasse. *American Journal of Orthopsychiatry*, 1950, *20*, 641–647.

Whitaker, C. A., Warkentin, J., & Malone, T. P. The involvement of the professional therapist. In A. Burton (Ed.), *Case studies in counseling and psychotherapy.* Englewood Cliffs, N.J.: Prentice-Hall, 1959.

Winnicott, D. Hate in the countertransference. *International Journal of Psychoanalysis*, 1949, *30*, 69–79.

Wynne, L. C., Ryckoff, M., Day, J., & Hirsch, S. I. Pseudomutuality in the family relations of schizophrenics. *Journal of Psychiatry*, 1958, *21*, 205–220.

Zuk, G. K. Critical evaluation of triadic-based family therapy. *International Journal of Psychiatry*, 1969, *8*, 539–548.

APPENDIX:
WORKS BY CARL WHITAKER

BOOKS

The roots of psychotherapy, with T. Malone. New York: Blakiston, 1953.
Psychotherapy of chronic schizophrenic patients (Editor). Boston: Little,
    Brown, 1958.
The family crucible, with A. Y. Napier. New York: Harper & Row, 1978.

CONTRIBUTIONS TO BOOKS

Critical incidents in psychotherapy. S. W. Standal & R. J. Corsini, Eds. Engle-
    wood Cliffs, N.J.: Prentice-Hall, 1959.
Strategy and structure in psychotherapy. O. S. English, Ed. Philadelphia: East-
    ern Pennsylvania Psychiatric Institute, 1965.
Stream and structure of communicational behavior. A. E. Scheflen, Ed. Phila-
    delphia: Eastern Pennsylvania Psychiatric Institute, 1965.
*The therapeutic relationship and its impact: A study of psychotherapy with
    schizophrenics.* C. A. Rogers, Ed. Madison: University of Wisconsin
    Press, 1967.
Psychiatry: East and West. J. H. Masserman, Ed. New York: Grune & Stratton,
    1968.
Creative developments in psychotherapy (Vol. 1). A. Mehrer & L. Rearson, Eds.
    Cleveland: Case Western Reserve University Press, 1969.
Family dynamics and female sexual delinquency. O. Pollak & A. S. Friedman,
    Eds. Palo Alto, Calif.: Science & Behavior Books, 1969.
Psychotherapy from the center. R. B. Corlis & P. Rabe, Eds. Scranton, Penn.:
    International Textbook Co., 1969.
The puzzled body. C. Kent. London: Vision Press, 1969.
Black ghetto family in therapy: A laboratory experience. C. J. Sager, T. L.
    Braybog, & B. Waxenberg. New York: Grove Press: 1970.
*Family interaction: An encounter between family researchers and family thera-
    pists.* J. L. Framo & I. Boszormenyi-Nagy, Eds. New York: Springer,
    1970.

The book of family therapy. A. Ferber, M. Mendelsohn, & A. Napier, Eds. New York: Science House, 1972.
A family therapy notebook. B. B. Peck. Roslyn Heights, N.Y.: Libra Publishers, 1974.

CHAPTERS IN BOOKS

Multiple therapy and psychotherapy, with T. P. Malone & J. Warkentin. In J. L. Moreno & F. Fromm-Reichmann (Eds.), *Progress in psychotherapy.* New York: Grune & Stratton, 1956.

The involvement of the professional therapist. In A. Burton (Ed.), *Case studies in counseling and psychotherapy.* Englewood Cliffs, N.J.: Prentice-Hall, 1959.

Anxiety and psychotherapy. In M. R. Stein, A. J. Vidich, & D. M. White (Eds.), *Identity and anxiety.* Glencoe, Ill.: Free Press, 1960.

The ongoing training of the psychotherapist. In M. P. Dellis & H. K. Stone (Eds.), *The training of psychotherapists.* Baton Rouge: Louisiana State University Press, 1961.

First-stage techniques in the experiential psychotherapy of chronic schizophrenic patients, with R. E. Felder, T. P. Malone, & J. Warkentin. In J. Masserman (Ed.), *Current psychiatric therapies* (Vol. 2). New York: Grune & Stratton, 1962.

Countertransference in the family treatment of schizophrenia, with R. E. Felder & J. Warkentin. In I. Boszormenyi-Nagy & J. Framo (Eds.), *Intensive family therapy.* New York: Harper & Row, 1965.

Time-limited therapy for an agency case, with J. Warkentin. In A. Burton (Ed.), *Modern psychotherapeutic practice.* Palo Alto, Calif.: Science & Behavior Books, 1965.

Acting out in family psychotherapy. In L. E. Abt & S. L. Weissman (Eds.), *Acting out—Theoretical and clinical aspects.* New York: Grune & Stratton, 1965.

Serial impasses in marriage, with J. Warkentin. *Psychiatric Research Report* (20). Washington, D.C.: American Psychiatric Association, 1966.

The secret agenda of the therapist doing couples therapy, with J. Warkentin. In G. H. Zuk & I. Boszormenyi-Nagy (Eds.), *Family therapy and disturbed families.* Palo Alto, Calif.: Science & Behavior Books, 1967.

The therapist as a prototype, with J. Warkentin. In J. F. T. Bugental (Ed.), *The challenges of humanistic psychology.* New York: McGraw-Hill, 1967.

The growing edge—An interview with Carl Whitaker. In J. Haley & L. Hoffman (Eds.), *Techniques of family therapy.* New York: Basic Books, 1968.

Experiential or nonrational psychotherapy, with T. P. Malone. In W. S. Sahakian (Ed.), *Psychotherapy and counseling—Studies in technique.* Skokie, Ill.: Rand McNally, 1968.

A commentary on Rollo May's contributions of existential psychotherapy. In A. R. Mahrer & L. Pearson (Eds.), *Creative developments in psychotherapy* (Vol. 1). Cleveland: Case Western Reserve Press, 1971.

Multiple therapy and its variations. In G. D. Goldman & D. S. Milman (Eds.), *Innovations in psychotherapy*. Springfield, Ill.: Charles C Thomas, 1971.

The staff team and the family square off, with E. Olsen. In G. M. Abroms & N. S. Greenfield (Eds.), *The new hospital psychiatry*. New York: Academic Press, 1971.

Family interaction: An encounter between family researchers and family therapists, with J. L. Framo. New York: Springer, 1972.

Problems of beginning family therapy, with A. Napier. In D. Bloch (Ed.), *Techniques of family psychotherapy: A primer*. New York: Grune & Stratton, 1973.

Teaching open communication and commitment to intimacy, with A. Napier. In S. J. Marks & S. Berg (Eds.), *Doing the unknown*. New York: Dell, 1973.

New approaches to residency training in psychiatry, with G. Abroms. In G. Farwell, N. Gamsky, & P. Mathieu-Coughlan (Eds.), *The counselor's handbook*. New York: Intext Educational Publishers, 1974.

The symptomatic adolescent—An AWOL family member. In M. Sugar (Ed.), *The adolescent in group and family therapy*. New York: Brunner/Mazel, 1975.

The patient as a person, with T. P. Malone. In A. G. Banet, Jr. (Ed.), *Creative psychotherapy—A source book*. La Jolla, Calif.: University Associates, 1976.

The learning tree. In S. Kopp (Ed.), *The naked therapist*. San Diego: Edits, 1976.

The hindrance of theory in clinical work. In P. J. Guerin, Jr. (Ed.), *Family therapy: Theory and practice*. New York: Gardner Press, 1976.

A family is a four-dimensional relationship. In P. J. Guerin, Jr. (Ed.), *Family therapy: Theory and practice*. New York: Gardner Press, 1976.

Psychotherapy with couples. In G. D. Erickson & T. P. Hogan (Eds.), *Family therapy: An introduction to theory and technique*. New York: Jason Aronson, 1976.

Counseling the dissolving marriage, with D. V. Keith. In R. F. Stahmann & W. J. Hiebert (Eds.), *Klemer's counseling in marital and sexual problems* (2nd ed.). Baltimore: Williams & Wilkins, 1977.

Symbolic sex in family therapy. In G. P. Sholevar (Ed.), *Changing sexual values and the family*. Springfield, Ill.: Charles C Thomas, 1977.

The technique of family therapy. In G. P. Sholevar (Ed.), *Changing sexual values and the family*. Springfield, Ill.: Charles C Thomas, 1977.

The divorce labyrinth, with D. V. Keith. In P. Papp (Ed.), *Family therapy—Full-length case studies*. New York: Gardner Press, 1977.

Cotherapy of chronic schizophrenia. In M. M. Berger (Ed.), *Beyond the double bind: Communications and family systems, theories and techniques with schizophrenics*. New York: Brunner/Mazel, 1978.

The use of videotape in family therapy with special relation to the therapeutic impasse. In M. M. Berger (Ed.), *Videotape techniques in psychiatric training and treatment* (rev. ed.). New York: Brunner/Mazel, 1978.

Add craziness and stir: Psychotherapy with a psychoticogenic family, with D. V. Keith. In M. Andolfi & I. Zwerling (Eds.), *Dimensions of family therapy*. New York: The Guilford Press, 1980.

Symbolic–experiential family therapy, with D. V. Keith. In A. Gurman & D. Kniskern (Eds.), *The handbook of family therapy*. New York: Brunner/Mazel, 1981.

Family microevents: Communication patterns for problem solving, with J. Metcoff. In F. Walsh (Ed.), *Normal family processes*. New York: The Guilford Press, 1982.

PAPERS

Prepsychotic personality in alcoholic psychoses, with E. Davidoff. *Psychiatric Quarterly*, 1940, *14*, 103–120.

Treatment of neurosyphilis in a psychiatric clinic, with E. Davidoff. *Diseases of the Nervous System*, 1940, *1/2*, 113–121.

Without psychosis—chronic alcoholism. *Psychiatric Quarterly*, 1942, *16*, 373–392.

Ormsby Village: An experiment with forced psychotherapy in the rehabilitation of the delinquent adolescent. *Psychiatry*, 1946, *9* (3), 239–250.

Induced regressive behavior as therapy for adults. American Orthopsychiatric Association, 1947. (Unpublished with movie.)

Compensation for psychiatric disabilities in industry. *Occupational Medicine*, 1948, *5*, 391–395.

Group interviewing as a method of evaluating applicants for medical school, with H. Wood & H. Ades. *Journal of the American Medical College Association*, 1949, *24*.

A philosophical basis for brief psychotherapy, with J. Warkentin & N. Johnson. *Psychiatric Quarterly*, 1949, *23*, 439–443.

Teaching the practicing physician to do psychotherapy. *Southern Medical Journal*, 1949, *42* (10), 1–11.

The psychotherapeutic impasse, with J. Warkentin & N. Johnson. *Journal of Orthopsychiatry*, 1950, *20* (3), 641–647.

Why a state mental hygiene program?, with G. Rice. *Journal of the Medical Association of Georgia*, 1951, *40*, 259–262.

Symposium on group psychotherapy, theory and practice. *Group Psychotherapy*, 1951, *4* (1, 2), 38–40.

A comparison of individual and multiple psychotherapy, with J. Warkentin & N. L. Johnson. *Psychiatry*, 1951, *14* (4), 415–418.

Preverbal aspects of psychotherapy with schizophrenic patients. *Archives of Neurology and Psychiatry*, 1952, *67*, 834–837.

Doctor-patient relationship in therapy: A round table discussion. *American Journal of Psychoanalysis*, 1955, *15* (1), 3–21.

Communication in brief psychotherapy with the nonpsychotic patient. *Diseases of the Nervous System*, 1957, *18* (2), 2–7.

Psychotherapy with couples. *American Journal of Psychotherapy*, 1958, *12* (1), 18–23.

Social origins of delusions, with J. Warkentin & T. P. Malone. *Southern Medical Journal*, 1959, *52* (11), 1418–1420.

Organic psychosis as picked up in psychiatric examination, with R. E. Felder, T. P. Malone, & J. Warkentin. *Journal of the Medical Association of Georgia*, 1960, *49* (2), 56–59.

The ambulatory schizophrenic patient. *Journal of the Medical Association of Georgia*, 1960, *49* (3), 125–126.

Rational and nonrational psychotherapy—A reply, with T. P. Malone & R. E. Felder. *American Journal of Psychotherapy*, 1961, *15* (2), 212–220.

The usefulness of craziness, with J. Warkentin, R. E. Felder, & T. P. Malone. *Medical Times*, 1961, *89* (86), 587–589.

The use of aggression in group psychotherapy. *Journal of the Los Angeles Group Psychotherapy Assocation*, July 1962.

The psychotherapy of the acting-out schizophrenic, with T. P. Malone. *American Journal of Psychotherapy*, 1963, *17* (3), 417–426.

Experiential psychotherapy: Evaluation of relatedness, with J. Warkentin, T. P. Malone, & R. E. Felder. *Journal of Existential Psychiatry*, 1963, *3* (11), 248–254.

The one-to-one therapeutic relationship in the treatment of schizophrenia, with J. Warkentin. Presented at the Eastern Pennsylvania Psychiatric Institute Conference, 1964.

The psychotherapy of married couples. Lecture delivered at the Cleveland Institute of Gestalt Therapy, Cleveland, Ohio, January 1965.

The community of psychotherapists, with T. P. Malone. *International Journal of Group Psychotherapy*, 1965, *6* (1), 23–28.

Marriage—A model of intimacy in our society, with J. Warkentin. Presented at the Eastern Pennsylvania Psychiatric Institute Conference on Treatment of Marital Problems, April 1965.

Open communication from the psychotherapist. *Existential Psychiatry*, January 1966.

Sauna bath and snow plunge. *Voices*, 1966, *2* (1), 33.

The administrative ending in psychotherapy. *Voices*, 1966, *2* (2), 69–70.

The marriage: A secret ally for the physician. *Kentucky State Medical Journal*, 1966, *64*, 1012–1014.

Family treatment of a psychopathic personality. *Comprehensive Psychiatry*, 1966, 7 (5), 397–401.

Process koans, with J. Warkentin. *Voices*, 1966, *2*, 91–92.

Training for the unreality experience. *Voices*, 1966, *2*, 43–46.

The commitment to intimacy. *Existential Psychiatry*, 1967, *6* (23), 182–183.

The contribution of individual and family therapy to the psychotherapy of schizophrenia. Presented at the Eastern Pennsylvania Psychiatric Institute Conference on Psychotherapy of Schizophrenia, April 21–22, 1967.

The impasse. *Voices,* 1968, *4* (3), 5–8.

Existentialism in American psychiatry: Ten years later, with M. Miller & C. Fellner. *American Journal of Psychiatry,* 1969, *125* (8), 1112–1115.

Dyads and triads—A critical evaluation of "Triadic-Based Family Therapy" by Gerald Zuk. *International Journal of Psychiatry,* 1969, *8* (2), 566–567.

Family psychotherapy of a psychopathic personality: Must every member change?, with J. Burdy. *Comprehensive Psychiatry,* 1969, *10* (5), 361–364.

A reevaluation of psychiatric help when divorce impends, with M. H. Miller. *American Journal of Psychiatry,* 1969, *126* (5), 611–618.

The territory chart as a platform for family therapy. *Voices,* 1970, *6* (2), 95–97.

The family enters the hospital, with C. H. Fellner & G. M. Abroms. *American Journal of Psychiatry,* 1971, *127* (10), 1363–1369.

Process techniques of family therapy, with A. Napier. Presented at the Family Therapy Conference, Montreal, Fall 1971.

Commentary: A longitudinal view of therapy styles where $n = 1$. *Family Process,* 1972, *11* (1), 13–15.

Out of Janet's magic into limbo. *Voices,* 1973, *9,* 50–51.

My philosophy of psychotherapy. *Journal of Contemporary Psychotherapy,* 1973, *6* (1), 49–52.

Técnicas del proceso de terapía familiar, with A. Y. Napier. *Neurología-Neurocirujía-Psiquiatría,* 1973, *14* (2–3).

Power politics of family psychotherapy. Presented at the American Group Psychotherapy Association Conference Symposium, February 17, 1974.

Counseling techniques and the person of the counselor. *Conciliation Courts Review,* 1974, *12* (1), 1–5.

Alternate treatment systems for psychosis. *Voices,* 1974, *10,* 60.

Techniques de processus en thérapie familale. *Cahier de Thérapie Familiale,* 1974, No. 1.

Psychotherapy of the absurd: With a special emphasis on the psychotherapy of aggression. *Family Process,* 1975, *14,* 1–16.

Comment: Live supervision in psychotherapy. *Voices,* 1976, *12,* 24–25.

Yoga and psychotherapy—The evolution of consciousness: A review. *Voices,* 1976, *12,* 59.

Sex, love and the committed relationship. *Journal of Sex and Marital Therapy,* 1976, *2* (4), 263–264.

Family therpay and reparenting myself. *Voices,* 1976–1977, *12* (4), 66–67.

Process techniques of family therapy. *Interaction,* 1977, *1* (1), 4–19.

Psicoterapie dell'assurdo: Con particolare referimento alla psicoterapie dell' aggressivita. *Terapia Familiare,* June 1977, No. 1.

Struggling with the impotence impasse: Absurdity and acting in, with D. V. Keith. *Journal of Marriage and Family Counseling,* 1978, *3,* 69–77.

The importance to the family therapist of being impotent. *The Family,* 1979, *4* (2), 120–126.

Family therapy as symbolic experience, with D. V. Keith. *International Journal of Family Psychiatry,* 1980, *1,* 197–208.

Play therapy: A paradigm for work with families, with D. V. Keith. *Journal of Marital and Family Therapy*, in press.

CASSETTE TAPES

Couples and family psychotherapy. 30 ½-hour-long tapes.
Preparation for marriage. 10 ½-hour-long tapes.
Facilitating divorce. 6 ½-hour-long tapes.

> Available through Instructional Dynamics Incorporated, 450 East Ohio Street, Chicago, Illinois 60611.

The process of family therapy. Black-and-white videocassette.
Family therapy consultation. Two-part videotape demonstrating a family therapy consultation, and a debriefing session with therapist and consultants.
Three-generational family consultation. Two-part videotape demonstrating the consultation and debriefing of a multigenerational family therapy system.

> Available through IEA Productions, Inc., 520 East 77th Street, New York, New York 10021.

Affinity. Family consultation videotape.

> Available through Philadelphia Child Guidance Clinic, Philadelphia, Pennsylvania, for rental or purchase.

INDEX